Archaeology and History of Toraijin

This new 2022 version of *Archaeology and History of Toraijin*
by Rhee, Aikens, and Barnes replaces the 2021 version

Archaeology and History
of
Toraijin

Human, technological, and cultural flow from the Korean Peninsula to the Japanese Archipelago c. 800 BC–AD 600

Song-nai Rhee
C. Melvin Aikens

with

Gina L. Barnes

ARCHAEOPRESS ARCHAEOLOGY

Archaeopress Publishing Ltd
Summertown Pavilion
18-24 Middle Way
Summertown
Oxford OX2 7LG
www.archaeopress.com

ISBN 978-1-78969-966-1
ISBN 978-1-78969-967-8 (e-Pdf)

This book is available direct from Archaeopress or from our website www.archaeopress.com

Contents

List of Figures and Tables

List of Maps

Stylistic Notes

• **Romanization of Asian words**

For many decades, writers around the world used the McCune-Reischauer (M-R) system for romanization of Korean words. Unfortunately, most readers unfamiliar with the M-R system have rendered Korean words and especially Korean personal and place names confusing or unrecognizable. Consequently, in 2000, the Korean government officially adopted the Revised Romanization system (R-R) of Korea. Since then, the latter is used as the primary romanization system in South Korea to the exclusion of the M-R system.

In this book, we use both the M-R system (without diacritical marks) and the R-R system: the former for *some* Korean personal and place names already well-established in Western literature such as Koguryo, Paekche, Kaya, Pusan, Taegu, Pyongyang, Kyongju, Kimhae, Inchon, Kim, Lee, Rhee, and Park and the latter for less known personal and place names and all common Korean words. In some cases, we have romanized Korean authors' names as preferred by the authors themselves. Chinese words are romanized according to the Pinyin system that replaced the older Wade-Giles system in 1989. Romanization of Japanese words generally follows the modified Hepburn system without macrons.

*Asian names

When Asian proper names are cited in full, the surname precedes the given name as in the Asian practice. To make it crystal clear we show these surnames with small caps (Example: KIM Won-yong and KADOWAKI Teiji).

* Translated passages

The English translations of the *Nihon Shoki*, quoted in this book, are from W. G. Aston's *Nihongi* (Tuttle 1972). Those of the *Samguk Sagi* and the *Samguk Yusa* are from translated texts of YI Pyong-do (1972: 1977) and Jonathan Best (2006). All other translations are our own.

Acknowledgements

From its inception to completion, this book is indebted to a countless number of people around the world in the field of archaeology and history of ancient Korea and Japan. As our research led to Japan and Korea, we met, listened, and dialogued with numerous frontline researchers and scholars shedding light on the subject of our inquiry. In-office discussions, guided field trips to archaeological sites, and research publications which they provided us became the basis of this book.

Our thanks are due the following (in alphabetical order); in Korea, Ki-dong BAE, Seung-ok BAEK, Sung-rak CHOI, Wan-gyu CHOI, Jang-geun GWAK, Bo-shik HONG, Yeong-nae JEON, Gu-Geum KIM, Gyeong-taek KIM, Jang-suk KIM, Seong-gu KIM, Seung-ok KIM, Jae-hyun LEE, Seong-ju LEE, Joong-hwan PARK, Kyeong-cheol SHIN, Ui-jeong SONG, and Duk-hyang YUN; in Japan, HIRAKORI Tatsuya, HIROSE Yuichi, ISHINO Hironobu, KINOSHITA Wataru, KOHAMA Sei, KOYAMADA Koichi, MATSUMOTO Kazuo, NISHITANI Tadashi, TANAKA Toshiaki, TOMOIKA Naoto, and YOSHI'I Hide.

We are also indebted to the research staff of various museums and research institutes for the generous assistance provided during our research; in Korea, Paekche Culture Research Institute, Bokcheon Museum, Buyeo National Museum, Buyeo National Research Institute of Cultural Heritage, Gongju National Museum, Daeseong-dong (Kimhae) Tumuli Museum, Haman Museum, Kimhae National Museum, Kyongju National Museum, Naju National Museum, Gwangju National Museum, National Museum of Korea, the Pungnap Toseong Research Center, Pusan University Museum, Seoul National University Museum, and Yeongnam University Museum; in Japan, Itokoku History Museum in Maebara City (Kyushu), Yoshinogari Rekishi Koen Center in Yoshinogari (Kyushu), Kashihara Archaeological Institute Museum, Nara National Research Institute of Cultural Properties (Nabunken), Okayama Ancient Kibi Cultural Research Center, Osaka Chikatsuasuka Museum, Osaka Yayoi Culture Museum, and Shiga Azuchi Castle Archaeological Museum.

With our heartfelt gratitude we wish to lift up several scholars and frontline researchers around the world, who have been indispensable in the writing and completion of this book. Mong-lyong CHOI of Seoul, Korea, has regularly kept us informed of the most recent archaeological findings and academic discussions regarding prehistoric and ancient Korea through his latest publications and personal conversations. His vast knowledge of the archaeology of the Peninsula's Mumun, Mahan, and Paekche periods, in particular, have been invaluable.

Jong-cheol LEE of Jeonju, Korea, a specialist on the Songguk-ni type culture, has enlightened us with his insights regarding the Initial Toraijin who arrived in the Archipelago with the Songguk-ni type culture during the first millennium BC. In addition, he has graciously assisted in the preparation of several illustrations included in this book.

SHODA Shinya of Nara, Japan, a highly informed scholarly bridge between the Archipelago and the Peninsula has shared his time, knowledge, and insights on the archaeology of the Peninsula's bronze age and the Archipelago's Yayoi period, one of the central topics of this book. With his publications and online conversations, he has helped elucidate numerous issues including those of the Yayoi chronology.

KAMEDA Shuichi of Okayama, Japan, a renowned authority on the archaeology of the Toraijin of the Kofun period, has generously provided us the results of his research on the history of the Toraijin and their contributions to the Kofun society, especially in the development of the iron industry in the Archipelago. We are deeply grateful for the time he gave us in Okayama and the guided site trips provided by his staff.

Finally, we wish to thank the University of Oregon Knight Library for its generous and efficient service in acquiring published monographs and journal articles from around the world, essential to our research, through the interlibrary loan and electronic access system, Jeffrey Hanes, Mara Epstein, and Holly Lakey of the Center for Asian and Pacific Studies for their support in the completion of this book.

Preface

In the ongoing saga of Japan-Korea relations, the years of 2000 and 2001 witnessed two extraordinary events. In the former, INOUE Mitsuo (2000, 16-18), a prominent scholar of Japanese history, highlighted the special place of the Toraijin in Japanese history with the publication of a provocative essay, "Without the Toraijin, Japanese history would have been delayed by 200 years". In the latter, Emperor Akihito publicly announced: "Those who immigrated or were invited to come to Japan from Korea introduced culture and technology... It was truly fortunate that such culture and technology was brought to Japan through the enthusiasm of the Japanese people and the friendly attitude of the Korean people. I also believe that it contributed greatly to Japan's subsequent development" (Kunaisho 2001; French 2002).

Indeed, one cannot review the development of society in the Japanese Islands without being astonished at the debt Japanese culture and people owe to early societies on the Korean Peninsula. The arrival of immigrant rice-agriculturalists from the Peninsula in the early first millennium BC was the first of three major waves of technological transfer between the continent and the Islands. The second brought bronze and iron-working to the Archipelago around the 4th century BC, and the third brought elite crafts and administrative technology as well as Confucianism and Buddhism in the 5th and 6th centuries AD.

Until the 1970s, the information on the Toraijin (immigrants to the Japanese archipelago mainly from the Korean Peninsula) was based largely on a few ancient historical texts such as the *Kojiki* (Records of Ancient Matters, compiled in 712), the *Nihon Shoki* (Chronicles of Japan, 720), the *Shoku Nihongi* (Chronicles of Japan Continued, 797), and the *Shinsen Shojiroku* (New Records of Family Registers, 815), documents compiled long after the actual events pertaining to the Toraijin.

Beginning in the early 1980s, however, thanks to massive salvage archaeological excavations undertaken throughout the Archipelago, unprecedented amount of archaeological data has been collected and analyzed, shedding much light on the Toraijin: their beginnings, their settlements, their life, and their contributions to the early Japanese society and the beginnings of Japanese civilization. Likewise, similar excavations in the southern Korean Peninsula of the past four decades, are providing much information on the historical and socio-cultural background of the Toraijin.

Dissecting this information is the task of this book, to document whence, when, and why Peninsular people emigrated and how they and their descendants changed the population structure and material culture within the Archipelago. In doing so, it is important to note that such waves of technology transfer and population movement are common in prehistory, exemplified also by the history of the British Isles. The inhabitants of the Korean Peninsula were also subject to such intrusive waves from the China Mainland, Steppe region, and Northeast Asia.

This is not to say that Korea and Japan did not and do not have unique cultures then and now. Periods of migratory quiescence allowed the autochthonous flowering of new forms of material creation and social behavior that became indigenous to the Pen/Insulae. The time-period covered herein can be compared with the Meiji period (1868–1912) in Japan when Western culture was voraciously acquired and consumed. No one can say today that Japan does not have a unique Japanese culture despite its overt Western appearance. So, what is being offered here is not a denigration of Japanese culture but an explanation of some of the roots and ingredients that made Japan what it was historically.

There are people within and without Japan (Egami, Ledyard, Covell and Covell, Hong), who speak of conquests and subjugation of the Archipelago's inhabitants by militant Peninsular peoples in the 4th–5th centuries. There are also people (SUEMATSU Yasukazu and his followers), mainly in Japan, who believe that early Japan developed its society by gaining advanced culture and technology of Korea through invasion. In fact, the history of early relations between the Peninsula and Islands is far more nuanced, complicated, and variable than that, with no evidence of a massive state-sponsored military invasion either way at any time. Unpicking those relations is a fascinating task, and every year that passes, with new excavations and analyses, allows us to delve in deeper than before. The Toraijin story is a major key unlocking the box containing the mysteries of Japan's beginnings

Introduction

I. IMPORTANCE OF THE SUBJECT: TORAIJIN

Toraijin (渡來人), a term meaning 'people who have crossed over', has ethno-cultural and historical nuances. It is used more in Japan than in other countries in East Asia. In China and Korea, it is rarely mentioned, and their general public would not understand its meaning until they are given an explanation. In Japan it is used primarily to designate people who immigrated to the Archipelago from the Korean Peninsula over two millennia from c. 800 BC to 600 AD.

In the context of such ethno-culturally-driven cognitive differences, Kyoto Bunka Hakubutsukan (Kyoto Museum of Culture) published, in 1989, an attractive photo-laden book with an eye-catching title, 海を渡つ て來た人と文化 (*Umi o Watatte Kita Hito to Bunka* [The People Who Crossed the Sea and Their Culture]), as a part of its first anniversary celebration. Its primary focus was *Toraijin*, "the people 人 who crossed 渡 the sea to come 來" [to the Archipelago]) and their cultural, technological, ideological, and demographic contributions to Japanese society.

The book was based on a series of special lectures presented by Japan's prominent archaeologists and historians, including MORI Koichi, professor of archaeology at Doshisha University, NISHITANI Tadashi, professor of archaeology at Kyushu University, UEDA Masaaki, professor of ancient history at Kyoto University, KADOWAKI Teiji, professor of ancient Japanese history at Kyoto Furitsu University, and INOUE Mitsuo, professor of ancient Japanese history at Kyoto Sangyo University.

These five foremost scholars of Japan's ancient history and archaeology firmly believed that the Toraijin phenomenon was of such significance that an authentic history of Japan could not be written without telling its story.

Toraijin were mentioned in Japan's ancient records as a continental people coming into the Archipelago, normally in groups and at various times, with advanced technical skills of varying kinds, long intriguing the Japanese imagination (N Nakamura 1915; Kanno 1932; Maruyama 1934). The initial interest led to serious scholarly investigations in the post WWII Japanese academia (Takeuchi 1948; Seki 1956; Shida 1959; Ueda 1965; Egami 1967; Imai 1969; Kadowaki 1973; Yamao 1977; S Nakamura 1981). Through the 1960s, the ancient aliens were described as Kikajin (歸化人) ('naturalized people'). Beginning in the 1970s, however, the term has been replaced by Toraijin mainly because not all aliens who came to the Archipelago became naturalized (Ueda 1991: 45-80). Nevertheless, Hirano (2018) has recently published *Kikajin to Kodai Kokka* (Kikajin and the Ancient State), focusing on the role and the position in ancient Japan of the Toraijin and their descendants who became naturalized citizens of Japan under the auspices of the Yamato state.

In the early 1980s, massive nationwide archaeological investigations in Japan began to shed unprecedented light on the Toraijin, prompting publication in Japan of several archaeological reports on the critical role of the Toraijin during Japan's formative period (Kyoto Bunka Hakubutsukan 1989; OYBH 1999, OYBH 2004; SKAKH 2001; OFCAH 2004). Along with these, KAMEDA Shuichi (1997: 2000, 2003a, 2003b, 2004a, 2004b, 2004c, 2005, 2010, 2011, 2012, 2016) and others (Iwanaga 1991; Kataoka

1999, 2006; Shichida 2005, 2007a, 2017b; Saga-ken Kyoiku I'inkai 2008; Sakai 2013; Hashino 2014; K Miyamoto 2017) have made significant contributions on the archaeology of the Toraijin.

The archaeological discoveries have revealed that the first significant wave of Toraijin first appeared in the Archipelago in the early part of the first millennium BC, though individuals may have arrived earlier (Bausch 2017), and that they had helped Japan's prehistoric hunting-fishing-gathering society become a food producing one and acquire bronze and iron technology during the Yayoi period. In the 5th century, the Toraijin helped Japan advance upward to another level with new hitherto unknown technologies. "The 5th century is viewed as the century of technological revolution," states KAMEDA Shuichi (2011: 116):

> The arrival in Japan of Sueki stoneware, equipments related to war and military power such as horse paraphernalia, weapons, helmets and body armors, new iron forging techniques and gilt-bronze craftsmanship, and (advanced tools) for agriculture, land reclamation, and public works greatly changed the technology of Japan. Furthermore, the horse and the arrival of new cooking facilities including *kamado* (clay cooking-stove) significantly altered the lifeways of Japan.

The revolutionary changes, Kameda continues,

> did not happen because certain *mono* (things, objects) came into the country. They happened because of the coming of the people who possessed techniques and technologies. In the earlier days also, cultural exchanges took place through the movement of people, but particularly the revolutionary changes of the 5th century cannot be considered without the large number of people coming in, namely 'the Toraijin.' Therefore, the 5th century may be called 'the century of Toraijin'.

Echoing Kameda, SHIRAISHI Ta'ichiro, Director of the Osaka Furitsu Chikatsu Asuka Museum, has summed up the significance of the Toraijin in Japanese history (2004: 7-14):

> The Toraijin... brought to Wa (Japan) new technologies including horse breeding and horse-riding, metallurgy, a Sueki (stoneware pottery) industry, and weaving skills, along with civil and architectural engineering, astronomy, calendar, arithmetic, Chinese writing, and religious and political ideologies among other things. It goes without saying that these new cultural and technological contributions propelled the advancement of Japanese civilization... The role of the Toraijin in civilizing Wa was immense (*kiwamete okii*).

By 'Wa', Shiraishi means ancient Japan, which was described in the ancient Chinese records as Wo (倭) or Woguo (倭國) (J. Wa, Wakoku). According to the *Xin Tang Shu* (The New History of Tang Dynasty, compiled in 1060), the Archipelago came to be called Nihon (日本) for the first time in 670.

Some of the 5th-century Toraijin were officials on a diplomatic mission, or temporary resident scholars and teachers (somewhat similar to British and American advisors brought in by the Meiji government in the late 19th century); but the majority comprised the general population including farmers, bronze and iron smiths, potters, craftsmen, military personnel, and even elites who fled their homeland for one reason or another in search of a new haven. They settled permanently and became Kikajin (naturalized immigrants).

In time, some of them became powerful magnates (*gozoku* 豪族) while others became government officials, technocrats, and political functionaries, playing a critical role in the advancement of politics, economy, and culture of ancient Japan (Ueda 1965: 86-96, 180). YAMAO Yukihisa (1977: 39-50) observes that "without the Toraijin, it is impossible to consider the process of state formation [in Japan] during the 6th–7th century", highlighting the vital role which the Toraijin played in social, economic, agricultural, industrial, and political transformation of ancient Japan. They also became ancestors of many modern Japanese.

In "Japan and Continent," a chapter in *The Cambridge History of Japan* Vol. 1, OKAZAKI Takashi highlights Japan's indebtedness to the Asian continent for its civilization (1993: 268):

> Japan's prehistory was marked by the gradual transmission of techniques and artifacts from the continental civilizations of Asia... Imported technology – the cultivation of rice in paddies, and bronze and iron technology – enabled the Japanese to create a settled and stratified society, and...contributed to the formation of the Japanese state.

This was a part of a grand civilizational drama taking place in a corner of the world aptly named the 'Yellow Sea Interaction Sphere' (Map 0.1); it was also the final phase of the formation of the great East

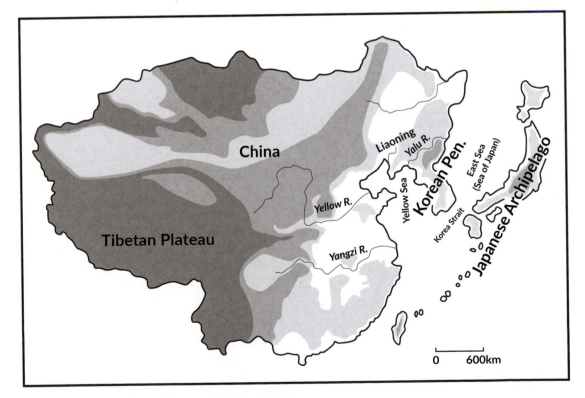

Map 0.1. Geographical map of East Asia (by Lucas Pauly).

Date	China	Korea	Japan
B.C. 14,000	PALAEOLITHIC	PALAEOLITHIC	PALAEOLITHIC JOMON Incipient
10,000 9000 8000 7000 6000 5000 4000 3000 2000 1000 900 800 700 600 500 400 300 200 100 0 AD 100 200 300 400 500 600 700 800 900	NEOLITHIC Yangshao		
		NEOLITHIC (Chulmun)	Initial
			Early
	Longshan SHANG W. ZHOU	BRONZE AGE (Mumun)	Middle Late Final
		Early	
	E. ZHOU	Middle	YAYOI Early
	WARRING STATES	Late IRON AGE GO CHOSON (WIMAN CHOSON) SAM HAN/LELANG-DAIFANG	Middle
	QIN/W. HAN		
	E. HAN		
		KOGURYO	Late
	THREE KINGDOMS (222-280) SIX DYNASTIES (420-581) SUI (581-618) TANG (618-966)	PAEKCHE, SILLA, KAYA LATER MAHAN	KOFUN Early Middle Late ASUKA
		UNIFIED SILLA	HEIJO (Nara) HEIAN (Kyoto) (794-857)

Table 0.1. Chronology of East Asia (by Lucas Pauly).

Asian civilization which began more than 10,000 years before in the Asian mainland (Barnes 2015: 361-383) (Table 0.1).

In the transmission of the continental civilization to the Archipelago, many hands were involved, including traders, travelers, diplomats, immigrants, and even soldiers on foreign expeditions. Certain technologies absolutely essential to the advancement of Japanese civilization, however, had to wait for the arrival in the Archipelago of skilled technicians with their technological know-how. The history of iron technology in the Archipelago is a good case in point.

II. IRON, A CASE STUDY

Ever since the inhabitants of the Archipelago discovered the superiority of iron over stone and wooden tools in the 3rd century BC (or even earlier), they sought to develop their own iron technology (Murakami 1999: 84-150, 2007: 9-138). With skills learned from the continent as well as with their own ingenuity the Archipelago smiths made a variety of simple iron implements with raw iron materials imported from the continent. By the Early Kofun period, they were using the improved forging method (*tanya*) to produce useful iron tools such as iron axes, chisels, sickles, hoes, arrowheads, knives, daggers, and swords (Murakami 2007: 123-126).

Iron implements requiring complex technology such as riveting, however, had to wait until the arrival of skilled Toraijin technicians in the 5th century. It was the latter that helped revolutionize the iron technology of the Middle Kofun period in the production of advanced weapons, horse paraphernalia, iron helmets and body armor, which became the new status symbols of the emerging elites (Murakami 1999: 128-129, 188-189; Kameda 2000: 165-169).

Most critical in the development of the Archipelago iron technology, however, was its lack of success in iron production. Even around 550, the technology essential to iron production (*seitetsu gijutsu*) was still in a state of infancy or nil after more than eight or nine centuries of attempts by the Archipelago artisans to produce the raw iron locally (Murakami 2007: 47-50, 170-175). Consequently, for iron supplies, the Archipelago had to depend almost completely on the continent through much of the Late Kofun period (Murakami 1999: 60-120, 2004: 70-75, 2007: 110-135). This changed after 550 with the arrival in the Archipelago of skilled iron technicians from the continent who helped develop the iron production industry (Kameda 2000: 174-179; SKAKH 2001: 34-36). For their insatiable demands for the iron, the Wa elites still had to depend on the continent for the supply of raw materials (Murakami 2007: 304-305), but the groundwork was laid by the Toraijin technicians for development of the local iron production industry (Kameda 2000: 174-179; SKAKH 2001: 34-36).

Therefore, ancient Japan, in order to advance into a settled and stratified society and eventually into an enduring state, required from the continent not only advanced goods and technologies (wet-rice farming technique, bronze and iron technology, horse breeding and horse-driven transportation, civil engineering, etc.) but also technicians and engineers who could transplant the vital technologies *in situ*.

III. WHO WERE THE TORAIJIN, WHERE DID THEY COME FROM, AND WHAT DID THEY CONTRIBUTE TO THE ARCHIPELAGO?

KATAOKA Koji (1999: 177) defines Toraijin as "the people who came from the Korean Peninsula to the Japanese Archipelago crossing the sea and their descendants who continued to live with the lifeways and traditions [of their parents and grandparents]." INOUE Mitsuo (1991: 96-97) is more specific: "Stated succinctly, they are the people who came from Korea *in groups and with a distinct purpose* (集團 で意志をもつて)" (italics added).

Scholars at the Kyoto Museum of Culture relate them to the origins of Japanese civilization (Kyoto Bunka Hakubutsukan 1989: 9):

> In seeking the source of Japan's ancient culture, many will look to China, but the quest will finally lead to Korea where China's advanced culture was accepted and assimilated. In actuality, the people who crossed the sea [Toraijin] were the people of the Korean Peninsula and their culture was the Korean culture.

World historians – Murdoch (1910), Sansom (1958), Reischauer and Fairbank (1958, 1960), Hall (1970), and Brown (1993) – have stressed the pervasive influence of China and its advanced culture in the rise of Japanese civilization. In this narrative, the Korean Peninsula, situated between China and Japan, has been portrayed as a mere bridge or a conduit through which the advanced continental civilizations passed on their way to the Japanese Archipelago.

Such a perception of the Korean Peninsula is both simplistic and erroneous. Barnes (2015: 331), while discussing the emergence of Korea's early states, observes that, for example, the Peninsular polities that arose from the late 3rd century were neither mere extensions of [Chinese] dynastic power nor copycat borrowings of those dynastic systems...their internal dynamics and material representations are all substantially different, attesting to cultural creativity and local solutions for administrative problems. Regarding the early kingdom of Paekche, Walsh (2017: 161), in light of her analysis of its ceramic production, usages, and exchange, concludes that "the kingdom clearly deployed autochthonous political, economic, and social strategies to integrate and administer its territory, rather than relying on imported Chinese bureaucratic models."

Accordingly, world historians are warned against their tendency to view the Korean Peninsula as no more than a conduit through which Chinese civilization flowed into Japan (Barnes 2007: 1-3). As with other peoples, the ancient Peninsula inhabitants advanced their civilization by close interaction with their neighbors. Archaeological and historical records reveal clearly that they adopted advanced cultural elements from China and its northern neighbors. However, in the course of evolving, they assimilated the borrowed cultures and technologies and further refined them according to their own needs (Okazaki 1993: 271; SJ Lee 2007: 164-185; Barnes 2015: 331). Likewise, in the Archipelago also, the Peninsular culture, as it arrived along with the Toraijin, was adopted and adapted through time to become specifically Japanese, as shown in later chapters.

In the course of time, some of these Peninsular inhabitants became the Toraijin, the people who crossed the sea for one reason or another, reaching the Japanese Archipelago. Some of them were temporary residents, but many (more than a million over several centuries) settled permanently throughout the Archipelago, becoming critical contributors in the building of the Japanese civilization. Already by 600, many ancient Korean immigrant communities were well established in the Osaka–Kyoto–Nara area, playing an indispensable role not only in transplanting vital technologies of the continent in the Japanese soil but also in ancient Japan's accessing the continent and its rich civilization. The *Song shi* (the official account of the Liu Song Dynasty, 420–479, compiled in 488) reports that during the 5th century, five kings of Wa came to the Liu Song court in southern China to pay an official visit. "Without the information and knowledge of the Toraijin," states ICHIMURA Kunio (2004: 49), "even the diplomatic mission of the Five Kings of Wa to [Liu] Song China would have been impossible." Likewise, when the Yamato court sent an official cultural mission to Tang China in 608 to acquire the best parts of Chinese civilization, seven or all eight members of the mission were from the Yamato Aya Clan comprised of Korean immigrants and their descendants (*Nihon Shoki*: Suiko year 16).

In sum, about three thousand years ago, when the Archipelago's indigenous people were still engaged in lifeways based on fishing, hunting, and gathering, the Toraijin came and transplanted wet-rice farming in the Archipelago, transforming the Japanese lifeways forever. Six hundred years later, they brought and transplanted bronze technology. In the 5th and 6th centuries, they added the vital technologies of horse breeding and horse driven transportation, stoneware pottery, high-temperature iron-working and hi-tech iron tool-manufacturing, a writing system, and the ideologies of Confucianism and Buddhism critical to nation-building.

These observations in the archaeological and ancient historical records have led Japanese scholars (Ueda 1965; Yamao 1977; Okazaki 1993; Kataoka 1999; Sakai 2013; Hashino 2014; K Miyamoto 2017; Shichida 2017) to conclude that each major epoch in Japanese history, from the advent of the Yayoi rice farming society to the emergence of metallurgy of the Middle Yayoi, and the revolutionary socio-cultural dynamism of the Kofun period, coincided with the appearance of the Toraijin. The Toraijin, by their crisis-born fate, thus became cultural agents during Japan's formative period (c. 8th century BC–AD 600), which is the central theme of this monograph. Essentially, they acted as transmitters as well as transplanters of the advanced continental civilization in the Japanese Archipelago. But it is essential to acknowledge that the peoples on the Korean Peninsula themselves had undergone similar previous transformations with the introduction of millet and rice agriculture, bronze and iron objects and technologies from further west and north. Japanese development is not unique in this way; however, the one thing that cannot be countenanced is to ignore or even reject such continental influences, nor should they be overstated as in the Horserider Theory which we will revisit in later chapters.

IV. PUSH-PULL DYNAMICS IN MIGRATION

Human migration in ancient times around the world has long been a subject of serious interest among archaeologists and historians as an event as well as a process (Haury 1958; Rouse 1986; Anthony 1990; Burmeister 2000; Lyons 2003; Manning 2013). Tracking methods of the immigrants' movement and migration markers are well developed.

"In general, migration is most likely to occur when there are negative (push) stresses in the home region *and* positive (pull) attractions in the destination region..." states Anthony (1990: 899, italics added). The negative (push) stresses may be economic-environmental (climate change, shortage of arable land), or socio-political (population pressure, internal strife, civil wars, invasions, and wars). The positive (pull) attractions may also be environmental/economic – open fertile land, better climate, more material resources, and opportunities for a better life – or socio-political such as the relative absence of war and a host population welcoming the immigrants for what they might have to offer to improve their life. Add to these the presence of previous immigrants, kin or not.

Migration is integral to human adaptive strategies for survival and improvement of life; it is a rational process. Decisions are made about questions of where, when, and how. Information on the destination is gathered, networks are established, and logistics are developed. The structure of many migrations, according to studies on migration in history resembles a stream more than a wave, as stated by Anthony (1990: 903):

> Migrants tend to proceed along well-defined routes toward specific destinations... Earlier migrants create pathways by overcoming obstacles and providing routing information for later migrants. The route is therefore often just as finely targeted as the destination. Archaeologically, this ... result [s] in artifact distributions that follow a specific line of movement.

Through the study of cultural remains left by the immigrants, researchers are able to map the point of their origin, their initial arrival, spread, settlement, and economic and other activities. Historical records, if available, provide valuable complementary information. In Japan, through extensive archaeological researches (Kameda 2000, 2004a, 2004c, 2010, 2016; OYBH 1999; SKAKH 2001; OFCAH 2004; Okuno 2012) much is known about these aspects of the Peninsular immigrants, the Toraijin of ancient Japan. Through environmental, archaeological, and ancient historical records, the push/

pull dynamics can be identified in the migrations of Korea's Middle Mumun people to the Japanese Archipelago across the Korea/Tsushima Strait.

V. PRIMARY OBJECTIVES OF THIS BOOK: THE *SEVEN* QUESTIONS

More than three decades have passed since the Kyoto Bunka Hakubutsukan highlighted the Toraijin and their extraordinary significance in ancient Japan. Since then the Toraijin has become a major subject of scholarly interest *within* Japan, and Japanese archaeologists and historians have shed more light with publications of their research result, as mentioned above. Nevertheless, not a single monograph in English, focused on the Toraijin, has appeared. We can only speculate on the reason.

In this book, we present a panoramic bird's eye view of the fourteen centuries-long Toraijin story, from c. 800~600 BC to 600 AD or thereabouts, on the basis of our own archaeological and historical researches over several decades in Korea and Japan as well as reports and insights provided by Korean and Japanese scholars.

Specifically, we seek to answer the following seven questions:

(1) Where did the Toraijin come from?

(2) What was their historical and socio-cultural background?

(3) Why did they leave their homeland, risking their lives on the turbulent and notoriously dangerous waters of the Tsushima Strait?

(4) Where did they live in the Archipelago?

(5) What did they do in the Archipelago?

(6) How did the Archipelago people treat the Toraijin?

(7) What contributions did the Toraijin make to the ancient Japanese society?

We explore these questions in five chapters, with each chapter focused on a major period in Japanese history: Incipient/Early Yayoi (Chapter 1), Middle Yayoi (Chapter 2), Late Yayoi/Early Kofun (Chapter 4), and Middle/Late Kofun (Chapters 4 and 5). In the way of enhancing the flow of the Toraijin story, we have chosen "From the Peninsula to the Archipelago" approach. Therefore, in each chapter, first we meet the Toraijin in their Peninsular homeland archaeologically and historically (where historical records are available), and then we meet them in the Archipelago archaeologically and historically (where historical records are available).

As we meet them in the Peninsula, we observe their settlements, their lifeways, houses they built, tools they made and used, their weapons, pottery vessels, their mortuary practices, and the character of their social organization. As we meet them in the Archipelago, we locate their settlement sites and examine the Peninsula cultural complex which they transplanted in the Archipelago: houses they built, tools and pottery vessels they made and used, their mortuary practices, and how they interacted with the Archipelago people.

Of special importance, as we follow the Toraijin during each major period, we seek to answer three vital questions: (1) Why did the ancient Peninsula people leave their homeland to cross the South Sea and the Korea/Tsushima Strait? (2) How did the Archipelago people treat the Toraijin? And, (3) what did they contribute to the Archipelago society?

Finally, in the final section, Collaboration *Not* Conquest, we examine and assess major alternative explanations regarding the revolutionary socio-cultural transformations in ancient Japan and offer our own findings in light of the archaeological and historical evidences presented in the five chapters. Also, we assess the nature of Toraijin contributions to Japan's formative period.

VI. RESEARCH DATA: ARCHAEOLOGICAL AND HISTORICAL

Archaeological Data

For the Toraijin-related archaeological data in the Archipelago, this study relies *primarily* on the evidence presented by Japanese scholars for the Japanese data and by Korean scholars for the Korean data.

Due to logistic difficulties accessing field excavation reports, we have relied largely on the publications of research staff and archaeologists at various museums, universities, and field research institutes inside Japan, who, on the basis of their examination of the field excavation reports or their own field work, have published informative monographs. A conscious effort has been made to convey *their* observations in *their own words*, albeit in translation by the authors unless otherwise noted. This, therefore, is the story being told by scholars and front-line researchers in Japan and Korea, *not by outside observers*.

For the Korean archaeology, we have incorporated our own field research results along with information embodied in monographs and journal articles published by field researchers, research institutes, museums, and university archaeology faculties.

The theoretical principle underlying our evaluation of archaeological data is the anthropologically informed notion that during migration *a culture moves with people from one region to another – not as isolated artifacts or trade goods but as integral components of well-established and socio-economically integrated systems* (Haury 1958: 1-7; Burmeister 2000). Kameda and others have identified archaeological markers of the Toraijin settlements in the Archipelago in terms of the pottery used in daily life, culinary features including especially the *yeonjil* earthenware, mortuary practices, and/or residential patterns unique to the Toraijin's pre-migration life-ways (Kameda 2003a: 1-14, 2003b: 55-65, 2005: 1-16, 2011: 116-119; K Tanaka 2004: 88-95; Kyoto Bunka Hakubutsukan 1989; OYBH 1999, OYBH 2004; SKAKH 2001; OFCAH 2004; Iwanaga 1991; Kataoka 1999, 2006; Shichida 2005, 2007a, 2017; Saga-ken Kyoiku I'inkai 2008; Sakai 2013; Hashino 2014; K Miyamoto 2017).

For example, the Songguk-ni type residential buildings and the mortuary culture of dolmen construction, unique to the Peninsular Middle Mumun society, serve as archaeological markers for the Early Yayoi-period Toraijin when these features occur archaeologically in mutual association (i.e., linked into a settlement system, not emulated individually). Likewise, a sudden appearance of Peninsular Jeomtodae pottery (pots with a clay ring around their rim) and the wood-coffin burial system would indicate the presence of the Middle Yayoi Toraijin (Kataoka 1999, 2006).

Also, residential buildings equipped with an attached Peninsular-style cooking oven and supported by four posts, buildings with thick walls, and buildings equipped with an *ondol* (an ancient traditional Korean under-floor heating system), accompanied by Yeonjil (soft earthenware) pottery of ancient Korea, serve as archaeological markers for Kofun period Toraijin settlements (Kameda 2003a: 1-14, 2004a: 75-94, 2005: 1-16, 2016: 283-321; Sakai 2013: 77-78; GGOB 1999: 60).

Along with these cultural features, human skeletal remains provide vital clues regarding the identity of the people associated with settlement sites (Shichida 2017: 41-42). Quantitative and qualitative differences in skeletal morphology distinguish between incoming populations from the Peninsula and the indigenous hunter-gatherer populations of the Archipelago. Intermarriage created a descendant population with combined features. Dental metrics of modern Japanese reveal ratios of immigrant/native influence as 3:1 in the Kanto region as opposed to 3:2 in the Ryukyus and 3:7 in the Hokkaido Ainu (Matsumura 2001).

DNA studies are clarifying gene flow from the continent but concentrate mainly on modern population compositions due to the lack of skeletal remains in the Mumun and Yayoi periods. Nevertheless, modern Japanese (including the Ainu) are assessed to have between 50–80% continental genes (the rest inherited from the indigenous hunter-gatherer population) with the latest study averaging more than 80% continental genes except in the far north (Kanazawa-Kiriyama et al. 2015).

Ethnologically the modern Japanese population is dual-structured, exhibiting "the native Jomon and immigrant Yayoi traits" (Hanihara 1991; 2000: 4; Allen 2008: 122). According to genetic researches, two different sets of Y chromosomes mark "the Jomon and the Yayoi populations in the Japanese paternal gene pool, going back over twenty thousand years and three thousand years respectively" (Allen 2008: 122-123). Of special significance, while the Jomon chromosome markers are rare among the population of Korea, they are more common among the Ainu and the Okinawans than in the population of Honshu. On the other hand, the Yayoi markers are common in Korea and Japan except in Okinawa and among the Ainu. "This," Allen concludes (2008: 123), "supports the hypothesis that the peninsula migrants and their descendants prevailed in many parts of Japan while the native population and culture remained predominant in northern and southern spheres." Thus, the migration of Toraijin did not end with changing the culture of the Japanese Archipelago but it effected a transformation of the population that survives to the present day.

Historical Sources

The archaeological data are complemented with gleanings from ancient Chinese records including the *Shiji* (Historical Records) compiled by SIMA Qian (145–85? BC), the *Hanshu* (History of the [Former] Han Dynasty), compiled by BAN Gu at the end of the 1st century, and the *Weizhi* (Records of the Wei Dynasty), compiled by CHEN Shou (233–297) and existing as part of the *Sanguozhi* (History of the Three Kingdoms, c. 220–265).

For the Three Kingdoms period of Korea (Koguryo, Paekche, Silla, and Kaya) and Kofun period Japan, we have drawn, along with rich archaeological data, useful information from the Stele of Gwanggaeto (414), the *Samguk Sagi* (Historical Records of the Three Kingdoms) (1145), the *Samguk Yusa* (Anecdotes of the Three Kingdoms) (1281), the *Kojiki* (Records of Ancient Matters) (712), and the *Nihon Shoki* (the Chronicles of Japan) (720).

The Gwanggaeto Stele has been subject to controversy ever since it was discovered around 1880, and questions regarding its contents will never end because many of the inscribed words are no longer legible and there are discrepancies among the extant copies of their original rubbings (SH Park 2007; HG Lee and RH Park 1996; JS Park 1996). Likewise, questions abound regarding the historical accuracy of the *Samguk Sagi* and *Samguk Yusa* in light of ancient historical texts from China as well as archaeological data (HS Shin 1981; Shultz 2005; McBride II 2006; Best 2003: 165-167; 2006: 31-35; 2016). Jonathan Best (2016) has found the early chronology of the *Samguk Sagi* unreliable and cautions against indiscriminate use of its narratives.

Equally questionable is the historicity of many accounts in the *Kojiki* and the *Nihon Shoki* (Tsuda 1924: 1948, 1950; Umezawa 1962, 1988; Mishina 1971; Yamada 1991; Furuta and Shibuya 1994; Piggott 2002; Shinkawa and Hayakawa 2011). Created as a political treatise rather than a historical narrative, for the purpose of legitimizing the Yamato hegemony, the *Nihon Shoki* suffers in historical accuracy. Aston (1972[1896]: xv-xvi) has observed that the early part of the *Nihon Shoki* is essentially fictional and that "trustworthy record of events" appear after the mid-5th century. Its compilers also transposed many of the ancient historical records, creating confusion about the actors of various historical events as well as numerous chronological discrepancies (Tsuda 1924, 1948, 1950). Problematic also are numerous cases of anachronism, rendering the 4th–5th century events according to the perceptions of the 8th century, such as describing ancient Wa as 'Nihon' (Japan) (first used in the latter part of the 7th century and the ancient kings of Wa as 'Tenno' (Emperor) (also first used in the latter part of the 7th century). Finally, the Japan-centered worldview, underlying the ideology of the *Nihon Shoki* compilers, resulted in skewed perceptions of Yamato's relationship with its neighbor states, especially those in the Peninsula.

Keeping in mind the inherent textual problems, we have sought to ensure that the accounts cited from the ancient records are not contradicted by other reliable historical records and archaeological investigations. Where their historicity is questioned, we have so noted.

Because of logistic difficulties in accessing voluminous excavation and fieldwork reports in various Korean and Japanese research centers the authors have relied on journal articles and monographs published by Korean and Japanese archaeologists and archaeological research centers, providing the essential information on their researches.

In addition to numerous publications by academicians, research institutes, museums, and universities, this volume also reflects on many conversations which the authors personally held with eminent Japanese and Korean researchers at research institutes, universities, and museums from Seoul to Kyoto.

Finally, we wish to remind our readers that the primary focus of this book is neither Korean history nor Japanese history. It is the Toraijin and their contributions to ancient Japanese society. Hence, we devote much of our narratives to the archaeology and history of the Toraijin. Korean and Japanese history are discussed only where they are relevant to the Toraijin.

CHAPTER ONE

RICE-BEARING TORAIJIN

I. THEIR HISTORICAL AND CULTURAL BACKGROUND: SONGGUK-NI TYPE CULTURE OF THE PENINSULA'S MIDDLE MUMUN SOCIETY (C. 900–400 BC)

The Incipient Toraijin who migrated to the Archipelago at the end of the Jomon period were the farmers of the Middle Mumun period in the Korean Peninsula. The Mumun culture began with the appearance of the Mumun pottery at the end of the Neolithic Chulmun Period, c. 1,500 BC.[1] Mumun (無文) means 'without decoration' or 'plain'. Though not entirely without surface manipulations, the Mumun pottery was so named to distinguish it from the earlier Chulmun pottery which was elaborately decorated with a variety of comb pattern designs.

The Mumun society was an agricultural society based on an intensive agriculture (GA Lee 2011: S326). Agriculture first emerged in the Peninsula during the Chulmun Neolithic, around 3500 cal. BP (GA Lee 2011: S319-S322; Y Oh *et al.* 2017: 1766-1768), when the Chulmun broad spectrum economy began to engage in the cultivation of barley, legume, and rice in addition to foxtail and broomcorn millet, which had long been a part of the Chulmun diet (GA Lee 2003, 2005, 2011; Shin, Rhee, and Aikens 2012: 68-109).

Following several centuries of further development, the Mumun agricultural society entered its florescence phase during the Middle Mumun period, c. 900–800 BC. It coincided with the appearance of a new Mumun cultural system, known as 'the Songguk-ni type culture' in southern Korea. KIM Ha-Beom (2019: 2) defines the latter as "a particular type of recurrent assemblage in material records that is associated with a time and space" in the Korean Peninsula, c. 900–400 BC. Its distinctive features included houses with an oval pit in the center of the floor (Fig. 1.1A), (pottery jars with a flaring lip (*oeban guyeon*) (Fig. 1.1B-D), triangular stone reaping knives (*samgak hyeong seokdo*) (Fig. 1.1 E), straight-hilted polished stone daggers (*ildanshik seokkeom*) (Fig. 1.1F), and stone axes with a notch on the back of the stem (*yugu seokbu*) (Fig. 1.1G) (SO Kim 2006b: 51; HB Kim 2019: 26-48).

Emerging in the lower reaches of the Geum River in west-central Korea c. 900 BC or shortly thereafter (Kwak, Kim, and Lee 2017: 1092; JC Lee 2015: 33-37; HB Kim 2019: 18), the Songguk-ni culture spread to nearly all parts of southern Korea (Map 1.1), becoming the dominant Mumun culture of southern Korea during the Middle Mumun (JC Lee 2015: 77-198; GT Kim, Lee *et al.* 2015). As it expanded outward from the Geum River basin, it encountered various local cultural traditions formed during the Early Mumun Period. In most localities the two cultural traditions came to coexist, as evidenced in the archaeological remains of Daepyeong-ni near the southeast coast (GJIB/GSND 2001; HB Kim 2019: 11-12).

---

[1] Dates for the Mumun period including Mumun calibrated dates are from JC Lee 2015: 26-44 and HB Kim 2019: 2, 24.

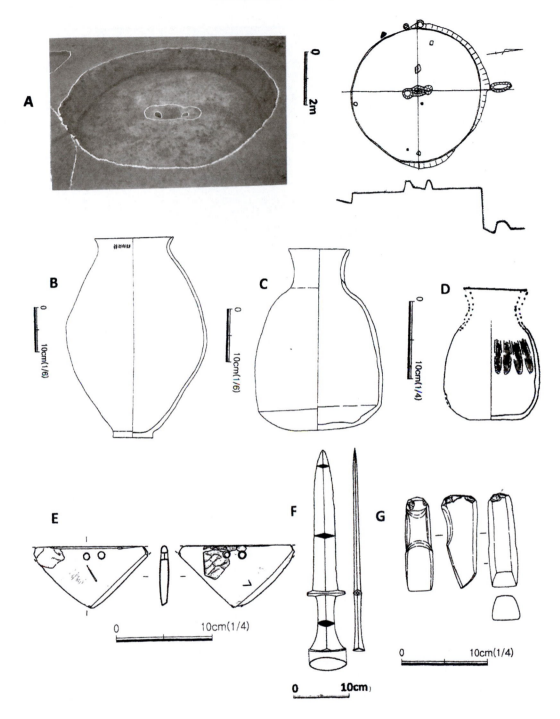

Fig. 1.1. Distinctive features of the Songguk-ni type culture. **A:** Residential floor plan with a central oval pit and two side post holes. **B:** Songguk-ni storage jar with an everted rim. **C:** Red-burnished globular pot (mainly used for mortuary purpose). **D:** Globular pots with a lobed design. **E:** Triangular-shaped stone reaping knives with alternating cutting edges. **F:** A polished stone dagger with a straight hilt. **G:** A stone axe with a groove. (After GT Kim, GS Lee *et al.* 2015: 48, 148, 153, 220, 252, 259).

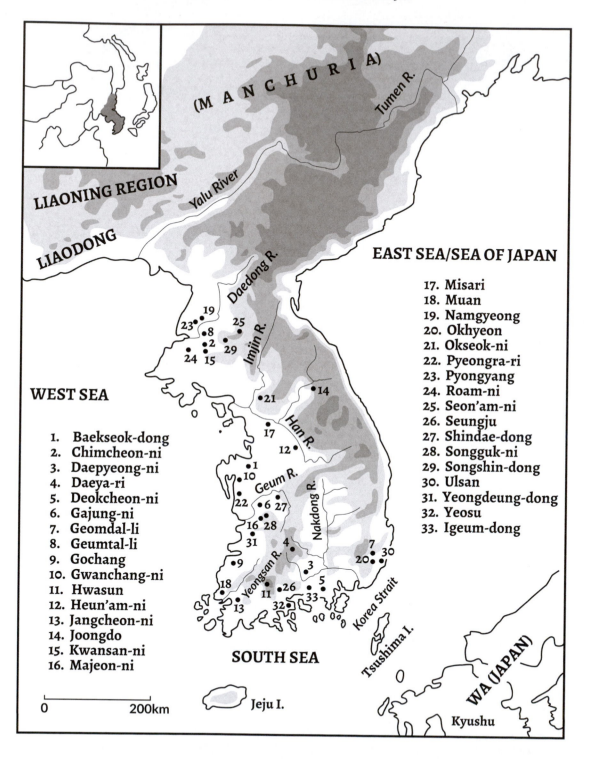

Map 1.1. Mumun sites in the Korean peninsula (by Lucas Pauly).

1. Pottery of the Songguk-ni-Type

The most conspicuous vessels of the Songguk-ni type pottery are jars and pots (Fig. 1.1B-D) (GT Kim et al. 2015). The primary diagnostic feature of the Songguk-ni type jar is the flaring lip (rim) of wide-mouthed jars, 20–40 cm tall. Normally, they have an egg-shaped body and a reduced, flat base. Prominent also in the Songguk-ni pottery repertoire are the globular red-burnished pots, which had first appeared during latter part of the Early Mumun (BS Kim 2003: 248). Made primarily for funerary purposes and found mostly in graves, they were apparently used to provide food or drink for the dead.

The globular pots with grey or black lobes (1.1D), which also had appeared during the Early Mumun as a part of its mortuary culture (BS Kim 2003: 248), joined the Songguk-ni pottery repertoire. Initially they were placed in the elite graves (cists, dolmens, and moat-surrounded tombs) as a set along with polished stone daggers and arrowheads, but gradually this custom was relaxed as evidenced by the frequent occurrence of a single jar in the elite burials along the southern coast during the latter part of the Middle Mumun (Hirakori 2013: 157-159).

With the expansion of the Songguk-ni culture throughout southern Korea its pottery came to coexist with that of local cultural traditions. For example, Daepyeong-ni, a major Middle Mumun village site, has yielded a variety of pottery types including those of the Songguk-ni and its local tradition. As the Songguk-ni culture interacted with various local traditions, the two also underwent a process of amalgamation in pottery forms (GJIB/ GSND 2001; JC Lee 2015: 138-143).

2. Settlements

Many Early Mumun settlements (Daepyeong-ni, Sangchon, and Pyeonggeo-dong in Jinju; Dongcheon-dong in Taegu; Songjuk-ni in Gimcheon) continued to thrive on the flat alluvial beds next to a river, but the Middle Mumun farmers also chose low-lying hillsides, 40–50m high, adjacent to streams and fertile plains, as in the case of Songguk-ni (HW Lee 2009: 111-112) (cf. Map 1.1).

In a recent study of the mobility and settlement pattern of the Songguk-ni people from the emic perspective, KIM Ha-Beom (2019: 98) observes that

> In river valleys, the slope had a definite strong constraining influence on the mobility pattern of the past Mumun population. On the other hand, the slope acted much less as a constraining factor in the plain regions. From the emic perspective of the Mumun people, people enjoyed relative freedom of movement unconstrained by the slope in plain regions, whereas their mobility was highly constrained by the slope of the topography in river valleys.

The Middle Mumun settlements consisted of pit houses with square, rectangular, or circular floor plans. The most distinguishing mark of these pit houses was an oval pit dug at the center of the floor, with postholes placed either inside or outside the pit (Fig. 1.1A) (GJUB 1979: 110-114; Weongwang University 2000: 338-350; JC Lee 2015: 51-58). There is much debate on the function of the oval pits. Some scholars believe that they served as central hearths while others treat them as waste disposal pits associated with stone tool manufacturing (HW Lee 2009: 127-132).

Gullipju (large raised buildings supported on posts) were also prominent in Songguk-ni-type settlements, as evident at the Igeum-dong site (Fig. 1.2). At the Yeongdeung-dong site on Korea's southwest coastal plain, five such buildings were grouped in an open space surrounded by residential structures (Weongwang University 2000: 349-350). At Jangcheon-ni, another coastal plain site also in southwest Korea, one such storage building was found among 12 residences (SR Choi 1986: 35-36, 48). Evidence from various excavated sites suggests that one of these large storage buildings was present for every four or five dwellings (GJIB 2002: 32; Fig. 1.2 Top). Clearly, Songguk-ni-type settlements produced substantial harvests of rice and other crops that were cared for on a communal basis.

The square footage of the residential buildings was reduced during the Middle Mumun. For example, while many Early Mumun houses at Baekseok-dong were over 40 m², the average floor size of 20 Songguk-ni type dwellings at Jinrari was 15.8 m² (HW Lee 2009: 121-124; SH Lee 2014: 23, 28). Simultaneously, the number of individual dwellings increased. JH Ahn (2006: 59), on the basis of agricultural expansion and population increase evidenced archaeologically, postulates that during the Middle Mumun the extended family system of the earlier period broke down leading to the emergence of nuclear families. Others (SO Kim 2006a; HW Lee 2009) suggest that it was the result of the breakdown of a communal living, prompted by the same socio-economic factors.

Regardless of the reason, the number of settlements grew explosively during the Middle Mumun on the low alluvial land as well as on the hilly ridges (SH Lee 2014: 19). A Middle Mumun settlement at Dongcheon-dong in Taegu was a large farming village comprising 60 contemporaneous residences while Jinra-ri in Cheongdo 93 houses (SH Lee 2014: 24). This was undoubtedly the result of expanding wet-rice farming discussed below (SH Lee 2014: 28).

In terms of community patterns, the Songguk-ni settlements displayed central planning, as shown by the discrete locations of residences, industrial complexes, cemeteries, and farmed fields. In some cases, Songguk-ni settlements were protected by fortification complexes including one or more encircling moats (JC Lee 2015: 206-234).

As revealed at Jinra-ri and Dongcheon-dong, large villages were spatially organized around a central plaza, near which all raised storage buildings (*gullipju*) were placed along with extra-large residential buildings (SH Lee 2014: 23-24). The person(s) living in the large residential building(s) near the storage buildings are believed to have been community leaders in charge of the collection and distribution system of surplus food.

Another Songguk-ni type cultural feature was the appearance, along with the outdoor storage *gullipju* buildings, of numerous outdoor underground flask-shaped storage pits. During the Early Mumun, the storage pits were inside the residential buildings, but now they were placed outdoor away from individual residences. LEE Su-hong (2014: 25-30) assumes that the purpose was to place surplus food under the control of the community rather than individual households. If so, along with the *gullipju* storage buildings, the outdoor storage pits facilitated the emergence of a manager class within the community, the beginning of a stratified society.

During the 7th to 5th centuries BC, a number of Songguk-ni settlements grew into mega-communities that could well be called towns, with large populations, multiple residences, expanded farming fields, and clear evidence of social stratification. Such sites include Songguk-ni in the lower reaches of the

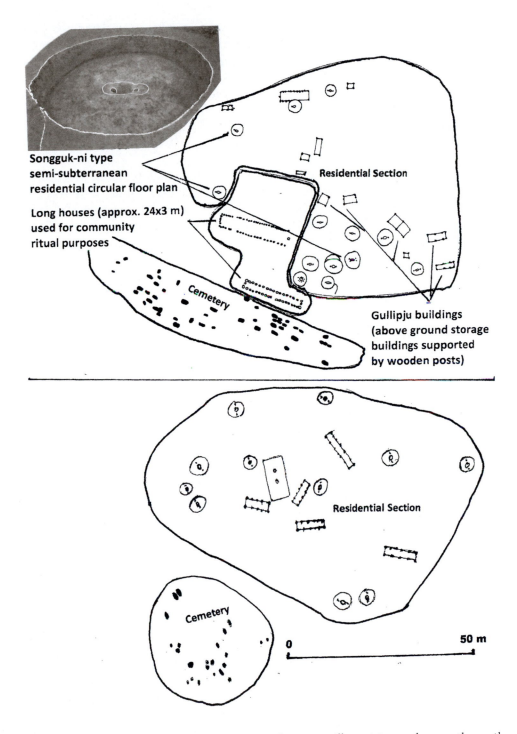

Fig. 1.2. Songguk-ni-type villages. **Top:** A Songguk-ni type village at Igeum-dong on the south coast of Korea (after HW Lee 2009: 233). **Bottom:** A Songguk-ni type village at Etsuji, northern Kyushu (after Mizoguchi 2013: 56).

Geum River, Yeoigok in the upper hinterland reaches of the same river, Gwanchang-ni on the central west coast, Shinpung and Galdu in the Tamjin River basin on the southwestern coast, Daegok-ni in the Seomjin River basin on the south coast, and Daepyeong-ni in the Nam Gang River basin on the south-eastern coast, among others. These large Songguk-ni culture communities were socially stratified, with one or two supersize residences typically occupying a central place in the community (MY Song 2006: 9-29; JC Lee 2015: 279-354).

3. Agriculture

Songguk-ni culture settlements were fully agricultural, based on multiple cropping of "a variety of upland crops, including foxtail and broomcorn millets, wheat, barley, bottle gourd, azuki, soybean, beefsteak plant, and melon species as well as rice" (Kwak *et al.* 2017, 27(8): 1091-1092. Among the Middle Mumun period sites, carbonized rice remains are known from Songguk-ni and Majeon-ni. Songguk-ni has yielded some 395 grams of carbonized *japonica* rice and *radiocarbon dates of c. 2665 and c. 2565 cal. BP.*

Gubong-Nohwari (Park, Lee, Habu, and Jeong 2004) and Majeon-ni (GGOB 2002: 40) have revealed a paddy, irrigation channel, water control dikes, and a reservoir. Gwanchang-ni in the same region has also revealed wet-rice fields and irrigation channels (KH Kim and JJ Kim 2001: 525-533). Rice, wheat, barley, and millet were all cultivated during this period by the people of the Songguk-ni culture at the site of Daepyeong-ni by the Nam River near the south coast (GJIB 2002: 58-59).

Wet-rice cultivation required geophysical and hydraulic engineering skills essential to levelling of a wildland, building dykes, preparation of the soil, and regulation of water supply at different points of the rice plants' growing, maturing, and preparation for harvesting. It was also highly labor intensive. Even in modern days, farmers in Asia treat wet-rice cultivation as a major undertaking, far more complicated and laborious than the upland cropping.

The fact that the farmers at Gubong-Nohwari, Majeon-ni and Gwanchang-ni were investing their time, energy, and resources into the development of rice cultivation in the irrigated fields indicates that already during the Middle Mumun Period, rice was a highly desired grain. *Analysis of carbonized grains found at Songguk-ni type culture settlements has shown that rice was ubiquitous, found nearly in every house* (MK Kim 2015: 838-853). *In time, in Korea and throughout Asia, rice emerged as the most important commodity, symbolizing wealth and power* (SH Lee 2014: 28-29).

4. Lithic Implements

A. Industrial and Farming Tools

The stone tool repertoire of the Early Mumun was continuously employed throughout the Middle Mumun Period for industrial and agricultural purposes. The industrial tools included small and large square- and oval-bodied stone axes with the cutting-edge ground on both sides, but the *hap'in seokbu* (oval bodied axes with a closed-up clam-shape cutting edge ground on both sides, Fig. 1.3A), which had become popular during the latter part of the Early Mumun, emerged as the most important (JS Bae 2007: 66).

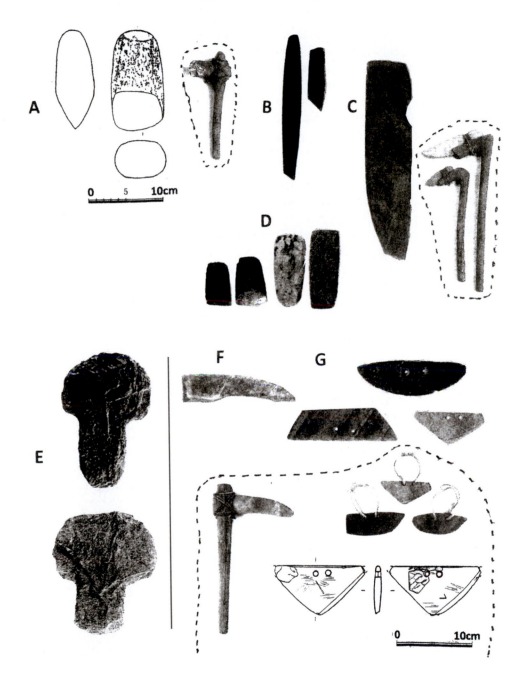

Fig. 1.3. Middle Mumun lithic implements. **Industrial tools** (**A**: Adzes. **B**: Chisels. **C**: Notched axes (left, 28.1cm). **D**: Planing blades (after National Museum of Korea 2003: 46-47). **Agricultural tools** (**E**: Hoes. **F**: Sickle (25.6 cm). **G**: Rectangular, boat-shaped, and triangular reaping knives (left, 12-18 cm) (after GJIB 2002: 68, 101).

During the Middle Mumun there was a phenomenal increase in the number of the wood-working-related tools such as chisels (Fig. 1.2B) and flat stone axes with the cutting-edge ground on one side (*pyeon'pyeong pyeon'in seokbu*) used as planing tools (Fig. 1.2D) (JC Lee 2015: 166-168). Newly added to these was the *yugu seokbu* (stone axes with a groove on its stem) (Fig. 1.2C). It was a stone axe with its cutting-edge ground only on one side as in the case of a chisel and was fastened to a wooden handle. The groove was made to enhance the fastening of the axe firmly to a wooden handle with a string (JC Lee 2015: 166). Unique to the Peninsula, the *yugu seokbu* was a significant contribution to the Middle Mumun industry, especially in the production of wooden implements and residential construction (JS Bae 2014: 66, 71-72).

The Middle Mumun farmers continued to use the flat stone reaping knives (rectangular, comb-shaped, and boat-shaped) of the Early Mumun Period for harvesting the grain. However, they invented new stone reaping tools in the form of triangular knives with reversible cutting edges and sickles to enhance harvesting (Fig. 1.2G). While the earlier reaping knives had the cutting edge only on one side, the triangular knives now had reversible cutting edges so that when one side became dull the knife could be slipped around so that the other cutting edge could be used. Such reaping knives were invented in response to agricultural expansion requiring greater efficiency in harvesting. Stone sickles (Fig. 1.2F) were invented for the same reason. However, for some unknown reason, the latter did not become as popular as the stone reaping knives (JC Lee 2015: 167-172).

B. Ritual Weapon

Ritual stone weapons of the Middle Mumun Period comprised polished stone daggers, spearheads, and arrowheads. In addition to the polished stone daggers with a two-step hilt of the Early Mumun Period, there appeared three new types: daggers with a node in the middle of the hilt (*yujeol byeongshik sekkom*), daggers with a straight hilt, and stemmed daggers (Fig. 1.4) (JC Lee 2015: 154-162). In the case of stemmed daggers, the stem was inserted into a wooden handle. Some of the Middle Mumun ritual weapons appear to have diffused to the Russian Maritime Province during the middle of the 1st millennium BC (Shoda, Yanshina, Son, and Teramae 2009). The length of the daggers with a node on hilt ranged from 21–29 cm to 45 cm. The dagger from Dolmen #3 at Jinrari in Cheongdo, measured to be 66.7 cm long, was an exception. On the other hand, the length of the daggers with a straight hilt ranged from 24.7 cm to 35.8 cm.

The polished stone weapons of the Mumun Period were made of slate, tuff, hornfels, or schist, which were easily split and broken (Shoda 2015: 156). Scholars therefore believe that they were produced primarily for ritual use among the elites than as real weapons. This view is strengthened by the fact that the majority of them have been found in the elite graves.

Several scholars (JS Bae 2007: 180-182; Hirakori 2013: 160-161, 180-194; JC Lee 2015: 151-153) posit that the polished stone daggers were manufactured by highly specialized craftsmen, traded between remote regions, used primarily for mortuary purpose, and closely related to megalithic burials (dolmens). As such, their possession was "highly restricted" and mainly belonged to the males (Shoda 2015: 156, 158). There was "clear regularity in the production technique," and "production regularities and funeral rites [were] shared within single river basins..." (Shoda 2015: 156).

Hirakori (2013: 180-194) observes that the polished stone daggers with a noded hilt (Fig. 1. 3A1) were integral components of grand public mortuary rituals rather than individual or family funerary act.

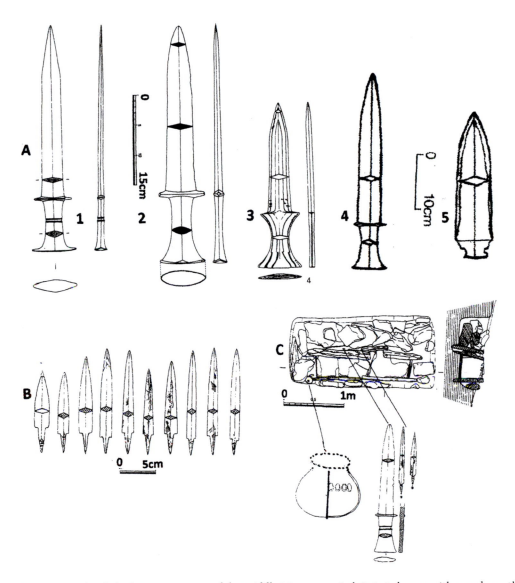

Fig. 1.4. Ritual polished stone weapons of the Middle Mumun period. **A-1:** A dagger with a node on the hilt. **A-2, 3, 4:** Daggers with a straight hilt. **A-5:** A dagger with a stem. **B:** willow leaf-shaped polished stone arrow points. **C:** A dolmen burial containing a polished stone dagger with a node on the hilt, willow leaf-shaped arrow points, and red-burnished pot, Shinchon-ni on the south coast (after Hirakori 2013: 111).

As such, they functioned as ritual property of the community, and the members of the community identified with each other through them. Stemmed daggers were tightly inserted into the tip of a wooden handle, while the stemmed spearheads inserted into the tip of a long wooden or bamboo pole (JC Lee 2015: 164-165).

As in the case of polished stone daggers, the polished stone arrowheads, especially those in the shape of a long willow leaf (Fig. 1.3B) were made primarily for the mortuary ritual and were placed in the elite graves along with the polished stone daggers (Fig. 1.3C) (JC Lee 2015: 162-164).

5. Bronze Daggers and Bronze Industry

During the Middle Mumun period, bronze daggers (Fig. 1.5) were status symbols of the elites and were placed in chiefly graves along with polished stone daggers and arrow-heads, tubular beads cut from semi-precious stones, and red-burnished pottery vessels. Bronze weapons have also been found in non-mortuary deposits, typically in remote spots overlooking a river or the sea. LEE Sang-gil (2000: 23-55) speculates that these were ritual offerings made in times of war, plague, or natural disaster, or in some cases for the ritual protection of water-borne voyagers.

Their morphology links them to bronzes of the Liaoning region in southwestern Manchuria, suggesting they spread from the region into Korea's northwest and west central coast regions, whence they were subsequently adopted in various localities throughout southern Korea (GJUB and GGWB 1992: 126-132). Because of their origin in the Liaoning region, they are called 'Liaoning bronze daggers." They are also called "mandolin-shaped bronze daggers" because of their shape in the likeness of the so-named musical instrument. Notably, among those found in the Korean Peninsula, many have a notched tang which sets them apart from those found in the Liaoning region of Manchuria. This characteristic, and the finding at Songguk-ni and other sites throughout the Peninsula of bronze casting molds cut from stone, have convinced scholars that Middle Mumun technicians had the skills to make their own bronzes. Found mainly within the Songguk-ni culture zone in southern Korea, bronze daggers appear to have been an integral part of that culture (YM Lee 1998).

Thus far over 100 Liaoning-type bronze artifacts have been reported from Korea, 58 of them being mandolin-shaped bronze daggers. The morphology of the mandolin-shaped bronze daggers changed through time: in the earliest specimens, the blade's protuberances were slightly above its midpoint, but they later moved farther upwards and the mandolin-shaped body became a narrower, slenderer dagger (Lin 1990).

Other bronzes found in Songguk-ni sites are spears (13), arrowheads (13), and fan-shaped adzes (10) (Fig. 1.5 bottom) (YM Lee 19983). Bronze mirrors of the Liaoning type are also found in Korea, but they are rare. A few reported finds had a flat surface, multiple attachment knobs and zigzag (or thunder) designs.

6. Spinning/Weaving Technology

Fundamental to human well-being is clothing, especially in geographical zones having cold winter seasons, as in the Peninsula. Spindle whorls began to appear during the Chulmun Neolithic period (c. 3,000 BC) at Seopohang III in the northeast and Gungsan in the northwest (GMUY 1991: 191-192, 468-480; YH Do and GD Hwang 1957). Found among residential remains and burial goods, they show that woven fabric clothing had become an integral part of Korea's Mumun culture. Normally made of stone or baked clay, spindle whorls were circular disks with a hole in the center, through which a wooden spindle was inserted. The whorl acted as a weight, or flywheel that would help weavers keep the spindle rotating conveniently as they deftly twisted together plant fibers into a continuous

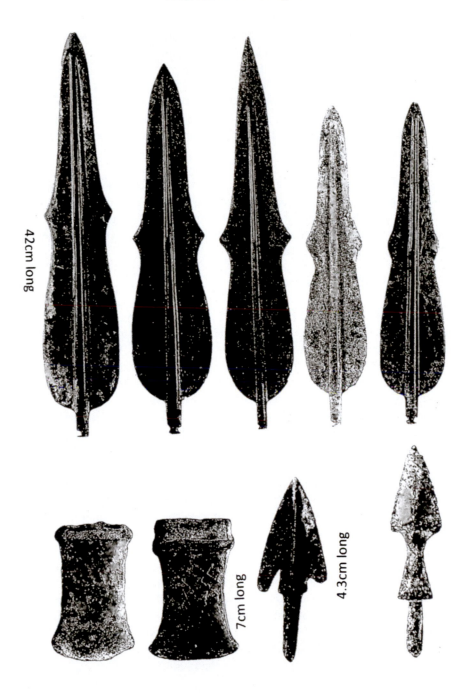

Fig. 1.5. Liaoning bronzes of the Middle Mumun period: daggers, axes, and arrow points (GJUB and GGWB 1992: 19, 22). Photo by Hanstudio.

thread and wound them onto the spindle. The thread thus made was subsequently woven on a loom into coarse fabric that could then be tailored into clothing (GJIB 2002: 114).

A bone needle uncovered in a shell midden at the Gungsan Site still had a piece of a thread twisted together from hemp fiber, indicating that hemp was one of the plant materials used to make clothes (YH Do and GD Hwang 1957). Spinning, weaving and tailoring was laborious, but less so than the Paleolithic method of hunting, killing, and butchering an animal whose hide had then to be stripped, tanned, cut, and sewn into a garment.

Recent studies of Korean Bronze Age spindle whorls indicate that after c. 800 BC, they became smaller and lighter, indicating that spinners had begun to produce fine yarn necessary for making tightly knit textiles. Investigators posit that such innovation was stimulated by a climate change from warmer to cool temperatures, as clothes made of tightly knit fabric could provide more warmth and comfort than porous textiles made of thick yarn (BW Park 2015: 5-31).

7. Symbols of Prestige and Political Power

Cist tomb #1 at Songguk-ni, dated to c. 800–700 BC with artifact typology (Shoda 2009: 129-133; Lin 1990), contained an impressive array of prestige goods, including a lute-shaped bronze dagger, a polished stone dagger, 11 willow leaf-shaped polished stone arrowheads, 17 tubular beads, two comma-shaped Amazonite stones, and a bronze chisel (Fig. 1.6). The grave goods were found in the positions where they were originally placed with or worn by the dead. A bronze dagger was placed next to the deceased person's left hand. The arrowheads were lying on the dagger. Two comma-shaped ornaments lay on each side of the dagger tip, suggesting that they once adorned a now-decomposed sheath, like two earrings. The tubular beads were scattered around the dagger between its midpoint and tip. The polished stone dagger lay at the waist of the tomb's occupant, with its tip toward the right foot, suggesting that it was attached to the waist.

The cist tomb is believed to have belonged to the highest-ranking leader of the Songguk-ni community (HW Lee 2009: 227-228). The daggers and arrowheads in particular, inspiring fear and awe, functioned as the symbols of social prestige and political power during the Middle Mumun period (JS Bae 2007: 172-191).

As shown in the above elite grave goods, certain jade ornaments, owing to their rarity, functioned as integral components of the social and political symbols (Shoda 2009: 187, 204). Specifically, they were comma-shaped amazonite stones, tubular beads made of jasper and amber, and small circular beads made of the amazonite, crystal or amber. In addition to the cist tombs, the comma-shaped jades have been found in dolmens (Usan-ni in Seungju; Pyeonggeo-dong in Yeosu; Weol'am-ni in Muan; Daepyeong-ni in Jinju on the south and southwest coast), and occasionally among Middle Mumun residential remains (Jodong-ni in Chungju; Changpyeong-ni in Ulsan).

In a dolmen at Usan-ni in Seungju a pair of curved amazonite stones and a tubular bead came to light along with a polished stone dagger, a bronze dagger, and small beads (GJUB and GGWB 1992: 13, 23). Most likely, those found singly were used as pendants, along with small tubular and circular beads, forming a necklace. The beads found in pairs are believed to have been used as earrings (GJIB 2002: 103; GSND-DADB 1999: 231).

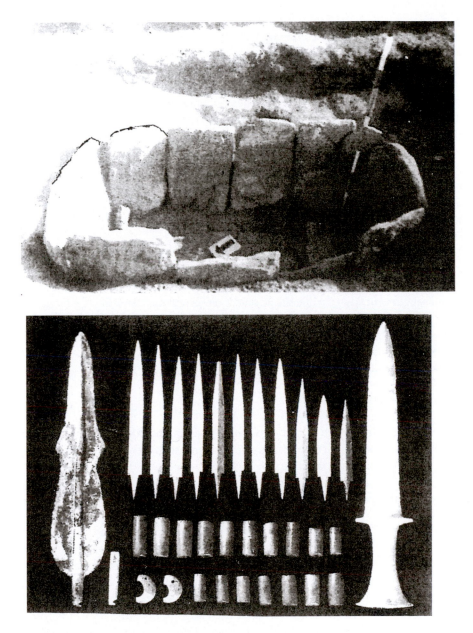

Fig. 1.6. Elite prestige goods from a cist tomb at Songguk-ni. **Top:** Cist tomb. **Bottom:** Prestige goods (**left:** mandolin-shaped bronze dagger, 33cm long. **middle top:** willow leaf-shaped polished arrows. **middle bottom:** from left, bronze chisel, tubular beads, a pair of Amazonite stones. **right:** polished stone dagger, 28cm long (GJUB 1986: 21). Photo credit: National Museum of Korea.

In terms of its origin, the curved amazonite stone has been related by some to curved dragon-shaped jades of the Hongshan Neolithic Culture (c. 4,500–3,000 BC) found in the far northern reaches of the Liao River basin (HG Lee 2004: 118-122). The temporal and spatial distance, however, has made most investigators, including authors of this book, skeptical about their genealogical relationship. The usual interpretation is that the form originated from the canine teeth of fierce animals, which were often used as pendants during the Neolithic period, or as a symbol of a half-moon sacred to moon worshippers, or as a symbol of fetus/fertility (HS Noh 1997).

During the 1995–1999 excavations of the Daepyeong-ni Mumun village site in Jinju near the southern coast, a team of archaeologists uncovered several industrial locations where tubular beads of jasper and comma-shaped ornaments of the amazonite stone were manufactured. Among the unearthed artifacts were finished and unfinished ornaments, raw materials, and grinding tools.

On the basis of his site analysis at Daepyeong-ni, Shoda (2009: 187-203) posits that the production of the prestige goods was carried out by the community through two specialized groups located at two different sections within the community, to enhance efficiency. The east section provided raw materials and roughly cut stones while the west section turned the latter into finely finished products.

The finished ornaments were distributed to other regions of southern Korea as part of a long-distance trade. Such prestige ornaments found along the southern coast at Yeosu, Seungju, Muan, and Ulsan were most likely manufactured at Daepyeong-ni (GJIB 2002: 103-109).

8. Middle Mumun Mortuary Practices

The farmers of the Middle Mumun Period employed four distinctly different types of burial structures: megalithic dolmens, stone cist tombs (seokgwan-myo and seokgwak-myo), moat-surrounded tombs (jugumyo), and ceramic funerary jar coffins.

A. Megalithic Burial Structures ("Dolmens")

Megalithic dolmens are found virtually in all parts of the Korean Peninsula and are more numerous there than anywhere else in northeast Asia. However, nearly 70% of 30,000 dolmens identified in the Peninsula are located along the southwest and south coast, suggesting that they flourished more in the southern part of the Peninsula (Map 1.3) (MUJC and SNUM 1999). Korean dolmens were essentially prehistoric burials closely associated with emerging agricultural communities. Beginning in the Early Mumun, the farming villages began to construct them for the burial of the village leaders and their family as a communal project. Through regular ritualization of dolmen construction, the agricultural communities sought to reinforce their communal solidarity and their relationship to the land which they farmed (SJ Lee 1999a: 423-441; BC Kim 2010: 5-24).

Korean dolmens broadly comprise three types: table-type (takjashik), propping-stone-type (gibanshik), and cap-stone-type (gaeseokshik) (YM Lee 1999: 938-939). The table-type, found mainly in northwestern Korea, consists of a flat cap-stone and two slabs supporting the latter on each side, giving the structure the table or desk-like appearance (Fig.1.7, top). When a corpse was placed inside the structure, two slabs were placed on its front and back, tuning the entire structure into a burial chamber. Some of the table-type dolmens were of monumental size. The capstones of the largest table-type dolmens are those of Gwansan-ni in Un'yrul (8.75 m long x 4.50 m wide x 0.31 m thick), Songshin-dong in Yeont'an (8.30 m long x 6.30 m wide x 0.50 m thick), and Roam-ni in Anak (7.70 m long x 6.00 m wide x 0.64 m thick) (Seok 1979). A number of table type dolmens in variant forms have been found in southern Korea along the west coast, on the island of Ganghwa, in Boryeong, and in Gochang, suggesting human migrations from the north to the south along the west coast during the Mumun period (HW Hong 1999: 213-224; ML Choi 1999: 128; YJ Park 1999: 1069).

The propping-stone-type dolmens were constructed primarily in southern Korea and for that reason are called 'southern-type dolmens' in contrast to the table-type, called 'northern type dolmens.' These are megalithic structures consisting of a large cap-stone, multiple propping stones, and an underground burial pit. In Type A (Fig. 1.7, middle left), the propping stones were in the form of upright columns, 2-5 feet high. They were firmly anchored in the ground, supporting the heavy cap-stone. Perched on such propping stones, the large cap-stones are visible from a distance. Essentially, they were intended to cover and protect an underground burial pit. In Type B (Fig. 1.7, middle right), the capstone, normally in the form of large boulders, is supported by a number of small circular, square, or rectangular-shaped stones, 1–2 feet long and 1–2 feet wide). They are placed around an underground burial pit, upon which rests the large cap-stone. Type B abounds along the southern coast, and it is also the main dolmen type found in northern Kyushu (Hashino 2014: 105).

The capstone-type dolmens (Fig 1.7, bottom) found in the northern and southern part of the Peninsula, are megalithic burials consisting of an underground burial pit and a large capstone (normally flat) without any propping stones. Because such dolmens have no visible supporting stones, they can be easily mistaken as naturally-occurring rocks or boulders.

Not all dolmens contain burial goods, and where they are present, they vary in kind according to dolmen types and their geographic location. The table-type dolmens, predominant in northern Korea, have yielded top-shaped (wide mouth and small base) and Mumun pottery, semilunar stone knives, tanged stone daggers, stone arrowheads, mace heads, and ground adzes (GJ Seok 1979). Propping-stone as well as cap-stone-type dolmens yield Mumun jars with perforated rims, red-burnished jars, polished stone daggers with or without a full handle, ground/polished arrowheads, and spindle whorls (ML Choi 1978). Liaoning Bronze daggers have been found in the propping-stone-type dolmens on the south and southwestern coast (YM Lee 1990).

Initially dolmens were small and simple but became larger and more grandiose over time (GJ Seok 1979; SN Rhee 1984; YN Jeon 1991; SJ Lee 1999a: 423-441, 1999b: 880). By the 7th century BC, in the northwest, the table-type megaliths had reached the level of monumental architecture, as in the case of the Gwansan-ni, Songshin-dong, and Roam-ni dolmens (GJ Seok 1979). By about 6th century BC, the same trend occurred for the propping-stone-type megaliths in the south, as shown by the mammoth dolmens in Hwasun of South Jeolla Province, in Gochang of North Jeolla Province, and in the lower reaches of southeastern Korea's Namgang River (SN Rhee 1984, 1999a: 927; YM Lee 1999: 1004; SJ Lee 1999b: 855-880). This trend coincided with the growing social complexity of the Middle Mumun Period.

Dolmen construction gradually came to an end in the north after c. 5th century BC and in the south by the 1st century BC. It has been postulated that the end of the megalithic construction coincided with

350 x 305 x 38 cm
Gochang, Dosan-ni

Type A
600 x 302 x 103 cm
Gochang, Sansuri

Type B
430 x 340 x 140 cm
Gochang, Ungok-ni

403 x 95 x 50 cm
Gochang, Jungrim-ni

Fig. 1.7. Dolmen types of the Middle Mumun. **Top:** A table-type dolmen. **Middle Left, Type A:** Propping stone-type with column-shaped supporters. **Middle Right, Type B:** Propping stone-type supported by small round, square, or rectangular-shaped stones. **Bottom:** Cap-stone type dolmen. Photo credit: Authors.

the continuing expansion of agriculture which increasingly demanded the communal labor more for production activities than for mortuary rituals (SN Rhee 2002: 214-252).

B. Stone Cist Graves

Stone cist graves were stone coffins built inside an earthen pit with slabs or cobble stones and without a large capstone. The most common cist grave was a rectangular stone coffin put together with four thin slabs, resembling a wooden coffin. Placed underground, it was covered by one to four slabs. Some stone cist graves had an extra space added to one end for the emplacement of mortuary goods.

A distinguishing characteristic of Korean cist graves was the emphasis on military implements among their mortuary goods, including *mandolin*-shaped bronze daggers. For example, a rectangular cist tomb at Songguk-ni in Buyeo contained one *mandolin*-shaped bronze dagger, one polished stone dagger, and 11 willow-leaf-shape polished stone arrowheads (Fig. 1.6). A six-slab cist tomb at Daea-ri (Baekcheon) in the northwest contained a *mandolin*-shaped Liaoning bronze dagger, a winged bronze arrowhead, and seven-winged ground and polished stone arrowheads. Stone cist tomb #1 at Seon'am-ni, Shinpyeong yielded a *mandolin*-shaped bronze dagger and four-winged polished stone arrowheads (JYYDPW 1989: 48-49). Another common feature of cist tombs, especially those bearing Liaoning bronze weapons, is the presence of prestige ornaments such as tubular jades, circular beads, and curved amazonite jewel.

Along the south coast, the funeral items were placed either inside or outside the coffin itself (Hirakori 2013). At Shinchon-ri Area-1 in Masan, a polished stone dagger, a stone arrow point, and a red-burnished jar were placed as a set outside a cist-type enclosure. They are believed to have been placed before the body was placed in the coffin to help magically secure the coffin (Hirakori 2013: 100, 124). The use of red-burnished jars for mortuary purpose became especially popular along the south coast around Kimhae and Mahan (Hirakori 2013: 100).

Skeletal remains found intact in the Middle Mumun Period burials at Daepyeong-ni near the southern coast reveal that bodies were placed in the burial enclosure in various positions including both extended and flexed forms. Those in the extended form were normally in a supine position. In some cases, the deceased persons were buried without their head and/or teeth extracted, for some unknown ritual reasons (Gyeongsang Namdo 1998: 52; GJIB 2002: 132-137).

C. Jar Burials

The use of storage jars as coffins was a common practice in the Songguk-ni culture zone. While the practice was concentrated in the lower and middle basin of the Geum River, it also spread to other regions as far as the south coast, as evidenced at Igeum-dong in Sacheon. As coffins they were placed in an earthen pit vertically, horizontally, or in a slanted position. Toward the end of the Middle Mumun, the horizontal position, with two jars combined mouth to mouth, became more predominant (MH Lee 2016: 42-74).

In the Geum River basin, they normally used a typical Songguk-ni type storage jars with a flaring lip, ranging from 25 to 57 cm in height and 20 to 24 cm in diameter at the mouth. Their smallness has led to a hypothesis that they were used for infant burials, but their use for secondary re-burials cannot be ruled out. Toward the end of the Middle Mumun, however, two storage jars were combined to accommodate an adult corpse. Burial goods found in jar-coffins are usually of humble types, such as simple cylindrical beads, suggesting that such burials belonged to the common people (IG Gang *et al.* 1979).

9. Emerging Social Complexity

There is a general consensus among Korean scholars that some of the basic elements of a complex society, at least at a simple chiefdom level, were present in the Middle Mumun society. In addition to emerging agrarian economy, they are population growth, and settlement expansion, some horizontal differentiation and a significant degree of vertical differentiation (Blanton 1981: 21; Chapman 1990: 169).

Settlement studies have shown that between the Early and the Middle Mumun periods, settlements expanded and population grew exponentially (JS Kim 2018: 34; JC Lee 2015: 191-194, 279-354; SH Lee 2014; MY Song 2006: 9-29). Ceramic vessels were varied, polished stone implements were produced by skilled experts, and prestige goods – mandolin-shaped bronze daggers, bronze spears, bronze axes, bronze chisels, bronze arrowheads, jade ornaments –increased (JYYDPW 1989).

These elaborations suggest the existence of craft specialists, and there were also religious professionals, such as shamans and priests, evidenced by the presence of bronze ritual bells similar to those used by modern-day shamans of Korea. These cultural features indicate horizontal functional differentiation (JS Bae 2006: 87-109; SG Lee 2006: 117-149; SO Kim 2006; BC Kim 2010: 5-24).

Vertical functional differentiation is readily identifiable in mortuary practices, which included differentiated dolmens, cist tombs, jar-burials, and earthen pit-burials. The associated grave goods or expenditure of energy in construction show that dolmens and cist-burials were for privileged members of the Mumun society; dolmens and cist tombs, in particular, provide useful information on differential status, both diachronically and synchronically (SO Kim 2006a: 39-82).

In a simple chiefdom, the chief is a part-time manager and facilitator in production and redistribution, operating in a close personal relationship with the people, who are normally of his kin group (Steponaitis 1978). He and his household are sustained by their own economic activities, but in his chiefly role he is also expected to act as a 'superiorly generous kinsman'. Consequently, the chief works harder than others to acquire what he gives away (Steponaitis 1978: 420). He is at best a *primus inter pares.* See discussions on Settlements, pp. 15-18.

In a recent study on the kinship-based dolmen clusters in the Yeongsan River Valley in the southwest, GANG Dong-seok (2019: 6-41) postulates that the chief occupied a centrally located place from which he could effectively facilitate production, redistribution, and critical information network among the various communities associated with the dolmen clusters.

10. Push-Pull Dynamics in the Middle Mumun Society

With the emergence of the mixed-crop agriculture, including wet-rice, the Mumun population began to increase rapidly (JS Kim 2018: 30-35; YJ Oh, M Conte *et al.* 2017: 1767-1768). At Sonam-ri in the lower Nam River basin near the southern coast, the number of dwelling structures increased from two in the Chulmun Neolithic period to fifty in the Mumun period. At Okbang #4 Area of Daepyeong-ni were found one Neolithic house and 65 Mumun dwellings (GSND-DDHB 1999: 54, 90-91).

During the Middle Mumun period, c. 800–400 BC, the Korean Peninsula underwent a further increase in population and settlements in conjunction with its agricultural expansion, with most settlements in the alluvial plains of major river valleys (JS Kim 2018: 34; JC Lee 2015: 191-194, 279-354; SH Lee 2014; MY Song 2006: 9-29). One investigator has estimated that the population of the Middle Mumun Period was seven times that of the Early Mumun (KK Kim 2003: 115-119).

Among 167 datable residences in Section C of the Jungdo site in Chuncheon, 14 belonged to the Early Mumun Period while 153 belonged to the Middle Mumun phase. Such numbers clearly show that the Mumun population continued to increase under the mixed crop agricultural regime of the time (Yemaek Munhwajae Yeonguweon 2014: 56-72). Along with the increase in agricultural expansion, population, and settlements, there appeared social divisions, internal stresses, and inter-communal conflicts. Strong indicators of major social divisions and internal stress are the elite residential precincts and fortification systems that began to appear in some places soon after c. 700 BC (JH Ahn 2000: 54-56; Pusan University 1995: 288, 295; MY Song 2001: 99-105, MY Song 2006: 9-29).

Moats have been found within the sites of Bangki-ri and Geomdal-li on the southwest coast); Saweol-li, Namsan, and Deokcheon on the south coast; and Daepyeong-ni and Songguk-ni in the south-central and the southern coastal region (JC Lee 2015: 279-354). Generally, the moats did not encircle entire settlements but only particular sections within a settlement, as shown in the Jungdo and Geomdal-li sites. It has been suggested that perhaps the moats were as much symbolic as military, but they manifestly did serve to set off special precincts for elite members of the community, and (not by accident) to sequester harvested grains and other communal wealth (Pusan University 1995; UD Jeong 2000: 97-137).

Evidence for social conflict and warfare is also clearly present in the Middle Mumun Period. At Songguk-ni, one of the largest Middle Mumun period settlements in the southwestern Peninsula, the majority of square pit houses were burned violently, with their unperishable household goods left intact, along with wooden barricades surrounding them, while only a small number of circular pit houses, spatially set apart from the square ones, suffered such fires. There was also a conspicuous contrast between square and circular pit houses at Songguk-ni in terms of the degree of destruction by fire they suffered, suggesting that conflicts existed within the Songguk-ni society (GS Kim 1994: 179-180).

Based on the accumulated evidence, MY Song (2000: 142-144) has posited that the continual increases in the Middle Mumun Period population and its growing social complexity resulted in a scarcity of land and other vital resources – and thus inevitably in social conflict and warfare. The percentage of such destruction by fire was even higher in north-western Peninsula, where up to 93.5% of Mumun houses excavated in the Pyongyang area were subjected to violent conflagration.

Daepyeong-ni, heavily inhabited by the people of the Songguk-ni culture, was abandoned sometime in the 6th–5th century BC, for reasons currently unclear, and it is unknown what happened to its people. In light of the many violent fires at Middle Mumun and later sites, however, it is reasonable to assume that the rapid growth of population and settlement sizes during the Middle Mumun resulted in social conflicts and warfare and, in turn, incited some of the Songguk-ni culture population to move and relocate. It was during this same interval of burgeoning settlements and violent destructions in the southern Peninsula that the Songguk-ni culture system began to appear in northern Kyushu.

Daepyeong-ni, in particular, was connected to the Korea Strait by an excellent riverine transportation network by way of the Nam River and the Nakdong River. In times of internal conflict or an emergency it would have been relatively easy for the people of the Songguk-ni culture at Daepyeong-ni to move from their home territory to the South Sea (Korea Strait) and beyond into northern Kyushu. The conjunction is too well marked to be mistaken, and no complex theorizing is needed to understand why Koreans in these circumstances would have been pulled to the vast uncultivated plains of northern Kyushu. Certainly, Kyushu was not an unknown land of mystery, as ample pottery and other evidence from both sides of the Korea–Tsushima Straits shows that people had been crossing back and forth since at least 6000 BC, trading goods from both sides (Jeong and Ha 1998: 1-90; DJ Lee 2000: 35-96).

In his detailed comparative studies of reaping knives, red-burnished jars, and dolmens found in northern Kyushu and in southern Korea, Hashino (2014: 86-107) has found the closest match between northern Kyushu and the Nam River basin. He therefore concludes that the home of the initial and early Toraijin was the Nam River basin. This includes the Middle Mumun people of Daepyeong-ni and the numerous Middle Mumun farming villages nearby.

Aggravating the population pressure and internal conflicts was the cooling of the climate in the Yellow Sea Interaction Sphere seriously affecting agricultural production and food supply. On the basis of data provided by Imamura and Fujio (2009: 47-58), K Miyamoto (2017: 240-241) posits that major cooling occurred three times in the 1st millennium BC: c. 2850–2720 cal. BP, c. 2680–2660 cal. BP, and c. 2420–2340 cal. BP.

The negative pressures occurring simultaneously – population increase, internal conflicts, and cooling of the temperature – pushed the Songguk-ni culture people of the Middle Mumun Period southwards even in the Peninsula, as indicated archaeologically by its spread toward the fertile plains such as Daepyeong-ni in the Nam River basin, and from there to the south coast and ultimately across the sea to the coastal plains in Fukuoka and Karatsu.

The positive pull of northern Kyushu included temperate climate and flat lowlands suitable for wet-rice farming, plenty of uncultivated land along the coast created by the retreating sea waters, and only a few Jomon people to contend with. The first arrival of the Songguk-ni culture people occurred in the eighth century BC (K Miyamoto 2017: 240-241). Hashino (2014: 110-114) believes that the initial Toraijin wet-rice farmers arrived in northern Kyushu around 730 BC when the sand dunes were formed along the northern coast of Kyushu under the cooling climate.

II. RICE-BEARING TORAIJIN APPEAR IN THE ARCHIPELAGO

1. New People from the Continent

For more than 14,000 thousand years, the islands of Japan were inhabited by a population known, archaeologically and historically, as Jomon people. Even though some of them cultivated foods (Crawford 2006: 77-95, Crawford 2008: 445-468; D'Andrea 2007: 172-174, Kaner and Yano 2015: 359-362) they were well adapted to their natural environment as hunters, fishers, and gatherers of wild nuts, roots, and plants (Aikens and Higuchi 1982: 182-185; Matsui and Kanehara 2006: 271; Kobayashi

2008: 27-39; Habu 2004: 61-62).). Some Jomon communities exhibited social hierarchy (Pearson 2007: 388), but this was without agriculture (Kobayashi 2008: 27-39; Aikens and Higuchi 1982. 182-185; Pearson 2007: 388). Throughout the Jomon period, "the degree of differentiation was minimal… [and] hierarchal societies did not develop" (Barnes 2015: 282-283). This is echoed by Mizoguchi (2002: 232-235). All this changed with the arrival of a new people from the continent.

As related by the Kyoto Bunka Hakubutsukan (1989: 27):

> Characteristics of the Japanese people began to change dramatically with the shift into the Yayoi period… In the northern part of Kyushu, it appears that people with the characteristics of the Jomon people and people with elongated faces, similar to the people who crossed the sea from the Korean Peninsula, lived in villages, near each other. Not only were the people who crossed the sea culturally superior, but it seems that a considerable number of them came in wave-like patterns.

The large and distinctive assemblage of more than 600 Yayoi period human skeletons from Kanenokuma in Fukuoka, Yoshinogari in Saga, and Doigahama in Yamaguchi, along with other accumulated evidences, has led Japanese archaeologists and anthropologists to affirm the arrival of a new people, marked by tall stature and a long face (Fig. 1.8), from the continent at the end of the Jomon period, who continued to multiply through interbreeding with the indigenous Jomon population (Hanihara 1993: 6-29; Nakahashi and Izuka 1998: 31-53; Hudson 1999: 62-81; Kataoka 2006: 13-50; Y Tanaka 2014: 24-44; Shimojo 2014b: 229-233; Shimojo and Tanaka 2014: 279-324; Hashino 2014: 79-115; K Miyamoto 2017: 151-179, 202-209).

On the basis of their morphological analyses of Yayoi skeletal remains from the Middle Yayoi period Nakahashi and Izuka (1998: 31-53, 2008: 131-143) have concluded that (1) only 10–20% of the Yayoi skeletons had Jomon characteristics, called 'Jomon-type Yayoi', while the majority (80–90%) had non-Jomon characteristics, called 'Toraijin-type Yayoi', and (2) the latter maintained the *overwhelming majority* of the Yayoi population throughout the entire Yayoi period. Echoing this observation, Hudson (1999: 80), in light of genetic studies, has noted that "although the Jomon people were not totally replaced by the incoming Yayoi migrants, their genetic contributions to the later Japanese was small, perhaps less than one quarter."

From these observations Nakahashi and Izuka (1998) posit that during the Yayoi period the Toraijin-type Yayoi population overwhelmed the native Jomon people in number and led the way in the commencement and development of the Yayoi farming society based on wet-rice agriculture. Demographic, economic, and social transformation of northern Kyushu during the Yayoi period, they conclude, could have been achieved only by the large Toraijin-type Yayoi population.

Accordingly, Kataoka (2006: 3-8) maintains that in northern Kyushu the primary actors responsible for the opening and development of the Yayoi society were the Toraijin rather than the native Jomon people. Y Tanaka (2014: 43), however, posits that the main developers of the Yayoi agricultural society were neither the Toraijin nor the Jomon people but the hybridized Toraijin-type Yayoi people plus the children of the Jomon people.

Nakahashi and Izuka did not pinpoint the geographical location from which the ancestors of the Yayoi-type Toraijin came while Hudson (1999: 68) suggests Korea's southern coast as the point of

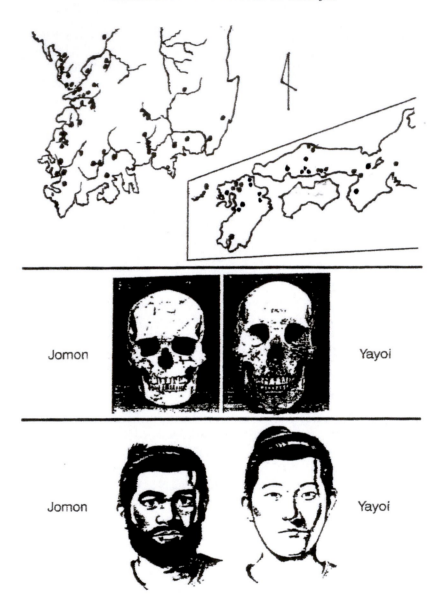

Fig. 1.8. Top: Distribution of Songguk-ni-type houses in the Archipelago (JC Lee 2015: 393; cf. OYBH 1999: 36) **Bottom**: Jomon and Yayoi skeletons and reconstructed facial features (after Baba 1997: 26-27).

their origin, noting that skeletons found along the southern coast of Korea "show a close affinity with Yayoi and Kofun populations in north Kyushu and Yamaguchi." The 200 plus skeletons of the 4th–7th century, found at Yean-ri in Kimhae near Pusan are strikingly similar to the Yayoi skeletons with "an average statue of 164.7 cm for males and 150.8 cm for females; with their high facial skeleton and flat naso-frontal region."

According to Shichida (2017: 41-42), more than 300 human skeletal remains unearthed at Yoshinogari and its adjacent area in northern Kyushu show an average height of 162.4 cm, 161.98 cm, and 164.27 cm for Yayoi males and 148.9 cm and 151.91 cm for Yayoi females. These numerical values are strikingly similar to those of the skeletal remains found in southern Korea described above. Largely on the basis of the closeness of the Yayoi skeletons to those of the Peninsula, in terms of height and facial morphology, Kataoka (1999: 177), Hudson (1999: 68), and Shichida (2017: 41-42) have suggested that the 300 human remains at Yoshinogari belonged to the immigrants (Toraijin) and their descendants from the Peninsula.

Additionally, as shown in the following pages, cultural remains associated with the new people unequivocally indicate that they were from southern Korea and no other parts of the continent. Specifically, they include Songguk-ni residential patterns, mortuary practices of southern Korean origin (megalithic burial structures knows as "dolmens" and the custom of placing certain funeral objects inside or near the burial pit including polished stone daggers and arrowheads and red-burnished jars), Mumun potteries of southern Korea, Mumun *ishibocho* (reaping knives), and spindle whorls of southern Korea, and most important, wet-rice farming technology of Mumun farmers of southern Korea (Kataoka 2006: 20-26).

In long-distance migration, a communication network is normally established between the migrant groups and their parent community, resulting in chain migration. As push factors continue in the parent community, others would follow the original migrant group in a stream-like flow (Anthony 1990: 895-914). Reflecting this anthropological observation on human migration in history, Hashino (2014: 109-110) has explained the arrival of the Mumun Toraijin in northern Kyushu in terms of multiple steps.

This was happening after the initial Toraijin had arrived at various sites along the north coast (Itazuke, Arita, Imakawa, Magarita, and Nabatake). Another group of Middle Mumun farmers headed to the low-lying ridges of the Mikuni Hills and the Saga Plain, the inland zones to the south (Map 1.2). Archaeological investigations in the two areas have revealed numerous dolmens and the Songguk-ni type settlements at Matsubara, Kansaki, Yoshino Rikitake, Yokoma, Misawa, Tsuko, Yoshinogari, Habu, Nabeshima, and other sites (Kataoka 1999: 103-113, 2006: 141-168; Shichida 2017: 15-18, 25-26; Y Tanaka 2014: 17-44; K. Miyamoto 2017: 151-179).

Kataoka (2006: 47, 121-124, 131-132, 141-168; cf. Shichida 2017: 25-26) posits that the move to the Mikuni Hills and the Saga Plain was prompted by a population saturation in the coastal plains by the food producing Toraijin and their first-to-third generation descendants. During the Middle Yayoi, Yoshinogari in Saga was emerging as the largest and most influential moat-surrounded Yayoi settlement in Japan (Shichida 2007a: 117-133, Shichida 2007b: 346-34, Shichida 2017: 33-34; Kataoka 2006: 192-193).

The cultural system which the initial Toraijin brought to northern Kyushu was that of the Middle Mumun society of southern Korea (Kataoka 2006: 13-50; Y. Tanaka 2014: 24-44; Shimojo 2014: 229-233; Shimojo and Tanaka 2014: 279-324; Hashino 2014: 79-115; K Miyamoto 2017).

2. New Residential Pattern

With the arrival of a new people there appeared a new residential pattern (Hashino 2014: 86-93). Early Yayoi residential structures were dominantly semi-subterranean pit houses of both square and circular floor plan, very much like those of southern Korea. A significant number of Early Yayoi

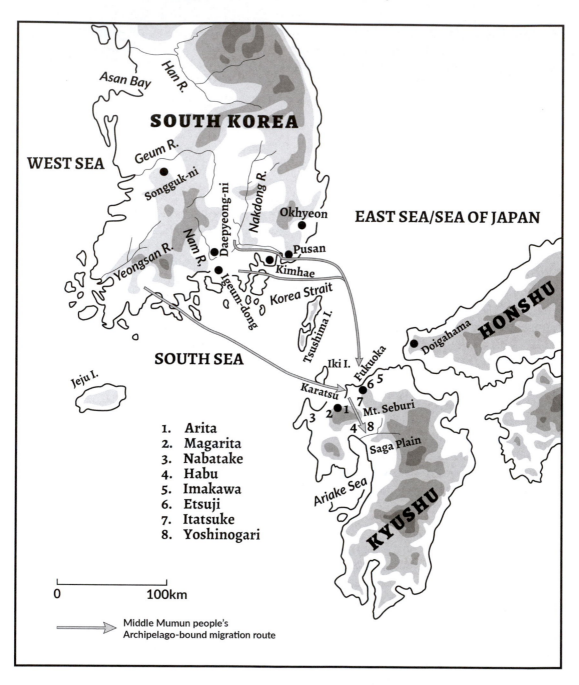

Map 1.2. Initial and Early Yayoi sites in northern Kyushu (by Lucas Pauly).

dwellings were specifically of the Songguk-ni type, characterized by a circular floor plan and an oval pit in the center, common in southern Korea between about c. 800 and 200 BC (Shintaku 1994: 118-135) (Fig. 1.2 Bottom).

On the basis of his settlement pattern studies of the Jomon and the Yayoi periods in northern Kyushu, Kataoka (2006: 6, 131-140) has observed that virtually no settlements existed on the Mikuni Hills north of the Chikushi Plains during the Jomon period but at the beginning of the Yayoi period (Itazuke Type I pottery) new settlements began to appear in the vicinity of rivers and streams and spread widely. Kataoka states (2006: 6):

> A representative site of such new settlements was the Rikitake settlement. Those who managed the new settlement were the Toraijin from the Korean Peninsula who not only possessed a highly developed wet-rice farming technology but also constructed Songguk-ni type dwellings, and practiced life-ways different from the Jomon natives.

Along with the semi-subterranean Songguk-ni residential types, the early Yayoi people also constructed, on the ground surface level, walled buildings with a rectangular floor and those with a raised floor as storage facilities (C Miyamoto 1986: 19-22). Like the pit houses, these were strikingly similar to those found in Songguk-ni-culture settlements throughout southern Korea, called *gullipju geonmul* (free standing buildings supported by rows of sunken post) and *gosang-shik geonmul* (tall buildings) respectively built for storage purposes (JC Lee 2015: 213-217).

As of 1987, more than 50 Songguk-ni-type dwellings were identified in Fukuoka Prefecture alone (Harunari 1990: 121-122; JC Lee 2000: 73-3, 2015: 392-397; C Miyamoto 1996: 128; Takesue 2001: 102-103). In Saga Prefecture, nearly 60 Songguk-ni-type dwellings have been excavated at Yoshinogari Site (Shichida 2005: 43-45). A number of the new Japanese farming settlements in the Yuusu/Itazuke I cultural context also had moats, another characteristic feature of large Mumun period settlements in southern Korea. In light of social conflicts in expanding agricultural societies, as in the Peninsula Middle Mumun society, the purposes of the Japanese moats appear to have been military defense, internal security, and social demarcation (Terasawa 2001: 26-28).

Of special significance is an incipient Yayoi village found at Etsuji in Kasuya-machi of Fukuoka, near the coast of northern Kyushu, facing the Tsushima Strait (Fig. 1.2 Bottom). Like the Songguk-ni culture type villages in southern Korea, it consisted of underground pit houses, granaries built above the ground, and a large rectangular building near the dwelling houses (Shintaku 1994: 118-135). It closely resembled Songguk-ni culture villages found at Daeyari in Geochang (Dongui University Museum 1998: 45; at Igeum-dong in Sacheon (HW Lee 2009: 233); at Jinra-ri in Cheong-do (SH Lee 2014: 24), at Jangcheon-ni in Yeong'am (SR Choi 1986: 56); and at Daepyeong-ni in Jinju (GJIB 2002: 31-35).

However, Etsuji did not appear to be a pure Songguk-ni type hamlet, for in it or associated with it were numerous Jomon tools and Jomon pottery vessels along with Middle Mumun *yugu seokbu* (stone axes with a notch in the stem) and Middle Mumun stone reaping knives. Also, the internal arrangements of the village were more akin to the indigenous Jomon pattern than that of the typical Songguk-ni village, suggesting that Etsuji was a village representing both Mumun and Jomon characteristics and an ethno-cultural hybridization in progress. The indigenous meaning, according to Mizoguchi, was incorporated into the physical forms coming from the peninsula (Mizoguchi 2013: 55-68, 81-86).

3. New Mortuary System

Ethnographic observations inform that in the ancient and traditional societies mortuary practices were essential to safeguarding and reinforcing "social identity and social memory" of the people and communities related to the person being buried (Joyce 2001: 13-26). Mizoguchi emphasizes this point by viewing cemetery "as a locale for communication and the constitution/preservation of memory" (Mizoguchi 2014: 848). Furthermore, Mizoguchi (2014: 849) stats that a cemetery:

> was a place where those who interacted and exchanged goods, people and information in the sodality-based network confirmed their individual and communal identities, their history and genealogy, and their social relationships, through the mediation of the materialized memory of the dead and the presence of ancestors".

As such the burial practices remained stubbornly traditional and were highly resistant to abrupt changes.

Accordingly, the Toraijin brought with them not only their residential but also mortuary culture (K Hirose 1997: 65-69; OYBH 1999: 42-47, 86; Sahara and Kanaseki 1981: 24; Nakayama 2003: 78; Mizoguchi 2013: 79; Hashino 2014: 101-106; K Miyamoto 2017: 151-178). The Toraijin culture comprised dolmens, stone cist graves, and jar burials, integral to the Middle Mumun mortuary culture.

They were not only new in northern Kyushu but also constituted a break between the old and the new. Mizoguchi (2013: 79) points out:

> Formerly in the Jomon settlements, burial grounds were often situated at the center of the settlement, due to which the residents were constantly aware of the presence of the dead, and possibly that of the ancestors.... With the onset of the Yayoi period, this level of intimacy between the living and the dead (and probably the ancestors) disappeared.

This was strikingly similar to the Middle Mumun settlements in the Peninsula, in which a clear boundary existed between the living and the dead, that is, between the residential compound and the burial plots (cf. Fig. 1.8).

A. Dolmens (Megalithic Burial Structures)

More than 700 dolmens are known from Kyushu, some 350 of them in Fukuoka and Saga Prefectures alone (Nishitani 1997: 56-150) (Map 1.3 Bottom). Considering that dolmens have been continuously destroyed in land-clearing efforts since ancient times, the original numbers were much higher.

The Kyushu dolmens, in their external form, were strikingly similar to *gibanshik*-type (*go* table-shape) dolmens common in southern Korea (Shim 1999: 153-210). They began to appear in the latter part of the Incipient Yayoi period. Soon after their arrival, they began to undergo local modifications (Hashino 2014: 101-106; K Miyamoto: 2017: 146, 151-167).

Burial goods in the dolmens, while fewer in comparison to those found in Korea, comprised jars and pots, including Songguk-ni type red-burnished globular jars, spindle whorls, amazonite tubular beads, and willow leaf-shaped arrowheads similar to those found in Korean dolmens (Nishitani 1997: 56-128). In the Munakata region of eastern Fukuoka Prefecture polished stone arrowheads and/or daggers were buried in the dolmens, as in Korea (Nakayama 2003: 80; K Miyamoto 2017: 163-167).

Several megalithic dolmens, with their cap stones longer than 6 feet, have been found in Shima-gun in Fukuoka. Their grave goods included large tubular beads and polished stone arrowheads made in Korea. Some of the dolmens are believed to have belonged to Korean immigrant elites who acted as the leader of the residents in the region (Yanagida 1992: 32). Some of the dolmens contained Jomon skeletons (K Miyamoto 2017: 178), suggesting that the indigenous Jomon people adopted the Toraijin mortuary practices. It is possible that some of the hybridized Toraijin-type Yayoi people carried Jomon physical characteristics.

B. Cist and Jar Burials

As they did in their Peninsula home land, the initial Toraijin and possibly their children in northern Kyushu appear to have buried their dead in stone cist graves and jar coffin burials. The cist graves were rectangular pits lined with thin vertically set stone slabs, identical to those known in southern Korea and like the latter contained polished stone daggers, red-burnished globular jars, and tubular jasper beads. Essentially, they were same as the *gaeseokshik* dolmens of the Middle Mumun consisting of a stone-framed burial pit and a cover stone (KK Kim 1999: 673-854; T Mori 1985: 73-74; K Miyamoto 2017: 156-163). As in the Middle Mumun society of southern Korea, the dead were placed in the graves in both supine and crouched position (Gyeonsang Namdo 1998: 49-52; K Miyamoto 2017: 160, 172-173).

Hashino (2003: 1-25) has suggested that the cists (stone-coffin burials) found in the region east of Fukuoka were dolmens which had lost their capstones. Actually, however, from the beginning they were constructed as cists in the manner of the mortuary practices in southern Korea. As known from the archaeological remains of Daepyeong-ni in the Nam River basin, the Middle Mumun people in the southeast coastal region constructed either dolmens or cists in accordance with their kinship mortuary tradition (GSND-DDHB 1999: 90-102).

As with the dolmens and cists, jar burials of the Middle Mumun began to appear in northern Kyushu during the Initial Yayoi period (Mizoguchi 2013: 59; Shichida 2017: 31). The use of storage jars as coffins was a common practice in the Songguk-ni culture, especially in the lower and middle basin of the Geum River. The jar burial practice diffused to other regions, as far as Igeum-dong near the southern coast. Jar coffins were placed in an earthen pit in a vertical, leaning, or lying position (MH Lee 2016: 42-74).

During the Initial Yayoi as well as in the first half of the Early Yayoi period, some people in northern Kyushu used small ordinary storage jars for infant burial as in the Middle Mumun society (Takesue 2012: 84). In the latter part of the Early Yayoi period, they began to use "globular jar shape-type (called Tsubo, 壺, in Japanese)" for adult burial as well (Mizoguchi 2013: 59). By the Middle Yayoi period, the jar coffins became numerically dominant and remained the most persistent type of

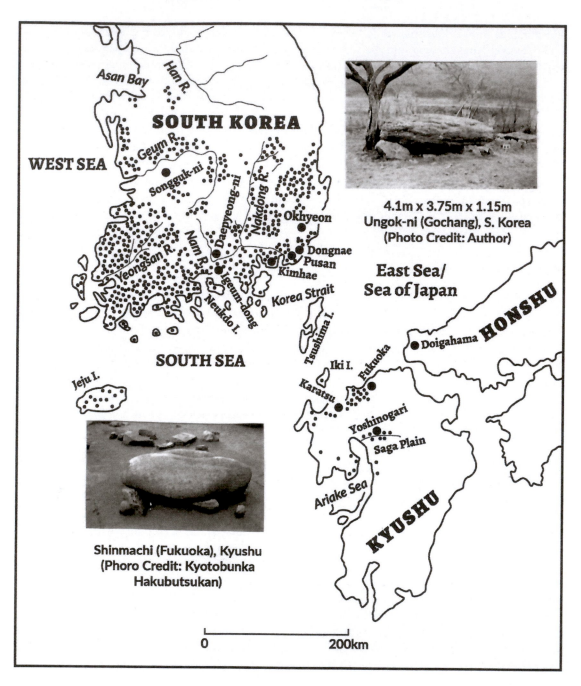

4.1m x 3.75m x 1.15m
Ungok-ni (Gochang), S. Korea
(Photo Credit: Author)

Shinmachi (Fukuoka), Kyushu
(Phoro Credit: Kyotobunka
Hakubutsukan)

Map 1.3. Geographical distributions of dolmens in northern Kyushu. The kibanshik-type in southern Korea and northern Kyushu (by Lucas Pauly). (After YM Lee 1993: 418; Nishitani 1997: 27, 57, 73, 82; K Miyamoto 2017: 165).

interment throughout the Yayoi period, as exemplified by more than 3,100 jar burials of the period from Yoshinogari (Shichida 2017: 30-31).

The globular jar shape-type was derived from the red-burnished globular jars of the Korean Mumun origin (Mizoguchi 2013: 59-61; Hashino 2014: 98-100). As in the latter, they comprised two types: small jars, normally 10–15 inches high, and large jars, about 30 inches high. Found in graves as well as in residential sites. As in Mumun Korea, they were also used to store rice grains for eating as well as sowing for new crops in the spring.

 In this dual role of the red-colored globular jars, Mizoguchi sees the symbolic meaning of death and renewal of life. In the connection between the dead, the rice grains, and the colour red, he sees "the metaphorical-transformative between the concepts of the death and regeneration of life of grains as well as human beings ..." (2013: 59). He further observes that its foreign origin notwithstanding, the red-burnished globular jars became incorporated into the indigenous pottery culture because of its compatibility in function and meaning (Mizoguchi 2013: 66).

4. Initial Toraijin Contributions to the Archipelago

A. Wet-Rice Farming in Northern Kyushu

The earliest evidence for wet-rice farming in Japan is found in the fertile plains around Hakata and Karatsu Bays near Fukuoka and Karatsu in northern Kyushu (Map 1.1 and 1.2). At Itazuke, within the present boundaries of Fukuoka City, various excavations from 1951 onward have revealed irrigation channels, water reservation ponds, and paddies that were divided by boundary ridges into small sections. More than a hundred human footprints preserved by volcanic ashes have been identified from excavated fields.

Rice grain imprints were found on sherds of Yuusu and Itazuke I pottery, as well as some carbonized specimens of short-grained *japonica* rice. Preserved also by waterlogged soils were various tools of Mumun Korean origin: wooden hoes, unfinished wooden rakes, and spindle whorls, found along with lithic adzes, planing knives, triangular reaping knives *(ishibocho),* sickles, axes, willow leaf-shaped tanged arrowheads, and polished stone daggers.

An Early Yayoi village with both inner and outer moats has been identified near the fields, as have numerous sherds of Yuusu-type jars, pots, bowls, mounted dishes, and a large burnished-red pot of the Itazuke I type (Fukuoka Kyoiku I'inkai 1995: 15-39; T Mori 1985: 48-55; Oda 1986: 143-145). At Arita, also in Fukuoka City, a partially excavated semi subterranean house yielded numerous carbonized grains of *japonica* rice. Yuusu and Itazuke I jars, pots, and bowls were common, most of the pots being of the burnished-red Itazuke I type. As at Itazuke, lithic tools included polished triangular reaping knives, grooved adzes, axes, and planing knives, stemmed willow leaf-shaped arrowheads, and polished stone daggers with handles of Korean type. Spindle whorls and chipped stone tools of Jomon types were also found (Oda 1986: 145-146).

At Imakawa, on the east side of Hakata Bay, excavations revealed evidence of a moat and a circular semi subterranean house. Yuusu and Itazuke I jars, pots, bowls, and mounted dishes were excavated from the moat, along with planing knives, axes, polished stone stemmed arrowheads, whetstones, grinding stones, spindle whorls, polished stone daggers with handles, and beads made of jasper and amazonite of Korean origin. Metal artifacts included a reworked bronze arrowhead, a bronze chisel, and an iron arrowhead. Chipped stone arrowheads and axes of Jomon types were also found (Oda 1986: 147-148).

Magarita, on a small rise in the coastal basin of Karatsu Bay, has given evidence of about 30 semi-subterranean houses with square floor plans. The pottery there is dominantly of the Yuusu type, though burnished-red pots similar to those of Itazuke I type were found as well. Associated with the settlement were also pottery jar coffins of Yayoi type and a small dolmen. Also found were carbonized rice remains, triangular stone reaping knives, sickles, planing knives, axes, whetstones, polished stone arrowheads with and without tangs, polished stone daggers with handles, tubular jasper and jadeite beads, and clay spindle whorls of Mumun Korean origin (T Mori 1985: 55-59; Oda 1986: 150).

At Nabatake on the western side of Karatsu Bay, archaeologists in 1980–1981 excavated 16 cultural layers that give perhaps the best available single picture of the Jomon/Yayoi transition. The lowermost levels 16–13 were dated to Early and Middle Jomon by characteristic pottery types. Through the Final Jomon levels 12–9, chipped stone tools of Jomon types diminished, to be increasingly replaced by polished triangular reaping knives, planing knives, daggers, and polished stone arrowheads of the Mumun Korean origin. The lower horizon of Level 8 was dominated by the pottery of the Final Jomon Yuusu type, with pots, shallow bowls, mounted dishes, and black-burnished as well as red-burnished vessels represented. There also appeared, however, the familiar Yayoi semilunar reaping knives, planing knives, and stemmed stone arrowheads, along with the further addition of polished stone daggers with handles, tubular jasper beads, axes, and stone chisels, all of which of the Mumun Korean origin. Finally, Level 8 added grooved stone adzes and more chisels of Korean origin, along with Itazuke I pottery (Karatsu-shi Bunka Shinko Zaidan 1993: 29-30).

Once established in northern Kyushu, the wet-rice farming spread throughout Kyushu and beyond along with Songguk-ni type cultural features. Already before the end of the Early Yayoi period, they were established throughout the Inland Sea, the Kyoto–Osaka–Nara regions, and beyond as far as the Nobi Plains around modern Nagoya (OYBH 1999: 36; K Miyamoto 2017: 256-257).

B. Pottery

The repertoire of southern Korean Mumun pottery comprised a variety of Mumun pottery traditions including the notched clay-band-type (gagmok doldaemun), the perforated rim-type (gongyeolmun), the Songguk-ni type, and the red-burnished globular jars. These pottery traditions all emerged with the initial Toraijin in Kyushu during the early Yayoi period (HJ Lee 2007: 31-33; Kawae 2014: 32-33).

The Early Yayoi communities in northern Kyushu almost invariably contained pottery of two new types: Yuusu and Itazuke, named for sites by the same names near Fukuoka in northern Kyushu (Aikens and Higuchi 1982: 200). Yuusu I and Yuusu IIa types are ascribed to the earliest phase of the Yayoi culture while the Itazuke I and II types, along with Yuusu IIb, are assigned to the Early Yayoi period. The two types are effectively indistinguishable in their basic fabric, but Yuusu jars are identified by a narrow and flattened base and incised bands encircling the shoulder and/or rim,

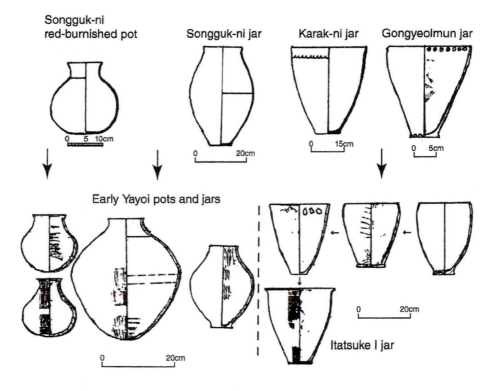

Fig. 1.9. Mumun pottery's influence on the Early Yayoi pottery. Top: Middle Mumun pottery (MY Song 2001: 83; Bottom: Early Yayoi pottery (Harunari 1990: 34, 39).

while Itazuke jars are characterized by a deep body, everted rim, and narrow flattened base (Fig 1.9 Bottom).

The Yuusu pottery, marked by *Dottaimon* design (incised bands encircling the shoulder and/or rim) resembles the *gakmok doldaemun*-type pottery of Korean Mumun tradition much more closely than it resembles pre-Yuusu Jomon types. Some Yuusu jars with perforated rims are considered to have been influenced by the perforated rim-type pottery (*gongyeol-mun*), which had coexisted with it in Kyushu and southwestern Honshu. Likewise, the globular storage jars prominent in the Yayoi pottery repertoire were clearly influenced by the same type in the Songguk-ni pottery (Kataoka 1999: 31-44).

Detailed comparative analysis has established that much of the earliest Yayoi pottery of western Japan had no precedents in the older Jomon pottery in terms of finger manipulation, clay, and firing and that it was derived from the Korean Mumun type (Takahashi 1987: 7-10; OYBH 1999: 34-37; Shim 1999: 47-56, 96-97; JH Ahn 2000: 56-58; HJ Lee 2007: 24-37; Mizoguchi 2013: 67-74).

Observing that Mumun and Yayoi cooking vessels "have coils merging in the opposite direction from Jomon pots, indicating a change in manufacturing technique," Barnes (2015: 273) suggests that "Peninsular men took Jomon wives after emigrating to the islands." If so, as a "marriage of Pen/

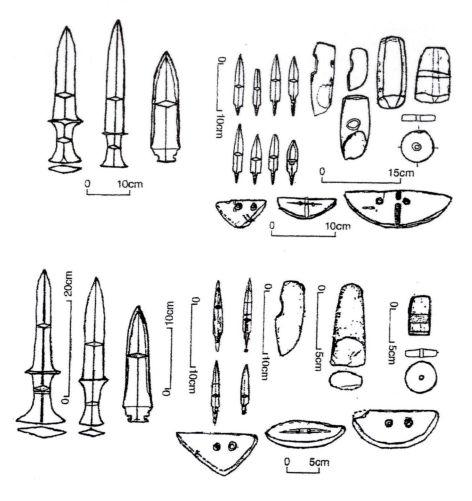

Fig. 1.10. Middle Mumun lithic implements from the Peninsula and the Archipelago: **Top:** From the Peninsula (after YN Jeon 1987: 202). **Bottom:** From northern Kyushu sites (after Oda and Han 1991: 160-167).

Insular potteries" (Barnes 2015: 273), it was indicative of the birth of the Yayoi people/culture, a process of ethnic and cultural hybridization highlighted by Mizoguchi (2013: 55-65).

C. Lithic Implements

Often found as a set at Initial and Early Yayoi sites including Tateiwa, the Mumun lithic implements include the stone axes with a notch in the stem (*yugu seokbu*), flat stone axes with the blade ground on one side only (*pyeonpyeong danin seokbu*), stone reaping knives (K., *banweol hyeong seokdo*; J., *ishibocho*), stone sickles (*seok gyeom*), hilted polished stone daggers (*yubyeongshik seokkeom*), stemmed polished stone daggers (*yugyeongshik seokkeom*), and willow-leaf shape polished stone arrowheads (*yuyeop seokchok*) (Shimojo 2014: 183-186, 199-205) (Fig. 1.10).

The stone axes with a notch in the stem and the willow leaf-shape polished stone arrowheads originated in the Middle Mumun Peninsula and were uniquely Korean. So were the hilted daggers (*ildan byeongshik*) and the hilted daggers with a nodal divide in the center of the hilt (*yujeol byeongshik*). The former was found mainly in the coastal plains to the west of Fukuoka while the latter in the regions to the east and the south of Fukuoka, suggesting that their origin involved different parts of southern Korea (K Miyamoto 2017: 168-173). As for the stone reaping knives, triangular shaped knives were the predominant. Some of them had alternating cutting edges like their counterparts in the Peninsula's Middle Mumun society (Shimojo 2014: 199-203).

D. Spinning/Weaving Technology

Discovery of spindle whorls among the artifacts of the early Yayoi farming communities indicates that the technology of spinning and weaving also arrived in Japan as part of the new culture from the Korean Peninsula (Aikens and Higuchi 1982: 202-203; OYBH 1999: 60; Kyoto Bunka Hakubutsukan 1989: 59-60).

5. Issues in Yayoi Chronology

This volume properly begins with the Jomon period, probably the longest archaeological period in the world, dating from 14,000–400 BC. The Jomon people were primarily hunter-gatherers, foragers and fishers, but they also cultivated and even domesticated some plants. However, their efforts in this last regard did not result in their being 'agriculturalists', as the species (e.g., barnyard grass, perilla, soybeans) were not those that could be relied upon as staples. Agriculture entered the Archipelago as a foreign technology: wet-rice cultivation as developed first in the Shanghai delta region of the China Mainland and then transferred to the Korean Peninsula in the mid-2nd millennium BC. This in itself is thought to have been accomplished through incremental migration, with the combination of plain (Mumun) pottery and agriculture coalescing in the Liaodong Peninsula before spreading into the Korean Peninsula before being carried to Japan by Mumun migrants. Their arrival signified great change in subsistence technology, population genetics, and material culture; the result was the formation of Yayoi culture.

Exactly when the changes based on the revolutionary wet-rice farming first appeared is currently a subject of huge debate within the Japanese archaeological community (Shoda 2007, Shoda 2010; Kuwabara 2015). In the 1950s and through the 1970s, Japanese archaeologists assumed that the Early Yayoi period began around 300 BC on the basis of ^{14}C dating as well as datable Chinese coins and mirrors found at Yayoi sites. The beginning of Yayoi at this time was defined by the appearance of Ongagawa-type pottery at the Itazuke site; thus, in parallel with the Jomon period, which was defined as the period of cord-marked (*jomon*) pottery (even though not all is cord-marked), Yayoi was defined as the period of Yayoi pottery but was understood to be based on rice agriculture.

Beginning in the early 1980s, however, Yayoi beginnings were modified as the result of finding rice paddies at Itazuke and Nabatake in northern Kyushu closely associated with Yuusu and Yamanotera type pottery of the Final Jomon traditionally dated to the 5th–4th century BC. SAHARA Makoto was instrumental in redefining the beginning of the Yayoi period to be based on agriculture rather than pottery, resulting in Yuusu and Yamanotera ceramics to be reclassified as Yayoi. Consequently, the

Japanese archaeological community adopted the 5th century BC as the beginning date of the Yayoi period.

In 2003, this date was challenged by the National Museum of Japanese History (NMJH) with an announcement that using the AMS ^{14}C dating method, it was able to date charred remains adhering to pottery samples to the tenth century BC. With the newly obtained ^{14}C date, NMJH posited that the Yayoi period began 500 years earlier, in the tenth century BC (Harunari, Fujio, Imamura, and Sakamoto 2003: 65-68).

Some (Shitara 2006: 129-54; S Fujio 2007: 7-19; Nishimoto 2006, 2007, 306; Fujio, Imamura, and Nishimoto 2010: 69-96) have accepted, but many, especially from the Kyushu University academia, rejected the AMS ^{14}C-derived date due to various unresolved issues relative to samples used, their context, and the broader East Asian archaeology (Iwanaga 2005: 1-22; Kataoka 2006: 19).

The most serious problem, according to YOSHIDA Kunio (2005: 54), was the charred material itself and its archaeological context. The charred remains were attached to a base piece of a pottery, and no one has been able to identify the pottery type. Also, known reservoir effects on charred remains making the latter 400 years older than those without the same effect have complicated the NMJH AMS ^{14}C dating. In addition, samples for "the earlier part of the Initial Yayoi" are too limited (only three). Noting these problems, Shoda observed that "The evidence NMJH presented is not enough to make many scholars understand and agree" (2007: 4). Still unresolved are the fundamental problems underlying the NMJH's long chronology based on the AMS ^{14}C dating: including the marine effect on the samples used, the nature of the charred samples and their context, and the paucity of samples. And there has been no new scientific evidence substantiating the long chronology with absolute certainty (SHODA Shinya, personal communication on 11/29/17).

In the meantime, the subject of the Yayoi beginning has largely become an exercise of academic guessing with each archaeologist suggesting or adopting a date on the basis of cross-dating of artifacts, climatic factors, and other considerations. Currently, it ranges from the 10th–9th centuries (c. 2900–2800 cal. BP) (Mizoguchi 2013: 34), the 8th century (c. 2800–2700 cal. BP) (K Miyamoto 2017: 239-242; Shoda 2010: 421-427; Hashino 2014: 112-113), and to the 5th century (c. 2500–2400 cal. BP) (Shichida 2017: 23).

As for Korean archaeologists, they view the NMJH AMS ^{14}C dating with much scepticism (BJ Jo 2010: 1-73). Archaeologically, the beginning of Yayoi coincided with the arrival in northern Kyushu of the Peninsula's wet-rice farmers of the Songguk-ni-type culture. Therefore, critically relevant to the discussions on Yayoi beginnings are the socio-cultural dynamics within the Songguk-ni-type culture society in southern Korea. Emerging in the 10th–9th century BC in the lower reaches of the Geum River in the west-central coastal area, the Songguk-ni culture first spread along the river toward its middle reaches (JC Lee 2015: 189-194). During the 8th–6th century, it expanded into all regions of southern Korea between the Asan Harbor on the west coast and the South Sea (Korea Strait). Spreading along the major rivers, the Songguk-ni culture settlements were established in the alluvial plains along the Yeongsan River and the coastal region in the southwest; along the Seomjin River, Nam River, and the southeast coastal region; in the upper reaches of the Geum River in the central highlands and along the Hwang and Nakdong Rivers in the east (JC Lee 2015: 189-194, 402-405).

The 8th–6th century BC was also the fluorescent period of the Songguk-ni-type culture. It was a period of rapid population growth, intensification of mixed crop agriculture including wet-rice farming, emerging social stratification, bronze technology, and inter-communal conflicts (MY Song 2006: 9-82). During this period, the Songguk-ni culture began to spread beyond the South Sea, appearing on the Jeju Island during the 7th–6th centuries BC (JC Lee 2015: 386-392). Most likely, it arrived in northern Kyushu around this time.

The earliest Songguk-ni-type farming settlement to appear in northern Kyushu was that of Etsuji in Kasuya, facing the Tsushima Strait. The residential structures of Etsuji were identical to the type found at the Igeum-dong site on the Peninsula (distinguished by an oval-shape pit in the center of the floor with a post hole on either side) (Fig. 1.2). Appearing first in the 7th century BC, the Igeum-dong type multiplied along the southeast coast at Igeum-dong in Sacheon, Daepyeong-ni in Jinju, and other southeast coastal sites (JC Lee 2015: 306). This area is believed to be the Peninsular region from which the initial Toraijin sailed to reach the Fukuoka Plains in northern Kyushu (Hashino 2014: 86-107).

Therefore, by comparison with Peninsular data, especially the beginnings and spread of Songguk-ni culture, it is deemed likely that wet-rice agriculture was initiated by Songguk-ni immigrants in the Archipelago no earlier than c. 600 BC. It is possible, however, that both individuals and crop products arrived before that, accounting for the finds of rice in Late and Final Jomon contexts.

In closing this Introduction, we would like to clarify that the Yayoi did not come from the Korean Peninsula, as is sometimes stated. Yayoi as a culture and as a people developed within the Japanese Archipelago through cultural interaction and intermarriage among the indigenous Jomon and the immigrant Mumun peoples. North Kyushu served as an incubator of this new Yayoi culture, and the mixed descendants spread through the Inland Sea as migrants (as opposed to immigrants) bringing new coastal lowlands under rice cultivation. Relations with indigenous Jomon groups as the agriculturalists expanded their territories were varied: some Jomon people acculturated and intermixed with the agriculturalists; some co-existed for a time pursuing their traditional lifestyle. Models of Yayoi expansion postulate that migrants made some inroads into coastal regions of eastern and even northern Japan, but overall, agricultural technology diffused into the northeast without substantial population input, resulting in less prominent continental genotypes in that area.

6. Other Controversies and General Consensus

The quest for the origin of the Yayoi society is tied up with Japan's long search for its national identity, specifically the origin of the Japanese people (Tsude 2005: 671-682; Y Tanaka 2014: 3-24). Recognizing the diversity of physical characteristics among the modern Japanese populations, early Western visitors of Japan wrote about the presence of two major races in the Archipelago. Chamberlain (1902: 22-24, 397-399), for example, spoke of the Mongol-type Japanese and the Aino [Ainu]-type Japanese. He viewed the Ainu-type as the aborigines of the Archipelago once occupying all the Japanese islands and the Mongol-type as immigrants (Toraijin) from the continent, gradually replacing the Ainus and emerging as 'lords and masters', starting in the southwest.

Since then, countless studies have been undertaken by Japanese historians, archaeologists, anthropologists, geneticists, and others regarding the immigrants, that is, the Toraijin. Where in the Asian continent did they really come from? When did they come? How many? What was their relationship with the indigenous population? What was their role in the formation of the Yayoi society and in the establishment of the initial wet-rice farming? (Y Tanaka 2014: 3-48; Shimojo 2014: 229-278; Shimojo and Tanaka 2014: 279-324; K Miyamoto 2017: 145-179).

These discussions have been endless and will continue endlessly (Mizoguchi 2002: 118-121, 2013: 19), blurring the picture and often moving into irrelevant directions in the study of the Japanese history and the Japanese identity. Nevertheless, Japanese scholars have arrived at a general consensus on the origins of the Yayoi society and the relationship between the Toraijin and the indigenous Jomon population.

On the basis of Japanese anthropological and archaeological researches presented in the foregoing pages, TANAKA Yoshiyuki (2014: 23) offers the following conclusions:

(1) The Toraijin came to the Archipelago not from the interior regions of the Asian continent but from the southern coast of the Korean Peninsula, specifically from the lower Nakdong and Nam river basin, that is, the area of modern day Kimhae and Daepyeong-ni. It was the Middle Mumun people of the Korean Peninsula that entered the Archipelago with their culture.

(2) The initial Toraijin population increased rapidly through interbreeding with the indigenous Jomon people. The result was the emergence of the Toraijin-type Yayoi people. The latter spread to all directions, further interbreeding with the local indigenous populations, resulting in various regional-type Yayoi populations.

(3) The leaders in the formation of the Yayoi culture were neither the Toraijin nor the indigenous Jomon people. They were the Toraijin-type Yayoi people.

In this regard, Etsuji, an incipient Yayoi village, was as an archetype of the so-called 'Yayoi phenomena', namely ethnic and cultural hybridization as well as change and continuity (Mizoguchi 2013: 55-65). The hamlet of Etsuji was unmistakably a Songguk-ni type village in its physical form but with Jomon elements in it. The builders of the Songguk-ni type residences grew rice in the nearby paddies as in Middle Mumun Korea, but inside the village an ethnic and cultural hybridization was taking place as Toraijin and local Jomon people were starting a new family and a new home.

The village of Etsuji also stands as a symbol of change and continuity. As observed by Mizoguchi (2013: 64):

> Although many material things were changed, there still remained a sense of continuity at the heart of the structuring principle, or the world view, of everyday life. In that sense, the beginning of the Yayoi was a kind of *becoming* rather than a *beginning*. It was not an event marking a break from the past but a process through which people, including the inhabitants of Etsuji and their ancestors, transformed themselves by maintaining continuity in their everyday life.

During the Initial and Early Yayoi period, the hybridization most likely progressed rather smoothly because the Toraijin offered something the indigenous people desired, and there was sufficient land for wet-rice farming obviating any conflict. Most of all, Mizoguchi (2013: 64) postulates that the

Toraijin and the Jomon people shared a similar worldview that "life was an endless cycle of death and regeneration of natural beings, including human beings"

Another controversy pertains to the beginning of wet-rice farming, specifically in regard to the question of "Who actively initiated the wet rice cultivation in the Archipelago?" (Shimojo and Tanaka 2014: 279-324). Some (Kanaseki and OYBH 1995: 236-247) have posited that Jomon people, already engaged in mixed-crop agriculture including dry field rice cultivation, were actively involved in the development of the wet-rice farming through their cultural interactions with the Peninsula; Barnes (1993) explored such options in a modelling exercise; however, archaeological evidence from Kyushu, where the wet rice cultivation first emerged, does not support such a view.

The Jomon hunting-fishing-gathering economy had been self-sufficient for over 10,000 years, and during the Final Jomon period, the population pressure in the Japanese Archipelago, especially in the southwest, was less than it had been in earlier times. Hanihara (1984: 140, 1993: 16) has estimated that Jomon population throughout Japan declined from 260,000 during the Middle Jomon to 75,000 during the Final Jomon, with only 10,000 of Japan's Jomon people in Kyushu. Furthermore, no evidence has been found for "the overexploitation of major subsistence resources... during the Late and Latest Jomon periods" (Mizoguchi 2002: 120).

A relatively small number of Jomon people living in a tolerably productive environment would have had no major incentive to engage in agriculture, let alone wet-rice cultivation, which was the most arduous, complex, and labor-intensive form of food procurement of ancient times, as graphically described by Mizoguchi (2013: 90-91). In fact, for these reasons the indigenous Japanese societies of central and northern Japan adopted wet-rice agriculture only slowly and reluctantly even as it was thriving in northern Kyushu (Akazawa 1982: 151-211; Barnes 2015: 280-284). Other Jomon societies, especially in the Tohoku region, are known to have tried and rejected it (Mizoguchi 2013: 28).

Furthermore, archaeological evidence from Kyushu shows clearly that the earliest wet-rice agriculture appeared there *suddenly and in fully developed form* (Mizoguchi 2002: 118; K Miyamoto 2017: 256-257). There is no evidence for Jomon trial and error experimentation with wet-rice cultivation, but instead a picture of highly sophisticated agricultural technology arriving suddenly with the Mumun farming people and their whole cultural system. In light of these observations, Mizoguchi (2013: 91) concludes:

> The [Yayoi] package consisted of not only material items but important know-how for dealing with various types of local topography, appropriately and efficiently positioning the necessary features and organizing labor to accomplish the required tasks. This suggests that the arrival of those who had plenty of experience in practicing sophisticated wet-rice agriculture essentially contributed to the changes that marked the beginning of the new era.

During the Kurokawa stage of the Final Jomon, some Jomon hunters and gatherers came down to the lowland to try food cultivation. Their stay, however, was brief, suggesting that they failed in their attempt at a new strategy for livelihood. For the Jomon people long dependant on stored acorns, food cultivation was too risky (Shimojo and Tanaka 2014: 295, 321). The arrival of the Toraijin with an efficient food producing technology, therefore, would have been welcomed by some Jomon people, resulting in a cooperative community in which the Toraijin and the Jomon natives worked together for common good, each engaging in what they knew and did best: Toraijin in farming and teaching wet-rice farming technology and the Jomon natives in hunting, fishing, and felling trees (Shimojo and Tanaka 2014: 314-315). Accordingly, as stated by TANAKA Yoshiyuki (2014: 33), the Yayoi society was created by neither the Toraijin nor the indigenous Jomon people. It was a Toraijin-Jomon cooperative venture.

Finally, the China connection. A number of Chinese and Japanese archaeologists have sought to relate the Yayoi wet-rice farming directly to the Yangtze River basin of southeast China (An 1985: 297-310; Higuchi 1986: 121-126, Higuchi 1995: 121-126). Noting that jade earrings, tall wooden structures, certain plants, the custom of tooth extraction, and certain lithic tools and ethnographic features observed at some Jomon and Early Yayoi sites are similar to those found in the Yangtze River basin, these scholars posit that the technology of rice cultivation diffused directly from southeastern China to Kyushu across the East China Sea. Others (Wasano 1995: 3-52), primarily on the basis of morphological analysis of rice grains found in China, Korea, and Kyushu, have also suggested a 'direct East China-Kyushu' connection to explain the origin of Japan's rice cultivation.

This hypothesis, however, remains untenable until it can adequately explain a number of crucial issues: (1) Why wet-rice cultivation appeared first in the Hakata Bay and Karatsu Bay – areas of northern Kyushu which are closest to southern Korea rather than along the southwest coastal region of Kyushu directly facing the East China Sea; (2) Why *only* the short-grain *Oryza sativa japonica* type, adapted to temperate climate and grown in Mumun Korea, first appeared in northern Kyushu, when both *Oryza sativa japonica* and the long-grain *Oryza sativa indica* types were grown in the Yangtze River basin; (3) Why grooved adzes, triangular reaping knives, polished stone daggers, willow leaf-shaped arrows, pottery vessels, settlement patterns, mortuary practices closely associated with the early Yayoi farming communities are found only in southern Korea but not in the Yangtze River basin; and (4) Why the initial wet-rice agriculture seen in Japan exemplified a whole complex identifiable with Mumun Korea's cultural system rather than that of the lower Yangtze River basin (Jeon 1986: 107-117; Takakura 1995: 283-288).

The China connection has been largely abandoned by the East Asian archaeological community as the result of extensive archaeological investigations in southern Korea since the 1980s, revealing much light on the Middle Mumun/Songguk-ni culture and the unmistakable connections between the latter and the initial and early Yayoi culture. Accordingly, YAN Wenming, China's foremost scholar on the development and diffusion of rice cultivation in East Asia, emphatically rejects the China connection. "Rice cultivation moved," he states, "from Korea to Japan with both its technology and the farmers who cultivated rice. They were the Koreans whom Japanese scholars call Toraijin, the people who crossed the sea" (Yan 1992: 95-100).

CHAPTER TWO

BRONZE-BEARING TORAIJIN OF THE MIDDLE YAYOI
(c. 350 BC–AD 50)

I. THEIR HISTORICAL AND SOCIO-CULTURAL BACKGROUND: PENINSULA'S LATE MUMUN SOCIETY (C. 400–50 BC)

In Korean history, the 4th–1st century BC is known as the Late Mumun Period. Several decades of archaeological studies have led Korean scholars to conclude that during this period, two major culture zones existed in southern Korea: the western zone between the Han River and the southwest coast and the southeastern zone comprising today's North and South Gyeongsang Provinces along the southeast coast. The two zones are separated by the massive Sobaek Mountain Range.

In addition, there is a general consensus among Korean archaeologists and historians that the western zone was the home of Early Mahan polities undergoing revolutionary socio-cultural transformation (GJEB 2000: 11-13), while the southeastern zone was in the waning stages of the Late Mumun cultural tradition. Thus, the Early Mahan people were essentially the descendants of the Songguk-ni culture people (JS Kim 2009: 52-54)

1. The Slender Bronze Dagger Culture of Early Mahan

Culturally, socially, and politically, the Early Mahan period was an era of dynamic and revolutionary transformations. They were, however, more the result of overwhelming external stimuli than of internally generated autochthonous dynamics. Incessant wars in China during its Warring State Period (403–221 BC) and the subsequent militaristic incursions of the Jin and Yan states into the northeastern regions, resulted in the dispersion of local populations of the Liaoning region.

During 300–250 BC, some of the dispersed people moved into the Peninsula with their culture including the variegated and slenderized type of Liaoning bronze dagger repertoire, iron tools, and new pottery vessels: the *heuksaek mayeon togi* (black burnished jars) and the *jeomtodae togi* (bowls with a clay striped rim) (Fig. 2.1) (SB Park 2009: 228-229). The Early Mahan people welcomed the new culture and soon developed it into the distinctive "Korean Slender Bronze Dagger Culture" (JS Jo 2005: 221-224; KM Lee 2007: 8-20).

Soon, the Korean Slender Bronze Dagger culture underwent three distinctive developmental phases: I (Early, c. 300–250 BC), II (Middle, c. 250–100 BC), and III (Late, c. 100 BC–AD 50) (KM Lee 1992b: 133-137; cf. JS Jo 2005: 200-212).

During Phase I, the bronze culture of the Liaoning origin was being established on the Peninsula with new indigenous features. Found in the elite graves at Goejeong-dong in Daejeon, Dongseo-ri in Yesan, and Namseong-ri in Asan, the Koreanized bronzes included weapons (bronze daggers, dagger hilt

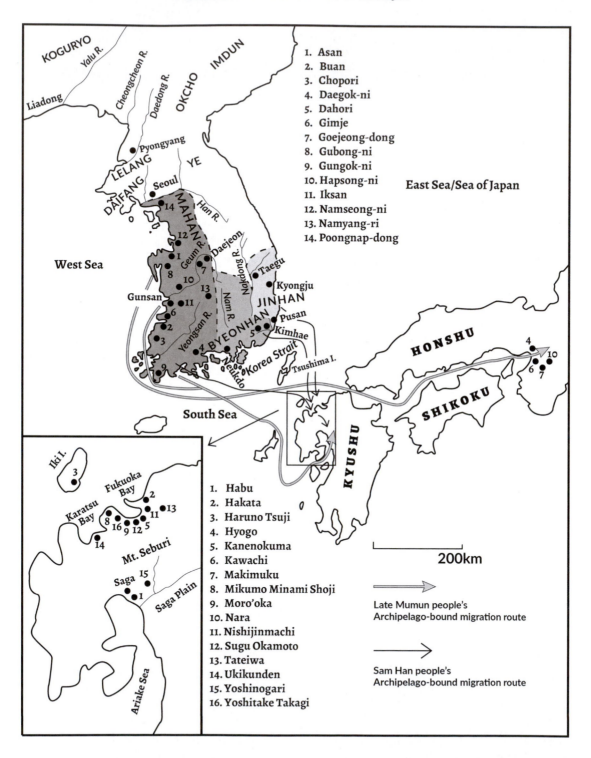

1. Asan
2. Buan
3. Chopori
4. Daegok-ni
5. Dahori
6. Gimje
7. Goejeong-dong
8. Gubong-ni
9. Gungok-ni
10. Hapsong-ni
11. Iksan
12. Namseong-ni
13. Namyang-ri
14. Poongnap-dong

East Sea/Sea of Japan

West Sea

1. Habu
2. Hakata
3. Haruno Tsuji
4. Hyogo
5. Kanenokuma
6. Kawachi
7. Makimuku
8. Mikumo Minami Shoji
9. Moro'oka
10. Nara
11. Nishijinmachi
12. Sugu Okamoto
13. Tateiwa
14. Ukikunden
15. Yoshinogari
16. Yoshitake Takagi

200km

Late Mumun people's
Archipelago-bound migration route

Sam Han people's
Archipelago-bound migration route

Map 2.1. Major sites of the Late Mumun/Sam Han and the Middle/Late Yayoi period, c. 300 BC–AD 300.

Fig. 2.1. Late Mumun pottery in southern Korea. **Top**, from left: *jeomtodae* (rolled rim) deep bowl, long-necked black burnished pot, bowl with a base, a mounted bowl. **Bottom**, from left: Songguk-ni-type jar, black burnished pot with ox horn-shaped handles, mounted bowl, steamer with a perforated base (GJUB 1993: 57-68). Photo credit: Hanstudio.

components, and shield-shaped bronze objects), industrial tools (fan-shaped bronze axes and bronze chisels), and ritual implements (bronze mirrors with coarse geometric linear design). In the case of bronze daggers, they assumed a straight body unlike the lute-shaped Liaoning daggers with the bulging base (KM Lee 1992b: 133-134; JS Jo 2005: 213-220) (Fig. 2.2).

During Phase II, the Korean Slender Bronze Dagger Culture blossomed (Fig. 2.3). First, there was a significant advancement in bronze technology involving the smelting of raw copper and tin ore in high heat, preparation of precision casting molds, and the chemical application of lead and zinc (KM Lee 1992a: 138-142). Second, it became thoroughly indigenized with new features and new objects. For example, decorative designs on bronze objects were transformed from the coarse to the fine-line geometric designs along with new design elements including sun rays, crosses, deer, hawk, human hands, and hunting scenes. Third, there was a special emphasis on the religious and ritual concerns. The ritual bronze implements included bells, multi-pronged rattles, and multi-knobbed bronze mirrors with fine-line geometric designs. Fourth, during this period, the bronze daggers and

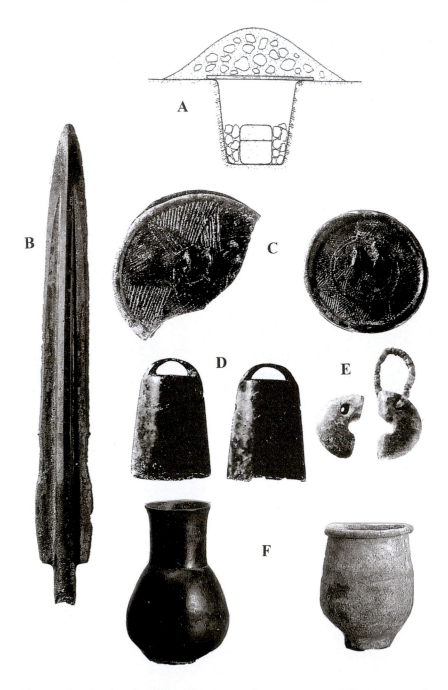

Fig. 2.2. A *Jeokseok mokgwanmyo* at Goejeong-dong in Daejeon and prestige goods placed in it. **A:** stone-framed burial pit (2.2-meter x 0.5-meter x 1.0 meter) containing a wooden coffin. **B:** a slender bronze dagger (length: 32.4cm). **C:** multi-knobbed bronze mirrors with coarse linear design (right, diameter: 11.3cm). **D:** bronze bells (heights: 11.4cm, 11.2cm). **E:** a pair of comma-shaped Amazonite stones (lengths: 3.2cm, 3.4 cm). **F:** a black burnished jar (height: 22cm) and a *jeomtodae togi* (pot with a round clay ring around the rim, height: 17cm) (GJUB and GGWB 1992: 28). Photo credit: Hanstudio.

bronze mirrors underwent several stages of further refinement, the former becoming slenderer and the latter with intricate geometric designs (KM Lee 1992b: 135-136; JS Jo 2005: 203-206).

The dazzling effect of the reflecting sunlight and images seen in a shining bronze mirror would have inspired awe and mystic veneration of the mirror as well as its owner. Furthermore, the multi-knobbed bronze mirrors were viewed as the communicative media of the divine will. They were buried in elite graves along with jade ornaments (curved jewels and tubular beads), as seen in the elite graves of Goejeong-dong in Daejeon, Gubong-ni in Buyeo, Namseong-ri in Asan, and Chopo-ri in Hampyeong (GJUB and GGWB 1992: 26-117).

Some of the elite graves containing bronze ritual bells along with bronze mirrors are believed to have belonged to religious heads or chief shamans of various Early Mahan communities while those bearing primarily bronze weapons (daggers, spears, and halberds) and bronze tools (axes and chisels) belonged to secular political chiefs (GMUY 2008: 237-238).

There also appeared new industrial bronze tools such as shouldered axes and heavy rectangular-shaped and closed clam shaped axes, pointed sculpting tools called *dongsa*, and awls. The bronze chisels, which had appeared during Period I, increased in quantity. They are often found in the elite graves as a set along with the shouldered bronze axes and the pointed sculpting tools. The new bronze weapons included, in addition to further slenderized bronze daggers, bronze halberds and bronze spear points, developed under the influence of mainland Chinese bronze weapons of the Warring Period.

Toward the end of Phase II, c. 200 BC, cast iron tools (axes, chisels, and pointed sculpting tools) were being produced at various bronze industrial sites such as Songsan-ni, Seoksan-ni, and Ihwa-dong. For the first time, there also appeared tubular glass beads made of lead and barium of Chinese origin (KM Lee 1992b: 136; JS Jo 2005: 206). It was during this period, c. 200 BC, that the slender Korean bronze dagger culture diffused to northern Kyushu. The multi-knobbed bronze mirror with fine-line designs found in #3 wood-coffin tomb at Yoshitake Takagi belonged to this period (JS Jo 2005: 205, 225).

Major sites of the Phase II bronze implements include Gubong-ni in Buyeo, Daegok-ni in Hwasun, Tanbang-dong in Daejeon, Solmegol in Bongsan, Jeongbong-ni in Shin'gye, Chopo-ri in Hampyeong among others. To the latter part of this period belong Hapsong-ri in Buyeo, Soso-ri in Dangjin, and Namyang-ri in Jangsu (JS Jo 2005: 94). As places of elite residences, these sites would most likely have functioned as political centers also.

Around 100 BC, the Korean Slender Dagger Culture began to decline, following Han China's establishment of its military/commercial outpost in 108 BC at Lelang (near modern Pyongyang) in northwest Korea. New advanced Chinese iron implements (iron weapons, iron horse paraphernalia, and Chinese bronze mirrors), available through Lelang, gradually superseded the Korean bronzes indicated among the archaeological remains of Jeongbaek-dong (#97), Sang-ri, Seok'am-ri. and Heukkyo-ri in the northwest and at Dahori (#1), Joyang-dong, Manchon-dong, and Sara-ri in the southeast (JS Jo 2005: 206-209).

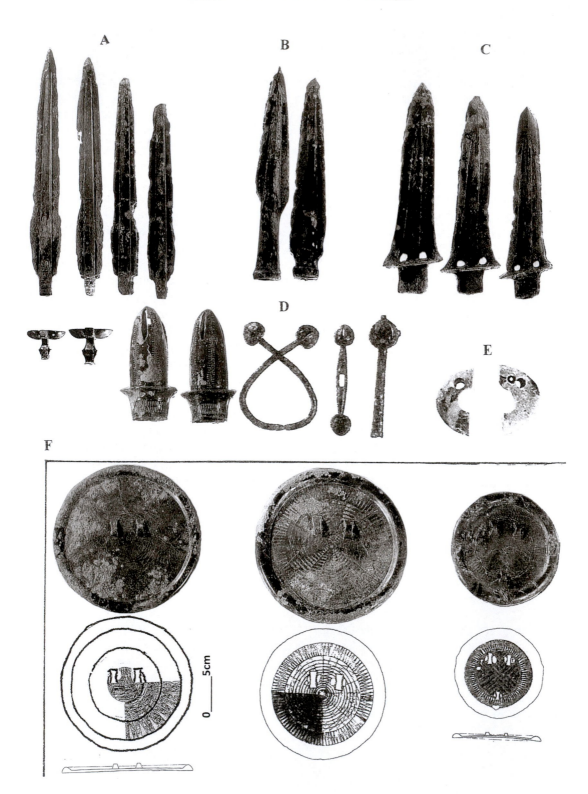

2. Iron Implements and Iron Tool Production

Iron tools first appeared in the northwestern part of the Peninsula sometime in the 3rd century BC at Yong'yeon-dong and Sejuk-ni, north of the Cheongcheon River. Comprised mainly of weapons and agricultural tools, they were imported from China's Yan State in southwestern Manchuria. The former included spears and arrowheads, while the latter included wedge-shaped axes, spades, hoes, sickles, needles, fishhooks, and semilunar knives. They were entirely of the cast-iron type. No forged iron tools appeared yet (MJ Sohn 2012: 15).

Soon the cast-iron tools, including heavy wedge-type axes of cast iron (*jujo cheolbu*) and iron chisels, spread rapidly throughout the Korean Peninsula, as evidenced by finds from Songsan-ni and Seokjang-ni in the northwest, Ihwa-dong in the northeast, and Soso-ri, Hapsong-ni, and Namyang-ni in the southwest (MJ Sohn 2012: 14-17). These cast iron tools were found in association with cast bronze implements suggesting that it was the elites in control of the bronze industry that acted as pioneers in the adoption and production of iron tools. They not only knew the superiority of metals over stone and wooden implements but also owned the technical knowledge of casting bronzes. Accordingly, the elite burials at Songsan-ni, Ihwa-dong, Soso-ri, Hapsong-ni, and Namyang-ni contained cast iron axes along with slender bronze daggers, bronze spears, and multi-knobbed bronze mirrors with fine geometric designs (MJ Sohn 2012: 15-18, 32; GJUB and GGWB 1992: 32-43).

The advantage of iron tools over stone implements common in the Mumun Period pushed for a greater demand for quality iron tools for agricultural and industrial purposes; consequently, at the end of the 3rd century BC, there now appeared for the first-time forged iron tools, not only more durable but more practical, including forged iron axes, long swords, daggers, spearpoints, chisels, sickles, and horse bits among others. From this time, the technology of iron forging became increasingly important through exchange and interaction among local elites. While the iron smiths continued to employ the casting method to produce certain non-utilitarian objects, they generally employed forging methods to manufacture the utilitarian implements (daggers, spearpoints, chisels, and sculpting tools) (MJ Sohn 2012: 16-24).

Around 200 BC, these iron tools spread to the Taegu region in the southeast along with smithing technology. The forged iron tools were placed in the early wood-coffin tombs at Paldal-dong (# 45, # 57, and # 77). During the 2nd century BC, iron forging workshops began to appear in the southeast region at Raeseong in Pusan and Gusan-dong in Kimhae. Initially, they were operated inside square-shaped residential buildings around a simple sintering furnace, in the form of a shallow dug-out pit without a tuyere (a blasting pipe) developed later (SM Kim 2019: 59-61).

Fig. 2.3. (Page 56) Advanced bronze artifacts of the Korean Slender Bronze Dagger Culture and Amazonite jewels from a *jeokseok mokgwanmyo* (underground wood coffin burial covered with a mound of piled stones) at Chopo-ri in Hampyeong. **A:** Slender bronze daggers with hilt knobs (lengths: 25.8-32.7 cm). **B:** Bronze spear points (lengths: 27.9cm, 26.1 cm). **C:** Bronze halberds (lengths: 27.6 cm, 26 cm, 20.5 cm). **D:** Ritual bells (left: height, 14.5cm, diam. 4.6cm). **E:** Comma-shaped Amazonite stones (lengths: 3.8cm, 3.85 cm). **F:** Multi-knobbed bronze mirrors with fine line geometric designs (from left: diameters 17.8 cm, 15.6cm, 9.7cm). (GGWB 1988a: 24-32, 114-116; GJUB and GGWB 1992: 40-41). Photo credit: Hanstudio and Gwangju National Museum.

3. Late Mumun Pottery

During the Late Mumun period, some of the plain coarse ware of the Middle Mumun (the later pottery of the Songguk-ni type culture) continued in use among the Peninsula's inhabitants. However, in the 4th century BC, there also emerged new pottery types in connection with new ethnic intrusions from southwestern Manchuria: the *heuksaek mayeon togi* (black burnished jars) and the *jeomtodae togi* (bowls with a clay striped rim) (Fig. 2.1) (SB Park 2009: 228-229). They are often found in the Late Mumun elite graves along with slender bronze daggers, bronze mirrors, and comma-shaped amazonite jewels (GMUY 2008: 1044-1045).

Long-necked black-burnished jars (*heuksaek mayeon togi*) were made of fine clay and distinguished by their long flaring neck, bulging body, small flat base, and burnished surface. By the 2nd century BC, the Late Mumun pottery vessels had undergone more formal changes. In the southwest, handles in the shape of lugs or rings were attached to their bodies, and vessels were diversified to include steamers, cups, and mounted dishes.

With the wide-mouth pots with a rolled clay rim (*jeomtodae togi*), the cross section of the rim was circular initially, and such vessels were the predominant type in both Korea's west-central region and the upper reaches of the Nakdong River in the southeast. Around 200 BC, clay rings with a triangular cross section began to appear and thereafter such vessels became the dominant form of *jeomtodae togi* all along the south coast.

4. Late Mumun Mortuary Practices

A. Northwest

In the northwest, cist tombs (coffins made of slabs) and stone-framed graves (with roughly cut stones) which had appeared during the Middle Mumun period were common. The third and 2nd century BC cist-tombs in Jeongbong-ni, Cheon'gok-ni, and Songsan-ni and the 2nd century BC wooden coffins in the Pyongyang area all contain an impressive array of prestige goods, including slender bronze daggers, bronze mirrors, bronze spearheads, and bronze axes (JYYDPW 1989: 81-86).

B. Southwest: Early Mahan (c. 350 BC-AD 300)

In Korea's west-central coastal regions, some of the Early Mahan elites constructed *jugumyo*, pit tombs partially encircled by a trench (Map 2.2, bottom left). The trench is believed to have functioned as a boundary marker and also as protection for a wood or jar coffin buried within the circle.

A large Late Mumun site at Gwanchang-ni in Boryeong has revealed 99 *jugumyo*. Some contained late Songguk-ni culture pottery while others yielded *jeomtodae togi* (pots with a round clay ring encircling the rim), black burnished jars, and multi-knobbed bronze mirrors of the Late Mumun Period (c. 400–100 BC). The artifact assemblages indicate that *jugumyo* first emerged during the 3rd century BC at the latest and continued on for several centuries as a prominent mortuary system in the southwest (OYBH 1999: 82-85; TG Lee 2008: 34-89).

There also appeared stone-framed wood-coffin burials (*jeokseok mokkwanmyo*). Prestige goods buried in them included an impressive array of bronze implements and jade ornaments. Such a tomb at

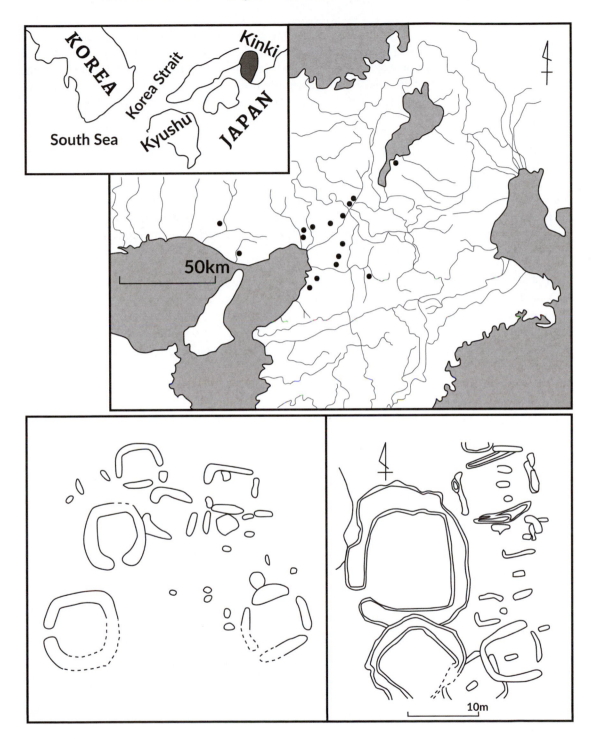

Map 2.2. *Jugumyo* (J. Shukobo) (moat-surrounded tombs) sites in the Kinki region (by Lucas Pauly) (after OYBH 1999: 82). Bottom left: Jugumyo excavated at Gwanchang-ni in Boryeong, west-central Korea (after OYBH 1999: 84). Bottom right: Jugumyo excavated at Higashi Muko in Hyogo (after OYBH 1999: 83).

Goejeong-dong (Daejon), from c. 300 BC, yielded one slender bronze dagger, two bronze mirrors with coarse-line decorations, three dagger handle-shaped bronze objects, one shield-like bronze ornament, one disk-shaped bronze object, and two bronze bells. There were also three triangular stone arrowheads, a pair of comma-shaped amazonite ornaments, some 50 small beads, and two pottery vessels (a deep bowl with a rolled rim and a black burnished jar with a long, flaring neck) (Fig. 2.2) (EC Lee 1968).

A stone-framed wood coffin tomb at Gubong-ni in Buyeo contained 20 bronze objects, including 11 slender daggers, two mirrors, two halberds, a spear, and a chisel (GS Lee 1987). A cist tomb at Dongseo-ri in Yesan contained nine slender bronze daggers, five bronze mirrors, and six bronze ritual implements along with tubular and circular beads (GG Jee 1979; GMUY 2008: 322-324). A cist tomb at Namseong-ni in Asan had nine slender bronze daggers, two bronze mirrors with thick geometric designs, a bronze axe, a bronze chisel, three bronze ritual implements, 103 tubular beads, and an amazonite curved jewel (BS Ham and KM Lee 1977).

Built about a century later in the 2nd century BC, a stone-framed tomb containing a split log coffin at Daegok-ni in Hwasun yielded five slender bronze daggers, three bronze mirrors, an axe, and four ritual purpose bells (GGWB 2013). Another stone-framed tomb at Chopo-ri in Hampyeong contained four slender bronze daggers, three bronze mirrors with fine linear geometric design, five ritual purpose bronze bells, three halberds, two spearheads, an axe, two chisels, and a pair of amazonite curved jewels (GGWB 1988a).

C. Southeast

In the southeast coastal region, dolmen construction was continuing, with some dolmen capstones enlarged to a mega size as in the case of Songseon-ni (8.00 m long x 6.00 m wide x 2.70 m thick), Moseo-ri (6.00 m long x 4.00 m wide x 2.40 m thick), and Dasan-ni (4.60 m long x 2.30 m wide x 2.14 m thick) dolmens (KK Kim: 1999: 743, 749) or constructed with a multi-level underground burial chamber as in the case of Deokcheon-ni Dolmen #1.

The latter, dated to the 4th century BC, was constructed within a large sacred precinct (56.2 m long x 17.5 m wide) demarcated with stone pavement and stone wall, the dolmen itself was distinguished by a large capstone and an underground chamber constructed in three levels. Also, it larger than all other dolmens in the region. At the bottom of the underground chamber was a wood coffin. The entire underground chamber itself was filled with cut stones and slabs. The dolmen contained twenty-two stemmed polished stone arrowheads, four tubular jades, and some wooden implements (SG Lee 1994).

In the vicinity of Dolmen #1, but just outside the demarcated precinct, were four other dolmens smaller in size. Most likely the sacred mortuary precinct belonged to the highest-ranking elite, that is, the chief of the region and his immediate family (SG Lee 1994). The chiefly status of the Dolmen #1 was conveyed not so much in buried goods but in the physical size of the mortuary structure and the amount of labor expended in its construction.

In the 2nd century BC, however, wood-coffin burials became dominant throughout the southeast region, as evidenced by the archaeology of Paldal-dong in Taegu and Imdang-dong in Gyeongsan,

Joyang-dong in Kyongju, Dahori in Changweon, and Yangdong-ri in Kimhae. They have yielded a large number of iron tools made of cast-iron (GMUY 2008: 210-212, 828-830; GJUB 2008; MJ Sohn 2012: 31-45).

Tomb #55 in the Yangdong-ri Cemetery, built in the 1st century BC, consisted of a wood coffin measuring 2.43 x 0.66 m, and 0.35 m deep, placed in an earthen pit measuring 2.93 x 1.23 m, and 1.12 m deep. The tomb contained an iron dagger, an iron axe, an iron sickle, iron arrowheads, a small jar of Wajil pottery, a circular bronze artifact, a necklace of small glass beads, and an imitation Chinese bronze mirror (HT Im and DC Gwak 2000). All throughout the Korean Peninsula integral to the Late Mumun mortuary culture was the burial of iron of many kinds. Iron had emerged as the symbol of wealth and power, and with it an iron cult elevating the iron to a form of deity.

5. 'Three Sacred Treasures': Dagger, Mirror, and Comma-shaped Jewel

During the Middle Mumun period, bronze daggers, comma-shaped jewels made of the amazonite stone, and tubular beads were valued as the symbols of the elite power, as evidenced in the remains of a chiefly cist tomb at Songguk-ni in Buyeo. In the Late Mumun period, bronze mirrors were added, so that three treasures in particular – daggers, mirrors, and comma-shaped jewels – now represented the ruling power (Figs. 2.2 and 2.3). This is evidenced in the prestige goods placed in the Late Mumun elite burials at Goejeong-dong in Daejeon, Yeonhwa-ri in Buyeo, Namseong-ri in Asan, and Chopo-ri in Hampyeong.

6. Push-Pull Dynamics during the Late Mumun Period

During the Warring States Period (401–221 BC), the Chinese state of Yan, located around modern Beijing, emerged as the strongest power in northern China. After solidifying its power internally, it launched wars of conquest against its northern and eastern neighbors, directly into the territory of ancient Choson spread across the land between the Liao River and the Han River (Byington 2016b: 33-46).

Yan state's northward and eastward push caused a domino effect in northeast Asia in the movement of disrupted and dislocated peoples and tribes eastwards as well as southwards. As the conquered and displaced tribes moved southwards into the Korean Peninsula, the newly displaced native tribes and polities also moved southwards, resulting in unprecedented socio-political turbulence in the Peninsula (WG Choi 2009: 247-258; SB Park 2009: 224-228).

In 222 BC, Wiman, a defeated official of China's Yan State, took refuge in the land of Go-Choson in northwest Korea with a thousand armed followers. After twenty-eight years of serving the court of Go-Choson, Wiman rebelled against King Jun of the Choson Kingdom in 194 BC, and in its place, he established his own kingdom, known as "Wiman Choson," in modern-day Pyongyang area. King Jun and his people fled southwards to the lower Geum River basin on the southwest coast. According to the *Hou Hanshu* (Account of the Later Han Dynasty), "[W]hen the Choson king Chun was defeated by Wei Man, he took several thousand of his remaining followers and fled by sea. He attacked [Early] Mahan and defeated it, then set himself up as the King of [Early Ma]Han" (Byington 2009: 151; brackets added).

The region which King Jun (spelled also as Chun) conquered is believed to have been the Iksan area in the lower Geum River basin on the southwest coast (JG Noh 2009: 215), a major population center since the prehistoric times. It included a wide area including the Gunsan harbour and the fertile Mangyeong Plains (JG Gwak 2017a: 23-59). His rule of the Iksan area, however, was short-lived because of the local people's rebellion, but the war which he waged against them would have left some of the Early Mahan people in the southwest devastated and displaced.

By this time, through the communication network established between the Initial–Early Toraijin in Kyushu and the southern Peninsula, northern Kyushu was well-known to the Early Mahan people on the Peninsula (Kataoka 1999: 112-113). As the pressure from the north increased, the Early Mahan people, who were essentially descendants of the Songguk-ni culture people (JS Kim 2009: 52-54), and familiar with seafaring as coastal people (JG Gwak 2017a: 23-59), sailed along the southwest coast and across the Korea Strait toward Kyushu, as their Middle Mumun ancestors had done. They settled in the Saga Plain at Habu, Yoshinogari, Ane, and Nabeshima Honmaru Minami among others, as evidenced by the presence at these sites of the Late Mumun pottery (*jeomtodae togi* and long-necked pots) (Kataoka 1999: 119-124, 149-150; Shichida 2007a: 118-120). The turbulent events in the Peninsula following Wiman's invasion and the appearance in northern Kyushu of the bronze-bearing Toraijin were contemporaneous, occurring around or shortly after 200 BC.

II. A NEW GROUP OF TORAIJIN COMES TO THE KYUSHU ISLAND

1. New Toraijin Settlements

A new group of Toraijin appeared in northern Kyushu and its adjacent areas between Yamaguchi in the north and Kumamoto in the south with wide-mouth pots with a rolled rim (*jeomtodae togi*) and long-necked black burnished pots (*heuksaek mayeon togi*), which were distinctive components of the Peninsula's Late Mumun pottery (c. 400–50 BC) (Kataoka 1999: 103-108) (Fig. 2.1). Thus, a new wave of Toraijin arrived in the Archipelago sometime during the Middle Yayoi (c. 350 BC–AD 50) (date according to Takakura 2011: 205).

Related to the Initial-Early Yayoi Period Toraijin, historically and culturally, the new Toraijin would not have found Kyushu Island to be a totally strange place. His/her feelings would have been similar to those of an Englishman coming to North America in the 21st century for the first time.

While some of the Toraijin called "the Moro'oka Type" (named after the Moro'oka site in Fukuoka) either returned to the Peninsula or moved to other sites, many others called "the Habu Type Toraijin" (named after the Habu site in the Saga Plain) converged on the Saga Plain and stayed permanently. Settling on a fertile plain, on the south side of the Seburi mountains, they established numerous colony-like settlements on the low-lying ridges between Habu and Yoshinogari (Kataoka 1999: 104-111, 119-124; Shichida 2007a: 118-120; Mizoguchi 2013: 111). According to Shichida (2007a: 121), most likely they arrived there by way of the Ariake Sea bypassing the north coastal areas of Fukuoka and Karatsu (Map 2.1).

The new Toraijin chose the Saga Plain for two reasons. First, at this time, the sea level on the north coast of Kyushu was several meters higher than in the Early Yayoi Period, resulting in the reduction of arable lands. Second, the Saga Plain was a vast stretch of fertile arable land suitable for wet-rice

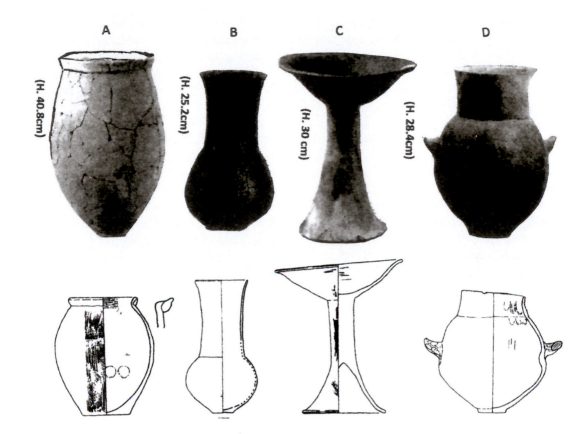

Fig. 2.4. Late Mumun pottery from the Peninsula and the Archipelago. **Top:** Late Mumun pottery from southern Korea (**A:** Storage jar with an everted rim. **B:** Black burnished long necked pot. **C.** Bowl attached to a tall mount. **D.** Wide-mouthed and long-necked pot with a pair of ox horn-shaped handles, (GJUB 1993: 57, 63, 65, 68. Photo: Hanstudio). **Bottom:** Late Mumun pottery from northern Kyushu. (After Kataoka: 1999: 86, 91, 122).

cultivation (Shichida 2007a: 121). This information would have been known to the Peninsula's farmers through the information network long existing between the Yayoi-type Toraijin and their Peninsula contacts (Kataoka 1999: 112).

Prominent sites among them were Habu, Yoshinogari, Ane, and Nabeshima Honmaru Minami in the Saga Plain. Their archaeological markers are the Peninsula Late Mumun pottery including the wide mouth pots with a rolled rim (*jeomtodae togi*), long-necked black-burnished pots (*heugsaeg mayeon togi*), and globular pots with attached ox horn-shaped handles (*ugakhyeong pasu togi*) (Fig. 2.4) (Kataoka 1999: 119-124, 149-150; Shichida 2007a: 118-120).

In the meantime, various Yayoi settlements in the Saga Plain which had emerged during the Early Yayoi Period, such as Habu, Nabeshima, and Yoshinogari, had grown into substantial agricultural communities.

Yoshinogari, the largest Yayoi settlement site in the Archipelago, has undoubtedly become the crown jewel of the Japanese archaeology. Excavations of the site begun in 1986 have revealed that the site, settled initially by the rice-cultivating Toraijin during the Early Yayoi period, as evidenced by the presence of Korean dolmens (Yanagida 1989: 120-121), emerged as an impressive village of 20 hectares during the Middle Yayoi period, with the influx of the bronze-bearing Toraijin (Shiga-ken Kyoiku I'inkai 2008: 15-20).

The village of Middle Yayoi Yoshinogari consisted mainly of the Songguk-ni type semi-subterranean houses distinguished by a central oval pit with two post holes near the pit and had numerous flask-shaped outdoor storage pits, closely resembling the Songguk-ni type settlements of the Middle-Late Mumun Peninsula. Along with the Songguk-ni type residential structures and potteries, archaeologists uncovered numerous bronze implements and bronze-casting molds. Particularly prominent among the Middle Yayoi Yoshinogari features is a *funkyubo* tomb, an artificially raised large earthen burial mound on a prominent hill containing 14 adult jar coffins. Eight of them yielded 16 slender bronze daggers and 79 tube-type glass beads. Excavators believe that on this earthen mound were buried Middle Yayoi chiefs over several generations (Shiga-ken Kyoiku I'inkai 2008: 19-20; Shichida 2017: 26-28).

From a moat, archaeologists uncovered numerous Peninsula-type lithic tools locally manufactured, including reaping knives, polished stone daggers, closed clam-shaped axes (*hap'in seokbu*) and hand axes with a notch in the stem (*yugu seokbu*), along with indigenous Jomon tools (Shichida 2017: 26-29). Undoubtedly, Yoshinogari and other Middle Yayoi settlements were inhabited by the new Toraijin as well as the descendants of the Initial Toraijin, now the hybrid Toraijin-type Yayoi people.

The Toraijin-related archaeological remains of Yoshinogari are so overwhelmingly of the Peninsula origin that Nishitani (1989: 127-132) has reported that "ancient Korea and its technology were greatly involved in the birth of Yoshinogari as well as in the process of state formation in the Saga Plains." In 2007, the Saga-ken Education Committee and the National Museum of Korea jointly held a special exhibit in Seoul with the publication of *Yoshinogari: Ilbonsogui Godae Hanguk* (Ancient Korea in Japan) (National Museum of Korea: 2007). The following year, in 2008, another joint archaeological exhibit was held in Saga, Kyushu, with the publication of *Yoshinogari iseki to Kodai Kanhanto: 2000 nen no Jiku o koete* (The Yoshinogari Site and the Ancient Korean Peninsula: Beyond 2000 years of Time and Space) (Saga-ken Kyoiku I'inkai 2008).

2. New Toraijin Contributions to the Middle Yayoi Society

A. Bronze Industry

From numerous stone molds for casting bronze implements found at various Middle Yayoi sites, from Habu to Yoshinogari, Japanese archaeologists (Kataoka 1999: 149-175; Shichida 2017: 38) posit that the bronze industry first emerged in the Saga Plain. As with initial wet-rice cultivation, the initial bronze technology appeared rather suddenly and in a close association with the Toraijin (Kataoka 1999: 176-201; Shichida 2007: 118-121; YS Lee 2007: 266-292).

According to JS Jo's classification (2005: 74-86, 221-226, 238), the bronzes produced in Kyushu (Fig. 2.5) belonged to the Period II of the Korean Slender Dagger repertoire which had appeared in the Peninsula

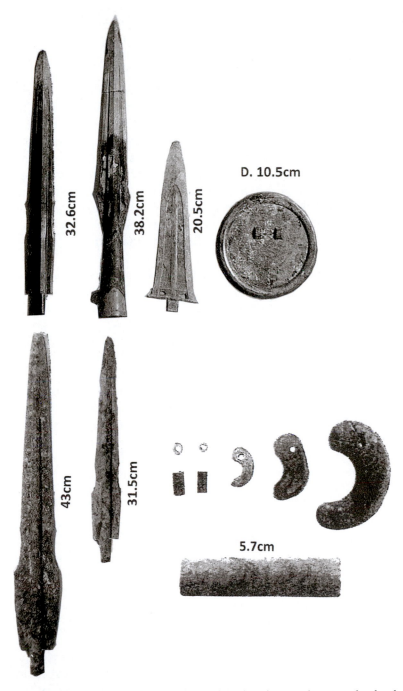

Fig. 2.5. Korean slender daggers and associated artifacts found in Kyushu. **Top:** slender dagger, spear point, halberd, and multi-knobbed bronze mirror from Middle Yayoi elite burials in Ukikunden jar coffins #6, #12, #17, # 41 (Saga-ken Kyoiku I'inkai 2008: 31, 38). Photo credit: Saga-gen Kyoiku I'inkai. **Bottom:** Korean slender bronze daggers and associated artifacts (small glass tubular beads, small glass beads, comma shaped magatama of glass and jadeite, and a long tubular bead of jadeite from Middle Yayoi elite burials at Yoshinogari (Saga-ken Kyoiku I'inkai 2008: 37, 45). Photo credit: Saga-ken Culture Exchange Office.

during c. 250–100 BC (e.g., Fig. 2.3). This indicates that the bronze industry emerged in northern Kyushu sometime during the Middle Yayoi, most likely c. 200 BC even though the bronze artifacts could have arrived in northern Kyushu as early as 300 BC through trade.

Major bronze industrial sites in Saga were located at Habu, Nabeshima, Ane, Hirabaru/Okubo, Soza, Yoshinogari, and other sites. Habu was a major Toraijin settlement site of about 10 ha in light of the Peninsula's Late Mumun pottery shards scattered over a wide area. A stone mold for bronze spearhead has been found, identical to those found in southern Korea. Mostly likely, it was brought from southern Korea. Nabeshima Honson Minami was another major Toraijin site with an abundance of the Peninsula Late Mumun pottery. In it were found a stone mold for a slender Korean bronze dagger from an earthen pit burial and a slender Korean bronze dagger from an elite burial. Ane, a site near Kuroi, another major Toraijin settlement has yielded bronze spearhead and a mold for bronze dagger. Hirabaru/Okubo, a site near numerous dolmens, contained a mold for bronze halberd. Soza, another Middle Yayoi site, yielded a double-sided mold for bronze spearhead and bronze dagger (Kataoka 1999: 156-164, 185-191).

Yoshinogari in the Saga Plains contained the largest number of stone molds: a mold for slender Korean bronze dagger, a four-sided mold for bronze dagger, and a four-sided mold for bronze dagger and bronze spearhead among others. Trench #154 contained remains of bronze casting workshops along with raw bronze materials, pieces of tin, and sections of bellows (Kataoka 1999: 157-158, 187-189; Shichida 2007a: 119). In light of the overwhelming number of the stone molds found at Yoshinogari, it is safe to assume that it was the center of Bronze industry.

As the unearthed stone molds indicate, the initial bronze implements produced at Yoshinogari and other bronze working sites in Saga were primarily weapons: daggers, halberds, and spearpoints. Highly valued by the Yayoi elites, they were placed in their elite tombs exactly as the Peninsula's Late Mumun society did for their elites (Shichida 2005: 35-42, 2017: 33-48). Furthermore, they were strikingly similar to those manufactured by the Late Mumun bronze technicians of southwestern Korea both in types and formal features (cf., Figs. 2.3 and 2.5). (Kataoka 1999: 149; YS Lee 2007: 277-283).

Shichida (2007a: 118-121) and KATAOKA Kōji (1999: 149-201) posit that the bronze factories in the Saga Plain appeared among the Toraijin settlements. Kataoka postulates that 80% of the population at Yoshinogari and in the Saga Plain, calculated by the number of the Songguk-ni type residences and sites bearing Songguk-ni type pottery shards, were the Toraijin-type Yayoi (the new wave of Toraijin and their children) who were in contact with the Peninsula. Accordingly, he posits that in acquiring the bronze technology it was this new wave of Toraijin that "acted as the main communication channel with the Peninsula" (1999: 112).

On the Peninsula, the production of bronzes during the Late Mumun was carried out primarily in the Geum River basin and in the southwest, that is, the home of the Early Mahan people. In the southeast region, no concrete archaeological evidence has come to light for bronze production activities by the Late Mumun period people (CG Lee 2002: 30-37). This suggests that the bronze industry in northern Kyushu was established by Toraijin technicians from the Peninsula's southwest and that the bronze-bearing Toraijin of the Middle Yayoi were the people of Early Mahan from the southwestern part of Korea, specifically from the modern North and South Jeolla Provinces between the Geum River and the southwest coast.

In the meantime, the Yayoi elites in the northern Kyushu coastal areas were importing bronze implements (daggers, halberds, and spearpoints) from southern Korea as indicated by their finds in Middle Yayoi elite burials in Yoshitake Takagi (#3), Nakabuse, Honmaru Bamai (#58), Harada, and Ukikunden (Tsunematsu 2011: 178). The earliest Yayoi pottery to appear in southern Korea (on the Neuk-do Island) was the Sugu I-II type pottery (dated to c. 220 BC–AD 1, Takakura 2011: 205). This suggests that Middle Yayoi elites' contact with southern Korea from Kyushu's north coastal area, began around 220 BC, which was about the time when the Toraijin technicians began their bronze production in the Saga Plain. In other words, while Middle Yayoi elites in the Saga Plain were producing their own bronzes, those on the north coastal area were sailing to Korea's southern coast to acquire Korean bronzes.

In the latter part of the 1st century BC, Peninsula's bronze production came to an end as the iron became increasingly dominant. As the flow of Korean bronzes stopped, the Middle Yayoi elites in the north coastal area began their own bronze production. By the latter part of the Middle Yayoi, c. 50 AD the Fukuoka region became a new bronze production center. Also, the bronze implements became increasingly naturalized with new innovations in the bronze tool repertoire according to local taste and needs. The slender Korean bronze daggers were now becoming wider in their body. There also appeared bronze bells (Kataoka 1999: 151).

By the middle of the Late Yayoi Period, about 300 years after its initial appearance in the Saga Plain, the bronze industry spread to all parts of northern Kyushu between the Saga Plain in the south, Yasumachi and Kasuya in Fukuoka in the north, and Karatsu in the west. Discovery of more than 200 stone molds, bellow parts, crucibles for casting bronze, bronze dregs, and bronze working facilities among others found on the foothills of the Kasuga Hills has led archaeologists to posit that the latter had become the new bronze industrial center in the Archipelago (Kataoka 1999: 150-152).

The Sugu-Okamoto site, in particular, became the most thriving bronze industry in Kyushu, as revealed by the finding of numerous remains of bronze working factories and stone molds for slender bronze daggers, spears, and halberds (OYBH 1999: 66-67; Kyoto Bunka Hakubutsukan 1989: 55-56). Also, at this time, local production began to take on its own distinctive character. Japanese-made bronze spearheads underwent a process of size exaggeration, even doubling in length and width, and were clearly intended for use in ritual rather than for practical purpose.

In the Kyoto-Osaka–Nara region, the emphasis was on bronze bells based on small Korean prototypes rather than on bronze weapons. As with the bronze halberds and daggers, they also underwent size exaggeration as an integral component of the elite religious rituals in the Kinki region.

B. New Mortuary Practices

a. Wood Coffin Burials (*mokkanbo*)

Beginning c. 300 BC, some of the elites of Korea's Late Mumun period began to construct wood coffin burials (K. *mokkwanmyo*; J. *mokkanbo*). By c. 200 BC, they became predominant in the southeast region as evidenced in the Yangdong-ni cemetery in Kimhae. The wood coffins were of two types: a box made of four wooden boards and a dug-out log coffin.

During the Middle Yayoi period, these elite burial types appeared in northern Kyushu. Of fifty-four burials at Yoshitake Takagi site, four were the wood coffin burials, three of which contained a slender bronze dagger. Wood coffin #3 contained two slender bronze daggers, a bronze spear, a bronze halberd, a multi-knobbed bronze dagger, a curved jade bead, and tubular beads (Fig. 2.6). Among the fifty jar burials, only four had a bronze dagger (Fukuoka-shi Kyoiku I'inkai 1996. At Yoshitake Oishi sit, 224 burials consist of 203 jar burials, twelve pit burials, and eight wood coffin burials. Among the 203 jar burials, three had a bronze dagger, while two of the eight wood coffin burials contained one. No pit burials had a bronze (Fukuoka-shi Kyoiku I'inkai 1996).

Thus, there appears to be differential prestige goods between the wood coffin burials and the other types. While the majority of the wood coffin burials contained bronze implements, only a small percentage of the jar burials contained them. Also, among the bronze-bearing burials, the wood coffin burials had more bronzes than the jar burials, as in Late Mumun Korea. Clearly, the wood coffin burials belonged to the top of the Middle Yayoi social tier, also as in the Late Mumun society.

b. Moat-Surrounded Tombs (*shukobo*)

The *jugumyo* system of Gwanchang-ni type (Map 2.2, bottom left) moved to western Japan first in the 3rd century BC with the Toraijin from west-central Korea and was in use until the Kofun Period. Known in Japan as *shukobo*, more than 4,000 of them have come to light between northern Kyushu and the Kinki Core region (Nara, Osaka, and Kyoto) (Watanabe 1999: 82-85; OYBH 1999: 85; cf. Takesue 2005: 69).

In the Kinki Core Region, the *shukobo* first appeared at Higashi-muko in Hyogo, at Higashi Nara, Ama, Kamei, Ikekami Sone, and Yottsu Ike in Osaka, and at the Oo Site in Nara. The *shukobo*, differentiated from each other by their size or the space they occupy within a cemetery, reflecting differentiated social statuses among the buried, were similar to those found at Gwanchang-ni in west-central Korea (M Watanabe 1999: 83-85).

At the Higashi-muko site in Hyogo, archaeologists have identified twenty-two *jugumyo* constructed during the interval c. 250–150 BC; among these, Tomb #2 contained Songguk-ni pottery ware made locally. Songguk-ni type dwellings belonging to the same period have also been identified in the Osaka region (M Watanabe 1999: 82). It is recognized among Japanese scholars that elite members of the Early Yayoi society living in the Kyoto–Osaka–Nara region used the Peninsula *jugumyo* as a new mortuary system for their ruling chiefs, and that the elite mortuary practice continued into the Kofun period and beyond (M Watanabe 1999: 85).

C. 'Three Sacred Treasures': Dagger, Mirror, and Comma-Shaped Jewel

In Japan's founding myths recorded in the *Kojiki* (Records of Ancient Matters), written in 712 AD, dagger, mirror, and comma-shaped jewel appear as "the three sacred jewels" with which Ninigi No Mikoto, the rice god and a grandson of Amaterasu Omikami, believed to be the sun deity and the ancestor of Japan's imperial family, descended to the earth to rule Japan (Phillipi 1968: 138-141).

The wood coffin grave #3 at Yoshitake Takagi contained two slender bronze daggers, one bronze spearhead, one bronze halberd, one multi-knobbed bronze mirror, one curved jade bead, and 95

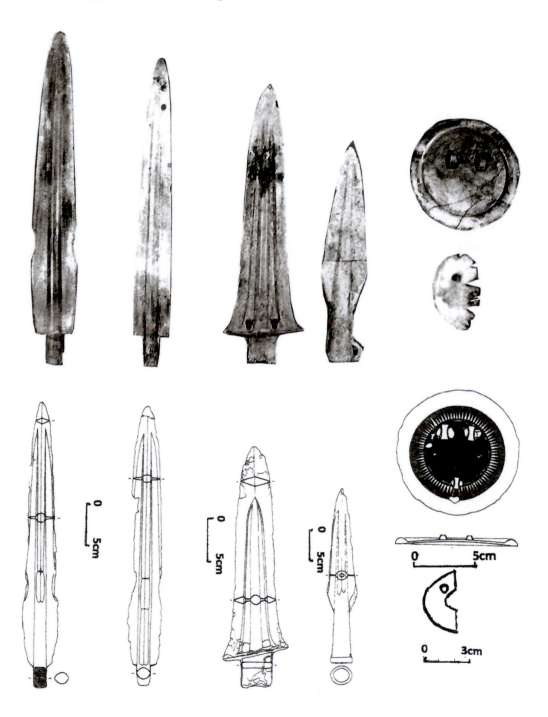

Fig. 2.6. Elite funerary goods in Korea and northern Kyushu. **Top:** From Wood-coffin Tomb #3 at Yoshitake Takagi (Fukuoka Kyoiku I'inkai 1986: 9. Fukuoka-shi Culture Office). **Bottom:** From a stone-framed wood-coffin tomb at Chopo-ri in Hampyeong, southern Korea (GGWB 1988a: 108, 109, 116, 117). Photo credit: Hanstudio.

tubular beads, all from Korea (F Oda, T Uno *et al.* 1986: 39) (Fig. 2.6). Buried as a set, as in the case of the Chopo-ri elite tomb in southwest Korea, these artifacts belonged to an elite leader. As in Late Mumun Korea, the bronze mirrors, bronze daggers, and curved jade became the symbols of power and authority in Middle Yayoi Japan. In time, they became the sacred symbols of Japan's imperial power in accordance with Japan's founding myth recorded in the *Kojiki* mentioned above.

The identity of the Yayoi elite buried in Wood Coffin #3 is intriguing. The tomb was a typical Late Bronze Age Korean elite tomb in the form of the wood-coffin burial (*mokkwanmyo*), popular in southern Korea at that time. The prestige goods placed in it (slender bronze daggers, a bronze spearhead, a bronze halberd, multi-knobbed bronze mirrors with geometric linear designs, and a comma-shaped jewel) were nearly identical to those found in an elite wood coffin tomb at Chopo-ri in Hampyeong in southern Korea (Fig. 2.6 bottom).

OYBH (Osaka Yayoi Bunka Hakubutsukan) suggests that the chief of Yoshitake was actually "the king of Sawara district" and that politically "he emerged in the context of the Korean immigrant culture, having succeeded in controlling the bronzes and the immigrants" (1999: 64).

3. Emerging Social Stratification in Northern Kyushu

The establishment of wet-rice agriculture brought about fundamental changes within Yayoi society – organizationally, economically, and politically (K Hirose 1997: 111-134; Komoto 1997: 104-110). By c. 300 BC, managers and leaders were appearing in Yayoi villages, a precursory event in the emergence of a stratified society. In this process, the bronze industry played a critical role, along with other cultural features brought by the new Toraijin.

On the basis of his studies on compound cemeteries in northern Kyushu, Mizoguchi (2012: 47-51) has concluded that the individuals buried in the early elite cemeteries of the Middle Yayoi were communal leaders emerging in response to intra- and inter-communal conflicts in an agriculturally expanding society. Rather than being 'kings', he considers them to have been more like 'big men' who sought to facilitate intra-communal ties and help resolve "rising tension in inter-communal relations associated with population pressure."

In light of his analysis of Yayoi jar burial patterns and household grouping, Mizoguchi (2005: 316) posits that social differentiation into chiefs (and their families) and commoners appeared at the end of the Middle Yayoi or in the early part of Late Yayoi. Accordingly, he views the Middle Yayoi "as an episode in the transition from tribal social organization to the system of chiefdom" (Mizoguchi 2000: 51).

Takesue (2002: 25-58) identifies the growth of social stratification in northern Kyushu during Middle Yayoi times through a comparative analysis of bronze-bearing elite burials. During the first half of the Middle Yayoi, in the Sawara Plains around Fukuoka, all bronze-bearing sites except one had only one or two bronze artifacts. The Yoshitake site, however, had twenty-four. Takesue accordingly posits a three-tier stratification for the area: a base tier of scattered villages with no elite residents owning bronze artifacts; a second tier of villages with several elite residents owning one or two bronze artifacts; and the top tier, comprised by Yoshitake, which had multiple elite burials and many bronze artifacts.

Emergence of chiefly classes inevitably involves regional conflicts. This was clearly the case in Middle Yayoi as indicated by archaeological evidences of violent warfare. Several Yayoi sites in Fukuoka in northern Kyushu have revealed human skeletons containing broken tips of a polished stone dagger and a bronze dagger, lodged in the head and the thoracic vertebra respectively (Hashiguchi 1986: 104). Numerous Middle Yayoi jar burials at Yoshinogari in Saga, for example, contained skeletons with stone arrowheads stuck in them, violently inflicted wound marks, or with severed heads. They are all believed to have been victims of war (Shichida 2017: 42-43). Also, as revealed by their prestige possessions, elites of Middle Yayoi period in northern Kyushu prized various lethal weapons including polished stone daggers, stone halberds, stone arrowheads, bronze daggers, bronze spearheads, bronze halberds, and iron arrowheads (Hashiguchi 1986: 104-111; Oda *et al.*: 1986: 35-57; OYBH 1999: 48-52, 64-68).

4. Beginnings of Pen/Insular Trade

The Middle Yayoi elites' demand for advanced weapons, prestige goods, and agricultural tools inevitably acted as a catalyser for the first and earliest Pen/Insular trade. Early Yayoi pottery is rarely found at Korea's Mumun sites (CH Lee 2011: 34-37; Takesue 2008: 259; C Inoue 2008: 238-239), suggesting that during the Early Yayoi period, when the wet-rice farming was being established in Japan, there was no Pen/Insular trade (Yanagida 1989b: 10-13). This changed during the Middle Yayoi.

The initial Yayoi traders' arrival in southeast Korea coincided with the appearance of Sugu I type potteries (c. 220-210 cal. BC). (Takakura 2011: 205; C Inoue 2008: 238-249; Takesue 2008: 258-302; CH Lee 2011: 33; Takakura 2011: 178). They came on behalf of their elites to acquire valued prestige goods to be used as the elites' status symbols. They included bronze daggers, bronze spearheads, bronze halberds, iron arrowheads, and multi-knobbed bronze mirrors with fine line geometric designs as well as comma-shaped jade jewels and tubular glass beads. They were integral components of Korea's Late Mumun elite culture. The initial Yayoi traders most likely comprised some of the Late Mumun immigrants and/or their descendants, that is, the Toraijin-type Yayoi people who are believed to have maintained a communication network with their parent communities along the southern coast of Korea (Kataoka 1999: 112; Hashino 2014: 107-110).

The advanced goods brought to northern Kyushu have been found in numerous Middle Yayoi elites' graves at Arita, Imori Tatagi, Iikura Karaki, Higashi Irube, Ukikunden, and Yoshitake sites (Oda *et al.* 1986: 39). What the Yayoi traders brought to Korea to exchange for the bronzes and iron is unknown. The findings of large Yayoi container jars at Korean sites suggest that they were perishable goods including rice and valued silk material (C Inoue 2008: 241; CH Lee 2011: 39).

The Gusandong site located near the ancient Kimhae harbor produced an unusually large number of Sugu I Type Yayoi pottery, to the exclusion of locally popular *weonhyeong jeomtodae togi* (jars with a circular clay ring attached to their rim), suggesting that it was a Yayoi hamlet where traders lived (Takesue 2010: 145-173; CH Lee 2011: 32).

The Archipelago's counterpart of Kimhae and Neuk-do was Haru-no-tsuji on the island of Iki, located between Tsushima Island and the north coast of Kyushu. According to Kataoka (2006: 51-63; also, GJIB 2016), starting in the latter part of the Early Yayoi Period, Korean Late Mumun period pottery began to appear on the southeast side of the Iki Island, at Haru-no-tsuji. It included a variety of the wide mouth pots with a rolled rim, mounted dishes, and the pottery with attached ox horn-shaped handles. They were made by the Peninsula's Late Mumun potters with the Peninsula pottery technology.

Some of the ceramics were identical to those found in the Peninsula while others exhibited Yayoi influence. These Late Mumun potteries indicate that Korean immigrants arrived at Haru-no-tsuji in the latter part of the Early Yayoi and continued to reside there, turning it into a Pen/Insular trade center on the Archipelago side throughout the Middle Yayoi.

CHAPTER THREE

IRON AND GLASS-BEARING TORAIJIN OF THE LATE YAYOI/ EARLY KOFUN PERIOD TORAIJIN (c. 50–350 AD)

I. HISTORICAL AND SOCIO-CULTURAL BACKGROUND OF THE LATE YAYOI/EARLY KOFUN PERIOD TORAIJIN: SAM HAN (C. 50 BC–AD 300)

1. Sam Han Society according to the *Sanguozhi*

In Chapter 30 of *Sanguozhi* (Chronicles of the Three Kingdoms, 220-265 AD) compiled in the latter part of the 3rd century AD, CHEN Shou (233–297) reported that during the 3rd century, the southern half of the Korean Peninsula was the land of Sam Han (三韓, Three Han): [Later] Mahan, Jinhan, and Byeonhan (Map 2.1), each of which comprised a number of semi-autonomous *guk*. The Chinese character 國 (*guk* in Korean; *guo* in Chinese; *koku* or *kuni* in Japanese) is an ambiguous term. In Western literatures it has been translated as 'state,' 'country,' 'nation,' or 'principality,' depending on the context (Barnes 1989).

From the *Sanguozhi* as well as from archaeological information, it appears that a *guk* of the Sam Han period was a polity consisting of several farming villages and towns within a geographical region bounded by rivers and/or mountains, which came together voluntarily for social, for commercial, for economic, and for military exigencies. Mahan comprised fifty-four such semi-autonomous polities while Jinhan and Byeonhan each twelve.

According to the *Sanguozhi* and the *Hou Hanshu* (Account of the Late Han Dynasty, 6–189 AD), in Mahan a large *guk* consisted of 10,000 households and a small one of several thousand. In Jinhan and Byeonhan, a large *guk* consisted of 4,000–5,000 households and a small one of 600–700 households. These figures are comparable to complex chiefdoms cross-culturally studied in other world regions (Sanders and Price 1968; Baker and Sanders 1972). (For the full texts on Sam Han in the *Sanguozhi* and the *Hou Hanshu*, see Mark Byington's annotated translations in *Early Korea: The Samhan Period in Korean History*, Korea Institute, Harvard University, 2009: 125-152; Byington and Barnes 2014.)

According to the criteria put forth by Service (1975), Steponaitis (1978), Carneiro (1970, 1981), Earle (1987), and others, the 78 *guk* scattered throughout southern Korea during the Sam Han period had not yet reached the status of state-level societies. None of them was a centralized polity, and their chiefs were *primus inter pares* at best.

2. Sam Han in Archaeology

A. Later Mahan Polities (c. 300-550 AD)

The Later Mahan polities, endowed with vast fertile plains along the west coast of the Peninsula, had been developing as a prosperous and dynamic agricultural society. Reportedly, (GJEB 2009: 120-125):

Already beginning in the 1st century BC, Mahan farmers cultivated their fields with iron hoes and spades for plowing and with iron sickles for harvesting, along with numerous wooden tools. In the 3rd century AD, the iron tools were diversified according to their function, replacing the wooden ones. This revolutionized agricultural production. Among the cultivated fields, wet rice paddies have been found at Jangsan-ni in Cheon'an along with water canals and reservoirs. A large number of carbonized grains of many kinds have been recovered from Mahan residential sites, indicating that agriculture was thriving in Mahan.

Iron implements of Later Mahan included, besides the farming tools, iron swords, iron daggers, iron spearheads, and iron arrowheads (SR Choi 2018b: 130). In light of the abundance of iron artifacts found in the graves of the Later Mahan elites it is assumed that the Mahan society produced iron. More than a dozen ancient iron production sites have been reported from the western part of the Peninsula, between the Han River basin and the southwest coast (DW Jang 2017: 3; EJ Song *et al.* 2014: 196-218; GJEB 2009: 110; GNB 2013: 78; YH Lee 1997: 101-105). The majority of them are dated to the 4th–5th century except Gian-ri in Hwaseong and Yeonje-ri in Cheongweon, both of which were located in the west-central part. At the former, archaeologists have found remains of bellows, iron ore, slags, and charcoal ovens, as well as numerous locally manufactured cast iron implements, dating to the 3rd–4th century. Likewise, at the latter, remains of bellows and iron slags have been unearthed (DW Jang 2017: 3; EJ Song *et al.* 2014: 196-218). The west central region came under the control of Paekche by 369, so until then Mahan technicians would have operated the iron production sites.

Later Mahan people still lived in semi-subterranean houses with a square (4~6 x 4~6 m) or circular floor plan and a thatched roof supported by four posts. The former was concentrated along the west coast while the latter in the eastern montane region. The houses were equipped with a cooking stove and in some cases with an *ondol* (underfloor) heating system. In some cases, such as Jungryang-ri in Hampyeong and Taemok-ni in Damyang, a Mahan village comprised about 200 houses (SR Choi 2017b: 128; GJEB 2009: 55).

In pottery, Later Mahan people made significant advancements in production technique and vessel types with new ceramic technology introduced from China. Foot-operated turntables and closed kilns enabled the Mahan potters to produce higher quality vessels at faster speed. The Later Mahan potters made both low-fired (*yeonjil*) and hard-fired (*gyeongjil*) earthenware vessels marked by cord and lattice *tanalmun* paddle impressions (Walsh 2017: 16, 87) (Fig. 3.1).

Depending on the clay, kiln types, and the firing methods used, Later Mahan ceramic vessels appear red, reddish-orange, grey, or greyish-blue. Encompassing a large territory, the Later Mahan pottery exhibited some regional variations in vessel-shape types and surface decorations (*Ibid.*). In the west-central part, globular storage jars and bowls of varying sizes were dominant. Mahan pottery vessels of the southwest included globular-shaped storage jars, steamers with ox-horn shaped handles, basins, bowls with double-up rims or a pair of ear-shaped handles, torpedo-shaped cooking pots, mounted dishes, and flower-pot shaped vessels. Storage jars were often decorated with lattice or mat-striated impressions.

As for the torpedo-shaped pottery used primarily for cooking in the Later Mahan region, KIM Jang-suk (2012: 38-45) finds its proto-type in the long-bodied "Yan-style cooking vessel" popular in the

(H. 28.0 cm)

(H. 25.8cm)

(H. 20.4.cm)

(H. 32.1cm)

(H. 28.6cm)

(H. 13.8 cm)

Fig. 3.1. Vessel types of the soft-fired (*yeonjil*) and hard-fired (*gyeongjil*) earthenware of Later Mahan. All vessels (steamers, water jugs, storage jars) except one (right, middle: globular storage jar in light grey) are *yeonjil* vessels in red or light brown. **Bottom:** *Tanalmun* (stamped cord and lattice designs) found on both yeonjil and gyeongjil vessels (GJEB 2009: 45, 57, 58, 59, 79, 80; GJUB 1993, 69). Photo credit: Jeonju National Museum and Hanstudio.

Liaodong region in Northeast China in the 1st century BC and postulates that the latter diffused to Korea's southwestern coastal region through maritime trade around 1 AD or shortly before. From the southwestern coast, according to Kim, it diffused northward to other parts of Mahan, first to the Geum River basin and then to the Han River region by 100.

Later Mahan people operated sericulture. Among numerous artifacts uncovered from a bog site at Shinchang-dong in Gwangju dated to the 1st century BC, a small piece of silk cloth

(2 x 3 cm) came to light along with a 5 x 6 cm piece of hemp cloth. Upon analysis the silk was found to have been made of strong yarn that had undergone multiple twisting and refining processes (YC Choi 2012). In light of the weaving tools found at the site, including spindle whorls, thread winders, and yarn guides, the investigator believes that the Later Mahan settlement of Shinchang-dong operated silk-weaving as well as silkworm raising factories. As a product of the 1st century BC, this silk piece is thought to be a century older than the oldest Chinese silk remains yet found in the Peninsula.

Later Mahan technicians made glass and glass beads. Molds for glass beads have been found at several Mahan sites including Songhak-dong in Iksan, Seonam-dong in Gwangju, and Taemok-ri in Damyang, while both a mold and glass slag were found at Pungnap Toseong in Seoul (Fig. 3.2) (GNB 2013: 67-69; GJEB 2009: 118-119). They produced clear and colored beads of many kinds and curved jewels. They have been found in both elite graves and dwelling sites. These findings reflect the *Weizhi* account that the people of Sam Han valued glass beads more than gold and silver.

In mortuary culture, Mahan people kept some of their Songguk-ni cultural traditions even as they adopted new cultural and technological elements. For mortuary practice, in particular, the Later Mahan people continued to employ cist tombs, stone-capped pit tombs, and jar coffin burials of the Songguk-ni tradition.

In the first century BC, the *jugumyo* (moat-surrounded tombs) which had first appeared in the 4th-3rd century BC gained popularity, becoming the dominant Later Mahan mortuary system. It now comprised two types: the Cheongdam-dong Type, whose moat resembles a crescent, and the Gwanchang-ni Type whose moat is square with an opening on one side.

In the course of time, many of the raised mounds surrounded by a moat disappeared under the impact of natural elements (rain and wind) and human activities (levelling the fields for cultivation). Funerary objects, including ritual pots, were also placed in the moat (WG Choi 2000, WG Choi 2001; JY Seong 2009: 235-238). Burial goods uncovered from early *jugumyo* at Cheongdang-dong in Cheon'an, Songjeol-dong in Cheongju, Songdae-ri in Ochang, and other sites included short-necked pots with a round base, iron weapons including long swords with a round pommel, spearheads, and arrowheads, axes, hoes, sickles, horse bits, bronze buckles, and glass and agate beads (JY Seong 2009: 241-245).

The *jugumyo* elites not only engaged in a thriving agriculture but also controlled maritime trade networks along the Yellow Sea (TG Lee 2008: 52). As skilful masters of seafaring, they accumulated great wealth as revealed in their construction of more than 30 impressive tumuli called *malmudeom* ('large tumuli' in the form of *jugumyo* and *bungumyo*) concentrated in the vicinity of Gunsan, a modern harbor city situated at the mouth of the Geum River (Map 2.1; Gwak 2017a: 32-53).

In 246, Mokji-guk, the head of the Mahan Confederation in west-central Korea, attacked the Daifang Commandery, killing its governor (JG Noh 2009: 220). This was a serious mistake because Mahan was no match against the militarily well-equipped Chinese. In the aftermath of its defeat, Paekche, a Mahan polity anchored in today's Seoul area, just south of the Han River, emerged as the new leader in west-central Korea and immediately moved to organize Later Mahan polities in the Han River basin into a new state.

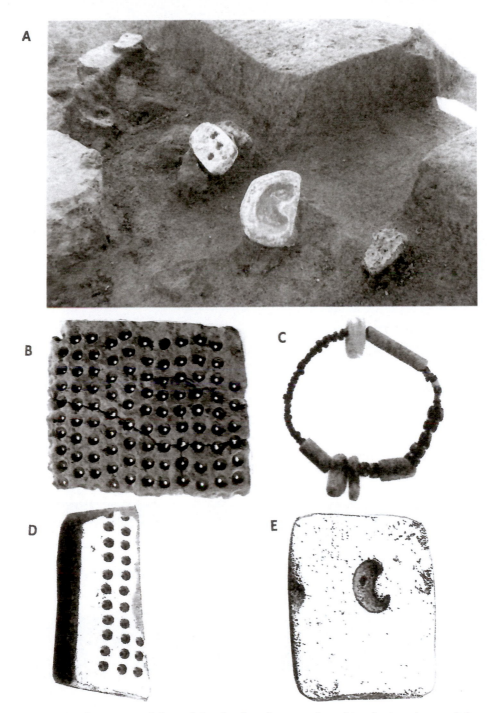

Fig. 3.2. Manufacturing workshop of glass beads and comma-shaped jewels. **A:** Mahan workshop remains at Seon'am-dong in Gwangju, manufacturing glass beads and comma-shaped jewels (GNB 2013: 65). Photo credit: by Honam Cultural Research Center. **B-C:** A mold for glass beads found at a Mahan workshop, Songhak-dong (Iksan) (GJEB 2009: 119). Photo credit: Jeonju National Museum. **D-E:** Molds for glass beads and comma-shaped jewels from a Late Yayoi site in Nishijinmachi, northern Kyushu (after OYBH 2004:13).

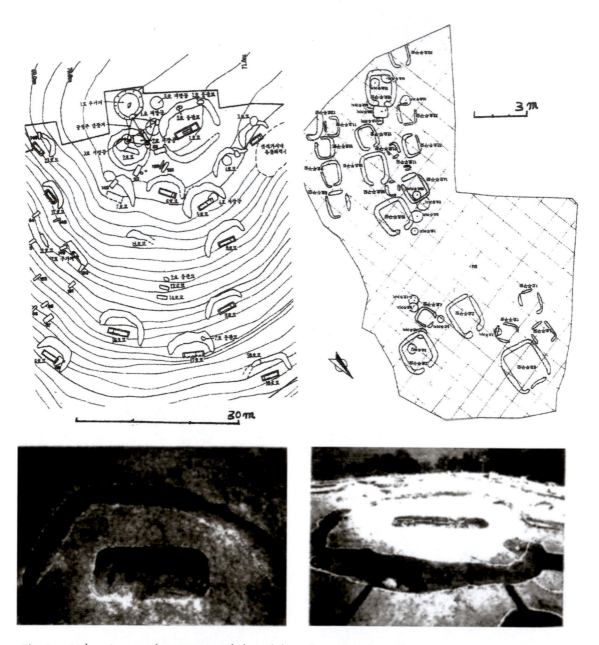

Fig. 3.3. Mahan *jugumyo* (moat-surrounded tombs) in the Peninsula. **Left:** Cheongdam-dong type. **Right:** Gwanchang-ni type. (After JY Seong 2009: 236-237; National Museum of Korea 2003: 68; GGOB 2002: 48).

There is much mystery surrounding Paekche origins. According to the narratives in the *Samguk Sagi*, Paekche was established by a group of elite refugees, who had migrated into the lower reaches of the Han River in west-central Korea in the 1st century BC from Buyeo state in the Sungari River basin in north-eastern China (SB Park 2000: 133-148; Best 1982: 344-445, 2006: 27-31). Historicity of this account is being debated among scholars (Byington 2016b: 264-267). In light of her study on ceramic specialization and exchange in Paekche and Later Mahan, Walsh (2017: 11-13, 162) emphasizes the "Mahanness" of Paekche, positing that Paekche's origin was in the context of Later Mahan which had had more than 600 years of dynamic cultural history (See Chapter Two: I).

What complicates this issue is the perception of the Paekche elites themselves inasmuch as in the 6th century AD, they identified themselves with the ancient Buyeo state, naming their new capital "Nam Buyeo (South Buyeo)" in 538, and using Buyeo as their surname.

What is archaeologically certain is that Paekche's beginnings were in the lower reaches of the Han River, at the northern end of Mahan territory. For strategic purposes, they established their colony on the south bank of the Han River, in the modern-day Seoul districts of Pungnap-dong, Bang'idong, and Seokchon-dong (SB Park 2000: 133-148).

In Paekche's early socio-political growth, its connections with China appear to have played a minimal role. Walsh, in light of her study of Paekche society's hierarchical and heterarchical complexity, based on the INAA (Instrumental Neutron Activation Analysis) analysis of Paekche's ceramic materials, their production, usages, and exchange, concludes that "the kingdom clearly deployed autochthonous political, economic, and social strategies to integrate and administer its territory, rather than relying on imported Chinese bureaucratic models" (Walsh 2017: 161).

In 278, Paekche sent an official diplomatic envoy to the Chinese State of Jin to establish its legitimacy (JG Noh 2003: 65-90; JG Noh 2009: 221-222). In the face of this newly emerging state of Paekche, fiercely assertive and aggressive, Mahan as a living political entity, ended and disappeared (SB Park 2009: 228; SR Choi 2017a: 289-291). However, the regional polities beyond the west-central part of the Peninsula continued to thrive and prosper as Later Mahan polities, primarily in the Yeongsan River basin of southwest Korea, until they were brought under the Paekche control around 550 one by one and group by group (SR Choi 2017a: 279-299; Walsh 2017: 20).

B. Jinhan Polities

In Jinhan, located southeast of Korea's massive Sobaek Mountain Range and geographically isolated from much of the Peninsula, the older indigenous dolmen societies continued on. Significant socio-political changes, however, commenced in the 1st century BC with the arrival of Choson (name for ancient Korea according to Chinese historical texts *such Hou Hanshu*) refugees from the north, with their advanced bronze and iron technology, in the aftermath of the Chinese invasion in 108 BC of the Choson Kingdom of Wiman in the Pyongyang (JW Lee 1982: 16).

Newly emerging local elites especially around modern Taegu and Kyongju fully took advantage of the advanced bronze-iron technology, and with their production of bronzes and iron tools as their power base, they established their leadership over the indigenous dolmen society. Those indigenous communities that aligned themselves to one of the new leaders became the constituents of a Jinhan *guk* (HH Lee 1984: 70-83; HH Yi 2009: 31-43).

Beginning in the latter part of the 1st century BC, iron emerged as the most important economic and political tool in the southeast region, the home of Jinhan and Byeonhan, which had abundant natural iron deposits. Iron's immense value as cutting-edge weapons and tools of daily life, and in agricultural and industrial workplaces, made the iron industry a major mover in economic and political development as well as in population increase. Those elites who succeeded in controlling the iron market would emerge as the dominant powers, and they displayed their power not only with the number of iron weapons they owned but with the number of *cheoljeong* (flat iron ingots) buried in their graves upon their deaths (HH Lee 1984: 146; HH Yi 2009: 31-43).

Bronze and iron artifacts related to horse-driven vehicles (parasol shafts, bells, horse bits etc.), found in the Taegu and Kyongju regions, were strikingly similar to those found in the elite burials of Budeok-ni, Galhyeon-ni, and Taeseong-ri around modern Pyongyang in the northwest, suggest that Jinhan elites actively traded with the Han Commanderies in the northwest (HH Yi 2009: 30; JYYDPW 1989: 194-209).

Archaeologically, the majority of significant elite burials in Jinhan appeared after c. 100 BC at Jisan-dong in Taegu and Joyang-dong in Kyongju (CG Lee 2002: 25-27). A major common characteristic among them is that they contained bronzes, iron, and Han Chinese mirrors. For example, the elite graves of wood coffin type such as the #5 and #38 tombs at Joyang-dong, dated to c. 50 BC, contained a bronze mirror, a bronze horse bell, an iron dagger, an iron halberd, and three bronze mirrors.

In light of the bronze and iron-bearing sites, some of the first Jinhan polities have been identified at Jisan-dong, Paldal-dong, and Pyeong-ri-dong in the Taegu area and at Joyang-dong, Angye-ri, and Sara-ri in the Kyongju region (CG Lee 2002: 28-29).

By the end of the 3rd century AD, the Saro-guk in Kyongju, with its thriving iron industries, emerged as the most powerful political and centralizing force in Jinhan. According to the *Samguk Sagi*, Saro-guk was frequently engaged in wars with other Jinhan polities in the process of territorial expansion and centralization (BH Choi 2015: 102-159). Military gear from two elite wood-framed burials in Gujeong-dong in Kyongju (Tombs #2 and #3), dated to c. 290–310 AD, contained 25 iron spear points, a long iron sword with a ring pommel, an iron axe, and a set of iron body armor.

A recent study on the mortuary system of the Kyongju area, especially its wooden chamber burials, has revealed the process of political centralization that was going on around the Saro polity before the full-fledged state of Silla emerged in Kyongju (BH Choi 2015: 102-159).

It thus appears that Saro-guk was on its way to emerging as the early state of Silla, and by the middle of the 4th century, the leaders of Saro Federation, now kings of Silla, began to construct monumental tombs for their elites, placing in them hitherto unknown gold crowns, gold waistbands, gold earrings, decorated swords, jade beads, and Roman glasses imported over great distances. LEE In-sook posits that during the 1st–3rd century, in northern Korea, some of these valuables were imported from China via Lelang, while in southern Korea, glass beads and Roman glasses, in particular, were acquired "via sea from Southeast Asia and southeastern China. Beginning in the 4th century, the valuable objects were imported "over the Silk Road, especially the steppe route via the Caucasus, southern Siberia and Northeast China" (Lee 1993: 12).

In the pottery culture, Jinhan and Byeonhan shared technology as well as vessel-shape types. As in Mahan, they made remarkable advances in its pottery-making technology with newly introduced advanced technology from China, including turntables, improved firing at a higher temperature up to 900–1,000 °C, and closed sloping kilns (Barnes 1992: 204). As in Mahan, the Late Mumun pottery evolved into soft-fired (*yeonjil*) and hard-fired (*gyeongjil*) earthenware. As a part of this evolution, there also appeared a new form of pottery called Wajil pottery, another form of hard-fired earthenware but comprising new vessels types. In its basic character, the Wajil pottery is a grey or greyish white earthenware made of finer paste than Plain [Mumun] Pottery. Two techniques characterize its surface finishing: paddling and/or clay slipping... The even coloration of the ware implies fine control over a reducing atmosphere during firing, and this implies the existence of a fairly sophisticated kiln. Wajil is assessed to have been fired at approximately 900 °C.

Wajil pottery underwent twofold processes (early and late) in the development of vessel-shape types before it evolved further into rock-hard stoneware called *dojil togi*. During the early stage, it comprised jars and pots with attached ox-horn shaped handles, pots with a round base, and bag-shaped pots. In the later stage, the vessels were fired at a higher temperature and there appeared new vessels including long-necked pots on a pedestal, brazier-shaped basins, and duck-shaped vessels (GJUB 1993: 69-97).

C. Byeonhan Polities

The territory of Byeonhan comprised the region in the lower reaches of the Nakdong River and the coastal zone along the South Sea. Geographically isolated from much of the Korean Peninsula by the massive Sobaek Mountain Range to the north and west and by the Nakdong River to the east, the Byeonhan region was little affected by the technological and socio-political revolutions taking place in other parts of the Peninsula. Around 100 BC, Korea was still in the waning phase of the Mumun culture. Bronzes were rare, and dolmens were still being constructed in the region for elite burials. At this stage, no elite person was wealthy or powerful enough to emerge as the leader of an independent polity (HH Lee 1984: 83-95).

Various prehistoric communities situated along or near the south coast had long been maritime-oriented in their economic activities. Coastal residents had also engaged in long-distance trade and exchange since Neolithic times, with distant islands as well as with Wa (IS Ha 2006; Y Hirose 2005). Furthermore, thriving trade and exchange was under way between coastal towns of Korea and northern Kyushu, as revealed among archaeological remains of Neuk-do Island dated to the 2nd–1st century BC (See Chapter Three: II, 4: Emergence of Thriving Peninsular Trade: Neuk-do/Kimhae-Kyushu/Kinki Connections) (M.L Choi 2009: 201-202; GMUY 2008: 229-230).

In these circumstances, some of the indigenous elites among the traditional dolmen societies began to expand their maritime trading ventures northward to Lelang. Yayoi people on the island of Kyushu were also eager to acquire Chinese goods from Lelang. In the face of newly emerging potentials for regional and international commerce, the elites residing on or near the coast, at Kimhae and Dahori, appear to have taken the lead, especially in the iron trade.

In the Byeonhan elite cemetery of Yangdong-ri, located at the mouth of the Nakdong River, Tomb #70, a wood coffin dated to the 1st century BC, was poor in burial contents. Tomb # 55, however, built in the 1st century AD, contained a rich array of prestige goods: an iron dagger, an iron halberd, an iron axe, an iron sickle, iron arrowheads, a jar, a circular bronze artifact, a necklace of small glass beads, and an imitation Chinese bronze mirror (HT Im and DC Gwak 2000; GMUY 2008: 828).

At Daho-ri, located about 20 km northwest of Kimhae and naturally connected to the sea and various communities in the region by way of the Nakdong River, Grave #1, dated to c. 50 BC, yielded an unprecedented array of rich goods revealing the importance of maritime trade and iron in the emergence of independent polities in the Byeonhan region (KM Lee 2008: 8-15; EJ Song 2008: 18-24).

Even after having been robbed, it contained three times as many artifacts (ten bronzes, forty iron implements, twenty-three lacquer ware items, and three *Wushu-ch'ien* Chinese coins) as did unrobbed Grave #6 (one bronze, sixteen iron implements, four lacquerware items, and no Chinese coins). The latter grave was also smaller (260 x 125 cm) than the former (278 x 136 cm) (YM Shin 2008: 135). Its bronze objects included weapons (daggers and spearheads) and ornaments (bells and rings). The iron specimens included weapons (daggers, spearheads, halberds, and knives) and woodworking and agricultural tools (axes and hoes). Among the iron-related remains were iron ore, iron manufacturing tools, and evidence of technologies used in cast iron as well as forged-iron manufacturing (GJUB 2008: 25). The lacquerware included weapons (bows, arrows, and a wooden mace) and vessels (bowls on stands and cups).

The grave also contained goods imported from foreign countries: multi-colored glass beads, a fiber rope, a *Wushu-ch'ien* coin of Han China, a Han bronze mirror, writing brushes for calligraphy, fans from China via Lelang, and a ritual bronze spearhead from Kyushu, Japan. These burial goods show that the person buried in Grave #1 at Daho-ri was the wealthiest and most powerful among all the elite personages discovered in the cemetery. At a time when iron was becoming the supremely valuable commodity item, he recognized its value and made it the supreme economic base and symbol of his personal power (40 iron implements vs. 10 bronzes).

Numerous farming-related tools such as iron weed cutters, iron sickles, and hoe-like tools found among his burial goods suggest that he was also an active promoter of the agriculture critical to his domain's economy along with the iron industry. (We assume the leader to be a male in light of the fact that the *Sanguozhi* does not mention any female chiefs in Samhan, while it recorded about Himiko, the female leader of Yamatai-koku in the Archipelago.) The many iron daggers, spears, halberds, arrowheads, and axes found among the grave goods show that he was also security-conscious and made a well-equipped military force a high priority for himself and his domain.

This personage was familiar with Chinese script and could write (or order others to do so) the documents essential to effective managerial and commercial enterprise. He was engaged in international trade and commerce and helped establish the southeast Peninsular coast as an important trading link from central China via Lelang to the land of Wa. In his outings he rode on horseback, wearing around his waist a slender bronze dagger in an elegantly lacquered scabbard, and while sitting in his office he was cooled by lacquered fans made most likely of imported ostrich feathers. At home he ate his meals in elegantly decorated lacquer ware. The investigators of Daho-ri and similar elite cemeteries in the southeastern region of Korea posit that the person in the Grave #1 was the chief a Byeonhan *guk* (KM Lee 2008: 11-12). Essentially, he was one of twelve chiefs of Byeonhan.

Being aware of the immense value of iron, Byeonhan polities also strengthened their position by importing iron technology from Saro-guk in Kyongju and/or Lelang, with which they had trade and commercial relationships. According to the *Weizhi,* by the middle of the 3rd century AD, Byeonhan had emerged as 'the iron capital of East Asia' as Chinese, Japanese, and others in Asia frequented it to acquire its iron. Byeonhan/Kaya earned this reputation not necessarily because their nexus produced the most iron in Samhan, but because the harbor in Kuya-guk/Kaya-guk in Kimhae served as the trading port for iron bought in from various local iron industries (HJ Lee 1998: 154-156).

Of about twelve Byeonhan polities, Kuya-guk in modern day Kimhae emerged as the paramount political entity, blessed by its location at the mouth of the Nakdong River and the excellent harbor that connected it to various inland regions and coastal towns as well as to more-distant Lelang and Japan. Archaeological remains from Yangdong-ri and Daeseong-dong in nearby Kimhae make it clear that by the end of the 3rd century AD, Kuya-guk had become the wealthiest polity in Byeonhan as the key intermediary in the East Asian trade and commerce between China, Korea, and Japan. Among the remains unearthed are such prestige goods as Han mirrors, bronze cauldrons, horse gear, and other items imported from Lelang, as well as bronze and stone ritual objects brought from Japan (Gyeongseong University Museum 2000a, Gyeongseong University Museum 2000b; KC Shin and JW Kim 2000).

As the paramount polity on Korea's southeast coast, Kuya-guk was able to bring neighboring polities into an alliance relationship so as to enhance their inter-regional trade and cooperation in times of emergency, but it never succeeded in outright political consolidation and centralization as Saro-guk did in Kyongju. Consequently, after 300 AD the various Byeonhan *guk*, numbering about twelve, continued to function as independent Kaya polities until the middle of the 6th century, never melding to become a centralized state.

3. LELANG and DAIFANG: Their Influence on SAM HAN (Map 2.1)

By the latter part of the 2nd century BC, Wiman Choson, centered in northwest Korea, had become wealthy through its over-lordship of nearby principalities. According to the *Shiji* (Historical Records) compiled by Sima Qian (145–85? BC), Wiman Choson's rising influence over the local chiefs, especially in regional trade and politics, and its defiant attitude toward Han China's court, prompted Emperor Wu Di to conquer it. In 109–108 BC, Wu Di sent 50,000 infantries and 7,000 naval forces against the Wiman Choson capital at Pyongyang, which fell after more than a year of fighting. Wu Di then established four Chinese commanderies – Lelang, Zhenfan, Xuantu, and Lintun – in the old territory of Wiman Choson, which comprised most of northwestern Korea and the region around Weonsan Harbor on Korea's east coast (Pearson 1976-78: 78; YC Oh and Byington 2013: 11-47; OJ Kwon 2013: 81-99; Barnes 2015: 313-314).

Wu Di's military incursion into the Korean Peninsula was met by fierce local resistance from the Choson people in the northwest, from Koguryo tribes in the northeast, and from native polities in the south. In the face of the local resistance, the Lelang commandery sought to maintain peace with local leaders by awarding them titles and ranks of nobility and cutting them in on profitable commercial transactions. However, as the Han Dynasty began to decline and became ineffective in the management of its faraway commanderies in the latter part of the 2nd century, the indigenous polities in the Peninsula such as Mahan began to assert themselves.

In the Liaodong Peninsula, the Gongsun warlord family became dominant, taking charge of the Lelang commandery (YC Oh 2006: 184-185). And in 204, it established Daifang, another military commandery, in the region between Lelang and the Han River to defend their outposts against local resistance, especially from the people of Mahan spread over the entire western farmland between the Han River and the south coast (YC Oh 2006: 184-185).

Four decades later, in 246 AD, the Mahan Confederation, a political alliance of various Mahan polities under the leadership of Mokji-guk, attacked Daifang and killed its governor (JG Noh 2009: 220). The ensuing Chinese war with Mahan and Koguryo, a newly emerging state in the middle reaches of the Yalu River, continued for 68 more years, until Koguryo finally succeeded in defeating the Chinese and establishing their own rule in Lelang and Daifang in 313–314 AD (KB Lee 2006: 33-43).

For 420 years Lelang had functioned as a multicultural polity comprised of Chinese residents and native Koreans, and Daifang did the same for 110 years after 204 AD. Their governors (*taesu*) were Chinese officials appointed by the Chinese emperor, but they chose their own local administrative officials from among local elites (Takaku 1995: 277).

China's commanderies not only secured Chinese frontiers with neighboring non-Chinese ethnic groups and polities but also functioned as Chinese embassies to various small polities in the Korean Peninsula, Japanese Archipelago, and elsewhere, receiving tributes and granting honorary ranks and gifts to local leaders. The commanderies were important trading entrepots for Chinese bronze mirrors, lacquerware, long iron swords, and bronze vessels, in addition to being points of dissemination of advanced Chinese technical, political, and intellectual culture to various centers throughout southern Korea and to some extent to northern Kyushu (Pearson 1979: 82-85; KB Lee 2006: 32-43).

Particularly significant in this regard was the commanderies' role in the advancement of iron technology among the Sam Han polities. In the 1st century BC, there appeared advanced forging workshops utilizing a high temperature. Found on the Neuk-do Island near Sacheon off the southeastern coast, inside as well as outside residential buildings, they comprised a distinct furnace and blastpipes of varying diameters (SM Kim 2019: 62-64).

At the same in the 1st century BC, the iron technicians of southeastern Korea began to mine iron ore at Dalcheon in Ulsan for the purpose of securing raw iron locally and becoming independent of iron imports from the northern regions (Liaodong in northeast China and the Chinese commanderies in the northwest of the Peninsula (SM Kim 2019: 65-67).

Whenever the Han rulers were having problems in the mainland during the 2nd century, there was a social unrest at Lelang, and many residents left and migrated to the prospering Sam Han territory to the south (OJ Kwon 2013: 93). The flow of Lelang residents was a boon to the advancement of Sam Han culture and technology throughout the 2nd century.

At 3rd-century iron factories in Gian-ri in Hwaseong and Yeonje-ri in Cheongweon, archaeologists have found, along with many Lelang potteries, remains of bellows, iron ore, slags, and charcoal ovens, as well as numerous locally manufactured cast iron implements. The bellows were critical to achieving high temperature to produce advanced iron tools (DW Jang 2017: 3; EJ Song *et al.* 2014: 196-

218). With advanced technology, the Sam Han became too powerful for the Lelang commandery to control. It was in this context that the Gongsun warlord clan in Liaodong asserted itself and moved into the region south of Lelang, establishing, in 204, another Chinese commandery, Daifang.

Han China's commercial expansion into the Korean Peninsula and the Japanese Archipelago through Lelang and Daifang is evidenced by the presence of *Wushu-ch'ien* coins at various sites dating about 100 BC–AD 200 Unseong-ni (Eunyul) and Hakkyo-ri (Hwangju) in the northwest; Songsan-ni (Masan), and Dahori (Uichang) on the southern coast; and Cheju Island (ML Choi 1992; KM Lee *et al.* 1989). Han bronze mirrors have been found at Pyeong-ri (Taegu), Joyang-dong (Kyongju), and Dahori in the southeast, and at Pyeongchang-ni (Iksan) in the southwest (YJ Yun 1981; KM Lee *et al.* 1989; YN Jeon 1987b). Also, *Wang-Mang-ch'ien* coins dated to 14 AD have been found at the southern coastal sites of Hoehyeon-ri (Kimhae) and Gungok-ni (Haenam) (ML Choi 1992; SR Choi 1993).

In the Archipelago, the Han Chinese coins, including *Wushu-ch'ien* and *Huoquan* have been found at numerous coastal sites in northern Kyushu (Shinmachi, Haru-no-tsuji, Moto'oka, Imajuku Koroue, and Aoya Kamiji) as well as at Takatsuka in Okayama and Kamei in Osaka (Takesue 2008: 262-263). It is not certain whether the Chinese coins found in Okayama and Osaka were carried there by Chinese or local Wa traders.

Actual political influence of Lelang and Daifang was limited largely to the Pyongyang area and adjacent regions in the northwest. South of the Han River, sociocultural evolution continued without direct Chinese domination, although it was increasingly affected by events in the northwest.

However, while Han China held – for nearly four centuries – its commercial, military, and political foothold in northwest Korea through Lelang and later Daifang, the sociocultural fabric of the Peninsula itself changed bit by bit as Chinese cultural elements found their way into the native Korean sociocultural milieu by way of the trade and population migration. For this reason, those local polities which, by reason of geography, had closer contacts with the Chinese commanderies reached political and military maturity much sooner than others, and this was especially the case with Koguryo and Paekche.

4. Push-Pull Dynamics during the SAM HAN Period

In 109–108 BC, Han China's Emperor Wu Di mobilized 50,000 infantries and 7,000 naval forces to conquer Go-Choson (the name for ancient Korea appearing in Chinese historical texts and the *Samguk Sagi*) centered in the Pyongyang area. The war lasted for more than a year before Go-Choson surrendered. In the course of armed conflicts, many Koreans fled the Daedong River basin toward the south.

Yeokkegyeong, the prime minister of Wiman Choson, for example, fled with 2,000 households to Jin Guk, believed to have been the region between the Han and the Geum River. The arrival in the south of a large population of refugees caused a considerable social disruption in Mahan (JG Noh 2009: 215-229).

Han China sought to appease the local polities by awarding them titles and ranks of nobility and cutting them in on profitable commercial transactions. However, as the Han Dynasty began to decline and became ineffective in the management of its faraway commandery in the latter part of the 2nd century, the indigenous polities in the Peninsula such as Mahan began to assert themselves.

Then, beginning around 200, the Peninsula was engulfed in violent conflicts. First, in 204, the Gongsun warlord family, dominant in Liaodong, invaded the region between the Daedong River and the Imjin River and there established a new commandery-trade center complex known as Daifang. The primary purpose was to check the growing power of local indigenous polities, especially Mahan, as well as to assume the lucrative trade with Sam Han polities and Wa as Lelang became preoccupied with Koguryo threats (YC Oh 2006: 185-186).

Four decades later, in 246 the Mahan Confederation attacked Daifang, killing is leader. Next, a major conflict erupted between the Mahan Confederation and Paekche, a newly emerging state in the lower basin of the Han River. As Paekche emerged as the victor, Mahan ceased to exist as a living political entity in west central Korea by 300. Only those Mahan polities in the southwest continued to exist as Later Mahan (SR Choi 2017a: 289-291; JG Noh 2009: 220-221).

In the meantime, the population was exploding in the southern coastal region. Investigators have uncovered more than 200 residential remains at Mahan villages of Jungryang in Hampyeong and Taemok-ri in Damyang (GJEB 2009: 55, 67). A Byeonhan village at Sonam-ri near the south coast had 161 dwellings (GSND-DDHB 1999: 54). Elsewhere, in the inland zone, a Mahan village at Yonggye-dong in Daejeon has revealed more than 350 residences.

As it happened in earlier times, the emergence of mega-size villages resulted in inter-communal conflicts and wars. In Byeonhan, the number of fortified villages dramatically increased, as seen in the archaeological remains of Ga'eumjeong-dong, Namsan, and Pyeongsan-ri (Changweon Province), and Dabang-ri (Yangsan Province). The V-shaped moats were reinforced with wooden barricades encircling the villages (GMUY 2008: 1317).

The conflicts and wars between the Chinese and local polities, especially Mahan, and between Mahan and Paekche as well as increasing population and inter-communal conflicts were the *push* factor in the *push-pull* dynamics underlying the migration of Mahan and Byeonhan people to northern Kyushu. The *pull* factor was the presence in northern Kyushu of their kinsmen and relatives who had established themselves in Kyushu earlier, namely an active migration network which had been operating since the arrival of the bronze-bearing Toraijin around 300 BC.

II. NEW TORAIJIN FROM SAM HAN

1. Toraijin from Later Mahan and Their Contributions

The discovery at Nishijin-machi in Fukuoka of Later Mahan settlements and Mahan pottery in a large quantity (Fig. 3.4) indicates that a contingent of Later Mahan people migrated from southwest Korea and settled in northern Kyushu, closest to southern Korea, during the Late Yayoi period (OYBH 2004: 9-11, 54-61; Takesue 2013: 340).

Of special significance, in terms of the Toraijin from Later Mahan, is the resurgence in northern Kyushu, during the Late Yayoi period, of the *shukobo* (moat-surrounded tombs) (Watanabe 1999: 82),

Fig. 3.4. Pottery vessel types of Sam Han from southern Korea and Nishijinmachi in northern Kyushu compared. **Top:** Mahan pottery from southern Korea, 3rd century (after: GJEB 2009: 49, 59, 79, 97; GGWB 2000: 43). **Middle:** Wajil pottery from Byeonhan (after GJUB 1993: 70, 88, 92). **Bottom:** Mahan and Byeonhan pottery found at Nishijinmachi in Fukuoka, Kyushu, 3rd century (after OYBH 2004: 10).

the primary mortuary system of Later Mahan. As in Mahan, elites were buried in enlarged *shukobo* during the Late Yayoi. A good example is Tomb Number One discovered at Hirabaru, 13 m long and 9.5 m wide. As in the case of Mahan elite *jugumyo*, it housed a wooden casket containing comma-shaped glass jewels, tubular and globular glass beads, and a long iron sword with a round pommel (Itokoku Rekishi Hakubutsukan 2004: 21, 25-26).

At Nishijin-machi, some of the Mahan people made glass beads and comma-shaped glass jewels while others worked at nearby Hakata forged-iron smithing workshops to produce locally needed iron tools, using raw iron imported from Korea (Murakami 1999: 106-107; OYBH 2004: 14-19).

During the Middle Yayoi period, iron tools were made in the Archipelago at relatively simple backyard smithing workshops with raw iron imported from the Peninsula (Murakami 1999: 91-101). This changed with the arrival of the Sam Han immigrants with an advanced bellow system which provided hitherto unattainable high heat to the metal-heating furnace. The improved furnace enabled the Archipelago smiths to produce a large quantity of forged iron tools, as evidenced in the piles of iron dregs and discarded pieces of forged iron. The new technology of forging iron based on high heat spread quickly to Makimuku in Nara, Minami Chohara in Kanagawa, and Okitsuka in Chiba (Murakami 1999: 106-109, Murakami 2007: 110-113).

During the Late Yayoi period, the Toraijin from the western part of Korea also migrated east to the Kinki Core Region either directly from Korea or by way of northern Kyushu, settling in Hyogo, Osaka, and Nara where earlier Toraijin from the same region had settled in the 3rd century BC. Like Toraijin of the Middle Yayoi period, the new immigrants constructed moat-surrounded *jugumyo* (J. *shukobo*) for their elites and helped establish local forged iron tool-making workshops (OYBH 2004: 24-27; Sakai 2013: 77-92). In Pit # SK 2480, dated to 200–250 AD at the Tomondo-Higashi Site in Shiki-gun, Nara, *yeonjil* pottery of south-western Korean origin has been found, suggesting that people from the region were settling in the area on the eve of the Early Kofun period (Sakurai Shiritsu Maizo Bunkazai Senta 2005: 8).

This may have been due to socio-political problems besetting northern Kyushu during the Late Yayoi period. According to the *Warenzhuan* (Legends of the Wa people) in *the Weizhi of Sanguozhi,* the land of Wa comprised about a hundred polities and the Wa people had frequent wars.

Excavations at eighteen sites in the Kinki region have revealed numerous burials of the Peninsula's Middle/Late Mumun type in the form of *jugumyo* (moat surrounded tombs) (M Watanabe 1999: 82-85). At Higashi-muko alone, twenty-two were uncovered. Assuming that #9, #10, and #15, occupying a land space 10–20 times larger than the others, belonged to the elites of the village, Watanabe posits that some of the Toraijin from west-central Korea emerged as elites during the Middle and Late Yayoi periods. By the Early Kofun period, c. 250 AD, they had securely established themselves as naturalized Japanese farmers as well as leaders of farming villages in the region. The person buried in a *shukobo* at the Miyataki site in Yoshino-cho (Nara) is thought to have been the chief/leader of a Yayoi farming village (NKKFH 1988: 33).

2. Byeonhan/Early Kaya People in the Archipelago: Byeonhan-Kaya Funerary Rituals, Iron, and Founding Myth

The presence of Kaya-type dwellings and Wajil pottery at Nishijin-machi, including brazier-shaped wares, indicates that the people from Byeonhan/early Kaya were also living in Fukuoka (Takesue 2013: 340; OYBH 2004: 9-11; Shirai 2000: 90-120). In addition, discovery of Byeonhan and early Kaya pottery remains in the Nara basin indicates that Toraijin from Korea's southeast moved into the Kinki region also during the Late Yayoi-Early Kofun period (Takesue 2013: 340).

Byeonhan-Kinki connections are attested by findings at Makimuku, the birthplace of early Yamato rulers (Barnes 2015: 351), of triangular wood arrowheads made as replicas of the distinctive triangular bone arrowheads of Byeonhan and Early Kaya (OYBH 2004: 29; Kameda 2011: 114). Pottery sherds found at Makimuku are also strikingly similar to the Wajil pottery from Byeonhan (Ban 2018: 76-78; OYBH 2004: 29; cf. GJUB 1993: 92-95).

The first Kofun tumuli built in Kinki during the Early Kofun period were similar to the 2nd century wood-framed chamber tombs of southeast Korea (OYBH 2004: 30-31; GMUY 2008: 828-829). For example, the wood-framed burial chamber found inside the Hokenoyama Kofun near Makimuku, dated to c. 250 and considered to be the oldest Kofun in Japan, was strikingly similar to wood-framed tombs of the same period found in the southeast region of Jinhan-Byeonhan area, including that of Gueo-ri (Fig. 3.5, bottom) (BH Choi 2015: 130). The Hokenoyama Kofun also contained a Korean *salpo*, a spade-like iron implement (Fig. 3.6B) (Kameda 2011: 112; OYBH 2004: 30-33). Attached to a long handle, it was used in ancient Kaya, Silla, and Paekche to control water flow to paddies absolutely critical to wet-rice-based agriculture. As such, it symbolized power and authority and was buried in chiefly graves along with other prestige goods (JH Kim 2006: 181-186; GGOB 2006: 101-105).

Another indication of Byeonhan/Kaya connection to Japan's early Kofun elite society is the presence of *yujarigi* scepters of southeastern Peninsula origin in the Kurozuka Kofun (c. 300-350 AD), one of the earliest keyhole tombs near Makimuku (OYBH 2004: 32). Appearing first during the Sam Han period primarily at southeastern coastal sites such as Yangdong-ni in Kimhae and Bokcheon-dong in Pusan, the *yujarigi* was a curlicued ritual iron scepter carried on a pole or staff that symbolized the commanding power and authority of its owner. Made of elongated flat pieces of iron (*pansang cheolbu*), 20–40 cm long, these scepters had one to four curlicues on each side and a bifurcation at the widened top end (Fig. 3.6D-E) (see Azuma 1999: 360-379). In time, the *yujarigi* became an important funerary ritual object, as it was used in the final sending-off ceremony of the dead elite personage in both Kaya and Silla. Normally it was placed in the grave of the highest chief in a given locale (HH Kim 2011: 39-76; BH Choi 2015: 129-130; also see PUM 1996b: 166; GSBD 1998: 174; Tokyo National Museum 1992: 75-76).

Another close similarity between the society of Kinki Core Region of the Late Yayoi/Early Kofun period and that of Korea's Byeonhan/Early Kaya is the practice of including iron implements and Chinese bronze mirrors in their elite tombs. For example, the Hokenoyama Kofun contained iron swords, iron daggers, iron arrowheads, and Chinese bronze mirrors, in addition to the iron *salpo*. This was strikingly similar to the wood-framed Kaya elite tomb #162 at Yangdong-ni in Kimhae, which contained a horde of iron spearheads and iron arrowheads as well as ten flat iron axes (*pansang cheolbu*) along with Chinese bronze mirrors (GMUY 2008: 828-829).

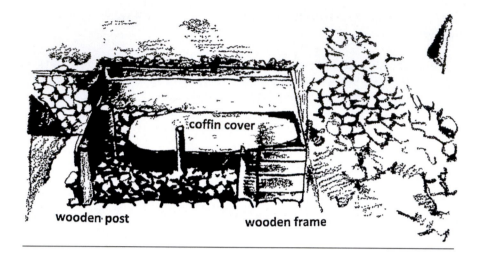

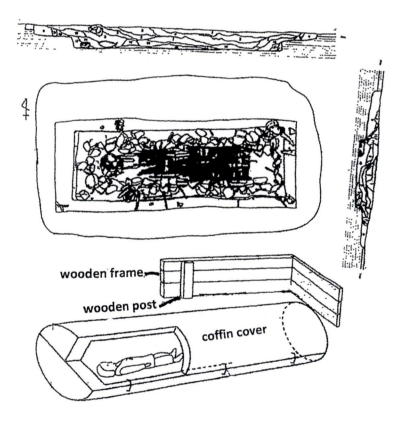

Fig. 3.5. Hokenoyama Kofun and a wood coffin tomb from Korean southeast. **Top:** reconstructed view of a wood-framed chamber containing a large wood coffin inside the Hokenoyama Kofun, c. 250 (after OYBH 2004: 31). **Bottom:** reconstructed view of the wood-framed chamber containing a large wood coffin at Gueo-ri in Kyongju, c. 200-300 after DC Kim 2010: 126-169, cited in BH Choi 2015: 117).

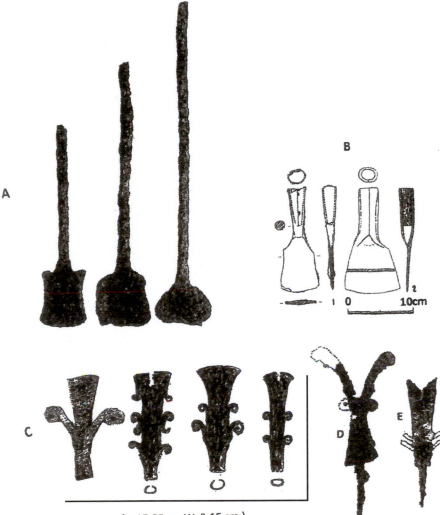

Fig. 3.6. *Salpos* (ritual iron spades) and *yujarigi* (curlicued ritual iron scepter). **A:** Salpos of ancient Kaya from Tomb # 27 at Dohang-ri, Haman, 4th century (after GKIB 1998: 86, 157). **B:** Salpos from Hokenoyama Kofun (after Kameda 2011, 112). **C:** Yujarigi found in early wood-framed chamber tombs in southeast Korea c. 200-350 (after: BH Choi 2015: 130; GSBD 1998: 174). **D:** Yujarigi found in the Kurozuka Kofun at Makimuku, 4th century (after: OYBH 2004: 32). **E:** Yujarigi found in the Azuchi Hyotanyama Kofun in Shiga, c. 400 (after: OYBH 2004: 32).

In light of these observations in the early Kofun funerary rituals, KOYAMADA Koichi (2004a: 29) states, "In the Kofun funerary rituals [*kofun saishiki*] established by the Yamato court are revealed various Torai-type information [*Toraikei joho*]. It is quite reasonable to think that there were learned men of the Torai origin [*Toraikei jishikijin*] [at Makimuku] who assisted in the establishment and organization of various rituals [*girei*]."

It was in this context that several forged-iron tool-making workshops appear to have been established at Makimuku during the Early Kofun period. Pottery remains distinctly of Kaya origin found at some of the Makimuku iron tool-making sites suggest that iron smiths from Kaya were at work in Makimuku (OYBH 2004: 30).

During the Late Yayoi and the dawn of the Early Kofun period, Kaya was the iron capital of East Asia. People from surrounding regions, including the Chinese of Lelang and Daifang and the 'Wa' traders were coming to Kaya to acquire iron. Until the latter part of the 7th century, the Archipelago was known to the Chinese and Koreans as 倭國 (C. Wo *guo* or K. Wae *guk*) and its residents as 倭人 (C. Wo people). 'Wa' is the Japanese reading of倭. As recorded in the Silla section of the *Samguk Sagi*, some Wa, known as pirates, raided Silla territory to acquire food or precious goods while others traded with the people of Kaya. Still others came at the invitation of Paekche and Kaya elites for help against Silla or Koguryo (Brown 1993: 140-144).

Kaya had already enjoyed iron technology for nearly five hundred years and had achieved a high level of skill in both its production and the manufacturing of cast iron and forged-iron goods. For the raw iron, the Archipelago depended entirely on material imported from Kaya. Likewise, most of the Archipelago's good quality agricultural tools (hoes, shovels, axes, sickles) and weapons (swords, daggers, halberds, spear points, arrowheads) were imported from Kaya. Under such circumstances, skilled artisans from Kaya, with their command of its well-developed iron technology, would have been eagerly recruited and coveted by the ambitious Yamato court, as at Makimuku in Nara.

A significant point, in considering the Kaya connection to the emerging Kofun society, is the fact that Japan's founding mythology shares common elements with that of Kaya, as noted in the following narrative on the origin of Karak Guk (Kaya nation) in the *Samguk Yusa: Karak-guk* section (Yi 1972: 198-199):

> Since the creation of the heaven and the earth there was no country or king with a name on the earth. There were only nine leaders called khans.... One day they heard a strange voice from a hilltop known as Kuji... When they, along with 200–300 people, approached the hill the voice asked: "Do you know where I am?" They replied: "Kuji... The voice said, "God has sent me here to establish a nation and become its king... Sing and dance, and you will meet your king."

> While they sang and danced a red rope appeared from the heaven, reaching the earth. At the end of the heavenly rope, they found in a golden box six golden eggs wrapped in a red cloth... Twelve hours later the golden eggs hatched. Ten days later, one of them grew nine feet tall and looked like a dragon... He was called Suro and became the king. He called his nation Dae Karak or Kaya-guk state. The others born of the golden eggs became the chiefs of other Kaya states.

According to the *Nihon Shoki* narrative on the origin of the Japanese nation (The Age of the Gods, II: 9-11; Iida 1912: 31-42; Aston 1972, Vol. 1: 69-70):

> Takami-mi-musubi no Mikoto wrapped his Grandchild, Amatsu-hiko-hiko-ho-nigi-no-Mikoto, with a cover and made him to descend... So, the Grandchild left... From the

floating Bridge of Heaven, he took stand on the twin summits of Kushihi... Then in search for a country/nation (*kunimaki*) he traversed Karakuni空國 [also read '*munekuni*'] of Sojishi until he came to the promontory of Kasasa... The Grandchild asked a man, "is here a kuni (country/nation) or not?" He said, "There is here a *kuni*." The Grandchild went and took up his abode there.

In both accounts a hill is mentioned as the starting point of a heavenly deity's nation building on the earth; it is called Kuji in the *Samguk Yusa* and Kushihi in the *Nihon Shoki*. Also, in both accounts, Kara or Karakuni is involved. In the *Kojiki* version of the same narrative (Advent of the Gods, I: 62), Kushihi is written as 久士布流多氣 and pronounced as Kujifurutake, which means 'hilltop of Kuji village'. Furthermore, 空國 is spelled as 韓國 (Karakuni or Korea) (Tsujita 1924: 223-224). There is little doubt that the Kaya founding-myth persisted among the Kaya immigrants and their descendants in Japan for many centuries, without losing two critical elements – Kuji and Kara – and became incorporated into the *Kojiki* and the *Nihon Shoki* in the early 8th century as the Yamato rulers sought to explain their origin.

3. Political Consolidation in Kyushu and Inter-Polity Warfare

Toward the end of the Middle Yayoi in the 1st century BC, the political relationships changed in northern Kyushu. A three-part stratification of the Middle Yayoi remained, but two new regional centers emerged: Sugu-Okamoto site in the Sawara Plains and Mikumi Minami-Shoji in the Ito region farther west and close to the northern Kyushu coast.

At this period, most other chiefly graves in northern Kyushu contained only a few bronze artifacts. Yoshitake, previously in the top position in the Sawara Plains, was now a member of the second tier under Sugu-Okamoto, and Mikumi Minami-Shoji became dominant over other chiefly centers in the Ito region farther west. In both areas the lowest stratum consisted of villages with no elite members, as before (Kyushu Rekishi Shiryokan 1980: 1-48; Takesue 2002: 25-58).

As the new political centers were emerging in the coastal plains facing southern Korea across the Tashima Strait, Yoshinogari was growing into a mega-size moat-surrounded settlement of more than 40 hectares in the Saga Plains to the south during the Late Yayoi. The V-shaped surrounding moat, intended for defense, was 6.3 meter wide and 3 meter deep. Inside the defensive moat were found an area devoted to rituals for the dead and a section devoted to chiefly residential buildings. Another section revealed remains of large elevated structures believed to have been used as community storage buildings. Also found were cist-type and wood-coffin graves, common in southern Korea during the Sam Han period (Shiga-ken Kyoiku I'inkai 2008: 21).

The *Weizhi* (*Record of Wei*), completed in 297 AD, reports that in western Japan there were 30 國 (C. *guo*; J. *koku, kuni*), during 250–300 AD and that in the earlier days there had been about 100 *guo*. It also reports that there were "disturbances and warfare" for "70 or 80 years" among the local polities. This account suggests that during the Late Yayoi period a process of political consolidation was ongoing in which many hitherto independent polities were brought into about 30 confederated *kuni*, each of which controlled a fairly large territory (Terasawa 2004: 26-43)

4. Emergence of Thriving Pen/Insular Trade: Kyushu/Kinki – Neuk-do/Kimhae Connections

It was in the context of this political turmoil in Kyushu that the Archipelago elites increasingly turned to the Peninsula's southern coast to acquire advanced goods, especially iron ingots, weaponry, and agricultural tools of the continent.

After a millennium of Toraijin's arrival and their naturalization in the Archipelago, the Peninsula was no longer a distant land shrouded in mystery to the Wa people. For the naturalized Toraijin, it was their homeland, and to the native Wa people it was a close neighbor. Middle Yayoi traders had been sailing across the Tsushima Strait back and forth. Having learned about the Peninsula' advanced culture and technology, the Archipelago elites increasingly commissioned their representatives to the Peninsula's southern coast to obtain Peninsula goods, undoubtedly guided by the Toraijin familiar with the Peninsula's language, customs, and infrastructure, and increasingly so in time, giving birth to a thriving Pen-Insular trade-exchange system.

Yayoi pottery in southeast Korea increased sharply with the Sugu II type belonging to the final phase of the Middle Yayoi, c. 75 BC–50 AD (date by Mizoguchi 2013: 34), suggesting that Yayoi traders arrived in an increasing number in southeast Korea during the first half of the 1st century BC and thereafter (C Inoue 2008: 236-255; Takesue 2008: 258-307; CH Lee 2011: 34-45). The Sugu II type vessels, however, were concentrated only at a few selective locations along the major south sea trade route (C Inoue 2008: 238-239; CH Lee 2011: 34.) Among them the Neuk-do Island and Kimhae were the most important.

Kimhae was a major harbor located at the mouth of the Nakdong River, while Neuk-do was about a midpoint between Ulsan in the southeast and Mokpo in the southwest. Neuk-do was an excellent point of meeting of traders from northern Kyushu and southeast Korea as well as from Mahan in the southwest and Chinese commanderies of Lelang and Daifang in the northwest of the Peninsula (C Inoue 2008: 239). Essentially, in the 1st century BC, Neuk-do Island emerged as the international trade center of East Asia (GJIB 2016).

The convergence of the three regions (Japan, southern Korea, and Lelang) on the Neuk-do Island and at Kimhae during the 1st century BC was the consequence of several epochal events developing in East Asia at that time. In northern Kyushu local bronze production was in full swing; on the Peninsula, the slender bronze dagger culture was on its way out in the face of an emerging local forged-iron industry; in China the Early Han Dynasty was on the move, projecting itself into Manchuria and the Korean Peninsula, militarily and commercially (C Inoue 2008: 239-240; Takesue 2008: 265-267).

Material items found at these major trading ports included the Sugu II Type Yayoi vessels from northern Kyushu and Chinese pots from Lelang. They were found with locally made Wajil ware. The Yayoi vessels, in particular, comprised jars (including some red-burnished ritual jars), pots, and mounted dishes used for storage, cooking, and funerary rituals (CH Lee 2011: 34-45).

In this regard, the Neuk-do Island and Kimhae, the main trading ports along Korea's south and southeast coast of this period, were strikingly similar to 'port-of-trade-type settlements' described by Mizoguchi as emerging across western Japan, during the latter part of the Late Yayoi period. They had "an abundance of material items which either were brought in from remote regions or were made by copying the originals from remote regions... [Their pottery repertoire included] pots of non-local origin (often including both transported and locally produced ones)," and most of the non-local pots were cooking jars (Mizoguchi 2013: 216-220). As in the case of the Late Yayoi port-of-trade-type settlements such as Nishijima, local and foreign populations lived together on Neuk-do Island and in Kimhae, mostly likely influencing each other culturally (CH Lee 2011: 36-47).

The Sugu II-period Yayoi residents on the Peninsula coast had twofold objectives: first, to acquire raw iron and iron implements (agricultural and industrial tools and weapons) from the southeastern Peninsula, which was then becoming a major iron producer in East Asia, and second, to acquire Chinese prestige goods including bronze mirrors, glass beads, and gilt-bronze ornaments (C Inoue 2008: 239). Iron was becoming increasingly critical for the Yayoi society as its rice-based agriculture was ever expanding. The Chinese bronzes were demanded by the Yayoi elites because the Peninsula was phasing out its own bronze production, supplanting it with iron industry. At the very same time, Chinese bronzes became available through its Lelang commandery in Pyongyang area, established 108 BC (Mizoguchi 2013: 105).

For about 200 years (c. 30 BC–AD 180), the Yayoi elites of northern Kyushu acquired Chinese bronze mirrors of various types, beginning with those of Early Han, for elite mortuary purpose. Importing them initially around 30 BC from Lelang, the Kyushu elites began to distribute them to other Yayoi elites throughout the Archipelago as far as central Honshu in the early part of the 1st century AD (Mizoguchi 2013: 224). After c. 50 AD, the number of Later Han type mirrors exploded, flooding the Osaka-Nara- Kyoto region where they were buried in the tombs of Late Yayoi chiefs (Okamura 1986: 70). While the Han bronze mirrors were venerated by the Yayoi elites for whatever power they were believed to hold for the dead and in their graves, iron was emerging as the most important instruments for their functional and practical advantages in daily life. For longer than six centuries (c. 50 BC–AD 600), the Wa/Yamato people would cross the Korea Strait at any cost to acquire the Korean iron absolutely critical to the advancement of their civilization, and the Korean iron would determine the nature and the course of Japan–Korea relations till 600 AD.

During the latter part of the Middle Yayoi and the Late Yayoi, the Yayoi elites in northern Kyushu, mainly in the Fukuoka and Ito areas, were acquiring the iron through their representatives residing at the major trading ports at the Neuk-do Island and Kimhae. As leaders of Yayoi settlements in these harbor towns, they appear to have interacted with the local elites who were in charge of iron production and its distribution network (C Inoue 2008: 235-255; Takesue 2008: 259-307).

The interaction between the Byeonhan elites and those of northern Kyushu is clearly evidenced by the presence in the elite graves of Byeonhan and Jinhan of ritual medium slender type bronze spearheads (*chusaikei hoko*) made in northern Kyushu during the latter part of the Middle Yayoi period. *Chusaikei hoko* found in elite tombs at Daho-ri in Changweon and Yongjeon-ri in Yeongcheon dated to c. 50 BC are good examples (C Inoue 2008: 236-238).

The *chusaikei hoko* and other similar bronze instruments were the most highly prized prestige goods among the Yayoi elites in northern Kyushu at this time and were placed in their tombs (C Inoue 2008: 239). The Yayoi elites therefore would have used them as elite exchange items. According to INOUE Chikara, the Yayoi elites sent the *chusaikei hoko* to their counterparts in southeast Korea to symbolize the special relationship between them rather than as payment for iron – believed to have been paid for with perishable organic materials such as rice and silk. This elite relationship accomplished twofold objectives. First, it facilitated the movement of iron (finished products as well as raw iron material including *pansang cheolbu*, the elongated flat iron plates used as an axe as well as raw iron material, and *jujo cheolbu*, the heavy cast iron axe also used as a tool as well as raw iron material) from the southeastern Peninsula to northern Kyushu. Second, it played a critical role in connecting the northern Kyushu elites with Chinese political and commercial functionaries at Lelang. This is evidenced in the simultaneous co-occurrence of Korean iron, the Yayoi *chusaikei hoko*, and Chinese prestige goods (bronze mirrors, *heki* green glass discs, and gilt-bronze ornaments) in the Yayoi elite graves of northern Kyushu and in those of Byeonhan and Jinhan (C. Inoue 2008: 239).

By c. 1 AD the sea trade route connecting northern Kyushu, southeast Korea, and Lelang was firmly established with a flourishing trade among the three regions, making the Neuk-do-Kimhae "the Northeast Asia Trade Center" where China, Korea, and Japan met for trade and exchange. Archaeological data from both sides of the Korea Strait indicate that iron was flowing from the Peninsula to northern Kyushu. From the latter, medium wide bronze spearheads (*chukokei hoko*) and large wide bronze spearheads and halberds (*daikokei hoko* and *daikokei doka*) were coming to Korea, as evidenced in elite graves at Bisan-dong and Manchon-dong in Daegu. Chinese prestige goods were flowing from Lelang (and later from Daifang as well) to the elites of south and southwest Korea and northern Kyushu via Kimhae on the southeast coast (C Inoue 2008; Takesue 2008: 260).

Of special significance in this regard are three Yayoi jar coffins from Hoehyeon-ri located in the vicinity of Kimhae's ancient harbor, which Yayoi people frequented (C Inoue 2008: 239-238). No. 3 jar, dated to the early part of the Middle Yayoi, contained two jasper tubular beads, two slender bronze daggers, and eight bronze engravers (K. *dongsa*; J. *dosha*) (Yanagida 1989b: 20-21). Undoubtedly the burial jar belonged to a Wa elite who lived and died in the trading town of Kimhae and was a leader in the bronze trade. The large jar coffins were either shipped from northern Kyushu or made locally (CH Lee 2011: 43; Takesue 2013, #228:1-19).

At this time, the Kinki core region was also starting to connect with Korea, as evidenced by the presence of Late Yayoi pottery, at Hoehyeon-ri site in Kimhae, from the Omi area in Shiga Prefecture (Takesue, Iba et. al. 2011: 257-268). Undoubtedly, as with the elites in northern Kyushu, those of the Kinki region were also beginning to recognize the power of iron for agricultural, economic, and military advancement. Soon, the Kinki region would emerge as the center of iron technology and production in the Archipelago, thanks to Korean iron technology and Korean immigrant technicians (Mizoguchi 2013: 199, 243).

Various Wa artifacts from the Late Yayoi period (c. 50–250 AD), including potteries, iron arrowheads, and imitation bronze mirrors, are found in the southwestern Peninsula, suggesting that the Yayoi people continued to cross the Korea Strait throughout this period to acquire iron (Yanagida 1989b: 23-38). However, other than common pottery vessels and a few iron arrowheads, no Yayoi artifacts of special value accompanied them. Most likely the Yayoi traders were still paying for the Korean iron with organic materials such as rice, silk, and unknown products, which have not survived.

CHAPTER FOUR

THE MIDDLE-LATE KOFUN PERIOD TORAIJIN: *IMAKI NO TEHITO* ("Recently Arrived Skilled Artisans") (c. 350–600 AD)

I. THEIR HISTORICAL AND SOCIO-CULTURAL BACKGROUND: KOREA'S EARLY STATES AND POLITIES (C. 300–700 AD)

1. A Brief Survey

Temporally, Japan's Kofun period corresponds to that of Korea's early states (Koguryo, Paekche, and Silla) as well as Kaya and Later Mahan polities (Table 0.1 and Map 4.1).

The history of early Korean states and polities, in terms of their origin and development, is a major subject of scholarly inquiry, and an innumerable number of publications on the subject already exists. General introductory texts on the ancient history of Korea readily available include *East Asia, The Great Tradition* (Reischauer and Fairbank 1958: 1960) and *Korea: Old and New History* (Eckert *et al.* (1990), and KB Lee (1988, 2006). *The History and Archaeology of the Koguryo Kingdom* by Mark Byington (2016a) is an excellent resource book on the origins and history of Koguryo. *A History of the Early Korean Kingdom of Paekche* by Jonathan Best (2006), along with his other scholarly monographs on Paekche (1982, 2003), is an invaluable resource in the study of Korea's early state which played the most important role in the Toraijin story of the Middle-Late Kofun period. *Early Kaya* (Byington 2012), a collection of scholarly papers, provides rich information on the illusive Kaya states: their history and archaeological remains. *Archaeology of East Asia: The Rise of Civilization in China, Korea, and Japan* (Barnes 2015), gives a panoramic view of ancient East Asian history and archaeology.

While Koguryo had an early start as a centralized state in the 1st century AD (Rhee 1992a, Rhee 1992b, Byington 2016a), Paekche, Kaya, Silla, and Later Mahan emerged after 250–300 BC (SB Park 2000; JW Lee 1982; TS Kim 1993, 2014a; ML Choi 2009: 199-214; JG Noh 220-223).

Through diplomatic and cultural interactions with various Chinese states as well as with each other, Korea's early states made rapid progress in their socio-political and cultural development. However, while Koguryo, Paekche, and Silla each became a unified and centralized kingdom or state, ruled by a hereditary monarchy, Kaya and Later Mahan polities remained as regional political confederations of a dozen or so autonomous polities with common culture but without the political centralization of early states (JG Noh 2009: 215-223; HG Lee 2020: 71-93). By 550 the Later Mahan polities were absorbed into Paekche as local prefectures (SR Choi 2017a: 279-299). As for Kaya polities, they were conquered by Silla beginning in 555 and by 562 were all incorporated into Silla's local administrative system.

2. Cultural and Technological Advancements of Paekche, Kaya, and Later Mahan

Culturally and technologically, Korea's early states underwent parallel development though exchange and interaction even as they exhibited their unique features with their own creativity. This is clearly observed in religion and ideology, iron technology, equestrian culture, stoneware pottery, gold

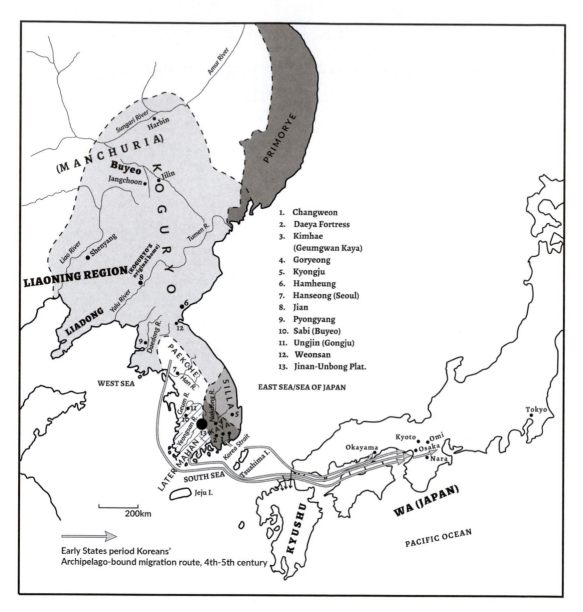

Map 4.1. Early states of Korea, c. 400 (by Lucas Pauly).

craftsmanship, and mortuary practices. Below, we present an overview of cultural and technological advancements of Paekche, Kaya, and Later Mahan whose citizens constituted the majority of the Middle to Late Kofun-period Toraijin.

A. Religion, Ideology, Art, and Architecture

Paekche's successful warring in 371 with Koguryo with 'thirty thousand crack troops,' even killing the king of Koguryo, suggests that by the time of King Geunchogo (346–375), Paekche had emerged as a powerful nation. The flow of literate Chinese into Paekche from Lelang, and Paekche's formal diplomatic and cultural relationship with the Chinese state of Eastern Chin (first established in 372), brought high Chinese culture into Paekche. The presence around 400 AD in Paekche of great scholars of Confucianism, including Ajiki and Wang In, and their close relationship with the ruling elites, suggest that Confucianism was an important ideology of the nation. It provided Paekche with political ideology and ethical codes essential to governing and management of the ruling bureaucracy and the society at large. In this, the Confucian principle of *chung-hyo*, loyalty and filial piety, was lifted up as the highest standard.

Buddhism was first introduced to Hanseong (Seoul) from Eastern Jin of China in 384. It was welcomed by the Paekche court and quickly became the religion of the nation. As a powerful, unifying force of the populace it supported the state in its governing of the nation (Best 2006: 79-84).

During the years of their national crisis, following the loss of Hanseong, its capital, in the Han River basin, Paekche kings doubled their efforts in their use of Buddhism "as a force to help centralize and strengthen royal dynasty" (Best 2003, 165: 189-209). To promote Buddhism, King Munyeong (r. 501–523) sent a group of bright Paekche students to India and China to study Buddhist scriptures. King Seong (r. 523–554), his son and successor, created a cabinet level department in charge of Buddhism. It was responsible for propagating Buddhism, training Buddhist priests and nuns, and constructing Buddhist temples in the capital and throughout the land. Paekche students who had gone to India and China returned and became leaders of Paekche Buddhist establishment, translating Buddhist texts from Sanskrit into Chinese, the language of the Paekche aristocracy. The various Buddhist literatures written by Paekche priests, including Gyeom Ik, Dam Wuk, and Hye In , became the basis for Buddhism's being established as Paekche's national religion.

As Buddhism became the state religion, Buddhist temples, pagodas, and schools were built and flourished throughout the land. Art flourished, architectural engineering employing stone foundations and tiles with lotus designs was advanced, and stone masonry developed. Countless number of learned priests and nuns served the nation, in the royal court as well as in villages and towns. Simultaneously Buddhist art and architecture saw the heyday of their advancement during the Sabi period.

As devout Buddhists, Paekche kings, Seong (r. 523–554) and Wideok (r. 554–598) actively sought to plant Buddhism in the Archipelago beginning in 538, succeeding in their efforts to have it officially adopted by the Yamato court as Japan's state religion also (for details, see Chapter Five, III:2).

King Mu (r. 600–641) zealously inculcated Maitreya Buddhism as a national priority in his effort to strengthen his throne and the central government, projecting himself as a living incarnation of compassionate and powerful Maitreya, believed by people as the savior Buddha to come. In 634 he completed the Wangheungsa Temple ("king's prosperity temple") begun by King Wideok in 577, and four years later he built in Iksan the Mireuksa (Temple of Maitreya Buddha) with three nine-story pagodas (a pair of stone pagodas and a wooden one standing in the center). It was the largest and most magnificent temple in ancient Korea, representing the finest architectural and artistic elements of the day, as revealed by recent archaeological investigations (GMUY 1989a).

Along with Buddhism, Daoism, especially its beliefs in immortality and supernatural powers, became popular from early on. A gilt-bronze incense burner of exquisite beauty, discovered in 1993 among the ruins of a Buddhist temple near ancient Sabi (Buyeo), was decorated with Buddhist and Daoist themes of joy, happiness, and eternal bliss. It had been placed in the temple by King Wideok (r. 554–598) to comfort the soul of his father, King Seong who had been slain by Silla forces. Along with the Mireuksa Temple, it represents the finest achievements of Paekche in art, sculpture, and gilt-bronze metallurgy.

As for Kaya and Later Mahan polities, little is known about their religion and ideology in the absence of reliable written records. However, in light of the fact that Kaya polities and Silla followed a similar trajectory in cultural and technological development, it is reasonable to assume that as with Silla, Buddhism and Confucianism took hold in Kaya somewhat slowly. Regarding the Later Mahan polities, archaeology informs that "conquered" by Paekche in 369, they became gradually Paekjeized in culture and technology between 369 and 550 (SR Choi 2017a: 279-299).

B. Iron Technology

Paekche advanced its iron technology in response to frequent wars with Koguryo and Silla. The iron weapons included long swords with a ring pommel, halberds, spear points, and arrowheads (winged and flat-headed) (Fig. 4.1) (GGOB 2006: 60-68, 124-137). As early as in the second half of the 4th century, c. 360, Paekche iron technicians were producing iron body armor of rectangular iron plates bound together with leather strings, exporting the technology to the Archipelago (HJ Kim 2020: 49-55).

Also, the rapid advances in agriculture increasingly demanded production of iron implements for farming, dike construction, and land reclamation. They included iron shovels, slender axes, flat axes, sickles, and chisels among others (GGOB 2006: 101-111). Prominent also among Paekche iron implements were horse gear including bits, stirrups, buckles, and decorative ornaments (GGOB 2006: 112-123).

Unique to Paekche iron tool inventory was the iron *salpo*, a 125 cm long staff fitted with a curling fern-like handle and an elongated narrow shovel at the other end. It was used to control water flow to rice paddies, absolutely critical to wet-rice cultivation. As a symbol of power and authority in a wet-rice-based agricultural society, it was carried by community chiefs (JH Kim 2006: 181-186; GGOB 2006: 101-111).

According to chemical analyses of the iron tools, technicians of Paekche succeeded in producing fine steel with heating and water-quenching methods and an advanced ventilation system capable of

Fig. 4.1. (Page 101) Iron implements of Paekche and two types of tuyeres used by Paekche iron technicians. **A:** long swords (left, 77.5cm long; middle, 73.5cm long). **B:** forked spear points (center: length, 41.5cm); straight spear points (center: length, 45.5cm); arrow points (lengths, 17-19.4cm). **C:** shovel blade (length, 20.9cm); axes (narrow and flat); sickles (blade lengths,18-21.6cm). **D:** horse stirrups (length, 27.4cm); horseshoe (width, 8.8 cm); bit (inside length, 23.7cm). **E:** Paekche tuyeres (L-shaped type, 56.7cm long and 18.3cm in diameter; straight type, 10.4cm long and 4.7cm in diameter). Their positions relative to smelting furnaces are conjectured. **F:** salpo (iron spade). (GGOB 2006: 106, 109, 134; GJUB 1999: 28, 41, 61, 74, 160; Cheongju National Museum 2017: 95, 100. Photo credits: Gongju National Museum; Hanstudio; Cheongju National Museum, Kimhae National Museum).

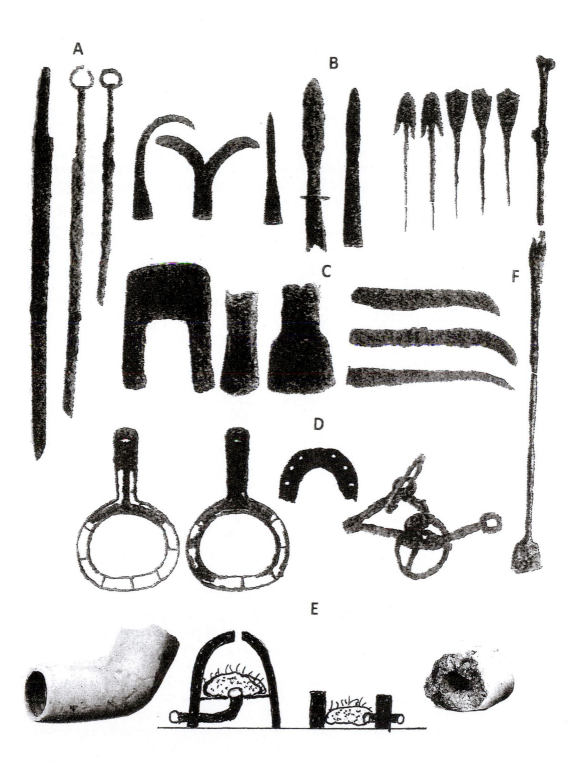

producing high heat reaching 1250–1270 °C. Also, in manufacturing weapons and tools of high quality, casting was largely replaced by the forging method (PJHGY and GDSGY 1985; JT Choi, EJ Jang *et al.* 2001; NG Lee 2008: 118-229; GH Shin, GS Jang, and NG Lee 2008: 234-271).

On the basis of iron slag and remains associated with smelting furnaces found in the Pungnap Toseong fortress in Seoul and its adjacent areas, archaeologists posit that Paekche produced its iron within its capital and at nearby locations (OY Kwon 2008: 11-18). Among them, the Gian-ri site in Hwaseong, south of Seoul, is believed to have played the "central role in the production of ironware during the Hanseong Paekje period," beginning in the latter part of the 3rd century (EJ Song *et al.* 2014: 221-222).

In the latter part of the 4th century, the now famous iron production complexes at Seokjang-ni in Jincheon and Chilgeum-dong in Chungju were added to Paekche iron industry, multiplying Paekche ironware (NG Lee 2008: 189). At least, eight iron production sites and 30 smelting furnaces have come to light at Seokjang-ni alone (YH Lee 1997: 101-105).

Archaeological remains from the west-central and southwest regions reveal that even as they lived under the shadow of the Paekche threat, the Later Mahan polities continued to thrive for 250 years, developing their culture autonomously and/or in interaction with Paekche (GJEB 2009: 36-101, 153-193; SN Rhee 1999b: 225-237). For example, they achieved extraordinary advances in iron technology both in iron production and in manufacturing high-quality iron farming/industrial tools as well as weapons. The new iron tools included long swords with a ring pommel, spearheads, arrowheads, hoes, axes, sickles, and horse bits (Fig. 4.2).

Among Korea's ancient states, Kaya is best known for its impressive array of iron implements recovered from its elite tombs. Beginning in the Sam Han period, Byeonhan, Kaya's predecessor, was already the major supplier of iron and iron implements in northeast Asia. A major question in this regard has been: Where did Byeonhan and Kaya get or produce all of their iron?

According to recent archaeological investigations, one of their primary sources of iron was the 80 km long section of the Sobaek Mountain Range which comprises the northern part of ancient Byeonhan–Kaya territory. It consists entirely of iron ore rich with nickel, one of the finest iron ore types. In numerous steep valleys on its western slope, which form the Jinan–Unbong Plateau (Map 4.1), archaeologists have identified more than 150 ancient iron production sites, the largest ancient iron-production complex ever found in the Peninsula (JG Gwak 2017b: 4-25). In light of more than 240 impressive Kaya-type mounded tombs found nearby, investigators have concluded that the iron mines and iron production facilities were originally developed and operated by the Kaya elites during 350–550.

The iron-producing apparatuses were all located in the immediate vicinity of iron ore mining sites, obviating problems relative to transporting the heavy chunks of iron ore. Preliminary excavations have brought to light remains of ancient bloomeries and large piles of iron slag.

Along with the bloomery remains were found at least 90 *bongsu* (fire signal towers) on the top of mountain peaks surrounding the iron ore mines and iron-producing factories and culminating in Jangsu, the administrative center of Jangsu Kaya elites (JG Gwak 2017b: 4-25). In light of pottery remains, those on the western slope were maintained by the Jangsu Kaya elites for over a century and

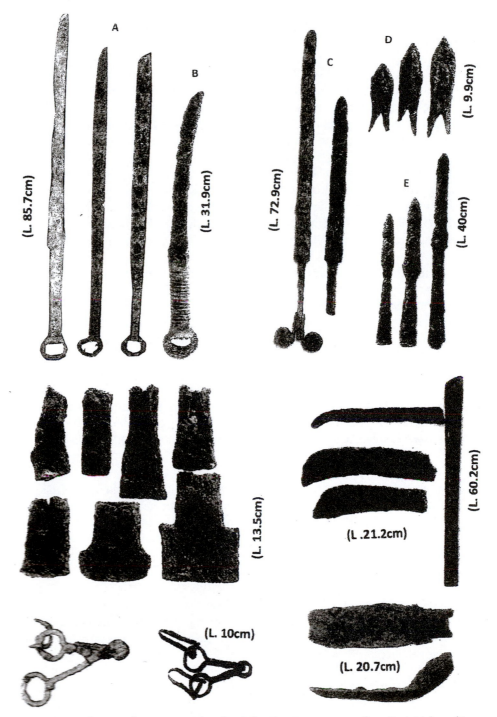

Fig. 4.2. Iron implements from Later Mahan/Paekche. **Top:** Iron weapons from Post-Mahan elite burials. **A:** Long swords with ring pommels. **B:** A sword with a decorated hilt. **C:** A sword with a decorated pommel and a dagger **D:** Winged arrows. **E:** Socketed spearheads (GJEB 2009: 66, 74-75, 160). **Middle left:** Iron axes (GJEB 2009: 123, 160). **Middle right:** Sickles (GJEB 2009: 122-147). **Bottom:** Horse bits and an iron spade (GJEB 2009: 116). Photo credit: Jeonju National Museum.

half from the latter part of the 4th century till the early part of the 6th century, when Paekche took control of them.

The *bongsu* towers were strategically positioned and were clearly intended to guard and protect the iron-making factories as well as the iron ingots produced on the sites (JG Gwak 2017b: 17-19). In light of KIM Do-yeong's thesis (2015: 32-68) that the early Peninsula states guarded the technology of iron production as state secrets and refused to share it with the outsiders, it may be postulated that the *bongsu* towers were also intended to safeguard the secrets of iron production technology.

Kaya iron implements include iron body armors and helmets, weapons (daggers, swords, spearheads, arrowheads), agricultural and industrial tools (hoes, picks, shovels, sickles, plows, axes, knives), horse gear (bits and stirrups), iron-working tools (forceps, anvils, and hammers), and raw iron materials (Fig. 4.3) (GCHB 1997: 58-68). Kaya's iron industry was essentially that of Byeonhan. As Byeonhan polities gradually became Kaya states, the latter continued to advance their Byeonhan cultural heritage.

Initially, appearing in the 4th century, the Kaya iron body armor and iron helmets (Figs. 4.3 and 4.4) were in the form of vertical-plate cuirasses, which consisted of long and narrow iron plates fastened together, first with leather strings and subsequently by riveting. Soon their number multiplied along with the growth of regional political powers, as evidenced in the archaeological remains of Yean-ri (Kimhae), Yangdong-ni (Kimhae), Daeseong-dong (Kimhae), and Bokcheon-dong tumuli (Pusan) (JW Jeong and KC Shin 1984: 273-297).

Around 450, with the introduction of riveting technology from Koguryo, further advanced helmets and body armor appeared. They included helmets with an extended visor, keeled helmets, and cuirasses with horizontally riveted rectangular or triangular plates, along with neck and shoulder guards. To them were added head guards and body armor for horses (Fig. 4.5; JW Jeong and KC Shin 1984: 275-288).

Gradually, the vertical and triangular-plate armor was replaced by lamellar armor made of 2.5 cm x 5~9 cm iron plates, which provided much greater flexibility in the heavily armed cavalry warfare. (JW Jeong and KC Shin 1984: 288; GSBD 1998: 332-338; Bokcheon Bangmulgwan 1999: 67; TS Kim and KH Song 2003: 276-302; KC Shin 2000: 261-276; JS Song 2003: 3-7, 54-75).

C. Equestrian Culture and Cavalry

Especially significant in the early Paekche society was the development of horse-related culture including horse-breeding, horse-riding, horse-driven transportation, mounted soldiers (cavalry), and horse paraphernalia (bits, stirrups, buckles). By 330 AD, the horse trappings were being buried in elite tombs, increasing in number through time.

Soon, there emerged in Paekche formidable mounted troops as evidenced in military gear and the horse trappings, including horse stirrups, found together in the early Paekche elite graves of Bongmyeong-dong in Cheongju (Ryu 2010: 143-145; JY Seong 2003: 1-28). The 4th century mounted troops were armed with bow/arrows or long spears. In the 5th century there also appeared cavalry soldiers fortified with an iron helmet and an iron body armor. Generally limited in number, the latter are believed to have been the cavalry leaders (Ryu 2010: 145).

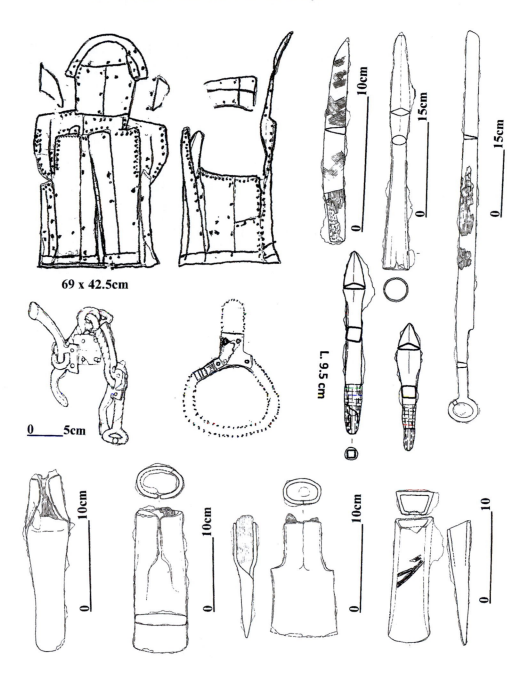

Fig. 4.3. 4th century iron implements of Kaya from Bokcheon-dong tumuli #57 and #60 in Pusan. **Top row** (from left): Riveted vertical plate cuirass; knife; spear point; a long sword with a round pommel. **Middle row:** horse bit; stirrup; arrow points. **Bottom row:** spade; forged iron axe; flat forged iron axe; heavy cast iron axe (PUM 1996b: 63, 65, 76, 78, 85, 86, 87, 90). Photo credit: Pusan National University Museum.

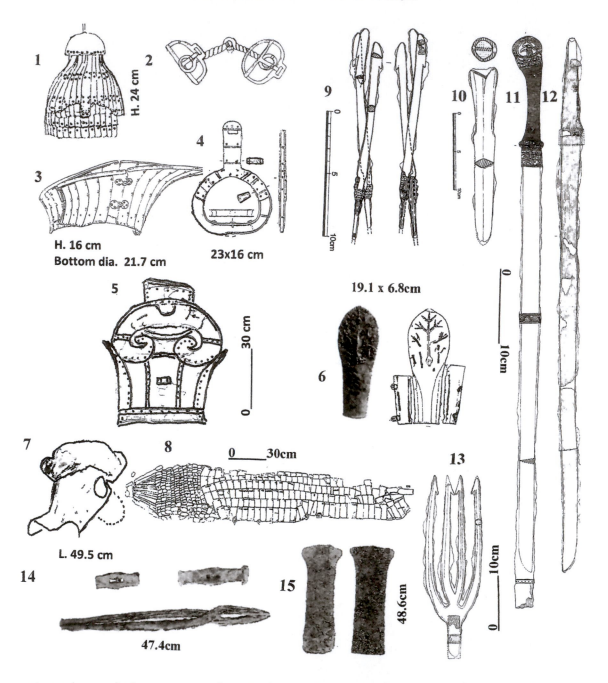

Fig. 4.4. (Page 106) 5th century iron military implements of Kaya and iron forging tools. **Cavalry Paraphernalia (1-8): 1,** Thonged vertical plate Mongolian type helmet. **2,** horse bit. **3,** neck guard. **4,** stirrup. **5,** riveted vertical plate cuirass. **6,** a pair of arm guards. **7,** chamfron. **8,** horse body guard (#1-#7 from Bokcheon-dong tumuli (after JW Jeong and KC Shin 1984: 279-286; TS Kim and KH Song 2003: 291, 266; #8 from Haman (after TS Kim and KH Song 2003: 301). **Iron Weapons (9-13 from Okjeon Kaya tumuli): 9,** arrow points. **10,** spear point. **11,** decorated long sword with a phoenix design pommel. **12,** long sword. **13,** four-pronged spear (Gyeongsang University Museum 1990: 46, 66, 89, 93. Photo credit: by Gyeongsang University Museum). **Iron Forging Tools (14-15): 14,** forceps and hammers. **15,** iron ingots (after GSBD 1998: 366, 367).

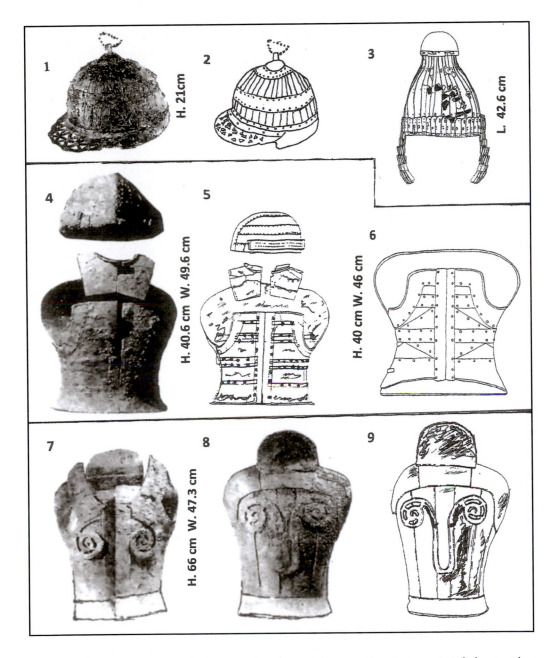

Fig. 4.5. 5th century cuirasses, helmets, and neck guard from southeast Korea. **1-2:** helmet with a visor from Jisan-dong (GSBD 1998: 334). **3:** Thonged Mongolian type vertical plate helmet with face guards (Bokcheon-dong Tomb #21, PUM 1990: 26-28). **4-5** (from top): keeled helmet, neck guard, and riveted horizontal rectangular plate cuirass from Jisan-dong (after GSBD 1998: 331). **6:** Riveted horizontal triangular plate cuirass (Sangbaek-ni) (after JW Jeong and KC Shin 1984: 280). **7, 8, 9:** vertical plate cuirass reported from Kimhae (GKIB 1998: 67). Photo credits: Yeongnam Cultural Research Center; Pusan University Museum; National Kimhae Museum.

While it is generally recognized that the horse culture of Koguryo influenced that of Paekche (Ryu 2010), that of Xianbei nomadic tribes in the Mongolian steppes is also believed to have contributed to the beginnings of Paekche' horse culture through long-distance trade relations during the 4th century (JY Seong 2003: 16-28).

The emergence of horse-riding was a momentous event in the history of ancient Korean civilization as were the first automobiles in the modern world (JY Seong 2006: 214; GGOB 2006: 112-123).

Kaya, under the influence of Koguryo and the Xianbei nomadic tribes, is especially noted for being the first in the Nakdong River region in ancient southern Korea to develop horse culture and heavily armed cavalry (Ryu 2010: 147). Along with the iron body armor and helmets the ancient Kaya society produced extensive horse paraphernalia including bits, stirrups, horse shoes, saddle components, harness fittings, and horse body armor/head guards. Found in Kaya elite tombs, they serve as evidences for horse-riding and mounted warfare in ancient Kaya (TS Kim and KH Song 2003: 227-315).

An early Kaya horse bit from Tomb #38 at Bokcheon-dong near Pusan, dated to 350, is a jointed wire mouthpiece with double offset twists and is strikingly similar to that found in an elite Xian-bei tomb in the Liaoning region. The majority of early Kaya horse bits belong to this type (TS Kim and KH Song 2003: 249-251).

After 350, Kaya iron technicians developed round-headed iron nails and riveting technology essential to production of lamellar body armor/helmets, reinforced stirrups, and saddle components. In the aftermath of Koguryo's devastating invasion of Kuya-guk in 400 with 50,000 troops supported by heavily armed cavalry, Kaya states embarked upon creating their own cavalry equipped with lamellar body armor and helmets as well as advanced iron stirrups, bits, and saddles, thanks to the iron and horse gear technology which they had been developing for a century (TS Kim and KH Song 2003: 256-270).

After 450, the horse gear further evolved to include highly decorative elements. Some of the harness fittings and saddle components were now of dazzling gilt bronze while the bits and stirrups became standardized with emphasis on their decorative aspects. At the same time, the horse-riding culture expanded throughout much of the Kaya territory, becoming an integral component of Kaya civilization (TS Kim and KH Song 2003: 270-275).

D. Stoneware Pottery

Early Paekche pottery, emerging in the Hanseong (modern Seoul) area in the 3rd century AD, was distinguished by high-fired (at 1000 °C) black burnished jars with a short straight neck, broad-shouldered jar, and tripod dishes (*heugsaeg mayeontogi*) (SB Park 2002: 86; Walsh 1917: 18). Paekche state developed them in the course of their diplomatic contact with the Chinese state of Jin and used them as prestige goods with political nuance, awarding them as gift items so as to strengthen political ties among the elites (SB Park 2002: 86).

On the other hand, the Later Mahan polities developed a variety of low-fired (*yeonjil*) and hard-fired (*gyeongjil*) earthenware, including round-based and short-necked jars. Earthenware cooking vessels, found in abundance, included jars with lug or ox horn-shaped handles, jars with a hole on the side, steamers with a perforated base, and torpedo or egg-shaped pots. Many of them were paddled-marked on the body surface with a rope or lattice pattern (JS Kim and JG Kim 2016: 64-70; GJEB 2009: 78-91; Walsh 2017: 16-17). On the basis of its highly standardized pastes, Walsh (2017: 142) speculates that the *gyeongjil* pottery was produced by a specialize system while *yeonjil* pottery was a part of non-specialized economy.

Some of the surface designs of Mahan storage jars from the southwest resembled bird footprints (*jojokmun*), giving such pottery the name, *jojokmun* pottery (YJ Choi 2007: 79-114). It first came into vogue in west-central Korea during the second half of the 4th century (350–400), and in time it spread all the way to the Yeongsan River valley in the southwest as well as to the Japanese Islands (Shirai 2001: 76-93; YJ Im 2001: 62-64; YJ Choi 2007: 79-114; SO Jeong 2012: 109-134). Another ceramic object unique to the southwest culture was a U-shaped guard attached to the opening of cooking ovens. This and the *jojokmun* pottery serve as archaeological markers for the Later Mahan people's migratory routes and destinations, particularly in the Archipelago (Fig. 4.6) (Ichimura 2004: 48-49).

After 400, as the interactions of Later Mahan and Paekche increased, the pottery of the southwest became increasingly hybridized; consequently, Later Mahan pottery is sometimes called Mahan/Paekche pottery (Fig. 4.7). Noteworthy is the barrel-shaped vessel with an opening on its top, called *dogi janggun* in modern Korea. Found throughout Paekche and Later Mahan, it was influenced by a Chinese vessel of similar shape, called *jianxinghu*, of the Han Dynasty and used in Paekche and Later Mahan for holding liquid and often for funerary or religious rituals (NH Shin 2019: 252-253).

In Kaya, the stoneware pottery first appeared around 300 as an advanced form of the hard-fired grey-bluish (*gyeongjil*) earthenware of the Samhan period, gradually becoming its dominant cultural feature during 300–562 (Fig. 4.8) (GJUB 1997: 55-80). Kaya potters employed the same technology as used by their Silla counterparts in the production of their stoneware, including potter's wheel and high firing, sloping tunnel-type kilns designed to achieve reduction or deoxidation at high heat of 1100–1200 °C, or even higher (Barnes 1992: 197-208; SJ Lee 1991: 251-258).

Kaya stoneware was produced primarily for mortuary rituals, that is, to be buried with the dead, among the elites. As such, its repertoire included pottery stands, mounted dishes, long-necked jars with stand, and cups with or without handles.

A prominent feature of the Kaya stoneware, as in the case of Silla and Paekche, was the decorated mounted stands in varying forms, sizes, and heights. Attached to the pottery stands were vessels ranging from a large basin or brazier to small dishes, which were intended to hold a variety of funerary offerings. Always found in the tombs of high elites they were made primarily for funerary rituals related to material offerings to the dead (GKIB 1999: 10-11).

The unusually tall tubular pottery stands have been found normally in the tombs of the highest elites throughout the Kaya region, suggesting that they were used as a symbol of high socio-political position of the dead. Their geographical distribution reveals the political and trade relationships existing among regional polities (CS Park 1999: 93-106).

Initially Kaya stoneware was similar to that of Silla in vessel form, style, and types. But after 400, they began to exhibit distinctly different forms and decorations, as shown in the stoneware produced at Ham'an and Goryeong. The elements deemed uniquely Kaya included mounted dishes with trumpet-

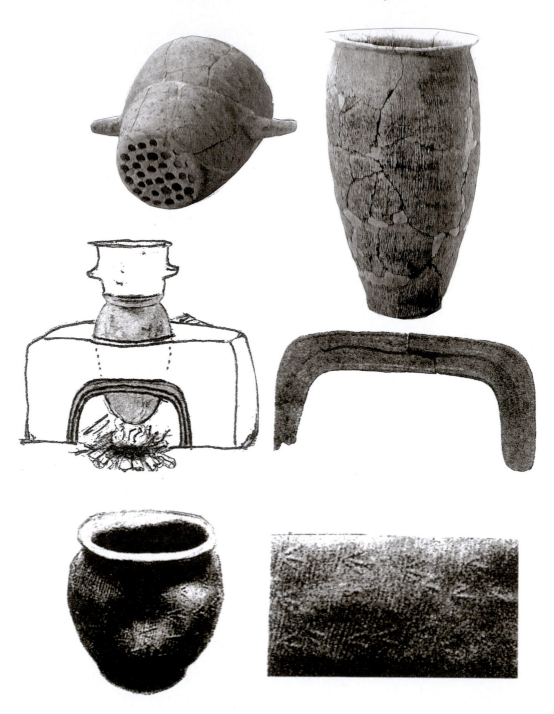

Fig. 4.6. Later Mahan kitchenware, an oven frontal guard, and jojokmun (bird foot prints) design (GNB 2013: 59, 106). Photo credit: National Naju Museum.

Fig. 4.7. Vessel types of Later Mahan/Paekche stoneware. **Top A:** A pottery stand holding a jar from Suchon-ni, c. 450 (stand only, height, 21.0cm). **Top B:** Stand and jar from Nonsan (height, 60cm). **Top C:** Mounted jar from Gongju (GGOB 2006: 141; GBUB 1992, #51; GGOB 1981: #84). **Middle A:** *Janggun (barrel-shaped)* jar from Gwangju (height, 14.1cm). **Middle B:** A jar with a side hole from Muan (height, 20.5cm). **Middle C:** A storage jar from Wanju (height, 24.5cm) (GJEB 2009: 164, 176-177). **Bottom A:** Two pedestaled mounted bowls, one with a lid, from Geumsan (heights, 12.3cm, 6.5cm); two handled cups from Gongju (right, height, 6.9cm). **Bottom B:** Small dishes (most likely with lids originally) from Gongju (height, 4-8cm) (GJEB 2009: 163, 176-177; GGOB 2002: 67, 71; GGOB 2006: 161). Photo credit: Gongju National Museum and Jeonju National Museum.

Fig. 4.8. Vessel types of Kaya stoneware pottery. From Bokcheon-dong tombs, c. 400. **A:** tubular stand holding a jar from Tomb #119 (48.7cm high). **B:** stand holding a jar from Tomb #31 (mouth circ., 24.5cm; 51cm high). **C:** a stand holding a jar (44.8cm high; mouth circ., 48.2cm). **D-E:** storage jars from Tomb #57 (15.5cm high; mouth circ. 24cm), c. 350-400. **F:** mounted dishes (right, 18.1cm high). **G:** cups from Tomb #57 (right, 11.5cm high), c. 350-400. (GKIB 1999: 20; PUM 1996a: 82, 83, 86; 1996b: 130-131; GJUB 1997: 66-67). Photo credit: Kimhae National Museum, Pusan University Museum; Hanstudio.

shaped pedestals, pottery stands with vertically aligned triangular or rectangular holes, and long-necked jars decorated with wavy lines on the neck (GJUB 1997: 55-80).

The greatest significance of the Kaya stoneware is the historical role it played as the ancestor of Sue pottery, which revolutionized the ceramic industry of Kofun-period Japan. In the course of close interactions between the Wa merchants and the Kaya polities for iron trade the Japanese Archipelago learned about Kaya stoneware and its superior quality. Gradually the Kaya stoneware trickled into Kyushu and other parts of the Archipelago (Shirai 2000: 90-120).

E. Gold, Gilt-Bronze, and Silver Craftsmanship

Paekche's gold and silver craftsmanship is evidenced in the gilt-bronze crowns, funerary gilt-bronze shoes, gold and silver ornaments, and gold earrings from Paekche elite tombs of the Hanseong period as well as of the Ungjin (475–538) and the Sabi (538–660) periods (HS Lee 2006a: 166-170; BH Park 2006: 171-180). Intricately carved designs on the gilt-bronze crowns and shoes reveal that Paekche artisans had mastered the gold and silver working skills. Gold earrings of the Hanseong Paekche Period were plainer than those of Silla and Kaya, but they became more intricate in design during the Ungjin period (GJUB 1999: 78-172; GGOB 2006: 38-68).

In Paekche, its rulers used gold crowns, gold diadems, gilt bronze crowns, gold earrings, comma-shaped jades, and gilt bronze ritual shoes not only as physical symbols of their power and authority but also to define relationships between the ruling monarch and his subordinates (Fig. 4.9; HS Lee 2006a: 166-170; BH Park 2006: 171-180). As such, they awarded them to their vassals, allies, and friends (especially in the Mahan territory) as a symbol of their political relationship as evidenced in the archaeological remains of local elite tombs at Yongweon-ri in Cheonan, Suchon-ni in Gongju, and Shinbong-dong in Cheongju, Shinchon-ni in Bannam, Bujang-ri in Seosan, and elsewhere. More often than not, the crowns awarded to the local vassals were those of the gilt bronze type and decorated long swords of a phoenix head design or a damascened ring pommel. Dragon designs were normally reserved for the kings.

In Kaya, its artisans perfected gold craftsmanship as in the case of their Silla counterparts, their immediate neighbour. But unlike the Silla crowns, which were all made of gold and for ritual purpose, those of Kaya were of gilt-bronze. They were also simpler in design and more practical. The gold earrings of Kaya were as elegantly designed as those of Silla, but unlike Silla earrings, the hoops holding various decorative attachments were all slender.

F. The Culture of Swords

The interstate wars, begun during the 4th century, resulted in a martial culture emphasizing lethal weapons of war including daggers, spears, swords, arrow points, and military helmets and body armor (Figs. 4.1–4.4). Particularly prominent among them were the long swords with various pommel designs, including circle, palmetto, phoenix, dragon, and phoenix-dragon combination (HS Lee 2004, 2006a, 2006b; JB Gu 1996). They served not only as weapons but also as symbols of power and official positions.

In particular, long swords, elegantly decorated with a dragon or phoenix head in gold and/or silver or with a damascened ring pommel (Fig. 4.10) were used to seal and symbolize the political relationship between Paekche's central government and its allies or local administrators. As such, they functioned as instruments of political communication in the courts of Paekche and Silla (BC Woo 2015: 104-139; JY Seong 2006: 209-227; HS Lee 1997: 1-37).

A number of such swords have been found in the 6th century elite tombs of Late Kofun period in Nagasaki, Fukuoka, Okayama, Osaka, Chiba, and Nara (Fukuoka-shi Hakubutsukan 2004: 62, 92, 128).

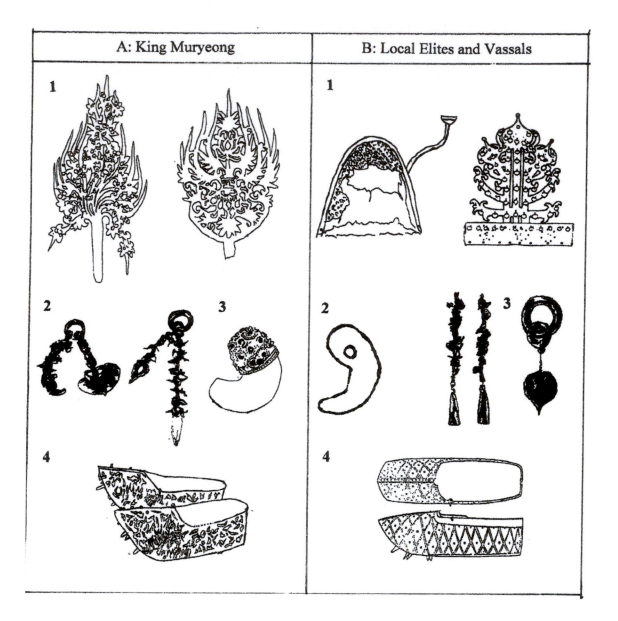

A: King Muryeong	B: Local Elites and Vassals

Fig. 4.9. Paekche instruments of political communication I. **A:** from King Munyeong's tomb: **1.** Left, gold crown diadem of the king; Right, gold crown diadem of the queen (heights, 30.7cm). **2.** Gold earrings (right, 11.8cm long). **3.** A gold-capped comma-shaped jade (3.5cm long). **4.** Gilt bronze ritual shoes (35 cm long). **B:** From local elites' tombs: **1.** Gilt bronze crowns: Left, from Ipjeon-ni (13.7cm high); Right, from Shinchon-ni Tomb #9 (25.5cm high). **2.** A plain comma-shaped jade from Shinchon-ni Tomb #9. **3.** Gold earrings: Left, from Ipjeon-ni (10 cm long); Right, from Beopcheon-ri (3.8cm long). **4.** Gilt bronze ritual shoes from Shinchon-ni Tomb #9 (29.7cm long) (after: GJUB 1999: 46, 112, 113, 122,123,127, 129, 136; GGWB 1988b: 251, 309).

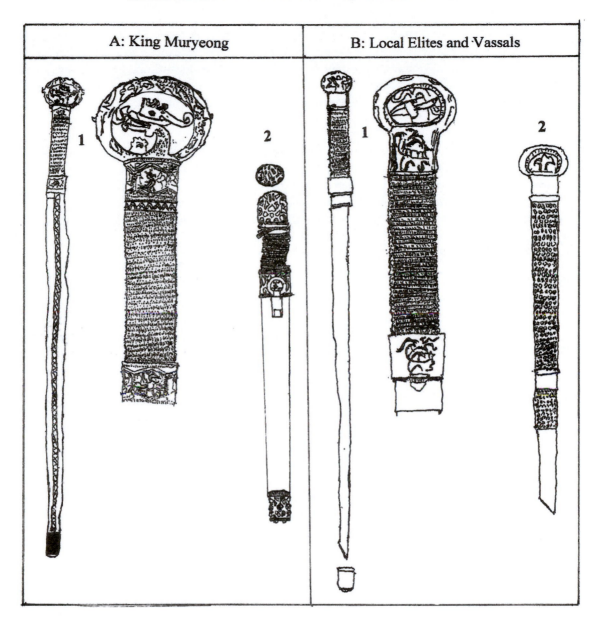

Fig. 4.10. Paekche instruments of political communication II: Decorated swords and daggers in gold and silver inlaid sheaths. **A:** from King Munyeong's tomb in Gongju **1.** A long sword decorated with a dragon's head (82cm long) and the enlarged view of its circular pommel decoration (after GJUB 1999: 124). **2.** A decorated dagger in gold and silver inlaid sheaths (16.5 cm long) (after GGOB 2004: 41) **B:** from a local elite Shinchon-ni Tomb #9 **1.** A long sword decorated with a phoenix head (89 cm long) and the enlarged view of its circular pommel decoration (GGWB 1988b: 99). **2.** A decorated dagger with a "three leaves" pommel (20.9 cm long) (after GGWB 1988b: 99).

The prestige goods of the Paekche elites, including the elaborately decorated long swords, were all made by skilled Paekche artisans in Hanseong, the Paekche capital, as well as at local elite centers (AS Moon 2007: 33-51; BC Woo 2015: 104-139). No precedents of the elegantly decorated swords, for example, have been found in southern China with which Paekche maintained close diplomatic and cultural contacts. Consequently, they are considered to have developed in Paekche (OY Kwon 2005: 179-180).

In the 5th century, Paekche' decorated swords diffused to Kaya where Kaya's skilled gold and silver craftsmen created more elegant swords (HS Lee 2006b). The handles were partly wrapped with exquisitely engraved sheets of gold and partly by fine gold threads. The pommels consisted of a ring and cast designs of a dragon, a phoenix, or a combination of a dragon and a phoenix taking up the central place of the ring. The sheaths were inlaid with silver and enclosed with flat gold bands.

G. Mortuary Architecture

During the Hanseong Period (c. 300–475), Paekche royal families first built *mokkwan bongtobun* (earthen mound tombs containing wood coffins), and later in the middle of the 4th century, as Paekche grew in its political power, they began to replace them with pyramid-shaped piled stone tombs (*kidanshik jeokseok-chong*), similar to those of Koguryo. As late as 1916, more than 60 such tombs existed on the south bank of the Han River within the boundary of modern Seoul City. Today only four remain (SB Park 2000: 133-148).

Beginning in the late 4th century, some Paekche elites began to construct corridor tombs called *heonghyeolshik seokshil-myo* (stone-lined or stone-framed chamber with a side entrance) in the vicinity of Paekche capital and at other early Paekche sites including Gwang'am-dong, Shinbong-dong, Ipjeom-ni, Mahari, Beopcheon-ri, and Suchon-ri.

Inspired by Koguryo and/or Han Chinese elite tombs with a side entrance/corridor leading to the burial chamber, the Paekche corridor tombs were intended to accommodate multiple uses (NS Lee 2000: 149-157; GMUY 2008: 307-309; JY Seong 2006: 209-227). After 475 BC, they became the dominant tumuli for all Paekche elites including the kings and their family.

Kaya's elite mortuary architecture also underwent formal changes in time. Its early form, as observed among the elite graves of Daeseongdong in Kimhae, dated to the 3rd–4th century, consisted of a large underground wood-framed chamber with no raised mound. Normally built on a ridge, they contained a rich array of prestige goods including horse trappings, body armor, helmet, and goods imported from abroad (GMUY 2008: 263-264). They also had associated graves containing human sacrifices.

Beginning in the 5th century, the Kaya elites began to build, also on mountain ridges overlooking elite settlements below, mounded tombs of varying sizes, as in the case of Jisandong graves of the Dae Kaya elites in Goryeong. Normally, under a raised circular mound were multiple elongated rectangular burial pits lined with stones. In some cases, smaller associated pit graves were built near the main raised mound burial. Tomb #44, a large raised circular mound, 27 m in diameter and 3.6 m high, had three burial pits under the center of the mound and 32 smaller stone-lined pits surrounding it. The central pit: 9.4 m long and 1.75 m wide, belonged to the highest elite of Dae Kaya. In the 32 smaller pits were buried his servants as human sacrifices (GMUY 2008: 1116-7; CS Park 2002: 195-218), although this interpretation is contestable. The circular raised mound tombs of Kaya contained a rich array of valued goods including iron body armor, helmets, and long swords.

Among the Later Mahan polities on the west coast, the elites continued to use *jugumyo*, which had become popular during the Sam Han and Early Mahan periods. After 300, the *jugumyo* burial mounds as well as the wooden coffins placed in them became quite large as seen at Bujang-ni and Giji-ri in Seosan; Sanweol-li in Gunsan; Sang'un-ni in Wanju; Haripseok I in Buan; and Bongdeok I, Mandong, Namsan-ri, and Seongnam-ri in Gochang. Because the *jugumyo* at these sites had square-shaped raised mounds, they are also called *bungumyo* ("burials with a raised mound"). In terms of architectural process, their builders first created a mound and next placed a coffin, wooden or jar, into the mound. In order to accommodate additional burials in the course of time, they kept enlarging the mound, as archaeologically observed in Tomb #9 at Shinchon-ri and Tomb #4 at Bok'am-ri (NJ Kim 2009: 34-50; GMUY 2008: 531-533).

Iron goods placed in these burials included long swords with a ring pommel, spearheads, axes, sickles, and knives. Special emphasis was placed on the iron spearheads, which formed a set together with iron axes and iron sickles. Iron tools and storage jars in the elite graves were also larger than before. The number of buried iron tools began to increase in quantity as well as in quality, especially in the case of iron spears and long iron swords. Long swords with a ring pommel, iron axes, and iron sickles were buried as a set. Iron horse bits were added to the prestige goods.

In the Yeongsan River basin of Later Mahan in the southwest, jar burials became increasingly popular. By c. 300, especially designed jar coffins, 200 cm long, were produced. By 400 some of them became as long as 280 cm (GJEB 2009: 171-187). The jar coffins were buried in impressive square- or circular-shaped mound tombs built for the ruling elites (GGWB 1988a). Tomb #9 of Shinchon-ri and Tomb #3 of Bok'am-ri are excellent examples (NJ Kim 2009: 42-45).

As Paekche's power expanded into various Mahan polities to the south, the side corridor tombs also spread widely throughout Paekche kingdom. Powerful local Mahan leaders adopted them as a symbol of their Paekcheization, as revealed in the elite burials at Beobcheon-ri in Weonju, Juseong-ni in Ochang, Shinbong-dong in Cheongju, Bugang-ni in Yeon'gi, Mihari in Hwaseong, Jeoseok-ni in Bun'gang, Ipjeom-ni in Iksan among others, (GMUY 1989b; SB Park 2001: 32; JY Seong 2006: 212, 224; GGOB 2006: 141). Finally, around 450 AD, they spread even into the Yeongsan River basin as it came increasingly under the Paekche hegemony (NJ Kim 2009: 64-96, 309-310).

Around 475 AD, keyhole tombs appeared in the Yeongsan River basin. KIM Nak-jung (2009) has provided a detailed study of these Yamato-style keyhole tombs in terms of their structure, burial goods, their relationship with the Paekche corridor tombs, and the historical context of their appearance.

Views on their background and the identity of their builders are diverse and controversial. Some (Azuma: 1995; Ju 2000: 49-99) argue for Yamato officials hired by the Paekche court, while others (Okauchi 1996: 47-48) insist the tombs were for both Yamato personages and local Later Mahan elites. IM Yongjin (2000: 157-162; 2009: 263-267) posits that the keyhole tomb builders were Mahan-origin Toraijin returning home, while KIM Nak-jung (2009: 220-221, 331) and Walsh (2017: 156) argue for local elites seeking a degree of independence during Paekche's weakness.

Emphasizing the keyhole tomb's local connection, on the basis of a ceramic analysis of Later Mahan, its political economy, and its relations with Paekche, Walsh (*Ibid.*) posits that "The use of these tombs was a localization of the exotic intended in part to intimidate societies like Baekje [sic], to remind nearer neighbors of their importance in the Peninsula's connection with the Archipelago."

According to PARK Sun-bal (2000b: 115-156) the primary factor underlying their appearance in Korea's southwest was the conflict and tension which had long been simmering between Paekche and the Later Mahan polities since the 4th century. Especially, during its existential crisis following the loss of Hanseong and its territory north of the Geum River in 475, the Paekche court was actively seeking to strengthen its hold in the Yeongsan River valley, one of Korea's richest bread baskets. To accomplish this, on one hand, it actively fostered the emergence of new loyal political elites at Bok'am-ri, away from Naju, the center of the old established local power clique, that is, the so-called Bannam clique.

On the other hand, Paekche was seeking to check the old local elites entrenched in Bannam and prevent them from possible rebellion. To accomplish this objective, the Paekche court invited a half dozen military elites from Kinki and Kyushu to station at various strategic points surrounding the traditional Post-Mahan political centers. This would explain the reason why the keyhole tombs with corridor-style burial chambers were all built in the peripheral zones surrounding the Bannam clique. Furthermore, a gilt-bronze crown and elite silver prestige goods used by Paekche for its lord-vassal relationship vis-à-vis local elites, found in the Shindeok Tumulus, one of the largest and most impressive key-hole tombs, and in Bokam-ni #3 Tomb, an impressive square mound burial, respectively, indicate that the key-hole tomb builders were in a lord-vassal relationship vis-à-vis the Paekche central government in Gongju/Buyeo as were the elites buried in the Bokam-ni #3 Tomb (NJ Kim 2009: 324-327).

By 520, about 30 years after its first appearance, the construction of the keyhole tombs in the Yeongsan River basin ended suddenly and permanently. It coincided with Paekche's resurgence during the reign of its powerful monarch, King Munyeong (r. 501–523).

H. Agriculture and Hydraulic Engineering

Favorably located in Korea's fertile plains in west and southern Korea, Paekche's primary economic base was agriculture. Under the supervision and guidance of the state, Paekche farmers reclaimed vast areas of the broad plains between the Han River and the southern coast.

Due to many rivers and streams crisscrossing the plains, Paekche farmers developed hydraulic skills with which to control the flood and tidal waters by means of dams and dykes. Also, to provide water to the cultivated paddies in times of drought they constructed reservoirs and irrigation channels. These were critical to the cultivation of wet-rice requiring water during the growing season and dry bed during its maturing period.

An integral part of the Paekche hydraulic engineering was a technology known as *buyeop gongbeop*. It entailed spreading multiple layers of organic materials and tree leaves at the base of a dam or a dike and pounded earth. As early as 300 AD, the Mahan inhabitants in the far southwest sought to control tidal waters by building the Byeokkolje Dam and a canal system. Using the same *buyeop-gongbeop* method, the Paekche engineers constructed the Pungnap Toseong, the fortification system of Paekche's first capital in modern Seoul area (WG Choi 2013: 25-30). Paekche, therefore, was in a position to provide the technology and the tools necessary for Yamato's agricultural land expansion and various public works projects during the Middle Kofun period, including the construction of great keyhole-type mound burials (Koyamada 2001: 94-97; Shiraishi 2004: 81-82).

3. Push-Pull Dynamics: Pen/Insular Crisis

A. Crisis in the Peninsula

From the beginning of the early states period, the Peninsula became embroiled in violent warfare, destruction, carnage, and waves of fleeing refugees in search of a safe haven. The violent warfare was caused primarily by the early states' desire to expand their territory.

The year of 369 was the year in which the Peninsula violently shook, commencing four hundred years of Peninsula-wide tragedies until 670. In that year, Koguryo, following its defeat of Chinese garrisons in Lelang (modern Pyongyang) and in Daifang (modern Hwanghae Province) in 313–314, invaded Paekche and subsequently fourteen more times in the period of six years between 369 and 375 alone. (For the frequent armed conflicts between Koguryo and Paekche, see Best (2006: 74-77.) In that same year, Paekche, emerging as a powerful and victorious nation, in its war against Koguryo, embarked on its conquest of Mahan, in order to expand its territory into the fertile agricultural regions to its south.

In 400, Koguryo's 50,000 heavily armed troops, supported by its cavalry, marched all the way to the southeast coast, wreaking havoc on Geumgwan Kaya in Kimhae, the leader of Kaya polities, because it was in alliance with Paekche and Wa threatening Silla, Koguryo's ally (HG Lee and RH Park 1996: 85-93).

In 475, after several more wars with Paekche, Koguryo sacked Hanseong (modern Seoul), the capital of Paekche, and burned it to the ground, forcing thousands of Paekche citizens, nobles and commoners, to flee as refugees. By 500, Koguryo had emerged as the dominant power in the Peninsula (Map 4.2).

Following the loss of their capital, the Paekche leaders fled south to Kom-naru (熊津, modern Gongju) and then to Buyeo to re-establish the fallen Paekche state. In the face of the national crisis, however, the Paekche leaders became quickly embroiled in a devastating power struggle, rebellions, and assassinations (Best 2006: 103-110).

In the meantime, following Paekche's military campaigns of 369, the Later Mahan territories in the Yeongsan River Valley of the southwest region were suffering under the shadow of Paekche's political and military over lordship for several centuries until their complete demise (SR Choi 2017a: 279-299).

In the southeastern region, Silla, long confined in a narrow valley around modern Kyongju, decided to embark on territorial expansion. In 551, with the help of Paekche, Silla invaded Koguryo to expand northward to the Han River basin. Two years later in 553, it back-stabbed Paekche itself to bring Paekche's old territory under its control. Then, for seven years (555–562), Silla warred against Kaya polities, destroying Dae Gaya in Goryeong, the last remaining Kaya polity, in 562.

Becoming mortal enemies in 553, Paekche attacked Silla the following year at the Gwansan Fortress (modern day Okcheon area). It was disastrous to Paekche, as its king (Seong, r. 523–554) was killed

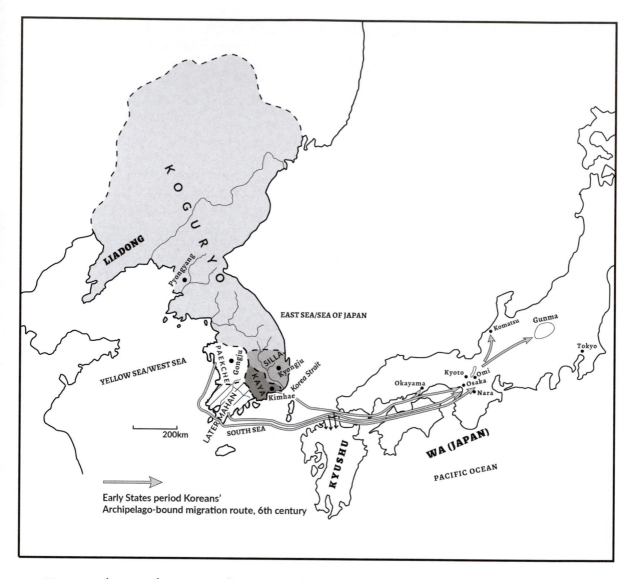

Map 4.2. Early states of Korea, c. 500 (by Lucas Pauly).

along with 30,000 Paekche troops. For revenge, Paekche invaded Silla eleven more times during 602–642.

Finally, in 660, four centuries of violence, carnage, and destruction turned the Peninsula into a hitherto unseen Armageddon. In that year, the allied forces of Silla and Tang China mounted massive assaults on Paekche from the sea and the land with several hundred thousand troops, destroying the kingdom of Paekche. This, however, was not the end of violence and carnage in the Peninsula. In 661, forces of Paekche Restoration Movement, assisted by 27,000 Wa troops dispatched by the Yamato government, attacked Silla and Tang forces, plunging the Paekche land into violent chaos once again. The war of resistance continued for three years until Silla and Tang forces prevailed in 663 (PD Yi 1977: 430; *Nihon Shoki* Tenji Year 2; Aston 1972, Vol. 2: 278-280). Seven years later, in 667, Silla and Tang did to Koguryo what they had done to Paekche.

The end of Paekche and Koguryo, however, did not bring peace to the Peninsula. In the aftermath of Koguryo's fall, Emperor Gaozong established six Tang commanderies in the Korean Peninsula, with the intention of turning them into Chinese colonies. Enraged, King Munmu of Silla declared war on Tang forces in Korea in 670. To crush Silla, Gaozong sent 200,000 reinforcements. Battles raged with more carnage and more destruction for six more years. By 676, Tang forces were defeated and withdrew to the Liadong region in Manchuria (Eckert *et al.* 1990: 43). This was the historical context which gave rise to the Toraijin of the Middle-Late Kofun period.

As indicated in the preceding pages, the majority of the Kofun-period Toraijin before 600 AD came from the southern part of the Peninsula, specifically from Paekche, Kaya, and Later Mahan polities, which were in a close relationship with the Wa people through exchange and interaction and/or through alliance. For Kaya and Later Mahan, the relationship was established already in the prehistoric and protohistoric times (C Inoue 2008: 236-255; Takesue 2008: 258-307; CH Lee 2011: 34-45; JS Jo 2019: 70-74). For Paekche, its formal friendship with Wa began in 371 during the reign of Paekche king, Geunchogo (INOUE Mitsusada 1973: 357-359; S Nakamura 1981: 48-49; Brown 1993: 121-122; T Tanaka 2001: 5; Kimura 2005: 74-80; Best 2006: 67-68).

Koguryo, occupying the northern half of the Peninsula, with its capital at Pyongyang, remained an adversary of Paekche, Kaya, and Wa throughout the Kofun period. While some merchants and diplomats of Koguryo visited Japan, little is known about Toraijin from Koguryo, prior to 600 AD except a few Buddhist priests on a religious or educational mission. As such, the role of Toraijin from Koguryo prior its demise in 668 AD was minimal in comparison to that of Kaya and Paekche. (S Nakamura 1981: 117-118) Likewise, Silla, though located in the southeast, relatively close to Japan, generally maintained an adversarial relationship with the Yamato elites in the Kinki region until the end of the 7th century; consequently, the number of Toraijin from Silla was limited (S Nakamura *Ibid.*).

B. Crisis in the Archipelago

At the same time, a crisis of different nature was emerging in the Archipelago. For more than a millennium, with the advent of agriculture based on wet-rice farming and metallurgy (bronze and iron), the Wa people had been making a steady progress culturally, economically, and socially. By around 250 AD, there had appeared throughout the Archipelago numerous organized polities as evidenced by the elite burials bearing bronzes and iron and the polities being mentioned in ancient Chinese records (the *Weizhi* section of the *Sanguozhi*, Chronicles of the Three Kingdoms, 220–265).

In competition with one another, these growing polities required tools and technology essential to their economic development as well as advanced weaponry critical to their military advantage (Takata 2014: 181-182). For nearly three hundred years since the 1st century BC, they had been acquiring advanced cultural items from China and Chinese traders at Lelang in the northwestern Korean Peninsula, but they ran into complications when the Han Dynasty disintegrated in 220, plunging China into chaos amidst interminable warfare among numerous rival petty states. Then in 313–314, the Chinese trade centers in Lelang and Daifang completely disappeared as the newly emerging state of Koguryo subdued and incorporated them into its territory.

Consequently, for nearly three centuries until about 600, culturally and commercially cut off from China, the growing number of Wa elites had to turn to the Peninsula. Okazaki states (1993: 308-309):

> The confused situation in China forced Japan to turn to Korea as a source of high culture, technology, and luxury items... Perhaps, the most important reason that the Japanese were anxious to maintain relations with southern Korea... was to guarantee access to Korean sources of iron.

Iron, scarce in Japan, was critical to farming and warfare (Okazaki 1993: 308-309). In the 3rd century, Kuya-guk on the southeast coast of the Peninsula was the iron capital of East Asia. Also, to the Wa elites, the southern Peninsula was known as "a land of gold and silver...a land of precious treasures" which the Wa elites coveted as prestige goods (*Nihon Shoki*: Ojin section, Year 15-16; Takata 2014: 30-32).

Without access to Chinese goods, the emerging elites of the Early Kofun period in the Kinki Core Region now redoubled their trading activities with Kuya-guk (Geumgwan Kaya) in the Kimhae-Pusan area to acquire Peninsular iron and other precious goods (Azuma 1999: 212, 429-433). This is evidenced by the presence of Early Kofun materials in the wood-framed elite burials at Daeseong-dong dated to 250–400. They include bronze staff ferrules, bronze spiral bosses, talc arrow point-shaped objects, curved beads of precious stones (KC Shin 1993: 99-119; Azuma 1999: 429-430; GMUY 2008: 263-264; Barnes 2015: 341). This exchange connection with the Kimhae–Pusan area also would end soon, following Koguryo's invasion of the southeast coastal area in 400, crippling Kuya-guk in Kimhae.

The two events, namely, the demise of Chinese trading posts in the Peninsula in 313–314 and Koguryo's crippling of Kuya-guk constituted a crisis among the emerging elites in the Kinki Core Region (Kyoto–Osaka–Nara) bent on establishing their hegemony over all the other local domains (H Suzuki 1996: 79-84). The expulsion of the Chinese trading posts in Lelang and Daifang deprived them of any access to Chinese goods. The demise of Kuya-guk cut them off from their primary source of iron (agricultural and industrial tools, advanced weapons, and especially raw iron) (TS Kim 2014b: 46-47).

The crisis equally affected the elites in northern Kyushu who had been acting for centuries as middle men in the iron market between the raw iron producers in the southeastern Peninsula and Wa elites throughout the western and central Archipelago. In order to overcome the crisis, the elites in the Kinki Core Region pursued a two-pronged approach. On the one hand, they sought to secure trading partners among the Kaya polities not affected by the Koguryo invasion of 400 AD, such as the outlying Goseong So Kaya, Ara Kaya, and Dae Kaya of Goryeong as well as among Later Mahan polities in Korea's southwest region and Paekche in the west-central Peninsula (GJEB 1994; KC Shin 2000: 190-191; SC Ha 2011: 95-140; TS Kim 2014a: 252, 258-264). On the other hand, as the Peninsula became increasingly embroiled in violent inter-state wars, the Kinki elites eagerly welcomed its people seeking to take refuge in the Archipelago – not only for their skills and technology to develop and advance their culture but also their military/political standing (Shiraishi 2004: 9-14).

II. *IMAKI NO TEHITO* ARRIVE IN THE ARCHIPELAGO

1. Late 4th – Early 5th Century: "The Century of Toraijin"

Even after the collapse of the Han Dynasty in 220 AD the Wa elites continued to import Chinese goods from Lelang and Daifang (See Chapter Three: II, 4: Neuk-do/Kimhae – Kyushu/Kinki Connections), but that also came to an end in 313–314 when Koguryo sacked the Chinese trading posts and incorporated them into its territory.

 In 369, Paekche, threatened by aggressive Koguryo from the north, began its military incursions southward into Mahan territory. The clash between Paekche invaders and Mahan people resulted in the uprooting of numerous Mahan elites and their people.

Even as Paekche was invading Mahan, putting the people of Mahan on the run, Koguryo began to invade Paekche from behind. Between 369 and 400, Koguryo invaded the latter nine times (in 369, 371, 475, 377, 386, 391, twice in 392, and in 396). The Koguryo–Paekche war of 396 was most devastating. After humiliating Ashin, the king of Paekche, in his own capital (modern Seoul), Gwanggaeto carried away more than a thousand Paekche citizens including ten of the highest Paekche officials. Four years later, in 400, he invaded Kaya in Kimhae on the southeast coast, an ally of Paekche, ravaging the wealthy seaport.

These frequent wars during the second half of the 4th century left major population centers in the southern Peninsula devastated, resulting in a huge number of refugees. Among them were farmers, merchants and traders, dam builders, iron smiths, horse breeders and horsemen, stoneware pottery makers, weavers, gold and silver craftsmen, and defeated elites among others. They were victims of an existential crisis beyond their control and desperate refugees, very similar to millions of refugees of the Middle East in the 21st century.

In order to escape the conflagration, they headed to the sea to reach a land beyond – believed to be safer, as refugees often do – as individuals, families, tribes, or organized bands led by defeated elites, generals, and village heads. Almost always, their destination beyond the sea was the Archipelago of the Wa people across the South Sea and the Korea/Tsushima Strait. In light of the massive influx of the new Toraijin, Kameda calls the 4th–5th century "the century of Toraijin."

In their quest for the valued Peninsular goods and advanced technology, the Wa elites throughout the Archipelago welcomed and accommodated them, giving rise to Toraijin communities all over the Archipelago. In the new land, the refugees would re-establish themselves as farmers, merchants and traders, potters, iron technicians, horse breeders, horsemen, dam builders, gold and silver craftsmen, and weavers. The Wa people in the Archipelago called them *Imaki no Tehito* (今來才技: "recently arrived skilled artisans") (*Nihon Shoki*, Yuraku 7th Year, 8th Month; OFCAH 2004).

The Toraijin phenomenon was both encouraged and enhanced by the close friendship and alliance among Paekche, Kaya, and the Yamato court. They were trading partners and comrades in arms in the face of aggressive Koguryo and Silla, its ally. Paekche and Kaya were severely punished by Koguryo in 400 for threatening Silla with the help of Wa, and the latter welcomed their friends in trouble. In reality, however, the Archipelago elites needed the Peninsular peoples and their skills; accordingly, they actively welcomed them, helping them settle in their domain. This was particularly so with the Tsukushi elites in Fukuoka, Kibi elites in Okayama, and the Yamato elites in Kinki, seeking to establish an upper hand socio-politically in the Archipelago, as evidenced in the concentration of 5th century Toraijin in three locations (Ichimura 2004: 48-49; Kameda 2000: 2).

First to arrive in Japan were the people of the west-central Peninsula affected by the military clashes in the Han River basin – evidenced by the sudden appearance in Kyushu and the Kinki Core Region of Paekche and Later Mahan cooking culture (K Shirai 2001: 81-82; H Yoshi'i 2002: 112-118; Ichimura 2004: 48-49). Soon the people of Kaya and Paekche were flooding into the Japanese Islands in ever increasing numbers (Ishiwatari 2001: 81-87, 134-139).

Among the most conspicuous identifiers of this influx are the reddish-brown *yeonjil* earthenware and unique vessel forms from Later Mahan polities in the west-central and southwestern Peninsula that had been produced there since the 2nd century AD or even earlier. Pottery types included cooking vessels (steamers) with ox-horn handles, storage jars decorated with striated or lattice designs, jars with perforated handles on their shoulders, the *jojokmun* pottery decorated with bird-foot prints, and U-shaped guard for cooking ovens (Fig. 4.11; Ichimura 2004: 48; YJ Choi 2007: 79-114; H Yoshi'i 2002: 112-128). Called *karashiki* or *kanshiki* (Korean type) pottery in Japan, these types are decisive archaeological markers of Korean settlements in Japan during the Kofun period (K Tanaka 2004: 88-95).

Other archaeological indicators of Toraijin settlements include residential buildings equipped with an attached cooking oven and supported by four posts, buildings with thick walls (*okabe*), and buildings equipped with an *ondol,* an old traditional Korean under-floor heating system that survived well into recent historical times (Fig. 4.12) (Kameda 2003a: 1-14, Kameda 2004a: 75-94, Kameda 2005: 1-16, Kameda 2016: 283-321; GGOB 1999: 60).

Still other decisive archaeological markers are iron nails and braces and abacus bead-shaped spindle whorls. The iron nails and braces were made and used by the immigrants for building their wood coffins (Kameda 2004b: 29-38). The abacus-bead-shaped spindle whorls (Fig. 5.8) were popular in the southern Peninsula during the 3rd–6th century and are found at Toraijin settlements throughout Kyushu and the Inland Sea regions normally with "Korean type" pottery (SKAKH 2001: 22; K Tanaka 2004: 88-95).

These cultural features from the Peninsula moved into the Japanese Archipelago not as isolated artifacts or trade goods but as components of well-established and integrated cultural systems of the Torai immigrants (Kameda 2003a: 1-14, Kameda 2003b: 55-65, Kameda 2005: 1-16; Kameda 2011: 116-119; K Tanaka 2004: 88-95). According to the archaeological criteria developed by KAMEDA Shuichi for Toraijin settlements during the Kofun period, immigrants settled in various parts of the Archipelago, all the way from Fukuoka in northern Kyushu to Okayama on the Inland Sea, to the Kyoto–Osaka–Nara area, to Gunma north of Tokyo, and even to Sendai in northeastern Honshu (Kameda 2003a: 1-14, Kameda 2003b 55-65, Kameda 2005: 1-16).

As people from Later Mahan polities, Kaya and Paekche settled into the Japanese Archipelago, they put to use the knowledge and skills they had brought with them for themselves, for previous immigrant communities they joined, for their Japanese neighbors, and particularly for the local Japanese elites

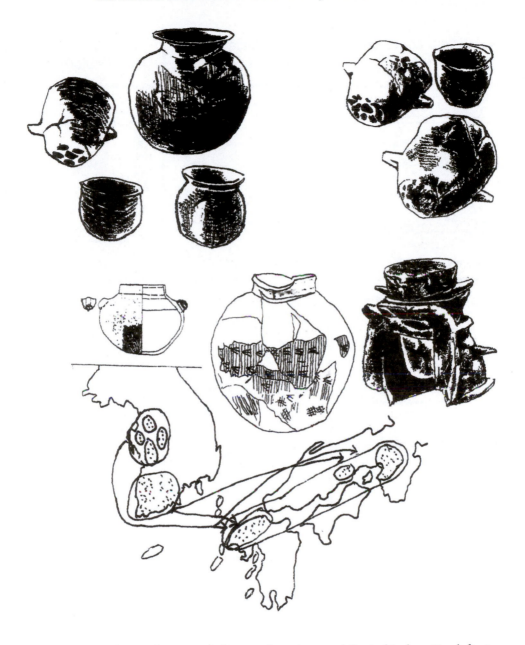

Fig. 4.11. Later Mahan cooking vessels from southern Korea and the Archipelago. **Top left:** steamer, jars decorated with striated impressions, and goblets from Nagahara in Osaka (after OYBH 2004: 47). **Top right:** Later Mahan cooking vessels and goblet from Yao Minami in Osaka (after OYBH 2004: 47). **Middle:** Later Mahan jar with perforated handles on shoulders from Fukuoka and Osaka, a Mahan storage jar with jojokmun (bird foot prints) design from Furyu, and a miniature cooking oven from Osaka (after Shirai 2001, 86, 90; Tenri University Sankokan Museum 2014; SKAKH 2001: 44). **Bottom:** geographical distributions of Later Mahan pottery in Korea and Japan (after YJ Choi 2007: 83).

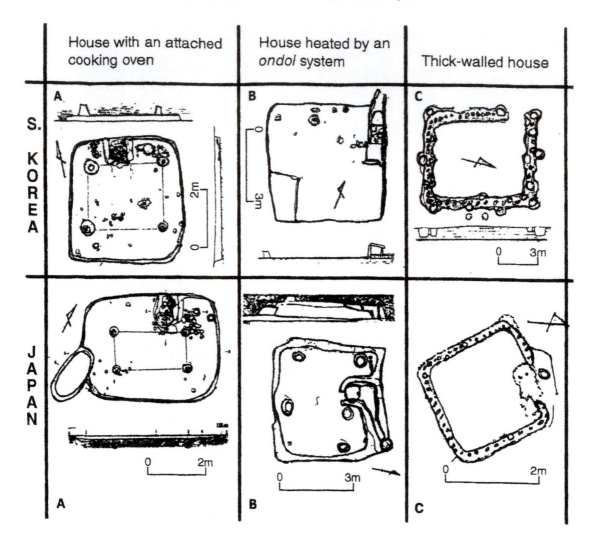

	House with an attached cooking oven	House heated by an *ondol* system	Thick-walled house

Fig. 4.12. Later Mahan/Paekche residential types from Korean southwest and the Archipelago. **Top:** Later Mahan/Paekche residential building types found in Korea. **A** (after Mokpo National University Museum 2003: 247). **B:** YC Lee 2002: 48. **C** (after JY So 2004: 68). **Bottom:** Later Mahan/Paekche residential building types found in Middle Kofun Japan. **A** (after Kameda 2004a: 70). **B** (after Kameda 2003a: 3). **C** (after GGOB 1999: 60).

who were eagerly seeking new skills and technology in their competitive relationships with other local and regional leaders (SKAKH 2001: 72-73; Kameda 2003a: 1-14, Kameda 2005: 1-16; Shiraishi 2004: 7-13).

2. Middle 5th–6th Century

The earth-shaking turbulence on the Korean Peninsula was intensified in the latter part of the 5th century when Koguryo invaded Paekche in 475 AD and burned down its capital in Seoul, killing its king and wreaking havoc upon Paekche citizens. The kingdom of Paekche was crippled, and the people of Paekche fled in all directions. Many of them sailed across the South Sea and the Tsushima Strait, settling in Kyushu, Kibi, and Kinki (Kameda 2011: 116-120). The Japanese Archipelago was the most logical direction of their flight not only because of its close geographic proximity but also because of Paekche's long-established relationship with the Yamato court, going back to 369 AD or even earlier.

Other surviving elites of Paekche moved to a town in the middle reaches of the Geum River, re-establishing their new (temporary) capital at a river town called Komnaru (Bear's Landing) (rendered in Chinese as Ungjin, 熊津), located on the south bank of the river. During those fateful days of Paekche, the Yamato court reached out to help it re-establish itself. In 479, following the sudden death of Paekche king, Samgeun, Yuryaku, the king of Yamato, made a special arrangement for the return of Malda, a Paekche prince residing in Yamato to Ungjin, accompanied by 500 Wa soldiers, to assume Paekche kingship (*Nihon Shoki*: Yuryaku year 23, 7th month). For 22 years until 501, as King Dongseong (r. 479–501), the Paekche prince from Yamato successfully restored Paekche's socio-political stability.

In reaching out to Paekche during its national crisis, the Yamato court was hoping to establish a steady, reliable partner and source for the acquisition of iron and advanced technology essential to its emergence as a nation-state. Yamato's turning to Paekche at this particular time was prompted by Silla's aggressive encroachment on the lower Nakdong River basin, the traditional source of iron for Wa since the Yayoi period. The close relationship between the Paekche and Yamato court, further solidified during the reign of Yuryaku and Dongseong, enormously facilitated the migration of Paekche refugees to the Archipelago.

Beginning early in the latter part of the 5th century, Paekche-style corridor tombs (tombs containing an underground gallery chamber for multiple burials) (Fig. 4.13) began to appear in the Kinki region (Hashimoto and Kiba 2004: 86-87; Mizuno 1981: 143-158; K Mori 1982: 111-113; Mizoguchi 2013: 300-308). Their number increased explosively by 550 AD in the form of "tumuli clusters" (Mizoguchi 2013: 300). They include Takayasu Senzuka Kofun, Hiraoyama Senzuka Kofun, Asuka Senzuka Kofun, Toki Senzuka Kofun, Niizawa Senzuka Kofun, and Ichisuka Kofun, among others (Ishiwatari 2002: 238-239) (see Map 5.2).

In the Archipelago, the people from Paekche and Later Mahan polities as well as their culture were becoming homogenized as in the Peninsula after 300. Thus, many of the Paekche-style corridor tombs and Later Mahan polities cooking wares are found together (SKAKH 2001: 69-71). In Tumuli #1, #2, #3, #4, and #5 at Akao Kuzuredani was found a large number of prestige goods including Sueki, bronze mirrors, iron daggers, knives, gold earrings, and numerous objects of jade and glass. All except Tumulus # 2 (a circular mounded tomb), were of the square type (Hashimoto and Kiba 2004: 86-87). This reflected the 5th-century elite mortuary practices of the Later Mahan polities/Paekche in the Yeongsan River basin in southwest Korea. Also, some of the elite tombs among the Senzuka burial groups were impressively large. Differentiated burials, in terms of the size of the tombs and prestige goods indicate that there existed a hierarchical organization within the Toraijin society (Mizoguchi 2013: 300-304). Hashimoto and Kiba (2004) believe that the five tumuli bearing the rare prestige goods belonged to the chiefs of the Toraijin society.

Senzuka means 'thousand tombs.' It is a hyperbolic term used to describe the extraordinarily large numbers of ancient burials concentrated on hilly ridges in several discrete locations in Kinki. By the beginning of the 6th century, several huge tumuli groups had appeared southwest of Biwa Lake

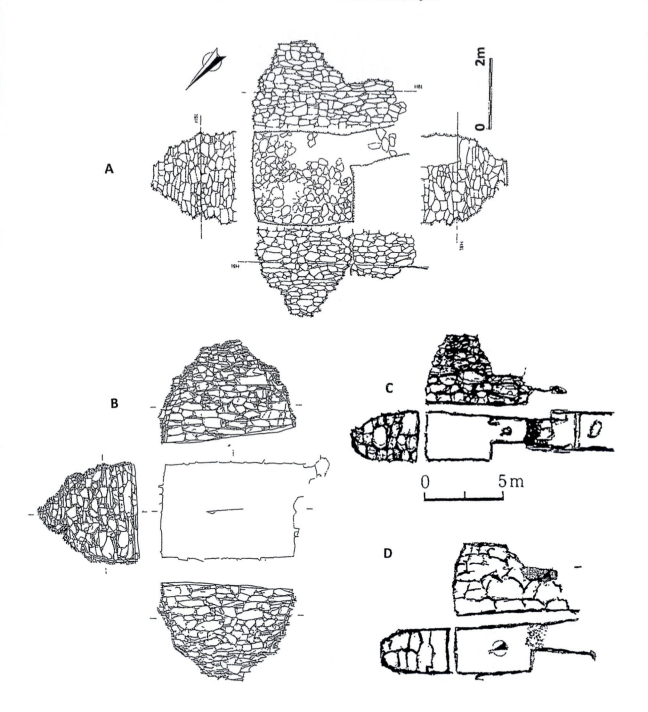

Fig. 4.13. Paekche corridor-style tombs in the Peninsula and the Archipelago. **A:** Corridor-style tomb with a side entrance leading to its underground burial chamber, Ipjeom-ri in Iksan (after Iksan-shi 2004, 60). **B-D:** Corridor-style tombs in southern Nara basin, 5th century (B: Miyayamazuka Kofun. C. Yorakukansuzuka Kofun. D: Numayama Kofun) (after Yoshi'i 2001: 116; Ban 2018: 126).

between the Yamagami-cho and Sakamoto districts of Otsu City. Some of the groups comprise more than 200 tombs. Thus far 700–800 tombs, many of which are the corridor-style tombs, have been identified. There are still several hundred burials to be excavated, suggesting that more than a thousand burials are located in this one area alone (Hori 2009: 13-22).

The exact number of Toraijin coming to the Kinki Core Region will never be known, but considering that those buried in many Senzuka (cemeteries of "thousand tombs") belonged to the Toraijin from the southwestern Peninsula and their descendants, Ishiwatari (2002, 239) postulates that at least a million people from the Peninsula arrived in the Archipelago during the years 475–600, a period of 125 years.

The tumuli clusters also suggest that the Peninsular immigrants not only maintained their clan solidarity through their own mortuary system but also organized themselves hierarchically according to clan lineages as they had done in their old homeland.

3. Major Toraijin Settlements

A. The Kinki Core Region (Osaka, Nara, Kyoto)

For more than a millennium since the 9th century BC, Peninsular peoples had headed south to the island of Kyushu and settled there to escape a crisis of one kind or another. Beginning in the latter part of the 4th century, however, they shifted their migration destination to the Kinki Core Region by way of the Inland Sea. Soon the Nara, Osaka, Kyoto, and Otsu region became saturated with the Toraijin (Map 4.3). Settling there, they developed the Kinki Core Region economically and technologically.

It was in the context of the Toraijin econo-technological dynamism that the Yamato elites were emerging as the dominant political power in the Archipelago, even constructing the great keyhole-shaped tumuli of Mozu and Furuichi. "In truth," states HIRANO Kunio (2018: 98, italics and brackets added):

> during the 5th century the Kikajin [immigrants] were concentrated in Yamato (Nara basin), Yamashiro, Kawachi, and Settsu among other locations, which were the political base of the [Yamato] royal power... Some of them were appointed as government officials. Others paid taxes, farmed the public lands, or constructed dams and dikes. Still others produced [essential] goods for the state. *It is not an exaggeration to state that the Yamato government owed them for its phenomenal development (飛躍的な發展) during the 5th-6th century.*

a. Toraijin in the Osaka (Kawachi) Plains

Nearly 100 sites around Kawachi Lake, between the Yodogawa River in the north and the Furuichi-Mozu districts in the south, have been identified as those bearing Korean *yeonjil* (earthenware) and stoneware (*dojil togi*) remains of the 5th–6th century (K Tanaka 2004: 90-91) (Map 4.3). The *yeonjil* pottery vessels, in particular, were an integral part of the Mahan/Paekche people's culinary culture; consequently, there is a consensus among Japanese scholars that archaeological sites bearing a significant amount of the *yeonjil pottery* remains were Toraijin settlements (K. Tanaka 2004: 88-95).

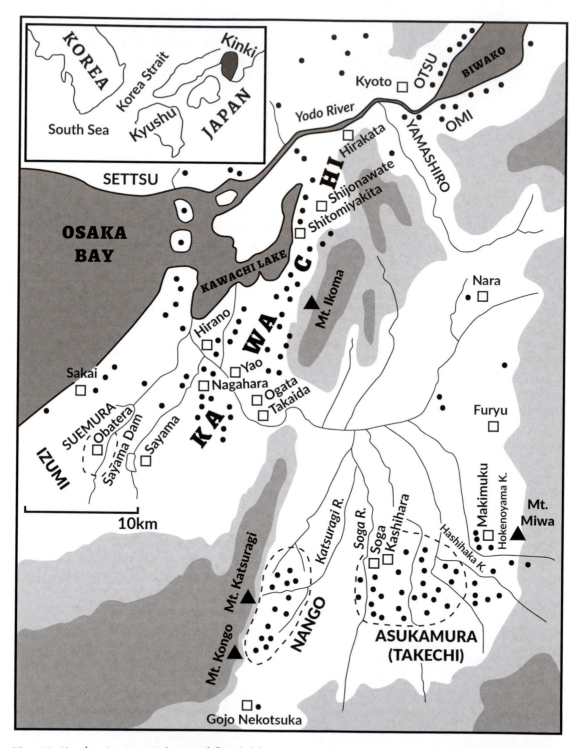

Map 4.3. Sites bearing Toraijin's yeonjil (kanshiki) pottery or other Toraijin cultural remains in the Kinki Core Region during the Kofun period, AD 400-700 (by Lucas Pauly). (After Kyomi Tanaka 2004: 91; SKAKH 2001: 24-48; Kyoto Bunka Hakubutsukan 1989: 118-148; Hori 2009: 13-22; Kaneyasu 1997: 63-66).

Beginning to arrive in this area in the latter part of the 4th century (Ichimura 2004: 48), the bearers of the Peninsula's earthenware and stoneware helped develop the Kawachi Lake basin, the home of ancient Kawachi, Izumi, and Settsu, which in time became the modern city of Osaka.

During the 5th–6th century, the Toraijin population became firmly established in the Osaka Plains as evidenced by numerous Toraijin settlements (Obatera, Doyama, Kosaka, Yottsuike, Dokiminami, Kokanda, Daisen-nakamachi, Fukada, Nagahara, and Tsujino etc.; cf. Pearson 2016: 46-48) and equally numerous Toraijin cemeteries (Doki Senzuka, Nonoi Kofungun, Ushi'ishi Kofungun, Hino-Otsukahara Kofungun, Shinoda Senzuka, Takaida Yokoana Kofungun, Doyama Kofungun, and Ichitsuka Kofungun etc.) (SKHB 2001: 95-98; Kamiobayashi 2004: 61-68).

The earthenware and stoneware belonged to the Later Mahan people of the Peninsula's southwest and the people of Kaya of the southeast respectively, suggesting that the earliest Kofun period Toraijin came from the Yeongsan River basin in Korea's southwest and as well as from the Nakdong River basin in the southeast. Toward the end of the 5th century, the people of Paekche joined and continued to increase in number, as suggested by the appearance of Paekche pottery and Paekche mortuary system (K Tanaka 2004: 92). This process is clearly evident in the archaeological records of the Doyama Kofungun in Kawachi, where the Kaya mortuary form and Kaya pottery preceded that of Paekche corridor-style tombs (Osakafu Kyoiku I'inkai 1994; IH Nam 2015: 140-159)

On the Kawachi plain (modern Osaka City), the Toraijin pursued five major enterprises: flood control and land reclamation, stoneware production, horse-raising, salt production, and advanced iron-tool manufacturing (Koyamada 2001: 94-97; Pearson 2016: 39-46).

From the prehistoric times, much of the Kawachi Lake basin was environmentally disadvantaged due to frequent flooding either by prolonged rainy reasons or high tidal waters pushing up inland from the nearby Osaka Bay (Pearson 2016: 8-12). With the technology of dam and dike construction and tools necessary such as U-shaped iron hoes and multi-pronged iron picks, which they brought with them or manufactured locally, they built sea walls, dikes along flooding rivers, and reservoirs, all for the purpose of protecting and/or expanding lands for habitation and farming. The Manda Dike, Kame'i Dike, and the Sayama Reservoir are excellent examples (Map. 4.3)

The Manda Dike, constructed in the 5th–6th century, was an embankment which ran along the Furukawa River flowing into Kawachi Lake. In construction, the builders incorporated natural embankments into the dike system, creating the longest flood water control system of the Kofun period. The Kame'i Dike in Yao City, built to prevent the flood water from moving upstream inundating the paddy fields, was a smaller version of the Manda Dike. It was 8 to 12 meter wide at the base, 6 m at the top, and 1.5 meter high. Such flood-control systems were unknown in the Archipelago prior to the Middle Kofun period (Koyamada 2001: 94-95). The civil engineering method used in the construction of both Nanda and Kame'i dikes was the same as the one used in the building of the Byeokkolje Dike in Gimje, southwest Korea, dated to the Later Mahan–Paekche of 330–370 (Koyamada 2001: 94-95; WG Choi 2013: 25-30).

The Sayama Reservoir in Sayama City, dated to 616 by dendrochronology, was created by damming the Nishi-Yukawa River. The dam itself is 5.4 m high, 27 m wide at its base, and about 300 m long. Its primary purpose was to drain and develop the land between the Nishi-Yukawa River and the Higashi-

Yukawa River for human habitation. The dam made it possible for the establishment of the Hirao settlement (modern Mihara-cho) which archaeologically has revealed rows of large buildings.

Construction of sturdy and durable dams able to withstand an enormous pressure of millions of gallons of water and the natural elements required highly sophisticated civil and hydraulic engineering. In light of an account in the *Nihon Shoki*: Suiko year 10 – reporting the arrival in 602 of Gwanleuk, a Paekche priest in Yamato bringing books on calendar-making, astronomy, and geography – Koyamada believes that Paekche provided the necessary technology. This belief is further enforced by that fact that Paekche officials were directly involved in the construction of a 1.2 km long massive riverine embankment in 664 to protect Dazaifu in Fukuoka (Koyamada 2001: 96-97).

While some of the Toraijin were building dikes and dams to protect and/or expand the land for habitation and agriculture in the Kawachi Lake basin, others were pioneering in the production and development of stoneware at Suemura, one of the largest Toraijin settlement complexes in the Archipelago during the 5th–7th century (Map. 4.3). First mentioned in the *Nihon Shoki*: Shujin year 7, Suemura (陶邑) is a collective term referring to the entire stoneware industry and the settlements associated with it. The Suemura complex was concentrated in an area, 10 km long (east–west) and 5 km wide (north–south), comprising modern Dokiyama, Takakura, Tomikumi, Toga, Onoike, Komyoike, Obatera, and Taniyama-ike – all concentrated in the Izumi section of southern Osaka. In its heydays, more than a thousand Sue stoneware kilns were operating in Suemura (SKHB 2001: 97).

Ceramic technicians on the Peninsula had developed the stoneware, known as *dojil togi*, in the latter part of the 3rd century under the influence of advanced ceramic technologies from China. Because of its durability and strong resistance to porosity, stoneware became popular in the emerging early Peninsular states, especially among their elites as an essential component of their mortuary culture. As valued objects, they moved with the immigrants arriving in the Archipelago at various locations including Fukuoka in northern Kyushu, Soja in Okayama, Takamatsu in Kanagawa, and in Sakai and Izumi in Osaka among others (Sakai 2004b: 69-73).

Upon arrival on the shore of the Osaka harbor, around 400 or shortly thereafter, the immigrants from Geumgwan Kaya (modern Kimhae) began to produce *dojil togi* at various sites, including Obatera in Sakai as well as Uedai and Kanancho in Izumi (Sakai 2004b: 69-73). Best known among these was Obatera settlement. Discovered in 1991, the site contained the oldest stoneware produced in the Archipelago, strikingly similar to those being produced on the Peninsula, and known in Japan as Sueki ('iron sounding vessel'). The kiln which produced the first and the oldest Sueki in Japan is identified as TG #232 after Toga, a section at Obatera (SKHB 2001: 96).

Along with residential remains of the Toraijin containing the earliest forms of the Sueki, Obatera settlement has revealed locations where finished Sueki vessels underwent quality inspection process. Among the Sueki vessels produced at Obatera were boat-shaped vessels, symbolizing the potter's long ocean voyage from the Peninsula, as well as tall cups and mounted dishes popular in Kaya (SKHB 2001: 96).

However, the initial Sueki stoneware repertoire also contained *dojil togi* types from the Later Mahan polities of the Yeongsan River valley in the Peninsula's southwest and Paekche, suggesting that from the beginning, the Archipelago stoneware had a complex origin. Throughout the 5th century, the

Later Mahan–Paekche type continued to increase, including three-legged dishes and pots with a pair of ear-shaped attachments (*yang'i buho*), gradually becoming the dominant type (SKHB 2001: 72-73). This change in the Sueki stoneware appears to have been caused by a steadily increasing number of immigrants from the Later Mahan and Paekche region of the Peninsula's west and southwest coastal region, beginning in the early part of the 5th century.

The stoneware quickly became popular and was highly sought after by the locals, especially among the elites as durable utilitarian vessels, and it also became an integral component of the Wa elite mortuary culture as on the Peninsula (Pearson 2009). Consequently, the number of Sueki kilns multiplied, operated by Toraijin technicians living in various settlements nearby, resulting in the emergence of the Suemura complex. Among the largest settlements of the Sueki technicians are Tsujino, Kokanda, and Tokiminami.

Utsuji site in Sakai, located on the bank of Tokikawa River, was an extraordinarily large settlement built around more than 50 above-ground-level buildings used as storage facilities during c. 450–700. Archaeologists have uncovered more than 2,000 pits and more than 1,000 boxes of artifacts including the Sueki remains, each box measuring 55 cm x 35 cm x 15 cm. More than 95% of the artifacts found in the storage buildings were discarded Sueki vessels of at least ten different types. The investigators posit that Utsuji was the inspection center, where Sueki vessels produced by the Suemura kilns were collected, inspected, and redistributed (SKHB 2001: 98).

Kokakuda and Toki Minami, two large settlements of Toraijin ceramic technicians, located in Tokiyama area in Sakai City, Osaka, appeared in the 6th century and continued the Sueki production through the 7th century. The presence of numerous above-ground-level storage buildings and a large quantity of discarded Sueki vessels suggests that these two sites also served as collection, inspection, and distribution centers (SKHB 2001: 98).

Surrounding the Suemura settlements are several cemeteries, including Toki Senzuka, Nonoi Kofungun, Ushi'ishi Kofungun, Hino'o Tsukahara Kofungun, and Shinoda Senzuka among others (SKHB 2001: 97). Built during the 6th–7th century, in structural form and burial contents they are similar to the Toraijin burials in Kawachi, the southeastern section of Osaka, such as Hiroyama Senzuka and Takayasu Senzuka.

In Kawachi, the Toraijin pioneered horse-raising and became heavily involved in the development of horse-raising farms and horsemanship as well as iron-tool production industry. In the *Nihon Shoki: Keitai* year 1 (507), Kawachi is mentioned as the home of Arako, a Toraijin in charge of horse-raising. In 2002, a team of archaeologists unearthed the remains of a 1500-year-old horse at Shitomiyakita site in Shijonawate City, located in the western slope of Mt Ikoma (Map 4.3). The horse remains were found along with wooden stirrups actually used. Nearby were also found remains of an ocean-going wooden boat, more than 30 feet long and more than 150 salt-making vessels essential to horse-raising, along with Peninsular stoneware and miniature portable cooking stoves associated with the Toraijin (Yamagami 2004: 74-75).

Having originated in the southern Peninsula, the miniature portable cooking stoves became a unique component of the Toraijin burial goods. In the south, including Paekche, they were only occasionally placed in graves. Upon arrival in the Kinki region, however, the Peninsula immigrants intentionally chose to make them an integral part of their mortuary culture to distinguish themselves from non-Toraijin population, who did not offer food or cooking-related vessels to the dead (Ban 2018: 77-80). "Upon arrival in the Archipelago," states BAN Yasushi (2018: 80 (italics added)), "the Toraijin developed the custom *in order to convey their identity as the Toraijin*".

In light of these finds, Yamagami (2004: 75) states,

> The Shitomiyakita site was a settlement closely related to the people and the technology of horse-raising during the second half of the 5th century... It is reasonable to posit that the Toraijin brought the horses from the Peninsula on a ship and transplanted in our country the technology of horse-riding and horse-raising and that they operated horse-raising farms with the local people of Kawachi. The plains spread out around the Kawachi Lake were perfect for the horse-raising pastures. The settlements between the mountain slopes and the Kawachi Lake appear to have been all related to horse-raising.

It is highly significant to note that Keitai, one of the prominent rulers of ancient Japan and the founder of a new royal dynasty, chose, in 507, Kawachi as his personal base of operation and the seat of his new dynasty. To begin with, he grew up as a member of a local elite family in the Echizen district in modern Komatsu City in the north-central region near the Sea of Japan, which had a strong connection with Paekche. The Echizen district was the home of many Toraijin as evidenced by the remains of houses equipped with an *ondol* (underground heating system) and artifacts associated with horsemanship. Also, striking similarities between the corridor-style elite tombs at Kodayama Kofungun near the Toraijin settlement and those of the Neungsan-ri royal tumuli of Paekche in Buyeo have led scholars to posit that there was an active interaction among the elites of ancient Komatsu and Paekche (K Mori 2001: 132).

When Muretsu died in 507 without a progeny to succeed him, Keitai was persuaded by his friends and supporters to assume the Yamato throne. Critical to Keitai's emerging as the new Yamato ruler was a supportive counsel given to him by Arako, a Toraijin in charge of horse-raising enterprise in Kawachi (*Nihon Shoki*: Keitai year 1). Upon deciding to become the new ruler of Yamato at the encouragement of Arako, Keitai chose Kusuba in Kawachi (modern-day Shijonawate) as the seat of his royal palace. Five years later, Keitai moved his capital to Tsutsuki-no-miya, which had long been the home territory of Nurinomi, a powerful Paekche elite as well as many Paekche immigrants (K Mori 2001: 132). In 518, Keitai moved his palace to Otokuni (*Nihon Shoki*: Keitai year 12). In 526, nearly twenty years after he had assumed the Yamato kingship, he finally settled at Ihara in the southern Nara basin, the home of the Yamato Aya, another group of influential Paekche immigrants, and there he died five years later in 531 (*Nihon Shoki*: Keitai year 20 and year 25).

Essentially, Keitai ruled Yamato from Kawachi, using the Paekche immigrants as his political base. This was by no means a historical accident. MORI Koichi (2001: 131) states:

> In the early 6th century, there was a rapid increase in the number of elite burials containing artifacts related to horsemanship, and there was a close connection between the rise of the Keitai Dynasty and the large-scale employment of horsemanship. Before he ascended the Yamato throne, Keitai consulted his confidant, Arako, the person in charge of horse-raising and horsemanship. Northern and Central Kawachi was the

land of horse-raising pastures, the place in the Archipelago where horses were first bred. Horses in the early 6th century corresponded to the automobiles, the immensely revolutionary invention in the early twentieth century. Keitai's focusing on the horses [of Kawachi] would have been similar to [an aspiring leader's] becoming interested in the emerging automobile industry... This indicates that Keitai and his supporters were the leaders of extraordinary foresight and enlightened perspectives.

As shown below, in addition to the horses, Kawachi provided Keitai with other essential ingredients needed to establish his political supremacy and advance his nation's economic, cultural, and social affairs, including expanded farm lands through large-scale land reclamation and cutting-edge iron tools and weapons. Essentially, through the Kawachi elites of Paekche origin, Keitai had access to all the best features of Paekche civilization. Most significant in this regard is the close relationship between Keitai and Munyeong, king of Paekche, revealed in the inscriptions of the Suda Hachiman Shrine mirror.

Along with the land reclamation, the Sueki stoneware production, and the horse-raising enterprise, the Toraijin in Kawachi were busily engaged in iron-tool production as shown among the remains of Nagahara and Ogata (Map 4.3). Nagahara was a settlement of the immigrants from Later Mahan and Paekche, as suggested by the presence of Mahan pots with *jojokmun* (bird foot print) designs and miniature portable cooking ovens (K Tanaka 2004: 92). The settlement occupied an area, 200 x 600 m, and contained various types of buildings including semi-subterranean pit dwellings, above-ground buildings (*gullipju*), and Paekche-style *okabe* (thick walled) buildings constructed on stone foundations. A prominent feature of the settlement was a building used as an iron-tool making workshop equipped with a smith's hearth and bellows, dated to 450 (K Tanaka 2004: 93-94). Nagahara was a typical Toraijin settlement where the iron tools were manufactured at a village level for the latter's consumption.

Ogata, on the other hand, was the site of a mega-size iron tool production complex. It was also one of the largest Toraijin settlements in Kawachi. The investigators of the Ogata site state (Kashiwara-shi Kyoiku I'inkai 1988: 54):

> There is a high density of Korean pottery in the settlement, dated to the Middle to Late Kofun period, reflecting the settlement's strong Toraijin connections. Also, forged iron-tool making workshop remains and artifacts from the Korean Peninsula abound... Several above-ground level buildings (*gullipju*), dated to the mid-6th to 7th century, were used as storage units.

Remains of more than 500 kg of slag, hearths, and more than a thousand pieces of tuyeres at Ogata, along with pottery remains dated to the 5th–6th century, have led the investigators to conclude that a major iron tool manufacturing center appeared in the Kawachi Plains in the middle of the 5th century and continued to operate through the 6th century in the production of tools for land reclamation, dam-building, public works, and agriculture as well as cutting-age weapons. Essentially, the Ogata iron-tool manufacturing complex, along with those in several other Toraijin satellite settlements (Ogata Minami, Taiheiji, Takaida, and Tanabe) supplied iron tools to the Yamato state.

As it became increasingly difficult for the Yamato elites to acquire critically needed iron tools and weapons from the Peninsula due to Koguryo's invasions and warfare, the Yamato elites actively sought to acquire Peninsular technology and accommodate the Toraijin technicians in their realm to produce the tools and weapons they needed. Especially critical to Yamato was the technology of iron refining essential to production of hard and durable iron tools and weapons. With the arrival of the Toraijin technicians this would have become possible. The Ogata iron tool-making factories were absolutely critical to the Yamato rulers seeking to establish their hegemony in the Archipelago through the 5th–6th century (Kashiwara-shi Kyoiku I'inkai 1997; Hanada 2002, Hanada 2004: 55-71).

A short distance from the Ogata settlement to its north is the Hiraoyama Senzuka containing more than 1,500 burials, making it the largest Toraijin tumuli group in Japan. Constructed between 500 and 700, with 550–650 as their peak period, the burials are mostly of circular mound type, averaging 10 m in diameter. Many of them house the corridor-style burial chambers and contain miniature portable cooking ovens, typical of the Toraijin mortuary practice. Along with the portable ovens were found gold earrings, jade jewellery, iron arrowheads, and horse paraphernalia (Kashiwara-shi Kyoiku I'inkai 1994).

In the vicinity of the Hiraoyama Kofungun there is also Takaida Yokoanabo Kofungun, comprising more than 200 tombs dug into vertical cliffsides. Resembling the corridor-type tombs, they were constructed during 550–650 (Kashiwara-shi Kyoiku I'inkai 1986). Of special significance is the Takaida-yama Kofun, a large corridor-type tomb built on the top of a ridge, set apart from all the other tumuli in Takaida. Inside the burial chamber were found two wooden coffins placed side by side along with a rich array of prestige goods. Next to the person lying on the west side were found gold earrings, jade jewellery, a bronze mirror, a long sword, spear, halberd, iron armor, keeled iron helmet, and horse paraphernalia. On the other hand, next to the person lying on the east side were found a few simple items including an ironing presser and jade arm and leg braces. Kamiobayashi believes that the tomb belonged to a powerful Toraijin leader and his wife of the Ogata settlement (2004: 65). More specifically, in light of the tomb's striking similarity to Paekche elite tombs of the 5th century found in Gongju (Paekche capital during 475-538), BAN Yasusi (2018: 56-60) considers the tomb to belong to a Paekche nobleman/official, suggesting that Paekche officials were residing in Kawachi as the official liaison between the Paekche immigrants and the Paekche court in Gongju (Ungjin) and later in Buyeo (Sabi).

Evidence for such liaison officials is found in the *Nihon Shoki*: Kimmei year 13 and year 14, according to which, an important court official serving King Seong of Paekche in Buyeo was Asabida of Kawachi Bu (河內部). Read Kawachi Bu (in Korean) or Kawachi Be (in Japanese), 河內部 appears to have been a Paekche Bureaucratic entity in charge of the affairs of Kawachi. In 552 and 553, Asabida came from Buyeo, the Paekche capital, to the Yamato court with Mokhyup Geumdon, another high-ranking Paekche court official, as King Seong's official envoy. It was immediately before and after King Seong sent his Buddhist mission to the Yamato court. Asabida of Kawachi Bu (or Be) appears to have been an official liaison between the Paekche court and the Paekche immigrants in Kawachi. It is, however, uncertain whether he was a Paekche official or a Wa official of Paekche Toraijin background serving King Seong (CH Park 2011: 167-189).

Hiraoyama Senzuka is surrounded by several other large Toraijin tumuli: Takayasu Senzuka in Yao City to the north and Habikonoshi Asuka Senzuka as well as Ichizuka Kofungun to the south. As in the case of other Toraijin cemeteries, they comprise mostly corridor-type tombs and contain the miniature portable ovens (Kamiobayashi 2004: 64-66). Together, these cemeteries suggest that Kawachi, the eastern and southeastern part of modern Osaka, geographically close to the southern Nara basin, was heavily settled by the Toraijin and their descendants, especially of Paekche origin, who began to multiply rapidly after 475, the year when Hanseong was destroyed by Koguryo. According to the *Shinsen Shojiroku* (New Records of Family Registers), an official genealogical record of ancient Japan, compiled in 815, 72 out of 124 Toraijin (clan) groups in 9th-century Japan – that is more than half – claimed their original home to have been in Kawachi (Shimomura 1993: 467).

With such a dominant presence in Kawachi, it was inevitable that powerful leaders would emerge among them as indicated by the elite tumuli of the Shishiyotsuka Kofun, the Akahage Kofun, and the Tsukamari Kofun built in the Hiraishi Kofungun complex in Kanan-cho. Constructed during 590–650 in a straight row on a ridge, from west to east (Shishiyotsuka › X(unknown) › Akahage › Tsukamari), overlooking a valley below, they represent four generations of powerful leaders. They were all corridor-type burials constructed on the top of pyramid-shaped three-tiered square earthen platforms, the lowest tiers of which measured 44.4 m long and 34.2 m long, on the west–east axis, for the Akahage Kofun and Shishiotsuka Kofun, respectively (Masumoto 2004: 76-85). By these measurements they were the largest tumuli found within a Toraijin cemetery complex.

Along with its extraordinary size, the Shishiotsuka Kofun contained long swords decorated in gold with dragon and phoenix, gold and silver rings, lamellar-type iron body armor, gilt-bronze horse paraphernalia, gilt-bronze waistband buckles, lacquerware, hundreds of multi-colored glass beads, and multi-colored jade ornaments among others (Masumoto 2004: 81). In consideration of the tombs' size, advanced masonry involved in their construction, and their burial contents as well as their setting within a Toraijin cemetery, Kamiobayashi (2004: 67) posits that these chiefly tombs belonged to "the leaders of the Toraijin clans from Paekche."

b. Toraijin in the Asuka District of Southern Nara Asuka-mura: Home of the Yamato no Aya

Asuka-mura (Map 4.3), located in the southeastern part of the Nara basin was one of the largest Toraijin settlements during the Middle Kofun period and was intimately connected with the emerging centralized Yamato state and the Asuka enlightenment period. It comprises the present-day Daihirada, Noguchi, Kurihara, and Abeyama (Kokushi Daijiten Henshu I'inkai 1993, 11: 968). The whole area is also known as Hinokuma (檜隈). Originally settled by the immigrants from Aya (=Anra) Kaya and later from Paekche, Asuka-mura soon became the home of the Yamato no Aya Toraijin including skilled technicians, scholars, artists, architects, and leaders of Buddhism. It is most likely that long before Buddhism became an issue in the Yamato court, it was already being practiced by the Toraijin in Hinokuma (Ban 2018: 122-127; Tamura 1981: 37-46).

According to the *Nihon Shoki:* Oujin year 20, "Aji no Omi, ancestor of the Atahe of the Aya of Yamato, and his son Tsuka no Omi immigrated to Japan, bringing with them a company of their people of seventeen districts" (Aston 1972, Vol. 1: 264-265). As in the case of other narratives in the Oujin (Ojin) section, this was a later event inserted there (Kamiobayashi 2004: 63; Yamao 1984: 47-50; Tsuda 1948: 79-86). Tsuka no Omi is mentioned properly in the Yuraku section, Year 7 (462), according to which he was the leader of newly arrived Paekche technicians including potters, saddlers, painters, brocade weavers, and interpreters being settled in Upper and Lower Momohara as well as in Magami-no-hara, all in Asuka-mura.

In light of these two narratives from the Oujin and the Yuraku sections, Yamao (1984: 47-51) posits that the Yamato no Aya Toraijin originally migrated from Aya (=Anra) Kaya to avoid violent warfare and were later joined by those from Paekche, including the Mokhyup Manchi family. According to archaeological remains uncovered from their residential sites and burials, the Toraijin communities were firmly established in Asuka-mura by the second half of the 5th century: 350–500 (Ban 2018: 119-122; Hashimoto and Kiba 2004: 87).

As the dominant population of Asuka, the Yamato no Aya Toraijin developed Asuka-mura. In the 6th century, they provided the land for the Hokoji (=Asuka Temple) and made Asuka the center of Buddhism in Japan. As pioneers in learning and scholarship, they led the Asuka enlightenment (Tamura 1981: 37-46). Within the Yamato Aya clan were great scholars acting in the Yamato court as officials in charge of translation of official documents and foreign affairs as well as high-ranking military leaders (Y Suzuki 1995: 58-59; Ueda 1991: 61-66). It became the home of Paekche technicians of various kinds including stoneware producers, iron tool makers, silk manufacturers, and saddle makers, among others. Essentially, Asuka-mura was emerging as a Paekche town or colony in the Kinki Core Region.

In the 7th century, the Yamato Aya Clan participated in the Sinification of the Yamato society as leaders of its cultural mission to Sui and Tang. Seven or all eight members of the cultural mission going to China in 608 were from the Yamato Aya clan. They were Fukuin, Yamato no Aya no Atahe; Kuromaro, Takamuku no Ayabito; Ohokuni, Imaki no Ayabito; Shoan, Minabuchi no Ayabito; Eon, Shiga no Ayabito; Kosai, Imaki no Ayabito (*Nihon Shoki*: Suiko year 16).

Early in the eighth century, Lady Takano Niigasa, a descendent from the Paekche nobility and a member of the Yamato no Aya clan, married the Yamato Prince Shirakabe (the future King Konin) and gave birth to Yamanobe in 737 in Nara. In 781, Yamanobe was enthroned as Emperor Kammu (r. 781–806), becoming in time the greatest monarch of ancient Japan (Ueda 1965: 15-19).

The Rise of the Soga Clan

The Asuka district was also the home of the powerful Soga clan which dominated Yamato during the 5th–6th century, and it was with the support of the Yamato Aya Toraijin that it emerged as the most powerful elite in Yamato in the middle of the 6th century, leading it for more than one hundred years during its most defining period (Ban 2018: 167-211; Kadowaki 1991: 168-184).

Students of the *Nihon Shoki* have long recognized connections between the Soga clan and Paekche, but it is KADOWAKI Teiji, a renowned professor of the history of ancient Japan, who has provided scholarly arguments establishing the Soga clan's Toraijin origin with the publication of *Soga-uji no shutsuji ni tsuite* (Regarding the origin of the Soga clan) (1973) and *Soga-uji to Toraijin* (The Soga clan and the Toraijin) (1991). Added to these are YAMAO Yukihisa's *Nihon Kokka no Keisei* (Formation of the Japanese State) (1977) and SUZUKI Yasutami's *Mok Manchi to Soga-uji – Soga-uji Kudarajin settsu ni yosete* (Mok Manchi and the Soga Clan – regarding the view that the Soga clan were the people of Paekche) (1981). Most recently, BAN Yasushi (2018: 115-116), in light of the Later Mahan's overwhelming cultural remains including the Later Mahan potteries, in the Asuka district in southern Nara, posits that the original home of the Soga Clan was in the Yeongsan River basin of southwest Korea.

In the *Nihon Shoki*: Oujin year 25, the original family name of Soga Manchi is mentioned as Mok or Mokra. In the *Samguk Sagi*, it appears as Mokhyup while in ancient Chinese records including the *Sui Shu* (Accounts of the Sui Dynasty) and the *Xin Tang Shu* (New Accounts of the Tang Dynasty) as Mok. The central element in these surnames is Mok, which was one of the 'eight powerful aristocratic families' of the Hanseong Paekche period. The ancient records connecting Mokhyup Manchi of the Paekche court and Soga Manchi of the Yamato court are the *Samguk Sagi*: *Paekche Bon'gi*, Gaero section (Year 21) and the *Nihon Shoki*: Richu year 2. According to the former, Mokhyup Manchi was from a powerful Paekche elite family and a high-ranking official in the Paekche court. When King Gaero was informed that Koguryo was planning to attack Hanseong, he bid his son Munju to flee and save his life for the sake of Paekche's future. "Accordingly, at this juncture Munju, together with Mokhyup Manch'i and Chomi Kolch'wi, fled southward from there" (*Samguk Sagi*, Chapter 25; Best 2006: 297). They arrived in Koma-naru (Bear's Landing), a river-side town located on the south bank of the Geum River, which would become Paekche's new capital.

As King Gaero had expected, Koguryo invaded and destroyed Hanseong in 475, killing the king. In Koma-naru, the new Paekche capital, Munju became the new king of Paekche. Only two years later in 477, however, he was assassinated in the midst of fierce power struggle between the old aristocratic factions of Hanseong and the newly emerging local power clique. About this time, Mok Manchi disappeared from the Peninsula. As Korean records go silent on Mokhyup Manchi from this point on, the *Nihon Shoki* picked up his story. He appears as Soga Manchi in the *Nihon Shoki*: Richu year 2, "administering the affairs of the state" with other Yamato officials (Aston 1972, Vol. 1: 306). According to KADOWAKI Teiji (1973: 88; 1991: 176-178), Mok Manchi changed his surname to Soga after the Soga River (also called Paekche River) near which he settled in modern-day Kashihara, as was the custom of the day. Mok Manchi thus became Soga Manchi in the annals of Japanese history.

The chronology of the *Nihon Shoki* prior to 461 is considered inaccurate by 120 years due to its compilers' primary interest in the exaltation of the Yamato legitimacy at the expense of history (Aston 1972: xviii; Tsuda 1950: 157-192: Yamada 1972: 247-254, Yamada 1991: 66-74; Kokushi Daijiten Henshu I'inkai 1993, Vol. 11: 194-195). Accordingly, adding 120 years to the reign of Richu (400–405) makes the second year of Richu AD 521. If Mok Manchi had left Paekche while in his thirties, he would have been in his late 70s or early 80s. SUZUKI Yasutani (1981) posits that Mokhyup Manchi left Koma-naru because he lost his beloved king, Munju, and also because the new Paekche capital was caught up in an unending power struggle between the old Hanseong aristocracy, to which he belonged, and the newly emerging local aristocracy. He sought to build a new life among the Paekche people already active and flourishing in Yamato.

According to the *Nihon Shoki*: Ojin, Year 25: while in Paekche, he was a powerful Paekche official exercising "absolute authority in Imna (i.e., Geumgwan Kaya in Kimhae) and frequently going to the Yamato court on official business. Such experiences made Mok Manchi a valuable asset to the Yamato court, especially in matters related to Paekche, Kara (Kaya), the military, and the finance (Y Suzuki 1981). Soga Manchi worked his way up in the Yamato court, becoming the minister of finance and establishing personal relationships with the king and elite members of the court. In his rise on the social ladder, he is believed to have received invaluable support from the Yamato no Aya Toraijin in Asuka-mura. Essentially, he emerged as the leader of the Paekche immigrants including scholars and technicians of various kinds (Ban 2018: 122-127, 130-134).

According to the *Soga-uji Keizu* (Genealogy of the Soga Clan), Manchi is recorded to have named his son Karako (Son of Korea). Karako named his son Koma (T Yoshimura 2016: 59). Koma named his son Iname.

Soga no Iname had two daughters and married both to Emperor Kimmei, during whose reign the Yamato court's relationship with Paekche flourished to an unprecedented degree. One of Iname's daughters bore a son who later became Emperor Yomei. Notably, the five Japanese emperors who came after Yomei all had a mother or wife related by blood to Soga no Iname, and with these royal connections, Iname wielded a powerful influence on Japan's sitting emperor, emerging as his Ohmi (Prime Minister) in 536. He essentially led Yamato Japan for thirty-four years, until 570.

One of Iname's lasting achievements was establishing the *miyake* system of estates throughout the Archipelago in the aftermath of the Lord Iwai of Tsukushi's rebellion in 527 in Kyushu. In order to prevent further rebellion in local regions, Iname placed under the direct control of the Yamato court what were formerly granaries, tax collection centers, and lands of the local elites, beginning with the Kibi region (Okayama), the most powerful regional center outside Yamato. This was a critical step toward the ultimate political centralization of the Archipelago and was similar to Paekche's regional control system put into effect by King Seong (523–554).

 Iname was also the first high ranking government official in Yamato Japan to espouse Paekche's Buddhism and become its active promoter against a reluctant Emperor Kimmei and several high-ranking Yamato officials; Mononobe-no-Oho-Muraji and Nakatomi-no-Muraji were dead-set against the new religion.

Of special significance, in his decision to propagate Buddhism in the Archipelago, King Seong appears to have relied on the assistance of Soga kinsmen in Paekche. For example, he sent Mokhyup Geumdon, a Soga kinsman and a high-ranking official of Paekche, to the Yamato court in May of 552, five months before he dispatched the initial Buddhist mission in October. Mokhyup Geumdon soon returned to Buyeo but in January of the following year he revisited Iname after the Buddhist mission had arrived in Yamato in October of the previous year. That was only two or three months following the arrival of the Buddhist mission in the Yamato capital (*Nihon Shoki*: Kimmei year 13 and year 14). King Seong sent Mokhyup Geumdon to the Yamato court to seek military assistance vis-à-vis Koguryo, but it is clear that he was seeking to influence the Yamato elites through the Soga clan.

Iname's son, Soga no Umako, became the new Ohmi in 572 following Iname's death; his full title was Ohmi, Umako-no-sukune, indicating his office (Ohmi) and his rank (*sukune*). Like his father, Umako was an ardent follower of Buddhism, and in 587 he succeeded in establishing it as the national religion of Japan by crushing Mononobe-no-Oho-Muraji, his chief political rival and leader of the anti-Buddhist faction. With his victory over the Mononobe, Umako emerged as the most powerful leader in the Yamato government. Like his father, Umako wielded extraordinary power over the Yamato throne through the marital relations which his father had established. When Emperor Yomei died, Umako put his nephew Sujun (his sister's son), on the throne. When Umako's relationship with the young Emperor Sujun went sour, Umako promptly had him murdered and placed his niece Suiko (wife of Sujun), on the throne. Umako then acted as the Empress' regent, becoming in this way the *de facto* ruler of Yamato Japan. In his new capacity as the regent, Umako chose, as his political confidant and comrade-in-arms, Shotoku Taisi, Emperor Yomei's son closely related to the Soga family. Together they promoted Buddhism and took various political, economic, cultural, and military actions in the advancement of the Yamato state.

Among the Toraijin clans with Korean roots, the Soga clan is the best known because of its connection with Paekche, its prominent role in the Yamato government, and its establishment of Buddhism as a national religion of Japan. The Soga dominated the Yamato state affairs for 114 years from 536–650, the most defining period in the formation of the centralized Japanese state. The Soga Clan's rise to the preeminent position in Yamato was made possible by the many Paekche immigrant communities already well established throughout the Kinki region in various social and economic roles: in the iron industry, in public works projects (dike construction and land reclamation), in prestige goods manufacturing industry, in Sueki stoneware production, in the development of equestrian culture, and mounted cavalry, and in the educated and learned establishment of Buddhist and Confucian scholars. The support of the iron-tool manufacturing complex at Ogata in Kawachi would have been particularly critical (Shiraishi 2009: 290-298).

During a century of Soga control of the Yamato court (c. 536–650), the relationship between Paekche and Yamato was also at its zenith. It was a century of heavy ocean traffic between Korea's west coast and Japan's Inland Sea via the Tsushima Strait. From the Paekche capital of Sabi (Buyeo), ships delivered official envoys, scholars of Confucian classics, Buddhist priests and teachers, metalsmiths, carpenters, artists, and tile makers to Asuka, the Yamato capital; in return, officials, priests, nuns, and students from Yamato travelled to Sabi. Along the way some of these travellers encountered storms, dangerous rocks, and high waves that led to many shipwrecks. Archaeological investigations at Jukmak-dong, a steep promontory in Buan on Korea's west coast overlooking the Yellow Sea, have revealed that during the 6th century, the place served as a sacred ground where representatives of Paekche and Wa maintained an altar at which to offer prayers and sacrifices to the deities of the sea for the safety of their sea-going countrymen (GJEB 1994).

The 6th–7th century was not only the era of the Soga dominance in Yamato but also the glorious Asuka period (592–645), and Asuka was Paekche reborn in the heart of the Yamato (Tamura 1978). For the people of Yamato, Paekche represented advanced technology and high culture. Paekche was a synonym for the best and the most desired. It was a time when the Yamato rulers readily identified with the Paekche culture. In 593, one hundred Yamato officials gathered in Asuka all dressed in Paekche robes to celebrate the construction of the Hokoji Temple. In 639 Emperor Jomei (r. 629–641) built a great palace and an impressive pagoda by a river named Kudara River (百濟川, Paekche River) and named it Kudara-no-miya (百濟宮, Paekche Palace), taking up residence there. When he died the following year an imperial resting hall was constructed next to the Kudara-no-miya and was named Kudara-no-Ohmogari (百濟大殯, the Paekche Great Temporary Mortuary) (*Nihon Shoki:* Jomei year 11, year 12 , and year 13).

In the Yamato society so deeply Paekcheized, no member of the Yamato society objected to the Soga clan's rise *because of its Toraijin origin*. According to the *Nihon shoki*, Mononobe-no-Oho-Muraji and Nakatomi-no-Muraji, became arch enemies of the Soga clan *not* because of its Paekche origin but because it was introducing foreign deities (Buddhism). Mononobe-no-Oho-Muraji himself depended on the Toraijin for his economic and political position (Shiraishi 2009: 290-298), and his opposition to the Soga clan was strictly for the religious reason.

In the modern era of heightened national consciousness, however, the Soga clan's Peninsular origin has been understandably questioned by some (Tamura 1981: 36-46; Kato 1983: 10-24; Toyama 2001: 219-223; T Yoshimura 2016: 61-63). With speculations and assumptions, these critics trace the Soga clan to Katsuragi in the southwestern Nara basin rather than to Paekche and consider Mok Manchi and Soga Manchi to be two different persons with the same personal name. In doing so, they have focused on one of the most clear-cut tell-tale evidences for Soga Manchi's Peninsular origin: naming his son Karako and his grandson Koma.

The critics argue that, in ancient Japan, Kara generally meant Korea and that "Karako" was no more than a common name used to refer to sons born of Japanese fathers and Korean mothers (Kato 1983: 19-20). There is, however, no evidence that all sons born of such marriages were called or named Karako. And there were many sons born of a Korean mother and a Japanese father. In the case of Soga Manchi, he most likely named his son after Kara (加羅) on the Peninsula, where he lived as an official representative of Paekche (*Nihon Shoki*: Oujin year 25). According to the *Nihon Shoki*: Jingo Year 49 and the *Paekchegi* (Paekche Records) cited in the *Nihon Shoki*: Ojin Year 25, Mok Manchi was the son of Mokra Geunja, a prominent Paekche general, and served as Paekche's plenipotentiary in Imna (Kara). In such a case, he would have intended for Karako to signify "Son of Kara" and thereby memorialize his special relationship with Kara.

The critics also argue that Soga Manchi, had he been a Paekche nobleman, would not have allowed his grandson to be named Koma (Koguryo, 高句麗), the arch enemy of Paekche. *Indeed, a Paekche nobleman would not have named his son or his grandson after Koguryo, which had destroyed Hanseong, the Paekche capital, and was still intent on destroying the Paekche state.* For the same reason, the Katsuragi, a Wa clan, would not have named its son Koma (Koguryo), inasmuch as Koguryo was just as adversarial to the latter as it was to Paekche.

Koma, as a shortened version of Koma-naru, was *actually* the name of Paekche's new capital, to which Manchi had taken refuge in 475 with King Munju, following Koguryo's destruction of Hanseong. Consequently, in the *Liangzhigongtu*, a pictorial accounting of foreign envoys who presented themselves at the court of Liang Dynasty around 530, Koma (固麻) is mentioned as the name of Paekche capital. It was the last place where Mok Manchi stayed before coming to Yamato.

Linguistically, *koma* was a variant form of a Tungusic word, *kom*, meaning bear. It has remained as *kom* in modern Korean and as *kuma* in modern Japanese. *Kom* (bear) appears in the Korean founding myth (Dangun Shinhwa) as the ultimate Mother of all Koreans and was the sacred totem (JW Lee 1994, 13-57).

When the Paekche court fled south, following its loss of Hanseong in 475, the Paekche capital, it had chosen a river-side town named Kom-naru ("Bear's Landing") on the south bank of the Geum River as its new capital ("Geum," the modern name of this river is a variant form of "Kom"). Accordingly, in the 5th century Yamato court, Paekche's new capital was known as Kuma-nari (rendered in Chinese as 熊津, also meaning "Bear's Landing") (*Nihon Shoki*: Yuryaku year 20; Aston 1972, Vol. 1: 367). In this light, it is understandable why Soga Manchi named his grandson Koma.

For unknown reasons, sometime during the Middle Kofun period, in the Yamato capital, Koguryo came to be called Koma; consequently, when the Soga clan genealogy was being written in the eighth century or later, "Koma" (熊, Bear) was mistakenly rendered in Chinese characters as 高句麗 (Koguryo). Most likely, for many generations, the Soga clan genealogy had been transmitted orally as in most ancient societies and was transcribed into Chinese characters in the eighth century. It was an anachronistic error similar to the *Nihon Shoki* compilers' rendering of Wa (倭) as Nihon (日本) in the same period.

Kara was the land where Manchi lived as a Paekche official, and Koma-naru was the last place where he stayed with his beloved king Munju as well as the new capital of his motherland. Kara and Koma were two places most endeared to Manchi; therefore, in longing for his motherland and in his desire to memorialize his and his family's Peninsula origin, he had every reason for naming his son Karako (Son of Kara) and his grandson Koma (Paekche). In other words, while the Katsuragi clan had no reason whatsoever to name its sons Kara and Koma, the Soga clan had every reason to name its sons by those names.

On the basis of his extensive study on the history and archaeology of the Katsuragi clan, BAN Yasushi rejects the latter's connection with the Soga clan. First, the two were geographically separated with the Katsuragi clan centering in the southwestern part and the Soga clan in the southern part of the Nara basin respectively. Second, they developed two distinctly different socio-political entities with their own territorial domain. While the Soga clan developed in a close alliance with the Yamato court, the Katsuragi clan operated outside it with its own territory and its own Toraijin technicians.

The Soga Clan is believed to have buried their members in the impressive Niizawa Senzuka which contains more than 600 Toraijin elite burials, including a number of keyhole tombs of varying sizes (Kadowaki 1991, 178). Tomb #126 contained an impressive array of precious goods that included a gold diadem, gold earrings, a gold arm bracelet, a decorated sword, a portable bronze brazier, and a rare glassware. Other tombs (#109, 115, 139, and 281) yielded long iron swords, daggers, iron body armor, and helmets (Fig. 4.14) (Nara-ken Kyoiku I'inkai 1977, Nara-ken Kyoiku I'inkai 1981a, Nara-ken Kyoiku I'inkai 1981b; NKKFH 1999: 61; SKAKH 2001: 32; OFCAH 2003: 76).

Tombs and Temples

Among the renowned archaeological remains of Asuka-mura are those of the Hokoji Temple (Asuka-dera), the Hinokuma Temple, the Teirin Temple, the Kurihara Temple, the Takamatsuzuka Kofun, and the Kitora Kofun among others (Kokushi Daijiten Hensho I'inkai 1993, 11: 968). While the Hokoji belonged to the Soga Clan, the Sakata Temple, located on the southeastern side of Asuka-mura, is believed to have been the private temple of the Kuratsukuri Clan also from Paekche in charge of producing saddles and other equipment related to horse-riding. Kuratsukuri no Tori, one of the Clan members, manufactured the famous gilt-bronze statue of Buddha still housed in the Hokoji (*Nihon Shoki*: Yuraku year 7; OFCAH 2004: 56). The Hinokuma Temple, located on the southwestern side of Asuka-mura, was the clan temple of the Yamato no Aya Clan, descended from Aji, a Paekche nobleman. Its remains are within the Omiashi Temple, which venerates Aji (*Nihon Shoki*: Yuraku year 7; OFCAH 2004: 56).

The Yamato no Aya Toraijin left their history not only among the remains of the magnificent temples but also in their community cemeteries, including the Hosokawa-dani Kofungun and the Akaokuzure-dani Kofungun in addition to the Niizawa Senzuka mentioned above. Located in the Hosokawa River

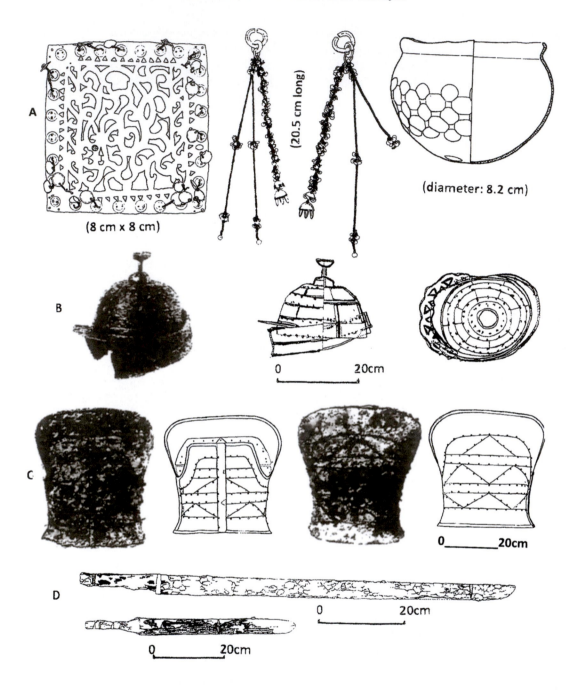

Fig. 4.14. Prestige goods from the Toraijin elite tombs at Niizawa, near Asuka. **A:** Prestige goods (open work gold pendant, gold ear rings, a Roman glass bowl) from Tomb # 126 (Nara-ken Kyoiku I'inkai 1977). **B:** Iron helmets from Tomb # 139 (Nara-ken Kyoiku I'inkai 1981a). **C:** Iron body armours from Tomb # 115 (Nara-ken Kyoiku I'inkai 1981b). **D:** A long sword and a dagger from Tomb # 109 (Nara-ken Kyoiku I'inkai 1981c). Photos and sketches credit: Nara-ken Kashihara Archaeological Research Institute.

valley, the Hosokawa-dani Kofungun contains more than 200 elite burials, built during the 6th–7th century. They are of the circular mound type and contain corridor-style burial chambers. As with other Toraijin tombs, those of Hosokawa-dani contained horse paraphernalia, gold finger and ear rings, and miniature portable cooking ovens (Tatsumi 2017, 1-20).

In the Akaokuzure-dani Kofungun, the investigators uncovered from five elite tombs more than 11,000 glass beads of varying colours, from red to blue and green, along with gilt-bronze horse paraphernalia, iron spearheads, silver and copper necklaces, and a large number of precious stones. Built in a straight row on the top of a ridge, Tombs #1, #2, and #3 belonged to the latter part of the 5th century, while #4 and #5 belonged to the early part of the 6th century. All except #2 were square-shaped mound burials, 11 to 16 m on a side. In light of the buried prestige goods and corridor-style tombs found nearby, containing potable miniature cooking stoves, the investigators believe that these tombs belonged to the chiefs of the Toraijin who settled in the area in the 5th century (Hashimoto and Kiba 2004: 86-87).

c. Elite Toraijin Technicians in Nango, Nara

Located about 5 km west of Asuka-mura and known as "the royal capital of Katsuragi," Nango was another major Toraijin settlement in the Nara basin. Its leaders and residents were also intimately involved in the development of the Yamato power, emerging as the largest settlement in the Archipelago during the Middle Kofun period, occupying an area of 2.4 km^2 (Ban and Aoyagi 2017: 4-16, 25).

Nango was essentially a Toraijin-supported settlement. As observed by Ban and Aoyagi (2017: 27):

> What makes the Nango site different from other large settlements is its deep connections with the Toraijin. It is not an exaggeration to state that Nango was undergirded and maintained by the Toraijin....Among the Toraijin were those who acted as *oyakata* [respected leaders and supervisors] who oversaw the production technicians... As possessors of the most advanced technology of the time, they were welcome and granted special privileges by the king of Katsuragi.

Underlying the Katsuragi political power were the Toraijin technicians and their advanced technology of iron-tool manufacturing, gold and silver craftsmanship, and architecture (Ban and Aoyagi 2017: 32-59, 72). Pottery remains from Nango include those from Kaya, Paekche, and the Later Mahan polities, suggesting that the Toraijin came from the southeast as well as the southwest regions of the Peninsula.

The most important production site at Nango was located at Nango Kadota site located in the center of the Nango settlement. Archaeological remains at the site have led the investigators to conclude that it was a specialized workshop where technicians produced weapons, including iron body armor and helmets, using the riveting method. Also produced at the site were glass beads of various kinds, prestige goods of gold, silver, and gilt-bronze belt buckles and gilt-bronze fixings on leather quivers, and deer-horn-carved hilts for daggers and knives (Ban and Aoyagi 2017: 54-58).

Immediately to the east of the central production center is Nango Yanagihara site which contains Peninsular soft-fired *yeonjil* potteries and Toraijin residential buildings. The latter consists of *okabe*-type structures distinguished by large, thick walls and constructed on stone foundations, similar to those found at other Toraijin settlements such as Hinokuma of Asuka-mura, Kankakuji site of Takatori-cho, and Anou site in Shiga (Ban and Aoyagi 2017: 62-66; Hanada 2000).

Inasmuch as similar buildings were constructed in ancient Paekche, they most likely belonged to technicians from Paekche. In contrast with the local preferences for pit-houses and pillared buildings, the Toraijin technicians were living in elevated sturdy buildings at the invitation of the 'king of Katsuragi' (Ban and Aoyagi 2017: 54-64). The investigators believe that the Toraijin technicians living in the *okabe*-type buildings were teaching supervisors of the commoner apprentices working at various iron tool manufacturing workshops, archaeologically identified at Nango Senbu, Shimochaya Gamada, and Sadayunoki sites among others (Ban and Aoyagi 2017: 68-76).

Closely related to Nango was a Middle Kofun-period settlement of Gojo located to its south. Along with *okabe*-type buildings, a large structure has been unearthed, yielding iron slag, tuyeres, and pieces of forged iron, suggesting that the Gojo settlement was an iron-tool manufacturing site. The presence of Peninsular *yeonjil* earthenware and early Sueki pottery at the site has led its investigators to conclude that Gojo was a Toraijin settlement of iron technicians. Nearby was found an impressive tomb of the square-mound-type, 32 x 32 m, which contained awesome prestige goods including two pairs of body armor, an iron helmet, gilt-bronze waistband buckles, a bronze mirror along with various tools used for forged iron tool making (Kamiobayashi 2004: 63; OFCAH 2004: 24).

Toraijin of Nango constructed their own tombs in the Koseyama Kofungun, one of the largest Toraijin tumuli groups, between the Katsuragi River and the Soga River. Among more than 700 tombs, many of which are the corridor-chamber type burials of Paekche origin, is Sakaidani #4, a circular mounded tomb belonging to a Toraijin elite. The tomb contained various smithing tools essential to forged-iron tool manufacturing, including pliers, an anvil, and a grind stone (Kamiobayashi 2004: 67-68).

d. Toraijin Settlement of Yamashiro (Modern Kyoto)

There is a consensus within the Japanese academia that the city of Kyoto was initially developed mainly by a Toraijin group known as the Hata Clan which settled in Kadono in ancient Yamashiro in the latter part of the 5th century (Kyoto Bunka Hakubutsukan 1989: 130-148; INOUE Mitsuo 1991: 103-111). The origin of the Hata Clan has been much debated among Japanese historians (Owa 1990: 196-226) The commonly held view, based on the *Nihon Shoki*: Oujin year 14 and the *Shinsen shojiroku* (The Newly Compiled Clan Genealogies), completed in 815, is that it came to Japan originally from Paekche, led by a Paekche elite, Prince Gungweol (Japanese: 'Lord of Yutsuki'). Others (Ueda 1965: 71-72; INOUE Mitsuo 1991: 103-111) suggest that the Hata came from Silla, on the basis of a linguistic consideration that 'Hata Clan' is a variant form of 'Bada Clan', a term originally used to refer to the Silla immigrants who had come across the sea (K. *bada*).

Owa (1990: 209-225), on the basis of his exhaustive analysis of ancient records, has concluded that the term, *hata*, is indeed a variant form of Korean *bada*. However, he reasons that *hata* or *bada* (sea) actually referred to 'Soe Bada' meaning 'Iron Sea' in Korean, which was the original name of Kimhae ('Iron Sea'), known as the iron capital of East Asia as early as in the 3rd century.

Kimhae was another name of Kuya-guk, the most powerful Kaya state on Korea's southeast coast. As well-known archaeologically and historically, Kuya-guk was invaded and destroyed in 400 by King Gwanggaeto of Koguryo, which caused some Kaya elites to flee to Japan along with their people. These Kaya people from Kimhae (Soe Bada) were called by the Japanese natives Bada or Hata (sea) people, that is the Hata Clan.

According to Owa, initially most of the immigrants from Kimhae settled in northern Kyushu, but some of them went to Wakigami in the southern Nara basin. Around 450 they moved to Yamashiro in the Kyoto basin (Owa 1990: 224-225). There the Hata clan organized various Korean immigrant communities for industrial production needed by the Yamato court, gradually emerging as one of the powerful immigrant cliques (Y Suzuki 1995: 57–58).

With superior engineering skills, they also built dams and dikes around Kyoto to drain and develop the Kyoto plains for agricultural expansion, and by 500 they emerged as the wealthiest and most powerful elite in the entire Kyoto basin (Yamao 1977: 43-46). With their wealth, the Hata clan built numerous temples and shrines in Kyoto, including Fushimi Inari Shrine, Matsuo Shrine, and the Koryuji Temple.

Beginning around 540, they became closely allied with the Yamato imperial family and the Soga clan, playing an important role in the rise of Buddhism under Prince Shotoku (Yamao 1977: 43-46; Ueda 1991: 66-71). They also formed a marriage alliance with the powerful Fujiwara clan, thereby exerting enormous influence in the Yamato government (Kyoto Bunka Hakubutsukan 1989, 131).

It should also be noted that when Emperor Kammu moved the Yamato capital from Nara to Nagaoka-kyo and eventually to Heian-kyo in Kyoto in 794, he depended primarily on the Hata clan for finance and engineering (Kyoto Bunka Hakubutsukan 1989: 131). The Hata clan built for themselves great keyhole-shaped tombs to house their megalithic corridor burial chambers in the Kyoto area. One of them is the Hebizuka Kofun designated as a national cultural relic.

e. Toraijin around Lake Biwa in Ancient Omi

In Otsu City (ancient Omi district), around Lake Biwa, a few miles east of Kyoto, archaeologists have reported on more than thirty Toraijin cemeteries of the 5th-6th century. These Middle Kofun period cemeteries, some of which contain up to 150 tombs are dispersed on the eastern slope of Mt. Hiei over a distance of 6 km between the towns of Nishikori and Sakamoto. Tombs in these cemeteries are the corridor-style similar to those found at Ichitsuka cemetery in Osaka. They contain portable miniature cooking stoves often found in Toraijin burials of the Middle Kofun period in the Kinki region (Hori 2009: 13-22). These multitudes of cemeteries indicate that a sizable number of Paekche immigrants settled in Omi in the early 5th century (400–450) and continued to thrive through the 6th century.

Yeonjil earthenware of the Later Mahan region of southwest Korea has been found along with early Sueki stoneware at numerous residential sites along Lake Biwa, also suggesting that the Toraijin from the southwestern Peninsula settled in the region in the early 5th century. Their settlements surround the lake: Minami'ichi Higashi to the northwest, Takatsuki Minami to the northeast, Irienai on the southeast, and Hattori at the south end (Kaneyasu 1997: 63-66).

During the 6th century, there appeared *okabe*-type buildings of Paekche style at numerous settlement sites on the southwest as well as on the south and southeast side of the lake – at Anau, Shigari, Minami Shiga, Namasu, and Kiso among others – suggesting that the number of new Toraijin from Paekche increased in the 6th century (Kaneyasu 1997: 66-71). Some of the buildings were equipped with an *ondol* (an underground heating system).

In the latter part of the 7th century, following the demise of the Paekche kingdom in 663, Emperor Tenji helped a large number of Paekche refugees, numbering 2,400, settle in Omi in 665–667. Having done so, he moved the Yamato capital from Asuka to Omi, bustling with Paekche people and flourishing with Paekche culture. Two years later in 669, he settled 700 more Paekche refugees in Omi (*Nihon Shoki*: Tenji year 4, year 5, year 6, and year 8). Among them were former high-ranking officials of the Paekche court. One of them, by the name of Guishil Jipsa, was appointed in 671 by Emperor Tenji as the Minister of Education in charge of the Yamato state's educational affairs.

Also, in Otsu, remains of numerous Buddhist temples built by various Toraijin families, including Kudara-dera (the 'Paekche Temple'), have been identified. A shrine built to honor and memorialize Gwisil Jipsa, the Paekche nobleman appointed as the Yamato Minister of Education, is still being revered by the people of Otsu (Kyoto Bunka Hakubutsukan 1989, 125-128).

B. Toraijin in Ancient Kibi (Modern Okayama)

Beginning in the late 4th century, the people of Kaya began to migrate to ancient Kibi and played a critical role in the development of iron industry there. In the vicinity of the ancient iron industry sites, immigrant settlements and their cemeteries have been identified (Kameda 2000: 165-184, Kameda 2004b: 29-38, Kameda 2004c: 3-14, Kameda 2016: 283-297; SKAKH 2001: 35). In the middle of the 6th century, more Kaya people arrived in Kibi and played a vital role in the development of Japan's first iron production.

Combined with the Toraijin iron-smiths who had arrived earlier, the new technicians helped Kibi emerge as the second most powerful polity in Japan, next only to Yamato (Kameda 2000: 172-174). The Toraijin of Kaya origin in Soja-Okayama, the iron industrial center, were so numerous that it was named Kaya-gun (Kaya Province) during the Kofun period and remained so for a millennium and half. Thus, the Okayama region became a major Kaya population center and remained the home of Kaya immigrants and their descendants for 1,500 years.

In the early part of the 7th century, a powerful Toraijin clique emerged in Maniwa, on the Kibi Plateau, in the northern part of Okayama. They built for themselves impressive large corridor-style tombs containing decorated long swords and gold jewelleries. The new tombs include Sada Higashitsuka, Nishitsuka, Sada Hokukobun, Otani #1 Tomb, and Sada #4 and #5. Of special significance, Otani #1 Tomb contained a gilt-bronze *salpo*, used by the elites of Kaya, Silla, and Paekche as the symbol of their political power. Believing that the corridor-style tombs belonged to the Toraijin, the investigators posit that the Toraijin elites in the Maniwa region, rich with iron ore, were exerting their power in alliance with the Yamato in Kinki (Maniwa-shi Kyoiku I'inkai 2008).

C. Toraijin in the Kanto Region

Besides the Kinai area, a large number of Korean immigrants also settled northwest of modern Tokyo in the Kanto region (Kameda 2012). In the area of modern Gunma Prefecture, they operated extensive horse-raising farms as well as advanced metallurgical factories, producing horse transportation gear, gold ornaments, and a variety of iron tools. In the 400s some of them emerged as powerful local chieftains, building for themselves impressive *jeokseok-chong* (tiered piled-stone tombs similar to those of Koguryo and the Hanseong period Paekche) such as Shimo-shibayatsu Kofun (SKAKH

2001: 50, 60, 74) as well as keyhole-type tombs such as the Watanuki Kannonyama and Hachiman Kannonzuka Kofun. Discovery in the Watanuki Kannonyama Kofun of a *sudaegyeong* (bronze mirror with animal boss), identical to one found in the tomb of Paekche King Munyeong, strongly indicates a close tie between Paekche and the Kanto region (Fig. 4.15) (SKAKH 2001: 74-83).

D. Toraijin in Kyushu

Kyushu's geographic proximity to southern Korea attracted Peninsular peoples since the ninth century BC of the Middle Mumun period with its favorable natural environment including temperate climate and fertile plains. Once communication was established between the immigrants and their parental communities in the Peninsula, the people of southern Korea continued to come to Kyushu for one reason or another, settling in various parts of the island.

A large number of *yeonjil* earthenware vessels from the Later Mahan polities in the southwestern Peninsula have been found in Early Kofun sites at Nishijin-machi in Fukuoka. They were found among ceramics from Kaya, Kinki, and the San'in district (northern coast of western Honshu) as well as local varieties, suggesting that the Toraijin from the Later Mahan polities coexisted with people from various regions, working as traders as well as producers of goods (Sakai 2013: 77-78).

During the Middle Kofun period, the number of the Toraijin in Fukuoka, especially from Kaya, increased – as shown by the presence of Kaya-type stoneware found at numerous locations including Yoshi'i Machi, Tsukando, Shingu Machi, Omori, Jonan, Ogori, Maebara, Munakata, Arajiada, Sawara, and Yoshitake among others (SKAKH 2001, 19-21; Shirai 2000: 90-120). Toraijin settlements were also established in Asakura (Fukuoka), as indicated by the Toraijin cemeteries of Kodera and Ikenoue in Amagi, which have yielded abacus-shaped spindle whorls of hard-fired clay and early 6th-century Sueki vessels. The Sueki stoneware vessels were produced by the Toraijin at the Asakura Sueki kilns (Sakai 2013: 78). Of special significance is the Tomb #6 at Ikenoue, which contained a rich array of prestige goods including horse gear, iron daggers, and iron hammers. It has been suggested that the tomb belonged to the leader of the Toraijin (SKAKH 2001, 19). Several other tombs at Kotera and Ikenoue containing abacus-bead-shaped spindle whorls of hard-fired clay that are believed to have belonged to women from Kaya (SKAKH 2001: 21).

In comparison, however, Kyushu was soon superseded by the Kinki Core Region as the first and primary choice of the Toraijin's destination despite the fact that it was less developed than Kyushu economically, culturally, and technologically (Hojo 2000: 41; Goyamada 2004: 6-19; Mizoguchi 2013: 225, 234-236). Also, it was ecologically less suitable for human habitation and agriculture. Many parts of the Osaka Plain were plagued by high tidal waters and frequent floods inundating the Kawachi Lake basin and the lands along the Yodogawa River and its tributaries (Koyamada 2001: 94-97).

Archaeological evidence clearly shows that beginning in the early 5th century, the Toraijin from Kaya and Paekche were flocking more to Kawachi, Izumi, Asuka-mura, Katsuragi, Omi, and Yamashiro than to Kyushu. Underlying this new phenomenon were two factors: (1) desire on the part of the refugees to flee as far as possible from the Peninsula engulfed in violent warfare, and (2) the welcoming mat spread out by the Yamato elites eager to have advanced culture and technology of the Peninsula (Ichimura 2004: 49).

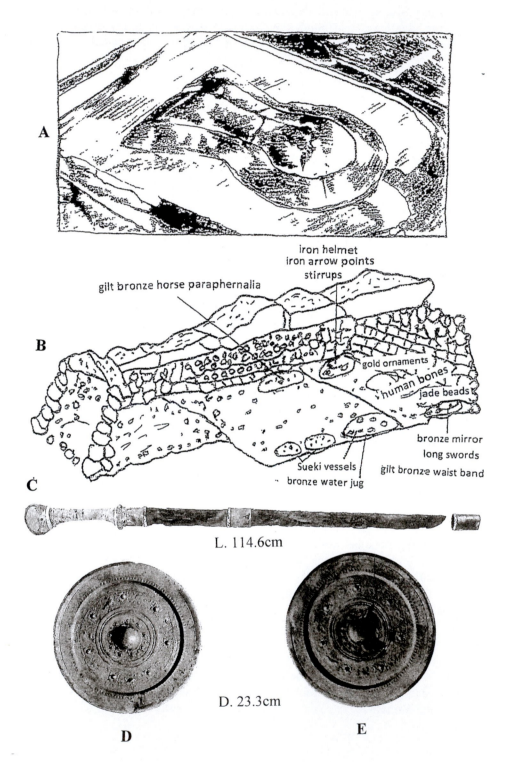

A

B

iron helmet
iron arrow points
stirrups

gilt bronze horse paraphernalia

gold ornaments

human bones

jade beads

bronze mirror
long swords
gilt bronze waist band

Sueki vessels
bronze water jug

C

L. 114.6cm

D. 23.3cm

D

E

Fig. 4.15. (Page 150) A Korean immigrant elite tomb in Gumma. **A:** Watanuki Kannonyama Kofun, 100m long, 6th century. **B:** A corridor tomb inside (12.5 meter-long, 2.2-meter high) containing bronze mirrors, a gilt-bronze bottle, gilt-bronze decorated swords, sueki, jades, iron arrows, and horse gear among other items. **C:** A gilt-bronze decorated long sword. **D:** A *sudaegyeong* (bronze mirror with animal designs) (SKAKH 2001: 55-58). **E:** An identical bronze mirror found in Paekche King Munyeong's tomb in Gongju (GGOB 2004: 62). Photos and sketches credit: Gunma Historical Museum and Gongju National Museum.

CHAPTER FIVE

IMAKI NO TEHITO'S CONTRIBUTIONS TO THE MIDDLE-LATE KOFUN SOCIETY

I. THE EARLY AND MIDDLE KOFUN SOCIETIES: COMPARED

Culturally and technologically, the Early Kofun period (250–400) has been viewed as an extension of the Late Yayoi. As with Yayoi, the Early Kofun society was primarily agrarian, religious/magical, and ritualistic in its sociocultural articulations, especially at the elite level. As stated by Wada (1986: 350–351):

> We characterize the Early Kofun period (fourth century) by its grave goods, some of a magical nature such as bronze mirrors, beads, swords, and jasper bracelets deposited in wooden coffins manufactured from split and hollowed-out logs... Research reveals many Early Kofun cultural elements to be a continuation of Yayoi social characteristics.

This observation has been emphasized by others. Egami (1967: 158-161) states,

> There is a fundamental difference between the culture of the Early Kofun period and that of the Middle and Late Kofun in terms of their basic character. There was an intimate relationship between the Early Kofun and Yayoi Cultures, such that UMEHARA Sueji wished to include the Early Kofun in the Yayoi cultural period.

In contrast, the elite culture of the Middle Kofun period emphasized iron weapons and horse gear, with a focus on military themes (Naoki 1992: 140; Pearson 2009: 6). Another striking point is that the Early Kofun tombs were constructed mainly in the Nara basin and mostly on the top of ridges or on foothills, while those of the Middle Kofun period were built in the Kawachi plains near present-day Osaka (Barnes 1988: 249-156; Naoki 1992: 140-142). Prior to the 8th century, "Kawachi Plains" comprised the entire Osaka Plains including Settsu and Izumi districts (Naoki 1992, 139-140).

Politically, the Japanese Archipelago of the Early Kofun period (3rd–4th century) was still a land of many regional powers or chiefdoms, with no central government. It was politically divided among four regional centers: Kyushu, Izumo, Kibi, and Kinki, with the last acting as the *primus inter pares* thanks more to its topographical advantages than to its cultural and technological foundation (Mizoguchi 2013: 225, 234-236).

Early Kofun society also lacked many of the cultural and technological elements that came to characterize Japan's subsequent unified Yamato state. It lacked a literate bureaucracy, efficient transportation, and critical technologies for iron production and steel-making. It lacked engineering skills for monumental construction of the Furuichi- and Mozu-type tumuli as well as for dam and dike construction essential to land reclamation. It lacked mounted cavalry and advanced military gear such as the iron body armor and helmet associated with the mounted warfare. It lacked a formal governmental structure with functional departments. There was no unified spiritual ideology undergirding the national unity other than animism. And the prestige goods which elite leaders and government officials needed to display their power and position, consisted of bronze mirrors and stone bracelets, lacking gold and silver paraphernalia and decorated swords, worn or carried.

Since it is increasingly recognized among Japanese scholars that during the Yayoi period, the Nara basin as well as the Osaka plains comprised a backward region technologically, especially in regard to iron (Hojo 2000: 31), how did the Kinki region attain *primus inter pares* status? In the early 3rd century AD, a supreme religious leader by the name of Pimiko/Himiko is attested in the Chinese chronicles, *Warenzhuan* (Legends of the Wa People) of the *Sanguozhi*. Barnes has proposed that she was "a charismatic avatar of the Queen Mother of the West of Daoism", attracting adherents from near and far and wielding an enormous power (Barnes 2014: 3-29). Archaeological remains including the large keyhole-shaped Hashihaka Kofun and highly valued Chinese bronze mirrors from elite tombs suggest that powerful political figures had emerged in the Miwa district, giving credence to the Queen Himiko references. (For more details on the emergence of early Japanese kings and the Miwa district, see J. Piggotts' *The Emergence of Japanese Kingship* 1997.)

The Miwa leadership emerged essentially in the context of the Late Yayoi socio-cultural context which had long emphasized the religio-ritual. As such, on their own cultural and technological base alone, the Miwa leaders could not emerge as the supreme political and military center of the Yamato state. Consequently, it collapsed by the middle of the 4th century following the demise of Lelang and decreasing influence of China. Instead, the Wa elites increasingly identified with a newly emerging technological society and culture in Kawachi that had Peninsular ties (Naoki 1992: 144, 153; also, Brown 1993: 125-132).

From the archaeological data, it is clear that the Toraijin communities were well established in Kawachi as early as 300 AD by the people of southwestern Korea, (Watanabe 1999: 82-85; Sakai 2013: 77-92). In the latter part of the 4th century, c. 370–400, they were joined by the *Imaki no Tehito*, from the same area, in the aftermath of Koguryo's devastations of Paekche in 369. (See Chapter Four, I, 3, A: Crisis in the Peninsula and II, 1: Late 4th–Early 5th century: Century of Toraijin".) In Kawachi, the *Imaki no Tehito* ("Recently Arrived Skilled Artisans") were active and thriving.

After Yamato elites' primary source of iron, namely Geumgwan Kaya (Kimhae) on Korea's southeast coast, was invaded and sacked by Koguryo in 400 AD, Yamato elites' source of iron was no more (See Chapter Four, I, 3, B: Crisis in the Archipelago). This created a crisis for the Yamato leadership. They now had to turn to the Toraijin in Kawachi in order to access economic and technological advantages offered by the Toraijin (Yamao 1984: 39-51; Ueda 1965: 69-143; Otsuka 1992: 50-68; Shiraishi 2004: 7-13; SKAKH 2001: 2-49).

Essentially, the emerging Yamato leadership was actively choosing to join those who, they believed, would help secure its future as it did repeatedly in later years: in 507 when Emperor Keitai decided to join the Toraijin in Kawachi, in 667 when Emperor Tenji moved his palace from Asuka to Omi, and in 794 when Emperor Kammu moved the Yamato capital to Kyoto. Along with Kawachi, Omi and Kyoto were Toraijin centers.

Having joined the Toraijin of Kawachi, the Yamato kings sought to increase their number by actively welcoming new Toraijin. ICHIMURA Kunio (2004: 49) states,

After the 4th century, the Yamato kings, taking advantage of the crisis situation in the Peninsula, actively invited and welcomed the Toraijin in order to promote their technology, knowledge, and scholarship. During the 5th century the Yamato court organized various professional guilds according to their technical skills. This enhanced the political organization of the Yamato court, enabling it to take new civilizational steps as part of the East Asian society... Without the information and knowledge of the Toraijin, even the diplomatic mission of the 'Five Kings of Wa' to Song China [in the 5th century] would have been impossible.

For this reason, KAMEDA Shuichi (2011, 116) calls the 5th century "the century of technological revolution" as well as "the century of Toraijin." "The revolutionary changes", Kameda states, "did not happen because certain *mono* (cultural things, objects) came into the country. They happened because of the coming of the people who possessed skills and technologies."

II. TECHNOLOGICAL REVOLUTIONS

Farris (1996, 1998), on the basis of his extensive research on the Kofun period archaeology, has "catalogued" in a lengthy article (1996: 3-13) all the cultural elements of Korean origin found in the Kofun society from iron to horse trappings, to wheel-thrown stone ware, to mortuary practices, to aristocratic accoutrements, to statecraft, and to iron-working, stoneware production, and dam building technologies. Some of them could have been brought from the Peninsula to the Archipelago through trade and exchange, while others were provided by the Toraijin in the Archipelago. In the following pages, we present technologies and cultural features transplanted in the Kofun society specifically by the Toraijin and the actors involved.

1. Iron Industry

At the end of the Yayoi period, iron had already emerged as the most important commodity in the Archipelago. For the newly emerging regional powers competing for political supremacy throughout the Archipelago, securing advanced iron implements, agricultural and military, was absolutely critical. As such, iron had become as much a symbol of wealth, power, and political authority as a practical tool and a means to more power (Murakami 1999: 114-120; Barnes 2000: 88-89). Accordingly, the iron became an integral part of elite mortuary culture as in the Peninsula.

For example, the Kurozuka Kofun, one of the earliest tumuli of the Kofun period, contained more than 27 iron single- and double-edged swords, 170+ iron arrowheads, and more than 600 small iron plates from a suit of lamellar-type body armor. The Mesuriyama Kofun, built during the Early Kofun period, contained 212 iron spear points and 236 bronze arrowheads along with iron double-edged swords, iron knives, iron axes, and iron sickles of Kaya origin (SKHB 2001: 90-91; OYBH 2004: 32).

 The Yamato #6 Tomb in Nara, a tomb classified as 'kingly tumulus type' and dated to around 450, included 872 iron ingots, 134 iron sickles, 139 iron hoes, 102 iron axes, 284 small iron knives, and 9 iron arrowheads, among other items (Azuma 1999: 152-163; Barnes 2000: 88; OFCAH 2004: 22). Ariyama Kofun, associated with the Oujin Mausoleum, is known to have contained 3,000 iron tools and weapons imported from the Korean Peninsula (Barnes 1988: 257).

Iron was thus being elevated to an exalted position by the elites of the Kinki Core Region vying for political supremacy. 'More and better iron tools and weapons!' became the clarion call of the day. The competitive social milieu of the growing Kofun society required an increase in the quality as well as in the quantity of the valued objects which had become the symbol of the elite prestige and power. The Kinki core elites, however, faced a doubled-edged crisis: limits in the Archipelago iron technology and complete dependence on foreign iron.

Since the latter part of the Middle Yayoi period, Archipelago artisans had been manufacturing simple but practical iron tools including axes, chisels, sickles, hoes, arrowheads, knives, daggers, and swords using iron forging skills (*tanya gijutsu*) on raw iron materials imported from the Peninsula (Murakami 1999: 89-103, Murakami 2007: 16, 123-126, 291-302). During the Final Yayoi in the 3rd century, the iron forging furnace (*tanya-ro*) was significantly improved with the introduction of tuyeres (*haguchi*) from the Peninsula, allowing high temperatures which enabled the Archipelago smiths to refine and harden raw iron (Murakami 1999: 106-107).

Nevertheless, unlike on the Peninsula, the Archipelago iron smithing technology became stagnant at the end of the Yayoi period with no innovation or production of specialized iron implements on the part of its technicians. This, according to Murakami, was largely due to the lack of transfer at this time of the advanced technology from the Peninsula (Murakami 2004: 75, Murakami 2007: 99-101).

Far more serious, however, was the inability on the part of the Archipelago technicians to smelt iron locally, preventing the Archipelago from becoming self-sufficient in iron supply. Since the Middle Yayoi period, the Archipelago elites and their smiths actually sought to develop the mining and production of the iron locally. Seven or eight hundred years of trial and error, however, failed in the effort. This also, according to Murakami, was due to the lack of necessary technology transfer from the Peninsula, whose early states guarded the technology of iron production as a vital state secret and refused to share with outsiders (Murakami 2007: 47-50, 170-175; DY Kim 2015: 32-69). "Friendship notwithstanding," states Murakami (2007: 305), "Paekche and Kaya did not share the technology of iron production and large-scale iron refining with the Wa polities." The Archipelago, therefore, had to depend almost completely on the Peninsula for the iron supply for another century or two until after 550 (Murakami 1999: 60-120, Murakami 2004: 70-75; Murakami 2007, 110- 135).

It is therefore no surprise that, as the Peninsula was caught up in violent turbulence, the Archipelago elites, especially those in the Kinki Core Region, actively sought to accommodate the Toraijin technicians in their domains during the Middle Kofun period, in order to acquire cutting edge iron tools they needed (Murakami 1999: 188). Major archaeological sites associated with the iron-tool manufacturing indicate that the Toraijin technicians skilled in iron technology played a critical role in establishing major iron workshops or factories throughout the Islands (Map 5.1) (Farris, 1996: 6; Ichimura 2004: 49; Azuma 1999: 419-438; Koyamada 2004b: 14-19).

In the Kinai region, smiths were established during the 5th century at Nango in Katsuragi, discussed above, located in the southwestern part of the Yamato Basin where the Yamato power was vying for political supremacy. Many locations there have revealed evidence of advanced iron-forging activities including slag, tuyeres, and pieces of iron left over from the making of forged tools such as iron daggers and knives (OFCAH 2004: 22-25). The presence of *yeonjil* and hard-fired (*gyeongjil*) earthenware, abacus-bead-shaped spindle whorls, and thick-walled residential structures at the Nango Site strongly

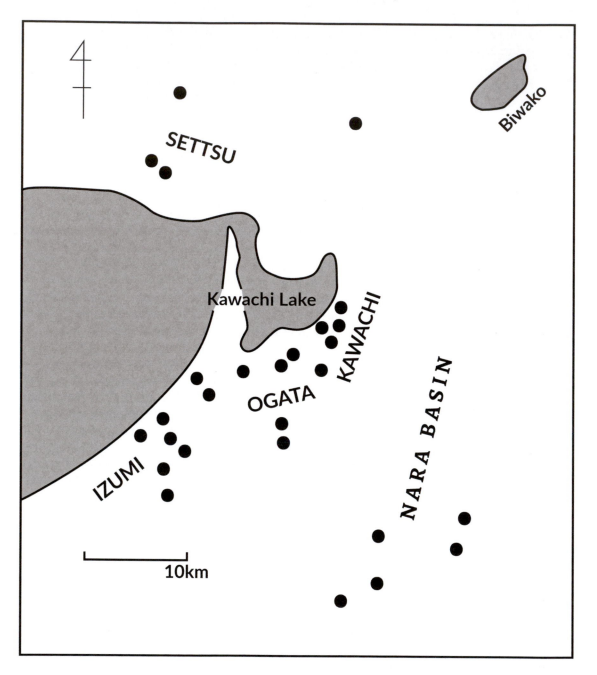

Map 5.1. New iron tool manufacturing sites in Kinki, 5th century (after Ichimura 2004: 49).

indicates that its forged-iron tool workshops were operated by Korean immigrants (SKAKH 2001: 37; OFCAH 2004: 23).

In the Nekozuka Kofun at Gojo City, dated to the 5th century and not far from Nango, was found a set of forged-iron smithing tools that included forceps, a hammer, chisels, and an anvil, along with an iron pitchfork (OFCAH 2004: 24), an elite mortuary phenomenon frequently observed in Kaya and Paekche as well as in Silla (Murakami 1999: 437).

Initially, immigrants from Kaya – the iron capital of East Asia during the 3rd and 4th centuries – were involved in the Archipelago's newly emerging iron industry, but from the mid-5th century onwards, Paekche immigrants became increasingly dominant, especially in the Settsu and Kawachi localities around Kawachi Lake in Osaka (Azuma 1999: 437). Archaeologists have identified nearly a hundred sites in the area bearing Kan-shiki or Kara-shiki (Korean-type) pottery remains (K Tanaka 2004: 90-92; JW Jeong and KC Shin 1984: 289-297).

Having engaged in iron smelting, production, and manufacturing since the late 3rd century, the iron technicians of Paekche, Later Mahan, and Kaya had mastered the skills of iron technology, even producing fine steel (GCHB 1997, 101-105). Many of the iron implements (daggers, swords, arrowheads, and hoes) found in the 5th–6th century tombs such as Yunoyama Kofun and Shichikan Kofun in the Osaka area are strikingly similar to those produced in Paekche, Later Mahan, and Kaya (Fig 5.2) (SKHB 2001: 44-51).

According to Kameda (2011: 294-296), the introduction of forceps in particular by the immigrants in the mid-5th century was a momentous event, for it revolutionized the iron-forging technology in the Archipelago. Hitherto unknown in the Islands, the forceps enabled local smiths to manipulate heated raw materials with ease, creating tools according to their wishes or as ordered by the elites. Along with the forceps, riveting technology was also introduced (Murakami 1999: 120-130). Diversification and quality improvements in the iron implements were now possible.

As part of the new iron tool repertoire, iron helmets and improved body armor began to be produced in the Archipelago during the Middle Kofun period. They included helmets with a visor, keeled helmets, and *obigane*-type (metal band framed) cuirasses, riveted together with horizontal rectangular or triangular plates (Fig 5.3; Barnes 2000; Yoshimura 2000: 104-111). They were strikingly similar, in form and manufacture, to those found in southern Korea (Fig. 4.5; JW Jeong and KC Shin 184: 273-294; Takesue 2013: 297-326). Coveted by the Yamato elites as prestige goods, they were produced in large numbers and were buried in the Yamato elite graves.

Observing that the keeled helmets and the *obigane*-type cuirasses occur overwhelmingly in the Archipelago, Yoshimura (2000: 110-111) and SUZUKI Kazunao (2013: 192-193) have posited that those found in southern Korea were made in Japan and that some of them were transported to the Peninsula as a part of trade and exchange. There is much debate on this issue (JW Jeong and KC Shin 1984: 291-292; Farris 1996: 8; Barnes 2009).

Underlying the factor of striking similarities in the iron weaponry including helmets and cuirasses were their historical context, the Toraijin phenomena, and especially the arrival of the *Imaki no Tehito*. Yamato elites were hungry for advanced iron tools including the advanced military gear, especially

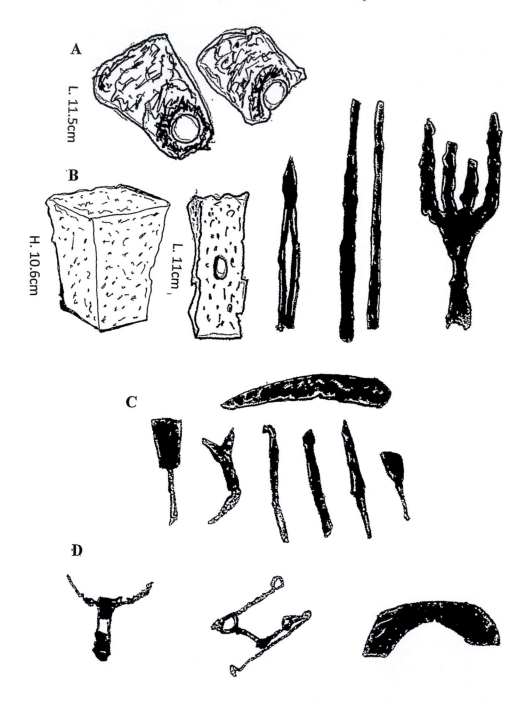

Fig. 5.1. Kofun period tools for forging iron and locally made iron implements from the Kinki core region. **A:** Blast pipes from Nango, 5th century (after OFCAH, 2004: 23). **B:** Forged-iron smithing tools from Gojo Nekozuka Kofun in Nara, 5th century (from left: solid iron block, hammer, forceps, chisels, and a 4-pronged spear (after OFCAH 2004: 25). **C:** Locally made iron tools (knives and chisels) from the Shitomiya Site in Shijonawate (Osaka) 5th century (after OFCAH 2004: 24). **D:** Horse gear from Nara, 5th century (saddle part from Haibara Cho; bit from Ouda Cho; stirrup from Uwanabe Tomb # 5) (after NKKFH 1999: 62).

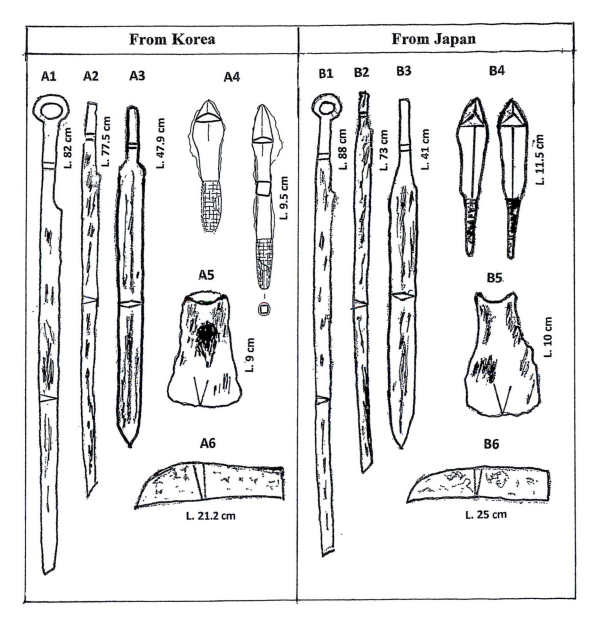

Fig. 5.2. Kofun period iron tools from southern Korea and Japan. **A1:** Long sword with a circular pommel from Pusan (PUM 1996b: 86). **B1:** from Osaka (after SKHB 2001: 48). **A2:** straight long sword from Yongweon-ri (after GJUB 1999: 134). **B2:** from Osaka (after SKHB 2001: 48). **A3:** dagger from Songdai-ri (After GJEB 2009: 75). **B3:** from Osaka (after SKHB 2001: 51). **A4:** long-stemmed arrow points from Bokcheon-dong (after PUM 1996b: 84). **B4:** from Osaka (after SKPB 2001: 48). **A5:** iron axe from Suchon-ri (after GGOB 2006: 108). **B5:** from Osaka (after SKHB 2001: 51). **A6:** sickle from Gijiri (after GGOB 2006: 106). **B6:** from Osaka (after SKHB 2001: 51).

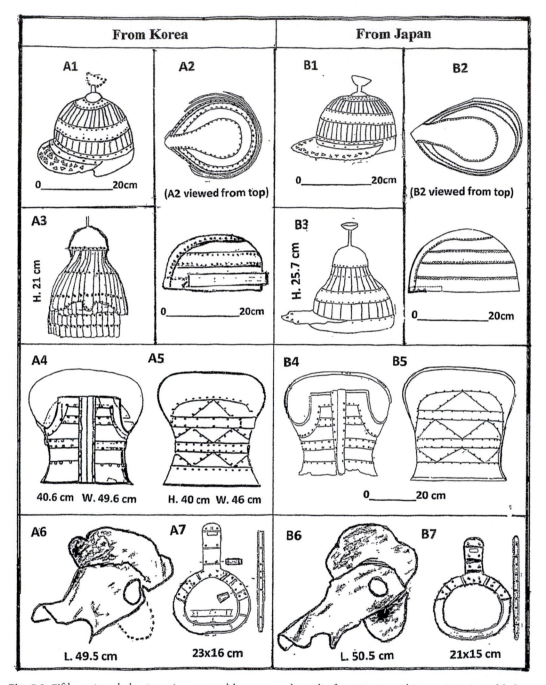

Fig. 5.3. Fifth century helmets, cuirasses, and horse paraphernalia from Korea and Japan. **A1**: riveted helmet with a visor from Jisan-dong (after GSBD 1998: 334). **B1**: from Fukui. **A2**: Keeled helmet (riveted) from Jisan-dong. **B2**: from Nara. **A3**: Mongolian type vertical plate helmet (thonged) from Bokcheon-dong. **B3**: Mongolian type vertical plate helmet (riveted) from Nara. **A4**: Horizontal rectangular plate riveted cuirass from Jisan-dong. **B4**: from Osaka (after JB Yu 2000: 378). **A5**: Horizontal triangular plate riveted cuirass from Sangbaek-ni (after Barnes 2000: 67). **B5**: from Nara. **A6**: Chamfron from Okjeon. **B6**: from Wakayama. **A7**: Metal encased wood horse bit from Bokcheon-dong. **B7**: from Shiga. **Source: B1, A6** (after Tokyo National Museum 1992: 113, 106); **B3, B6** (after Kyoto National Museum, 1987: 62,71). **A2, A3, A4, A7, B7, A8** (after JW Jeong and KC Shin 1984: 280-286); **B2, B5** (Kashihara Archaeological Research Institute).

those of Kaya and Paekche. For them, therefore, the arrival of Kaya iron technicians in the Kinki Core Region, soon after 400, was a momentous event. Soon, Toraijin-operated iron tool-making factories emerged throughout the Kinki Core Region at Furu, Ogata, Gojo, Nango, and at other sites. First, the Kaya technicians produced what they had been making in their homeland, but in the course of time they developed new tools as did their counterparts in the Peninsula, according to their own needs and preferences. After 475, they were joined by Paekche technicians.

Absolutely essential to the manufacturing of the Yamato keeled helmets and the *obigane*-type cuirasses was the *riveting technology*, which first appeared in the Peninsula and then moved to the Archipelago with the Kaya and Paekche iron technicians (JW Jeong and KC Shin 1984: 289-29, Murakami 1999: 128-129, 188-189; Kameda 2000: 165-169).

Around 550, the Toraijin iron technicians embarked on iron smelting and the production of iron; the earliest bloomeries in the Archipelago have been identified at the Senpiki Kanakuro-tani and Sago sites in Soja City, Okayama, in the ancient district of Kibi (SKAKH 2001: 35-36, 84-88). Located on sloping hills containing natural iron ore deposits, a dozen iron production sites have yielded chunks of iron ore mined from the hills, 140+ bloomeries, 68+ charcoal-making facilities, and numerous remains of tuyeres. Several forged-iron workshops were also identified nearby (SKAKH 2001: 84-88). During the Kofun period, the Soja/Okayama area of the Inland Sea became the iron capital of Japan.

On the Peninsula, the Paekche iron technicians employed two types of tuyeres, as revealed among the archaeological remains of smelting furnaces at Gian-ri of Hwaseong and at Seokjang-ni (Jincheon): the large L-shaped and the smaller straight tuyeres (Fig. 4.1E) (EJ Song *et al.* 2004: 215-218; Cheongju National Museum 2017: 95, 99, 100). Their length and inside diameter were approximately 56.0~58.0 cm x 18.3 cm for the former and 10.4 cm x 4.7 cm for the latter (measurements provided by Cheongju National Museum). In the Archipelago, the iron technicians generally used the smaller straight type (Fig. 5.1A) (OFCAH 2004: 24).

In the vicinity of the iron industry sites, immigrant settlements and their cemeteries have also been identified (Kameda 2000: 165-184, Kameda 2004b: 29-38, Kameda 2004c: 3-14, Kameda 2016: 283-297; SKAKH 2001: 35). After more than seven or eight centuries of vain attempts to smelt its own iron, the Archipelago finally had its own iron-producing industry after the mid-6th century. Combined with the Toraijin iron-smithing technicians who had arrived earlier, the *Imaki no Tehito* helped Kibi emerge as one of the most powerful polities in Japan (Kameda 2000, 172-174). Their role in iron production, therefore, was absolutely critical to the Yamato elites in Kinai in their emergence as the supreme leadership in the Archipelago.

It is no surprise that the first full-fledged iron production industries appeared in the Archipelago in the mid-6th century. Many centuries of exchange and interaction between the Peninsula and the Archipelago, including the arrival of the earlier Toraijin from Mahan, Paekche, and Kaya, had not aided Wa in its development of iron-smelting technology because the early states in the Peninsula guarded the secrets of iron production rigidly as state secrets, as in Han China. Inasmuch as iron trade was absolutely critical to the Peninsula states, they were willing to provide raw iron and finished iron products to the Wa elites but not the smelting technology (DY Kim 2015: 59-63; Murakami 2007: 189-190, 288-289, 304-305). The Peninsula elites of Kaya, Later Mahan, and Paekche knew that once the Archipelago started to produce its own iron and became self-sufficient, their most lucrative trade would come to an end, a major blow to the states' economy.

This changed during the first half of the 6th century because the Kaya states came under the threat of Silla and gradually met their demise one by one. In 562, Silla conquered Dae Kaya in Goryeong, the last remaining Kaya polity and the major iron manufacturing state in southern Korea. The *Nihon Shoki*: Kimmei year 23 reports that Silla "massacred the population" (Aston 1972, Vol. 1: 81). As with most war accounts, this was undoubtedly a hyperbolic rendering of the event, but it suggests a violent ending of the last Kaya state. With the demise of Dae Kaya, there was no longer any Kaya polity needing to safeguard the state secrets; consequently, some of the Dae Kaya survivors including the iron technicians fled to the Archipelago. Most likely, the people of Dae Kaya had begun to flee before 562 in anticipation of the Silla invasion.

Since 544, Dae Kaya had been enjoying a close relationship with Kibi through a Kibi official referred to by his rank as Kibi no Omi (*Nihon Shoki*: Kimmei year 5). Tomb #32 at Jisan-dong, the Dae Kaya elite cemetery site, contained a horizontal-band cuirass and a keeled helmet imported from the Archipelago, strongly indicating a close exchange and interaction between the Dae Kaya and the Archipelago elites (Barnes 2000; Tokyo National Museum 1992, 109, 151). Accordingly, it is no surprise that the Dae Kaya refugees migrated to Kibi when their state met its demise. This also explains why the Soja-Okayama area was called Kaya-gun (Kaya Province) for a millennium and half since ancient times. During the Kofun period, it became a major Kaya population center and remained the home of Kaya immigrants and their descendants for 1,500 years. In particular, it was in Asoko of Kaya-gun that Japan's earliest iron manufacturing industry was established (Kameda 2000: 8-14).

Finally, as in the Korean Peninsula, an almost cult-like focus on iron became an integral component of Kofun-period Yamato, as evidenced by the impressive arrays of iron objects buried in the elite tombs, including swords, spearheads, arrowheads, horse gear, body armor, helmets, and a range of agricultural tools (OFCAH 2002: 89-90).

2. Horse Breeding and Horsemanship

Horses were present in Japan during the Early Kofun period, as evidenced by the remains of horse teeth and horse gear uncovered from graves of the 4th century in Yamanashi Prefecture and Fukuoka (Fukuoka-shi Hakubutsukan 2004, 124). However, there was no organized horse-breeding culture in Japan until after 400 AD (Shiraishi 2004: 9). According to the *Nihon Shoki*: Oujin year 15, the Paekche court in Korea sent Ajiki, a Confucian scholar and official, to the Yamato court in 404 with two breeding horses, and Ajiki himself became the chief of Japan's horse-breeding enterprise during the Middle Kofun period. After his death Ajiki became deified and has since been worshipped in the Ajiki Shinto Shrine at Toyosato-cho in Shiga Prefecture.

The horse breeding practiced in early Japan was a direct outcome of Koguryo's late-390s military challenge against Paekche with an iron-armored cavalry. After confronting Koguryo's formidable mounted soldiers in Korea, Paekche undertook to build horse breeding farms to raise its own cavalry, both within Paekche and in Japan. Ajiki's mission was to start horse-breeding farms among the Paekche immigrants already in Japan, and the Yamato Court welcomed the effort for its own needs. Soon horse breeding farms were established by Paekche immigrants in Kawachi (present-day Osaka), in Tokyo and the broader Kanto region farther east, and in Gunma and Nagano Prefectures farther north. Horses, along with iron, quickly became the symbols of power in Japan and were regularly buried as prestige goods in elite tombs (SKAKH 2001: 74; Shiraishi 2004: 9-13; cf. JH Gweon and WY Jeong 2015).

A 5th century burial pit at Shitomiya-kita in Shijonawate City, Osaka, contained the remains of a five- to six-year-old horse. In addition to the horse remains, the site has yielded more than 1,500 pottery vessels used to make the salt which horse raising farms required, along with numerous horse haniwa and horse skeletons. (OFCAH 2004: 26-27). The current scholarly consensus in Japan is that Paekche immigrants not only established the first horse-raising farms but also developed horsemanship in Kawachi (K Mori 2001: 130-133; OYBH 2004: 48-49; K Tanaka 2004: 88-95; Shiraishi 2004).

The emergence of horse culture, like that of iron production, was a revolutionary event because of the practical power of horses in boosting mobility, transportation, and field warfare. It was analogous to the much later historical emergence of trains, automobiles, airplanes, and tanks. Consequently, those in charge of horse breeding, taming, and training wielded considerable power in the Kofun society. For example, according to the *Nihon Shoki: Keitai year 1*, a person named Arako, the leader of a horse-raising farm in Kawachi, was a close friend of Keitai, a royal aspirant. And it was with the active support of Arako, the Paekche immigrant in charge of horse farms, that Keitai ascended to the Yamato throne in 507 (K Mori 2001: 130-133), emerging as one of Japan's great emperors.

Arako's support was critical because whoever sought to have an upper hand militarily and politically in Japan of this period had to depend on horses and horse-driven transportation, and horse breeding was in the hands of the Paekche immigrants of Kawachi and elsewhere. Elite leaders who had a ready access to iron products and horse farms were destined to emerge at the top economically, militarily and politically. Throughout the 500s, the horse, dazzling in gilt-bronze trappings of Peninsular origin, became the key symbol of socioeconomic status and political power along with iron.

3. Flood Control, Land Reclamation, and Public Works

In Kofun society, based on an agricultural economy, the control of cultivable land was absolutely critical to political aspirants, and those who controlled the most such land had the greatest chance to emerge at the top. More lands could be acquired by war, but they could also be acquired by reclamation of swamps and wilderness, given relevant engineering expertise and proper tools.

Paekche had a long history of agriculture and land reclamation. As early as 300 AD, they had succeeded in draining vast wild and swamp lands in the Buan-Gimje region of southwest Korea by building the Byeokkolje Dam and an appropriate canal system. They also excelled in public works, as evidenced in the remains of the massive earthen fortress they constructed for their first capital at Pungnap-dong in southern Seoul. Paekche, therefore, was in a position to provide the technology and the tools necessary for Yamato's agricultural land expansion during the Middle Kofun period.

As early as 400, a number of Paekche elites as well as skilled Paekche artisans migrated to the Kyoto–Osaka–Nara region following Koguryo's military devastation of Paekche's old territory in 396 and 407 (T Tanaka 2001: 2-23; cf. *Nihon Shoki: Oujin years 14–20*). The majority of Paekche immigrants to Japan settled in the Kyoto–Osaka–Nara region, mainly in the Kawachi plains and southern Nara basin. There, they undertook the first large-scale dam-building and canal projects to drain the Kawachi wetlands for agricultural expansion, which was ultimately critical to the growth and sustainability of Yamato power.

According to archaeological investigations at the Manda, Kamei, and Sayama sites in Osaka, during the Middle Kofun periods Paekche immigrants built dikes and dams around the Kawachi Lake, employing their characteristic pounded-earth and dam construction technology known as *buyeop gongbeop*, which entailed spreading multiple layers of organic materials and tree leaves at the base of a dam or a dike (Koyamada 2001: 94-97).

Paekche immigrants with public works know-how are also believed to have supervised the building of the great keyhole-shaped burial mounds that remain today scattered across the plains of Kawachi. Archaeological evidence has revealed several temporary immigrant settlements (Daisennaka Machi, Mozu Sekiuncho Machi, Ryousai, and Asakayama) in the vicinity of these tumuli, which have yielded iron-making tools characteristically used by Korean immigrant technicians (SKHB 2001: 94-95).

4. Gold, Gilt-Bronze, and Silver Craftsmanship

According to the *Nihon Shoki*: Jingo section (Aston 1972, Vol. 1: 231), the land of Silla in southern Korea was long known to the people of Japan as "the Land of Gold and Silver... the Land of Treasure." As such, the Peninsula was much coveted by the Wa elites. Until about 500, Japan had no technology of gold, silver, and gilt-bronze smithing (Osaka Chikatsu Asuka Museum 2003: 80). Therefore, precious goods made on the Peninsula – including gold earrings, gold finger rings, ritual gold shoes, gold or silver belts, and long swords decorated with gold and silver – were highly coveted items of the elite families emerging in Japan during the Early and Middle Kofun periods. They were among the major items imported from the southern Peninsula (SKAKH 2001: 8-10, 61, 74-75; OFCAH 2003; Takata 2014: 30-138).

Nearly all the elite tombs of the Kofun period have yielded such precious goods of Peninsular origin in varying quantities (OFCAH 2003; Fukuoka-shi Hakubutsukan 2004). For example, Etafuna-yama Kofun at Kumamoto, Kyushu, built in the late 5th century, contained a gilt bronze crown, gold earrings, and ritual gilt bronze shoes of Paekche origin (Fig 5.4) (Fukuoka-shi Hakubutsukan 2004: 48, 49, 98, 101; OFCAH 2003: 41, 58, 88, 103, 108). A the east end of the Inland Sea, inside Tomb #126 in the Niizawa Senzuka near Asuka and also dated to the 5th century, were found a gold diadem, gold earrings, a gold arm bracelet, and a decorated sword, all most likely imported from the southern Peninsula (Nara-ken Kyoiku I'inkai 1977; OFCAH 2003: 64, 88, 108; Takata 2014, 180-302).

Upon their arrival in Japan the skilled craftsmen of Kaya and Paekche immediately began to produce such coveted precious ornaments (SKAKH 20011), establishing an intensive local craft industry (Pearson 2009: 5). As in the case of the iron industry, initially the newly arrived artisans replicated what they had made back home; consequently, it is impossible to ascertain whether many of the gold and gilt-bronze objects found in the 5th- and early 6th-century tombs were imported from Korea or made in Japan (Figs. 5.5 and 5.6) (Fukuoka-shi Hakubutsukan 2004: 135-138). In the course of time, however, the transplanted craftsmen and their Archipelago-born second generation technicians gradually developed their own styles, producing naturalized products that were unique to the Archipelago. Also, due to the scarcity of gold in the Islands, most of the prestige goods produced during the Middle and Late Kofun period were of gilt bronze (OFCAH 2003: 73-83). The specimens discovered in the Kamo Inariyama Kofun in Shiga (6th century), in the Fujinoki Kofun in Nara (6th century), and in Otani Ichigofun in Okayama (7th century), are excellent examples of the prestige goods made in Japan (Fig. 5.7) (Fukuoka-shi Hakubutsukan: 2004: 122-123).

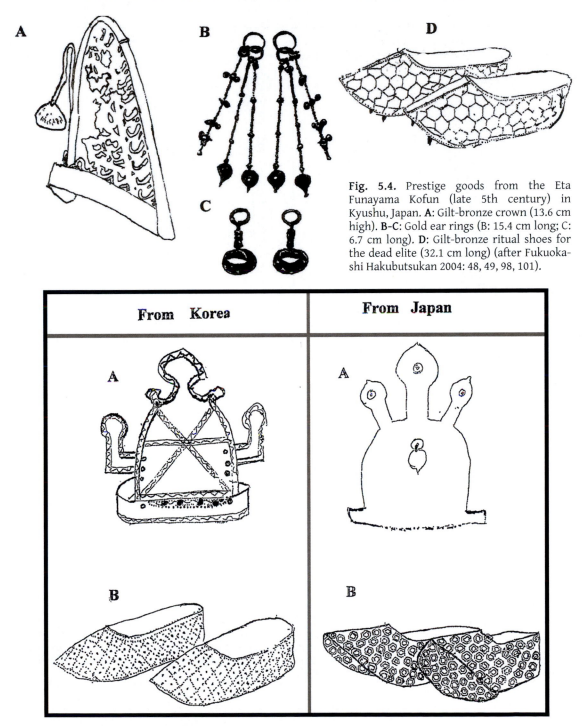

Fig. 5.4. Prestige goods from the Eta Funayama Kofun (late 5th century) in Kyushu, Japan. **A**: Gilt-bronze crown (13.6 cm high). **B-C**: Gold ear rings (B: 15.4 cm long; C: 6.7 cm long). **D**: Gilt-bronze ritual shoes for the dead elite (32.1 cm long) (after Fukuoka-shi Hakubutsukan 2004: 48, 49, 98, 101).

Fig. 5.5. Prestige goods made in Korea and those made in Japan compared (1). **From Korea:** A, Gilt-bronze crown from Kaya tomb # 32 at Jisandong in Goryeong (19.6cm high) (after GSBD 1998: 307). B, Funerary gilt-bronze shoes (30.2 cm long) from Ipjeon-ni, Korea (After Iksan-shi 2004: 15). **From Japan:** A, Gilt-bronze crown from Nihon Matsuyama Kofun in Fukui (23cm high) (after OFCAH 2003: 44). **B,** Funerary gilt-bronze shoes (38cm long) from Ichisuka Kofun in Minami Kawachi (after OFCAH 2003: 58).

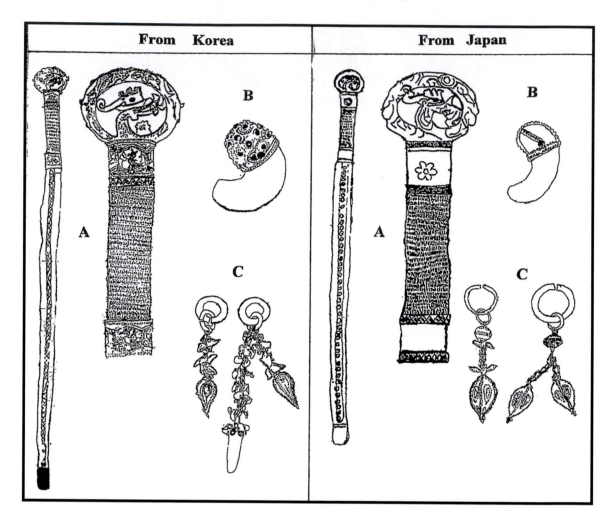

Fig. 5.6. Prestige goods made in Korea and those made in Japan compared (2). **From Korea: A,** A decorated long sword with a circular dragon-designed pommel from King Munyeong's tomb in Gongju (82cm long) (after GGOB 2004: 24). **B,** A decorated gold-plated comma-shaped jade (3.5cm long) (after GGOB 2004: 50). **C,** Intricately designed gold earrings (8.8 and 11.8 cm long) (after GGOB 2004: 36-37). **From Japan: A,** A decorated long sword with a circular dragon-designed pommel from Sannouyama Kofun in Chiba (after Fukuoka-shi Hakubutsukan 2004, 92). **B,** A gold-capped comma-shaped jade earring from Shakanokoshi Kofun in Wakayama (after Fukuoka-shi Hakubutsukan 2004: 103). **C,** Gold earrings from Kamo Inariyama Kofun in Shiga and Ichisuka Kofun in Minami Kawachi (after Fukuoka-shi Hakubutsukan 2004: 100).

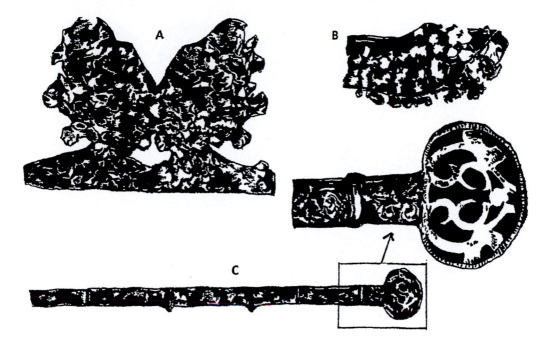

Fig. 5.7. Prestige goods, naturalized (Japanized). **A:** A gilt-bronze crown (52cm high) from Fujinoki Kofun in Nara, 6th century. **B:** A gilt-bronze shoe (29cm long) from Kamo Inariyama Kofun in Shiga, 6th century. **C:** A sword in a decorated sheath (110cm long) and an enlarged view of its decorated pommel from Otani Ichigofun in Okayama, 7th century (after OFCAH 2002: 49, 54, 63).

5. Silk Industry

According to the *Nihon Shoki:* Oujin year 14 (403), Ashin, the king of Paekche (392–405) sent to the Yamato court a seamstress named Jinmojin, who became the ancestor of fine silk weaving and sewing in Yamato Japan. By the 1st century BC, the people of Mahan were producing fine silk, as evidenced in the archaeological remains of Shinchang-dong in Gwangju. Most likely Jinmojin and others from Later Mahan polities and Paekche brought to Japan the know-how on silkworm raising and silk weaving using a loom.

Weaving technology had been first introduced to Japan during the Yayoi period, as evidenced by the presence of Mumun-type spindle whorls. Various Kofun-period sites have yielded the kinds of abacus-bead-shaped spindle whorls made of hard-fired (*dojil*) clay popular in Paekche, suggesting that the Paekche immigrants brought their weaving technology to Japan (Fig. 5.8; SKAKH 2001: 22) and that Jinmojin represented not the first fine weaving, but the arrival of a highly valued new level of silk-weaving skill from the Peninsula.

6. The *Sueki* Stoneware Industry

During the Middle Kofun period, a kind of stoneware pottery known in Japan as Sueki ('Sue vessels') suddenly appeared. Sueki vessels were the prestige ware of the elite classes during the Kofun period and included mounted dishes, covered dishes, jars, bowls, and tall pottery serving stands. Every

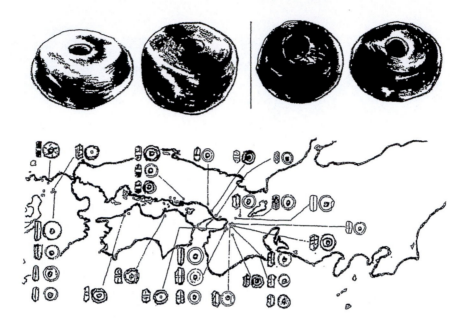

Fig. 5.8. Abacus bead-shaped spindle whorls of hard-baked clay (diameter, 4.0-6.0cm) from Korean southwest and the Archipelago. **Top left**: From Gongju (after GGOB 2006:163). **Top right**: From Toki Minami Sueki Production Site in Osaka (after SKHB 2001: 69). **Bottom**: Geographical distribution of abacus bead-shaped spindle whorls in the Japanese Archipelago (after SKAKH 2001: 22).

aristocratic Kofun grave contained Sueki, often in abundance. This was the industrially manufactured, wheel-thrown, high-fired stoneware made widely in ancient Korea and known there as *dojil togi* (stoneware), which was first introduced to the Archipelago by the Peninsular immigrants (Fig. 5.9).

When stoneware pottery was first produced on the southern Peninsula, natives descriptively called it *soe geureut* (iron vessels) because it was as hard as iron and made a metallic sound when tapped. When those peoples migrated to the Archipelago, they continued to call it *soe geureut*. As the Yamato scribes began to adopt the Chinese script to write their own language, they rendered the term as Sueki (SKHB 2001: 96).

As previously mentioned, one of the effects of Koguryo's devastating attack on Kuya-guk in 400 was to drive many Kaya people to leave their homeland. According to Shin and Kim (2000: 191-193), "The emergence of *Sueki* pottery in Japan was essentially a reestablishment of southern Kaya pottery technology.... There is no room for any doubt about the connection between the two.... When Geumgwan Kaya was destroyed by Koguryo forces in AD 400, people of Southern Kaya states migrated to the Archipelago."

The *dojil* stoneware began to be manufactured at various places in the Archipelago almost simultaneously between Kyushu and the Osaka Plains: at the Asakura kiln complex and Ichiba Minami Gumi sites in Kyushu, at Iyashiki in Ehime Prefecture, at Soja and the Okugatani site in Okayama Prefecture, and at the Suemura site in the Osaka region. Sueki pottery from the Obatera kilns near Suemura closely resembles the stoneware of the Pusan and Kimhae areas of eastern Kaya, while

Fig. 5.9. Vessel types of Early Korean States stoneware pottery found in the Archipelago. **Top:** Tubular and other pottery stands (60-95 cm high); mounted dishes and covers (15-25 cm high), early 5th century, from Kiln #TG232 in Osaka (after SKHB 2001: 60). **Middle:** Early Sueki barrel-shaped jars, jars with a side hole, and dishes and cups from Obatera in Osaka (after OFCAH 2004: 30). **Bottom:** Early Sueki jars, mounted dishes (most likely with lids originally), handled cups, and vases (after OFCAH 2004: 30).

the Sueki from the Asakura workshops in Kyushu resembles those made in the western Kaya area (Takesue 1997: 93-126).

It is also a widely held consensus among Japanese archaeologists and ceramic specialists that Sueki could not have been produced in the Archipelago without the on-site presence of Peninsular stoneware technicians and their direct technological contributions (Sadamori 1991: 167-176). The oldest Sueki in Japan has come from a square mound tomb at Kumeta in Kishiwada City (Osaka) (Torama 1993, 1994; Sakai 2013: 26-27, 46). The Kumeta repertoire includes vessels identical to the stoneware produced by various southern Kaya states as well as by potters of the Yeongsan River valley in southwestern Peninsula (KS Shin 2000: 180-181). This indicates that from the beginning, stoneware in Japan was produced by immigrant pottery technicians from the entire southern coastal region east to the west, including both Kaya and Mahan technicians.

It has been suggested that during the 4th century, Kuya-guk in Kimhae and Mahan polities were in a state of political alliance for mutual defense and commercial enterprise. Therefore, when Koguryo devastated Kuya-guk in 400, Mahan and Kaya elites migrated together to the Kinai region (KC Shin 2000: 194-198). Consequently, the Sueki from Obatera TG 232 kiln included vessel shapes of both Kaya and Mahan. The Sueki produced by Mahan technicians are distinguished by barrel-shaped jars and jars with a side hole and large mouth.

Even though the stoneware technology of Kaya and Mahan simultaneously commenced in the production of Sueki shortly after 400, Mahan technology was becoming increasingly more important (Sakai 2004a; Shiraishi 2004: 10; KC Shin 2000: 181-185). By the time TK-73 kiln at Suemura and ON-231 kiln at Nonoishi Site became operative, Mahan-type Sueki had become the dominant form of stoneware (Sakai 2013: 98-101; KC Shin 2000: 181-185). Sueki produced at the kilns in Osaka were distributed to regional power centers, even though those areas also produced their own stoneware for local uses.

The increasing dominance of Mahan technology in the Kinki region was the result of steady rise in the number of Mahan immigrants being pushed out by Paekche's encroachment upon their territory since King Geunchogo's military campaign into the Mahan territory in 369 AD. By the early 700s, the Sueki vessels became a part of ordinary people's daily lives, following a century of use as funerary ritual vessels of the elite classes. The Suemura kilns were continuously operated until the 800s, and the pottery tradition itself persisted into the 1100s (Takesue 1997: 87-119).

III. IDEOLOGICAL TRANSFORMATION

1. Confucianization of the Yamato Court

Planting Confucian ideology in the Yamato court was initially attempted by the Paekche court in 404. That year Paekche King Ashin sent Ajiki, a Paekche official, to the Yamato court with two breeding horses as a valued gift. Ajiki was also a scholar of Confucian classics and became the teacher of Yamato crown prince, Uji no Waka Iratsuko. The following year, Wang In, another Paekche scholar, was sent expressly to instruct the crown prince in Confucian learning (Nihon Shoki: Oujin year 15 and year 16). The study of the Confucian classics would acquaint government leaders with the Confucian ideology of governance and the wisdom and knowledge essential for administration and statecraft, while the ability to read and write, gained in studying the classics, would equip administrators and managers with recording and communication skills essential to their job performance.

The full-scale systematic and organized effort to bring about Japan's ideological transformation, however, began a century later during the reign of Paekche's King Munyeong (r. 501–523). According to the *Nihon Shoki*: Keitai year 7 and year 10, in 513 and 516, from his palace at Koma (Ungjin; modern Gongju) Munyeong sent to Yamato's Emperor Keitai teachers of Chinese writing and Confucian scholars. As a result of King Munyeong's efforts and those of others that followed, Yamato court officials, including the emperor and crown princes, became increasingly Confucianized. By the latter part of the 6th century, the Yamato court was firmly undergirded with Confucian political ideology, which emphasized the supremacy of the ruler, the loyalty of the ruled, and the enhancement of social order and harmony as the highest goal of the government. A national Constitution and other laws were promulgated in accordance with the Confucian ethical and political ideology.

2. Buddhism for the Nation

Further ideological transformation of Japan was undertaken by Munyeong's son, King Seong (r. 523–554), through his promotion of Buddhism with an unprecedented missionary zeal. The strongest proponents of the new religion were members of a Soga clan of Paekche origin that was descended from Mokhyup Manchi, introduced above as a high-ranking official from a powerful clan of the late 5th–6th century. These Soga were determined to propagate Buddhism in Japan at any cost, even by eliminating an emperor (Sujun) and other powerful rival clans standing in their way. Nor was it a mere coincidence that Mokhyup Geumdon, a powerful Soga kinsman in Paekche, was visiting the Yamato court at the very moment when the Paekche court was sending its first Buddhist mission to Japan (*Nihon Shoki*: Kimmei year 14).

According to the *Nihon Shoki*: Kimmei year 13, Paekche's King Seong commissioned a Buddhist delegation to Kimmei, the Yamato ruler, with a gilt bronze image of Shakyamuni Buddha, Buddhist scriptures, and Buddhist paraphernalia including flags and umbrellas. Along with these Buddhist objects King Seong also sent a personal letter to the Yamato king in which he said (Aston 1972, Vol. 2: 66):

> This doctrine is amongst all doctrines the most excellent. But it is hard to explain, and to comprehend... The doctrine... can lead on to a full appreciation of the highest wisdom... Myong, King of [Paekche] has humbly despatched his retainer, [Nuri Sa-chi], to transmit it to the Imperial Country, and to diffuse it abroad throughout the home provinces, so as to fulfil the recorded saying of Buddha: "My law shall spread to the East."

The exact date for this event has long been debated among scholars to be either 538 or 552 (Tsuji 1969, 34-42; Tamura 1981: 36-40; INOUE Mitsusada (1993, 171); Best 2006, 138-141). What is certain, however, is the fact it was King Seong (523–554) of Paekche that took the initiative of bringing the new religion to Yamato.

At first the new religion did not fare well in the Yamato court. According to the account recorded in the Nihon Shoki: Kimmei year 13, Emperor Kimmei was pleased to receive such rare gifts from Paekche, but could not decide on his own what to do with them. Soga no Iname, the then Prime Minister of the Yamato government and a man descended from Mokhyup Manchi of Paekche, highly praised and commended the new religion. Soga no Iname happened to be also Emperor Kimmei's father-in-law, giving him a considerable influence on the Emperor.

Okoshi, Mononobe-no-Oho-Muraji and Kamako, Nakatomi no Muraji, two other powerful Yamato leaders, however, fiercely opposed Buddhism in favour of worshipping only native deities. As recorded in the Nihon Shoki: Kimmei year 13 (Aston 1972, Vol. 2: 66-67):

> They addressed the Emperor jointly, saying, "Those who have ruled the Empire in this our State have always made it their care to worship in Spring, Summer, Autumn and Winter the 180 Gods of Heaven and Earth, and the Gods of the Land and of Grain. If just at this time we were to worship in their stead foreign Deities, it may be feared that we should incur the wrath of our National Gods".

To test its efficacy the Emperor asked Iname to take Buddha's image to his house and worship it, in effect making Iname's house the first Buddhist temple in Japan. When this was done, a deadly pestilence broke out in the capital, and so with the urging of Mononobe-no-Oho-Muraji and Nakatomi no Muraji, the Emperor ordered the image thrown into the Canal of Naniwa and its temple burned. As written in the Nihon Shoki: Kimmei year 13 (Aston 1972, Vol. 2: 67), "Hereupon, there being in the Heavens neither clouds nor wind, a sudden conflagration consumed the Great Hall [of the Palace]." Despite these fantastically unnatural events or because of them, the common people in Japan began to worship Buddha and chant Buddhist prayers, and the Emperor himself enthusiastically encouraged the new religion the following year, in 553.

In 554, King Seong of Paekche was killed during Paekche's war with Silla, and consequently King Wideok (r. 554–598), his son and successor, resumed Paekche's Buddhist mission to Yamato Japan. Encouraged by some positive effects generated by the earlier mission begun by his father, King Wideok sent in 554 a great Buddhist priest named Damhye, along with eight other Buddhist priests, to teach and propagate Buddhism to the people of Japan. He also sent a Confucian scholar, copies of Confucian classics, a specialist in the calendar, a physician, an herbal specialist, and a musician (Nihon Shoki: Kimmei year 15).

Due, however, to the persistent demands of the continuing state of war between Paekche and Silla, King Wideok had to wait eighteen years before he could dispatch another Buddhist mission to Yamato Japan. Wideok at length sent six more Buddhist missionaries in 587, including a temple architect, a maker of Buddhist images, two monks, a nun, and a reciter of Buddhist mantras, along with 200 volumes of Buddhist books (Nihon Shoki: Bidatsu year 6).

In the meantime, however, Buddhism had already been steadily growing in Yamato with the support of the powerful Soga clan. In 572 Soga no Umako, the son of Soga no Iname, had become the new Ohmi (Prime Minister) in the Yamato government, and as an ardent Buddhist himself, like his father he actively promoted the new religion, recruiting believers and training leaders for the new faith. In 584, Umako acquired from Paekche two stone images of Buddha, including one of Buddha Maitreya, popular in Paekche at that time as "the Saviour Buddha to Come."

Umako also recruited three young maidens – Zenshin, Toyome, and Ishime – as new Buddhists and paid with his personal funds for their training as nuns. Three years later he would send them to Buyeo, the Paekche capital, to receive advanced training in the Buddhist Law directly from Paekche priests. Umako built two Buddhist temples, one in Asuka near his dwelling and another one in Ishikaha, enshrining in the former the stone Buddha images he had acquired from Paekche (Nihon

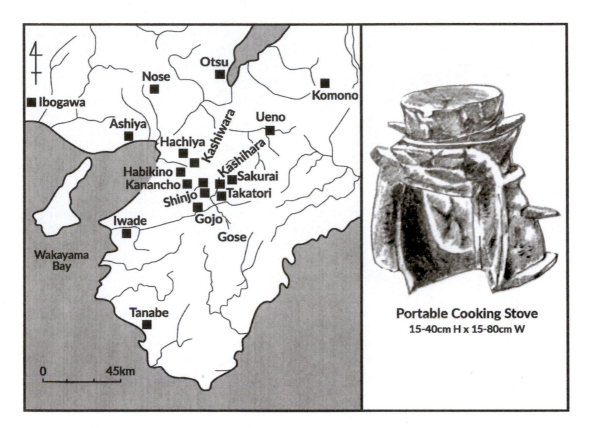

Map 5.2. Corridor-style tomb sites in Kinai and a miniature cooking oven placed in the corridor tombs (by Lucas Pauly). (After SKAKH 2001: 44, 69).

Shoki: Bidatsu year 13). In the meantime, he had also succeeded in persuading the Emperor Yomei to espouse Buddhism (Nihon Shoki: Yomei year 2).

The Soga clan, however, was not without opponents in Japan. Mononobe-no-Oho-Muraji and Nakatomi-no-Muraji, two powerful clans, vehemently opposed to Buddhism (Nihon Shoki: Yomei year 2). These two native clans had rejected the new religion from the beginning and were working in every way they could manage to destroy both the Soga clan and its Buddhism. When Umako built his own private Buddhist temple and pagoda near his house, the Mononobe-no-Oho-Muraji burned them down and crushed the stone Buddha images to pieces, throwing them into a nearby river (Nihon Shoki: Bidatsu year 14).

Subsequently, in the autumn of 587 Mononobe-no-Oho-Muraji and his supporters gathered a group of well-armed troops to attack and destroy Soga no Umako and wipe out his new religion. In the course of an intense battle, Umako prayed, making a solemn vow: "Oh! All ye Heavenly Kings and great Spirit King, aid and protect us, and make us to gain the advantage. If this prayer is granted, I will erect a temple with a pagoda... and will propagate everywhere the three precious things [Buddha, Dharma (Buddha's Teachings), and Sangha (the Buddhist Priesthood and Temple Establishment)]" (Nihon Shoki: Sujun; Aston 1972, Vol. 2: 114). Mononobe no Oho-muraji was killed in the battle, and his supporters fled in all directions.   Upon receiving the news that Umako had triumphed over his foes, King Wideok of Paekche dispatched to him twelve more Buddhist priests, headed by a monk named Hyechong; two temple architects; one temple smith; four specialists in roof tile manufacturing; and one painter of Buddhist art, along with three high-ranking court officials. The primary objective of this mission was to help construct Japan's first Buddhist temple (Nihon Shoki: Sujun year 1).

Soga no Umako himself also hastened to build a real temple he could be proud of, and in 587, according to the Nihon Shoki: Yomei year 2), "Soga no Ohmi erected the Temple of Hokoji in Asuka in fulfilment of his vow." Evidence suggests that he actually began the construction in the following year and completed it in 596, taking six years (Nihon Shoki: Sujun year 1 and Suiko year 4).

Hokoji Temple (also known as the Asuka Temple) was the first edifice ever constructed in Japan with stone foundations and roof tiles, and archaeological excavations of the temple site have revealed that the roof tiles of Hokoji—as well as those of all early Buddhist temples in the Kyoto–Osaka–Nara area—were local versions of Paekche tiles manufactured by Paekche tile specialists, suggesting that Japan's first Buddhist temples were all built by Paekche architects (BH Lee 2013, 35-15) (Fig. 5.10).

Umako then appointed his son as the head of the temple, and Hyechong and Hyeja, renowned priests from Paekche and Koguryo respectively, as resident priests. Following Umako's triumph in 587, Buddhism was established officially as the new religion of Japan. It would provide the Yamato leaders a new ideology, new ethical values, and a spiritual foundation on which to unify the people and the nation. Thus, with the pervasive arrival of Paekche culture, its arts, its architecture, and its Buddhist religion, Kofun-period Yamato entered the Asuka Era, the most brilliant cultural period in ancient Japan.

The propagation of Buddhism in Japan, which reshaped Japanese culture forever, was not a matter decided by the Yamato court, nor mutually between the Yamato court and the Paekche court, but rather between the Soga clan and the Paekche court for their own ulterior motives. On the part of the Soga clan, it sought to strengthen its own political base with the new religion. On the part of the Paekche court, still in the process of rebuilding its own nation in the aftermath of its catastrophic defeat by Koguryo in 475, it wanted to strengthen its political and military alliance with Yamato sharing a common ideology and a common spiritual force.

"Although [King Seong's] personal belief in Buddhism was doubtless a factor in sending the embassy to introduce the religion to Japan," Best (2003, 176, 2006, 140-141) perceptively observes, "the timing and the context of the mission allow little question but that political concerns formed his primary immediate motivation."

Throughout history political leaders have used religions, including Buddhism, to advance their political agenda. Buddhism, however, is doctrinally and ideologically universal, emphasizing the oneness of all existence and the unity of mankind and transcending national boundaries. Therefore, from the beginning, Buddhist leaders of Koguryo came to Japan to participate actively in Paekche's Buddhist mission work – to teach and propagate the new religion to the Japanese elites as well as to the common people, even though Koguryo and Paekche were mortal enemies.

In 595, Hyeja, a preeminent Buddhist scholar-priest of Koguryo, came to Asuka and, with Hyechong, an equally preeminent Buddhist scholar-priest from Paekche, became co-resident priests of the Hokoji Temple, teaching and propagating Buddhism to the Yamato elites as well as to the common people.

Fig. 5.10. Remains of Asuka Temple, the first Buddhist temple in Japan, built by Paekche architects and tile specialists. **Top left**: foundations of the middle gate leading to the temple. **Top right:** Remains of the foundation of the main hall (after Nara Kokuritsu Bunkazai Kenkyusho (no date), 52). **Bottom left:** Paekche roof tile ends found in Gongju, Paekche capital (diameter 14.5cm, 15.5cm) (after GGOB 1981: #96, #99). **Bottom right:** Tile ends found at the Asuka Temple site (after Nara Kokuritsu Bunkazai Kenkyusho (no date), 50).

For twenty years from 595 to 615, Hyeja served as the personal tutor of Shotoku Taishi, a prince and the regent of Empress Suiko, educating and enlightening him to become the greatest scholar-statesman in ancient Japan.

In 602, the Paekche court sent to the Yamato court, for the last time, an eminent Buddhist priest and books on the calendar, astronomy, geography, and divination. That priest, Gwan Leuk, remained in Asuka the rest of his life, training Japanese students (*Nihon Shoki*: Suiko year 10). Also, by this stage the Paekche court was satisfied with its accomplishments in helping Japan (and its large Paekche population) to arrive at a point where it could now go directly to China to further acquire the benefits of Chinese civilization.

Moreover, by 600 many Paekche communities were well established in the Osaka–Kyoto–Nara area, with Paekche people and their descendants leading in all walks of life within the Yamato power center and all of Japan's vital technological fields. According to the 8th-century census record reported in the *Shoku Nihongi* (Continuous Chronicles of Japan): Hoki, year 3, 80–90% percent of the people living in the southern Nara basin, the heart of Yamato power, were Peninsular immigrants, mostly from Paekche. Further, an entire section of the Osaka area in Settsu and Kawachi was designated as Paekche-gun (Paekche county). There the remnants of Paekche's ruling families, known as the O-clan, resided, building for themselves a powerful ally with the rulers of Yamato Japan, which would continue to benefit them for centuries to come (Furuichi 2001, 118-125).

3. Elite Mortuary System: From Vertical Pit-Chamber Burials to Corridor-Style Tombs

The corridor tombs were first introduced to northern Kyushu during "the late 4th or early 5th centuries" (Mizoguchi 2013: 256). After 475, they underwent structural changes under the influence of advanced corridor tombs of Paekche of the Ungjin period. Subsequently the Kyushu corridor tombs spread to other regions in the Archipelago as far north as Tokai and Hokuriku. "The time of the spread," Mizoguchi states, "corresponded with... conflicts of the Korean Peninsula... it also corresponded with the formation of local complexes of activities such as constructing and conducting rituals – all involving sophisticated technologies that had originated in the Peninsula..." (Mizoguchi 2013: 257-258).

Following the mass exodus of Paekche people, including the elites and commoners, to the Kinki region in 475 and thereafter, the corridor-style tombs began to appear in the region in an increasing number. By 550, thousands of the Paekche corridor tombs appeared on ridges in more than a dozen *gunshu-fun* ('packed tumuli clusters') (Map 5.2, cf. Fig. 4.13) (Ishiwatari 2002: 242-244; Mizoguchi 2013: 300-304).

Some of the corridor tombs built by immigrants in the Uzumasa District of Kyoto and in the southern Nara basin, centers of major immigrant colonies, were huge. For example, Hebizuka Kofun, 75 meters (or 225 feet) long, was built to house a mammoth stone corridor chamber (Kyoto Bunka Hakubutsukan 1989: 40; K Hirose 2013, 143-178). Equally large was the Ishibutai Kofun built in Asuka. These megalithic constructions were made by skilled stone masons from the Omi district, a major Paekche immigrant colony (OFCAH 2002: 91).

During this period, corridor tombs became popular with Wa elites. All the prosperous elites, from kings down to village chiefs, built corridor tombs for themselves (OFCAH 2002: 91-92; Shiraishi 2004, 11). The decisive event catalyzing this nationwide transformation was Emperor Keitai's personal decision to replace the vertical pit burial type of the preceding Oujin Dynasty with corridor tombs. This was to signal a dynastic change from the earlier Oujin to the later Keitai families (OFCAH 2002: 91).

With corridor tombs becoming normative in Kofun society, ideas relative to interment of the dead also underwent changes. Native Wa people who previously did not bury family members together began to do so, bringing a significant transformation in Japan's mortuary culture (Shiraishi 2004, 12). As Yamato society became ever more complex the unity and solidarity of the family, communicated through the new mortuary system, was becoming an important value.

According to Mizuno (1981, 158) and Mizoguchi (2013: 300-308), during the Late Kofun period the Yamato regime found the corridor tomb clusters useful as a political instrument to strengthen its direct control of the clan-based local power groups and fostered their adoption among them throughout the Archipelago. In the Peninsula, the Paekche rulers had already put this system in place by the beginning of the 6th century. As in Paekche, the transformation of Yamato's elite mortuary system was also as much political as ideological in its motivations. It not only changed Japan's elite mortuary practices but also communicated a dynastic change from Oujin to Keitai. Furthermore, it enhanced political centralization and control within the Kofun society as local elites adopted the corridor tombs following the Yamato court's lead (Yoshi'i 2001, 104-117; OFCAH 2002: 90).

IV. EXCHANGE AND INTERACTION BETWEEN PAEKCHE AND YAMATO ELITES (4TH-6TH CENTURY)

Singularly important in the cultural and technological revolutions of the Middle–Late Kofun period was the close exchange and interaction among the leaders of Paekche and Yamato (Best 2003; Takata 2014: 14-27). Underlying this phenomenon were also the *push-pull* dynamics.

Paekche needed military or diplomatic assistance from the Wa elites in the face of threats from Koguryo and Silla while the latter needed advanced Peninsular goods in their own socio-political and cultural development within the Archipelago. Accordingly, Takata (*Ibid.*) has explained the presence in Kofun-period elite burials of numerous prestige goods of Peninsular origin and/or manufacture (gold ear rings, elaborately designed gilt-bronze belt buckles, stirrups, and iron spearpoints, etc.) in terms of a formal exchange and interaction system between the Pen/Insular elites. Likewise, Paekche's Buddhist mission to Yamato, according to Best (2003), took shape in the context of the mutual needs.

1. KINGLY EXCHANGES

In 371, in the face of a Koguryo threat, Paekche King Geunchogo sent a seven-branched sword of friendship to the Yamato court (now in the Isonokami Shrine at Tenri) (INOUE Mitsusada 1973: 357-359; Brown 1993: 121-122; T. Tanaka 2001: 5; Kimura 2005: 74-80), and in 399 a combined force of Paekche and Wa soldiers became allies in a war against Koguryo (HG Lee and RH Park 1996: 85-93). In a concrete sense, the people of Paekche and Wa were linked by their shared histories as comrades in arms. Furthermore, in the course of their interactions with Paekche, the Wa people came to admire Paekche culture and technology. *That was an important reason why the welcome mat was spread out in Japan to the people of Paekche during the time of the latter's existential crisis.*

In the years 397 and 402, King Asin sent envoys to the Yamato court to strengthen the Paekche–Yamato friendship. This was followed by the arrival in Kinai of a large number of Paekche immigrants, as revealed by the sudden appearance in Japan at this time of Paekche–Later Mahan cooking culture and associated cooking tools including cooking stoves (K. *buttumak*; J. *kamado*) and cooking pots and pans with *jojokmun* (bird foot print designs). The Paekche refugees settled in northern Kyushu as well as in the Kawachi and Chikatsu Asuka area, turning the latter into a major Paekche Toraijin colony (YJ Im 2001: 48-73; Shirai 2001: 76-93).

Coinciding with this event is the appearance of the corridor tombs with a side chamber in northern Kyushu, soon spreading throughout western Japan as well as into the eastern part of the main island. Along with them there also appeared throughout the Archipelago an advanced iron forging technology and new prestige goods including horse trappings, long swords, slender arrowheads, body armor made of either lamellae or slats riveted together, and numerous gilt-bronze ornaments (TS Kim 2014b: 261-264). Three years later in 403, the Paekche king sent to the Yamato court a seamstress named Jinmojin who became known as "the ancestor of sewing" in Yamato Japan (*Nihon Shoki*: Oujin year 14).

Most of all, Paekche was eager to have a supply of effective mounted troops to help fight against those of Koguryo, so in 404, the Paekche court sent Ajiki to the Yamato court with breeding horses.

In 461, in anticipation of a Koguryo invasion, Paekche king Gaero (r. 455–475) sent Prince Gonji, his brother, to the Yamato court to seek military assistance and to plan a common defense against Koguryo. He was followed two years later (463) by a large number of skilled artisans from Paekche, including potters, saddle makers, painters, makers of multi-colored silk (*nishiki*), tailors, and interpreters. They were settled in the Momohara and Magamihara districts of the Yamato capital (*Nihon Shoki*: Yuryaku year 7). In time, they came to be known as the Yamato Aya Clan. Thus, already during the early period of Paekche at Hanseong (modern Seoul), Yamato was receiving an advanced culture from the Peninsula, including Chinese writing as well as various technologies including horsemanship and multi-colored silk fabric manufacturing.

Four years after the Hanseong catastrophe, in 479, Yuryaku, the king of Yamato, provided 500 soldiers to accompany Malda, Prince Gonji's son, as he sailed from Yamato to Koma-naru (Ungjin, modern Gongju) to ascend the Paekche throne, following the untimely death of Samgeun (*Nihon Shoki*: Yuryaku year 23, 7th month).

Essentially, underlying this exchange and interaction system were also *push-pull* dynamics caused more by the military exigency than by commercial interests. The existential crisis in the face of Koguryo invasions *pushed* the Paekche court toward the Yamato court to gain an ally. The need to have an advanced culture and technology *pushed* the Yamato court toward the Paekche elites and at the same time *pulled* in people of value.

In 513, Paekche King Munyeong sent Dan Yang'i, a learned scholar in Confucian classics, to the Yamato court. Three years later, Dan Yang'i returned, and the Paekche court sent Ko Anmu to Emperor Keitai to continue in the instruction of Confucian learning in the Japanese court (*Nihon Shoki*: Keitai year 7).

In 552 (or 538, Brown 1993, 171), Paekche King Seong dispatched a Buddhist delegation to the Yamato court, sending to Emperor Kimmei a gilt-bronze image of Shakyamuni Buddha, Buddhist scriptures, and various Buddhist paraphernalia (flags and umbrellas). As recorded in the *Nihon Shoki*: Kimmei, Years 13-14, (all quotes from Aston 1972, Vol. 2: 65-71), King Seong was determined to make Yamato a land of Buddhism like Paekche, for he believed that as a powerful spiritual force Buddhism would unify its people and greatly facilitate the process of Yamato state's centralization. In gratitude, the Emperor Kimmei reciprocated by sending precious gifts to Paekche including "two good horses, two travelling barges, fifty bows, fifty sets of arrows" Kimmei also sent a message to King Seong that he would send him "troops asked for". In Kimmei Year 14, sixth month, he asked the Paekche king to send "men learned in medicine, in divination, and in the calendar... books of divination, calendars, and medicines of various kinds".

King Seong quickly responded to Emperor Kimmei's urgent request. In February 554, he sent a large Paekche delegation consisting of an expert on Confucian classics, two experts on divination, two experts on calendar, one physician, two herbalists, four musicians, and nine Buddhist priests. Along with the cultural delegation, King Seong sent Kimmei a formal request for troops to assist him in an impending war which he was planning against Silla. In Kimmei Year 15, Kimmei swiftly responded with 1,000 soldiers, 100 horses, and 40 ships.

In actuality, the Paekche court's expectations from the Wa (Yamato) elites for military assistance ended in disappointment because that aid was too limited as well as ineffective against Koguryo and Silla forces combined with the heavily armed cavalry. This was particulary true in the days when Paekche was in its death and life struggle with Koguryo in 475, with Silla in 554 at the Gwansan Fortress, and with the combined forces of Silla and Tang in 660. Nonetheless, throughout its history the Paecke court viewed the Wa (Yamato) elites as allies.

2. Intermediary Role of Powerful Paekche Elites Residing in Yamato

Behind these extraordinary exchanges between the Paekche and the Yamato kings were powerful Paekche personages residing in the Yamato capital: Gonji and Mok Manchi and their descendants. Gonji, a Paekche prince, had gone to Japan at the behest of his brother, King Gaero, in 461, to "serve the Emperor," that is, to offer service in the Yamato court. He had five sons. According to the *Nihon Shoki*: Yuryaku year 23 and Muretsu year 4, two of his sons were Malda (spelled also Mata, Malta) and Sama (or Shima) born of different mothers. It is also suggested that Sama was the son of Gaero or Malda (Best 2006: 115). After a 15-year stay in the Yamato capital, Gonji returned to Paekche in 475 to help restore the Paekche court in crisis, leaving his family in Japan. Malda and Sama assumed the Paekche throne as King Dongseong in 479 and King Munyeong in 501 respectively.

Mok or Mokhyup Manchi, a member of the powerful Mok clan and a high scholar-official in the Paekche court left Paekche soon after King Munju, whom he personally served, was assassinated by the king's political enemies. His rich background as a Paekche elite and a high official in the Paekche court placed him in the Yamato court, working in the administrative and financial sector (Y Suzuki 1981). His great grandson, Soga no Iname, became the prime minister in the Yamato court in 536. Iname's son, Umako, emerged as the most powerful political figure in Japan, transforming its socio-cultural fabric during 572–626. (See "The Soga Clan" in Chapter Four, IV.)

Gonji and Mok Manchi, as members of the Yamato court, knew what the newly emerging Yamato nation needed to become an effective partner in the world of the East Asian civilization. Accordingly, as learned men of Paekche, they would have earnestly desired to transplant as much Paekche civilization as possible in the land of Yamato Japan. This would have been a major topic frequently discussed in their family and kinsmen gatherings as well as in their meetings with Yamato officials. It is therefore no surprise to learn from the *Nihon Shoki* that two years after Gonji's arrival in the Yamato capital, a large number of skilled artisans arrived in Yamato, as described above. Likewise, it is no surprise to learn that as soon as Sama, one of Gonji's sons, established social and political order in Paekche as King Munyeong and placed his nation on a firm foundation, he dispatched cultural missions to the Yamato capital, beginning in 513.

King Munyeong (r. 501-523) and Emperor Keitai (r. 507-531) were contemporary rulers of Paekche and Yamato respectively. According to the Suda Hachiman Shrine Mirror inscriptions, they had a close (fraternal?) relationship. This, undoubtedly, enhanced the migration of skilled Paekche people to Yamato during the early 6th century.

The cultural flow from Paekche to Yamato from 513 to 602, the year of Paekche's last cultural mission, resulted in the transmission of advanced technology in iron tool production, in farming, in land reclamation, in dam and dyke construction, in architecture, in tile-making, in stoneware pottery production, gold and gilt-bronze craftsmanship, and in horse breeding and horse-driven transportation along with arts, music, herbal medicine, calendar, learning in classics, art of governance, and new ideologies (Confucianism and Buddhism) among others.

In retrospect, it appears that Gonji and Mok Manchi were determined to Paekcheize Yamato culturally and socially. Their intent, it appears, was to help make Yamato become and look like Paekche culturally, technologically, and ideologically. And in this endeavour, Mok Manchi's descendants, now as the Soga clan, even went to war against the Mononobe and Nakatomi, two powerful native clans vehemently opposed to their endeavour. (See "Buddhism for the Nation" in Chapter 5, III:2)

The Soga clan's triumph over the Mononobe and Nakatomi clans in the war of 587 forever changed the colour and the texture of Japanese civilization through the glorious blossoming of Buddhism at Asuka and Prince Shotoku's proclamation in 604 of the Seventeen Article Constitution based on Confucian and Buddhist principles. In these endeavours, the Yamato leaders were immensely encouraged and helped by the elites of Paekche including Munyeong, Seong, and Wideok, the three 6th-century kings of Paekche.

V. SHOTOKU TAISHI, THE SEVENTEEN ARTICLE CONSTITUTION OF 604, AND THE TORAIJIN

Shotoku Taishi is revered in Japan not only as the greatest statesman of the 6th–7th century but also as the founder of Japanese Buddhism. (For details on Shotoku's life, see Kidder 1999: *The Lucky Seventh: Early Horyu-ji and Its Time.*)

According to the *Nihon Shoki* (Suiko, Year 12, Summer, 4th month), in 604, Shotoku Taishi (*taishi* meaning 'great prince' [Piggott 2002: 462]), as the regent of Empress Suiko and the most venerated Yamato statesman, opened a new chapter in the history of Japan with the proclamation of the Seventeen Article Constitution, designed to define the character of the nation culturally, socially, and politically and chart its destiny for ages to come. Its primary purpose was to help create and maintain a harmonious, orderly, and ethical society based on Confucianism and Buddhism.

Thus, the Constitution began in Article One with the injunction "to value harmony", and it emphasized in Article Three obedience to the Emperor as an absolute duty (because "The lord is Heaven and the vassal is Earth") (Aston 1972, Vol. 2: 129). These were the principles of utmost importance in the Confucian system of social and political ethics. In Article Two, the people of Yamato were bidden to revere three treasures of Buddhism – Buddha, the Teachings of Buddha, and the Buddhist priesthood – as matters of supreme importance in living a good and true life. In Article Six, the Constitution bid the people and the officials to "chastise that which is evil and encourage that which is good. This was the excellent rule of ancient times" (Aston 1972, Vol. 2: 130). For more details on the Seventeen Articles, see Brown (1993: 180-181).

The Seventeen Article Constitution represented the best of the enlightenment which the Archipelago had undergone since the dawn of history. Essentially, it was the culmination of cultural interaction between the Archipelago and the Toraijin for more than a millennium. But immediately underlying the Seventeen Article Constitution were the thoughts, ideas, and principles which the Toraijin had been transmitting to Yamato leaders since the 5th century with the arrival of Paekche scholars in Yamato, beginning with Prince Gonji in 461. Gonji was soon followed by Mok (Soga) Manchi. In 513, Paekche king, Munyeong, sent a scholar in Confucian classics, to the Yamato court. Three years later, he sent another Confucian scholar, this time to Emperor Keitai, to encourage and promote the instruction of Confucian learning in the Japanese court (*Nihon Shoki*: Keitai year 7). In 538 or 552, King Seong sent a group of Buddhist priests to Yamato to propagate Buddhism in its ruling family.

When Shotoku Taishi was born in 574 as the son of emperor Yomei, Buddhism had already become strong among the Toraijin residing in Asuka, the Yamato capital, including the Soga Clan. Related to the latter by blood (Kadowaki 1991: 185), Shotoku became a Buddhist. At age eighteen, in 587, he joined the Soga Clan in its war against the anti-Buddhist factions led by Mononobe no Oho-Muraji and Nakatomi no Muraji. Following their victory, they began the construction of Hokoji Temple (Asuka-dera), Japan's first Buddhist temple. In 588, a large number of Paekche scholars arrived in the Yamato capital including thirteen Buddhist priests and three Confucian scholar-officials.

Thus, by the time Shotoku became the regent under Empress Suiko in 593, Asuka, the Yamato capital, was bustling with Paekche scholars, Buddhist and Confucian. Beginning in 595 Shotoku became a student of three renowned scholars from the Peninsula: Hyechong, a Buddhist priest from Paekche; Hyeja, a Buddhist priest from Koguryo; and Hakka, a Confucian scholar (*Nihon Shoki*: Suiko year 1 and year 2). These Toraijin scholars were still instructing him in 604 when Shotoku Taishi issued the Seventeen Article Constitution, which, with unequivocal emphasis on the supreme importance of Buddhism, Confucianism, and imperial sovereignty, became Japan's socio-cultural foundation for the next fourteen centuries. Essentially, the Constitution was the culmination of 1,500 years of cultural and technological interaction between the Toraijin and the Wa people of the Archipelago, c. 800 BC–AD 600.

VI. LASTING FRATERNITY BETWEEN YAMATO AND PAEKCHE

By the 7th century, the Toraijin from Paekche were having a dominant influence on the Yamato government and its society. Yamato royal palaces and other important buildings were named after Paekche (Kudara).

In March, 660, when the Paekche homeland in Korea was invaded by the combined forces of Silla and Tang China, Empress Saimei (r. 655–661) of Yamato Japan undertook to help restore broken Paekche. In the spring of 661, she personally led ships from Asuka, loaded with soldiers, to attack Silla and Tang forces, but died on the outbound trip, temporarily halting the military campaign.

Upon succeeding his mother as the new ruler of Japan, Tenji (r. 661–671) sent war supplies, including 100,000 arrows, to the Paekche insurgents (*Nihon Shoki*: Tenji year 1). He also dispatched members of the Paekche royal family and Paekche elites then residing in Asuka to join up with and lead insurgent forces in the Paekche homeland. The following year, in March 663, Tenji mobilized 27,000 troops to help eject Silla–Tang allied forces.

On August 27, Japanese and Tang troops met at the mouth of the Baekchon River (believed to be the current Geum River) downstream from the Paekche capital, which was then in the hands of Tang and

Silla generals. A fierce battle commenced, and the outcome of the first Sino-Japanese War fought over Korea is told thus in the *Nihon Shoki:* Tenji year 2 (Aston 1972, Vol. 2: 280, brackets added),

> Tang closed upon their [Yamato] vessels from right and left, and engaged them from all sides. In a short space of time the [Yamato] Imperial force was defeated, and many fell into the water and were drowned. The ships were unable to maneuver either astern or ahead. Yechi no Takutsu [Yamato general] looked up to heaven and made oaths; he gnashed his teeth, and in his rage slew several tens of men. He then fell fighting.

According to the *Samguk Sagi,* on that day, August 27, 663, "the flames and smoke rose to scorch the heavens while the ocean's waters turned as red as cinnabar" (*Samguk Sagi,* Chapter 28; Best 2006: 407). In 661–663 Yamato was a fledgling nation-state, formed only about a half century before. It had lost every battle in the Korean Peninsula since it had first dispatched troops to help Paekche against Silla or Koguryo in the latter part of the 4th century and afterwards. The 27,000 troops of Yamato Japan were no match against the 180,000 powerful and battle-tested allied forces of Silla and Tang China.

Why did Empress Saimei and Tenji, her son and successor, decide to commit nearly 30,000 young Yamato soldiers to help restore the fallen Kingdom of Paekche when it was a clearly hopeless cause? The situation conjures up the modern-era image of the WWII Imperial Japanese government sending thousands of young *kamikaze* pilots against overwhelming U.S. naval forces in the Pacific, a similarly desperate and hopeless cause. Most probably, the Yamato court's decision was taken as a desperate attempt to protect its Japanese homeland against the fearsome allied forces of Silla and Tang because it believed they would invade Japan next if Paekche and Koguryo fell. Its fear of such an invasion from the continent was realistic and long-held, as shown by the massive defensive walls and fortresses, including the Onojo, that the Yamato court had constructed on mountain passes, near Fukuoka in Kyushu, that face the Korean Peninsula across the narrow Tsushima Strait.

Surely a powerfully important emotional factor in the Yamato court's decision to succour Paekche was the uniquely special place that Paekche occupied in the hearts and minds of Yamato Japan's ruling aristocracy. Paekche had helped build Japan's Yamato capital of Asuka and its glorious culture, and it had contributed mightily to the development of the Yamato state. Not only culturally but also ethnically, Yamato was inextricably intertwined with Paekche and its people, and for many centuries Yamato rulers identified deeply with Paekche – as in the case of Emperor Jomei who, in 639, built a great residential palace and an impressive pagoda by the Kudara River and named it Kudara Palace. Upon his death in the following year, the Yamato court constructed an imperial resting hall and named it the Great Kudara Hall (*Nihon Shoki:* Jomei year 12 and year 13).

For more than a hundred years, from 536 to 645, the Soga clan of Paekche immigrants and descendants were intimately involved in the rulership of Yamato. Even after Nakatomi-no-Kamatari and his compatriots brought an end, in 645, to the Soga rule by assassinating the tyrannical prime minister, Soga no Iruka, the Soga clan continued to wield power in the Yamato society through its marriage alliances with the Yamato rulers (*Nihon Shoki:* Kogyoku year 4). Paekcheization of the Yamato society was overwhelming, resulting in the birth of the glorious Asuka period in the 6th century. Ethnically, culturally, and technologically, the Kinki Core Region was Paekche reborn in the Archipelago. It was "an urban civilization that was definitely Korean in character," states Delmer Brown (1993: 176).

Viewed in historical perspective, we posit that the decision by Saimei and Tenji to help restore Paekche was as much out of fraternal feelings of obligation and responsibility as it was out of concern for the national defense of Japan. After all, many citizens of Yamato, especially its elite population, were of Paekche descent. Paekche was their motherland.

Following the military disaster at the Baekchon River, all high-ranking officials, generals, and members of the Paekche nobility not killed or captured by the Tang forces – which added up to a considerable number – sailed toward Yamato, along with learned scholars, Buddhist priests, skilled craftsmen, and ordinary citizens in their retinues. It was a massive and wholesale retreat of the best and the finest of the Paekche nation into Japan, to add their number to the Paekche immigrants already settled there (*Nihon Shoki*: Tenji year 2).

In 665–667, 2,400 of the new Paekche immigrants settled permanently in Omi (modern Otsu City), east of Kyoto, where earlier Paekche immigrants had carved out their colonies during the 5th century (*Nihon Shoki*: Tenji year 4, year 5, and year 6; Hiro 2009: 13-22). Simultaneously, in 667, Emperor Tenji moved the Yamato capital from Asuka to Omi. Two years later in 669, 700 more Paekche immigrants including former Paekche officials, Yeo Ja-shin and Guishil Jipsa settled in Omi, making the latter a new metropolis bustling with Paekche people (*Nihon Shoki*: Tenji year 8). Others, including scholars, priests, scribes, and generals, settled in the Nara–Osaka–Kyoto area and served the Yamato court in various official capacities. Surviving members of the Paekche royal family settled in Naniwa in the Kawachi area, a major center of earlier Paekche immigrants, in close relationship with the Yamato ruling family (Furuichi 2001, 118-125; OFCAH 2004: 7-13).

The infusion of such a large pool of experienced statesmen, generals, scholars, priests, technicians, and artists into the Yamato court, then still in its infancy as a state, was a boon of incalculable value that helped the new nation mature even more.

In 670, the Yamato court adopted "Nihon" (Land of the Rising Sun) as its formal name, and the nation we know today was officially born. Thus, while Paekche physically died in the Peninsula, its memory continued to thrive in the land of Nihon among countless number of Paekche immigrants and their descendants, becoming naturalized Nihonjin. A year later in 671, the Yamato court granted to those who had served as high-ranking officials in the Paekche court not only various ranks of Yamato nobility but also high positions in the Yamato government. Of particular prominence in this regard was Guisil Jipsa who was appointed by Emperor Tenji as the Minister of Education in charge of all educational institutions and programs of the Yamato state (*Nihon Shoki*: Tenji year 10).

In the *Shoku Nihongi* (Chronicles of Japan Continued, compiled in 797): Kammu Enreki Year 8, Japan's ancient historians recorded that the mother of Emperor Kammu (r. 781–806) ruling Japan from Nara was Lady Niigasa of a noble Paekche descent. In time Kammu became a monarch of ancient Japan (Imaizumi 1986: 1099-1100; Ueda 1965: 15-19). He subdued the indigenous residents in Honshu and Hokkaido. He carried out extensive reforms in the Yamato society of Nara, which had been overburdened by the powerful Buddhist establishment and an entrenched hereditary aristocracy. As part of an important reform in 794, he moved his palace and the seat of the Yamato government to the Yamashiro district, which was a major colony of the Korean Hata Clan. Built with the help of the Korean immigrants, he named his capital Heian-kyo, the 'capital of peace'; it remained the capital of Japan for more than a millennium until 1868, reborn as Kyoto (Kyoto Bunka Hakubutsukan 1989: 130-148).

Citing the *Shoku Nihongi* account, Akihito, the modern emperor of Japan, on his 69th birthday (December 18, 2001), solemnly reminded his nation, "I, on my part, feel a kinship with Korea [私自身 としては... 韓國とのゆかりを感じています]" (Kunaisho 2001; French 2002).

By the 8th century, the Toraijin, including the powerful Yamato Aya clan, consisting mostly of the Toraijin of Paekche origin, constituted the majority (80–90%) of the population in the southern Nara basin, the heartland of the Yamato power, according to the *Shoku Nihongi* (Chronicles of Japan Continued), Hoki Year 3. Clearly this was an overwhelming proportion of the Yamato capital area population and provides hints as to the role which ancient Peninsular peoples, particularly the Toraijin from Paekche, played during Japan's formative period.

All the Toraijin from Paekche and their descendants have, since long ago, become Nihonjin, but the memory of the Toraijin from Paekche still lives on in the Archipelago at various locations in the Kinki Core region, including Asuka-dera (飛鳥寺, Asuka Temple), Hyakusaiji (百濟寺, Paekche Temple), Kudara-mura (百濟村, Paekche Village), and Kudara-no (百濟野, Kudara Field), all in Nara; Kudara-Ou Jinja (百濟王神社, Shrine of Paekche King) and Minami Kudara-mura (南百濟村, South Paekche Village) in Kawachi; Kudara no Kori (百濟郡, Paekche District) in Settsu; Hyakusaiji (百濟寺, Paekche Temple) and Hyakusanjo (百濟山城, Paekche Mountain Fortress) in Shiga, among others.

In Miyazaki Prefecture in southern Kyushu, there is a lovely village called Nango-son (南郷村), a miniature look-alike of Buyeo, ancient Paekche capital, with Paekche-style buildings and halls. At the entrance of the village stands a sign that says, "Kudara no Sato" (百濟の里, Paekche Village) and a street guide sign pointing to Kudara no Yakata (百濟の館, Paekche Hall). A river flowing nearby is called the Kuma River after the Keum (or Geum) River that flows by Buyeo in Korea.

Every December, the people of the village, who believe that they are descendants of the ancient Paekche elites, observe a festival of sadness and happiness called Shiwasu Matsuri, consoling the souls of an ancient Paekche prince and his son from Buyeo forever longing for each other.

According to a sacred document kept at Hiki Shrine in Nango-son from generation to generation for longer than a millennium, Prince Jeongga and his son, Bokji, of the Paekche royal family, were fleeing their doomed homeland after Buyeo, the capital of Paekche, fell into the hands of the invading Tang and Silla forces. While sailing toward southern Kyushu, they were shipwrecked in a storm and became separated. The father eventually made his way to Nango-son while the son landed in a place about 90 km away. Longing for his father, Prince Bokji set out to find him. Likewise, longing for his son, the father also set out to find him.

Along the way, they found themselves in the middle of a war between government troops and rebels. While trying to fight their way out they were both killed and were buried in Nango-son. The souls of the father and the son whose longing for each other went unfulfilled are enshrined in the Mikado Shrine and Hiki Shrine respectively. In the annual festival of the Shiwasu Matsuri lasting two and a half day, the people of Nango-son re-enact the son's search for his father, ceremoniously walking 90 km. Japan's connection with Paekche thus lives on in a small corner of the Archipelago through a sacred ritual.

COLLABORATION *NOT* CONQUEST

The transformation of the socio-cultural fabric of the Yamato state was so revolutionary that some prominent historians (Egami 1967, Egami 1992; Y Mizuno 1967, Y Mizuno 1975; Ledyard 1975) have explained it in terms of invasion and conquest from the Peninsula.

According to EGAMI Namio, the primary promoter of the conquest theory, elite horse-riding warriors from Kaya in southeast Korea invaded northern Kyushu sometime in the 4th century, and subsequently their descendants marched eastward to the Kinki Core Region in alliance with local Kyushu forces, subduing the native ruling elites of the Kinki region and establishing there the Ojin Dynasty as well as constructing the enormous Kondayama tumulus in ancient Kawachi (modern Osaka) as Oin's tomb.

Besides various archaeological and chronological issues raised (T Suzuki 1975; Edwards 1983: 265-295; Sahara 1993; Kidder, Jr. 1993: 108-110; Egami and Sahara 2003; Barnes 2015: 354), the major weakness of the conquest theory is the absence of the 4th–5th century horse riders' ruling class mortuary system in the Kinki Core Region. Conquerors normally carry their own mortuary tradition into their conquered territory; therefore, we would expect to find the 4th century Kaya elite tombs of *mokkwak myo* (wood-framed tombs) similar to those found at Daeseong-dong in Kimhae and Bokcheon-dong in Pusan and the 4th–5th century circular mounded tombs appearing as the Kofun period rulers' tombs of the 4th–5th century. Instead, with the exception of the Hokenoyama Kofun dated to the 3rd century, the Yamato rulers of the Early and Middle Kofun Period in the Kinki Core Region constructed keyhole-shaped tombs surrounded by a water-filled moat.

Another critical factor is the lack of historical evidence. No ancient written records from Korea (*Samguk Sagi* and *Samguk Yusa*) or Japan (*Kojiki* and *Nihon Shoki*) mention invasion of the Archipelago by Korea's early states. Also, if the Archipelago had been invaded, conquered, and ruled by the horse-riding people from Korea's early states, contemporary Chinese historians such as PEI Song-zhi (372–451) and XIAO Zixian (early 6th century) would have noted it in their writings. Nothing supportive of the conquest hypothesis, however, appears either in Pei's annotations to the *Sanguozhi* (Records of the Three Kingdoms) or in the *Nanqishu* (History of the Southern State of Qi, 470–502).

Most of all, the Gwanggaeto Stele of 414 makes no mention of the conquest. King Gwanggaeto (r. 391–413) of Koguryo viewed the people of Kaya and the Archipelago as the enemy of Silla, his ally. As such, Jangsu, his son, recorded in the stele his father's invasion and routing of the Kaya and Wa elements on the southeast coast around Kimhae in 400 as one of Gwanggaeto's glorious achievements, but he mentioned nothing about the invasion and conquest of the Archipelago either by Kaya or by Gwanggaeto himself. Had the cavalry of Kaya or Koguryo invaded and conquered the Archipelago, Jangsu would have most certainly recounted the event in the stele.

In reality, Kaya had neither reason nor physical power to invade and conquer the Archipelago in the 4th century or thereafter. First, the people of Kaya and the Archipelago had long been friends and allies as mentioned in the Gwanggaeto Stele. Second, it was in no position militarily to launch an overseas invasion in the 4th century. For ten years (c. 315–325), eight coastal Kaya polities, including Geumgwan Kaya, were involved in a devastating civil war (SO Baek 2011: 76-87), and in 400 Geumgwan

Kaya in Kimhae was invaded and dealt a crushing blow by Koguryo's cavalry. These two events resulted in an influx of numerous Kaya immigrants into the Archipelago. This was repeated a century later on a massive scale as Silla began to invade Kaya states, destroying Dae Kaya, the last remaining Kaya state, in 562.

Following Egami's conquest hypothesis, Ledyard (1975) and HONG Wontack (2010: 25-26, 125-146), have focused on Paekche, rather than Kaya, as the conqueror of the Archipelago in light of the overwhelming Paekcheization of the Yamato society during the Kofun period.

Emphasizing Paekche's origin in the Buyeo nomadic tribes in the Sungari Basin, advocated by Egami, Ledyard posits that soon after its founding as a powerful state in the Han River basin in the 4th century, Paekche elites crossed the Korea Strait and conquered Kyushu, subsequently advancing eastward and conquering the Osaka–Kyoto–Nara region in the 5th century. The overwhelming influence of Paekche's culture on the Yamato society observed archaeologically, according to Ledyard, resulted from this conquest of the Kinki region by Paekche.

Hong, on the basis of his personal rendition of the *Kojiki* and the *Nihon Shoki* narratives, posits that King Geunchogo of Paekche and his son, Geun Gusu, emerging as powerful military leaders in 371, dispatched an army led by a Paekche general, Homuda, to invade the Archipelago. After their successful landing on Kyushu, Homuda and his troops moved eastward, completing their conquest of the Kinki region in 390, taking nearly 20 years. Thereupon, the Paekche conquerors, according to Hong, established a new ruling dynasty (the Ojin Dynasty) in Yamato with Homuda as its first ruler. Thus, in Hong's eyes, Emperor Ojin was thus none other than a conquering Paekche general, and the Yamato state was essentially a Paekche colony state.

The narratives of Ledyard and Hong suffer the same pitfalls as those of Egami. They lack archaeological and historical evidence for invasion and conquest. Most compelling in this regard is, as in the case of Kaya, the absence, in the Osaka region, of the 4th-century Paekche elite tombs in the form of pyramid-shaped piled stone tumuli.

Indeed, as demonstrated in this monograph, the Paekcheization of the Yamato society was overwhelming. Numerous Paekche elites, scholars, and high-ranking officials were residing in Yamato. The Soga clan of Paekche origin was leading the socio-political and cultural affairs of the Yamato state. The establishment of Buddhism as Japan's national religion took place through the pro-Paekche party's military triumph over the native Yamato elites. The Paekcheization of the Kinki Core Region, culminating in the glorious Asuka period during the 6th century, was essentially Paekche reborn in the heart of the Yamato power. *However*, in its making, the overwhelming socio-cultural transformation was not a result of military invasion or conquest. Rather, it was an event and process unfolding in the context of *push/pull* dynamics in migration *in the course of three centuries*.

Under the crises created by the devastating Koguryo invasions beginning in 369 and ending in the destruction of the Paekche capital in 475, as well as by other interstate wars, many Paekche people, including elites, learned scholars, and technicians in various fields, fled the Peninsula (the *push* factor) as did those of Kaya and Mahan, and the Wa elites in the Kinki Core Region, eager to advance their culture and technology and also to outpace their rivals, intensified their welcoming move (the *pull* factor). This move was all the more urgent inasmuch as the Wa elites could not access China during the 4th–6th centuries. The welcoming of the refugees, technicians, and elites from Kaya and Paekche was facilitated further by the friendship that had long existed between them and the Yamato state. After all, they had been allies in war and trade. Essentially, it was the *push-pull dynamics* which had given rise to the initial Toraijin phenomena and the Yayoi revolutions in the 8th century BC even though the nature of the push-pull factors differed.

On the flip side of the horseriders' conquest hypothesis, some writers, beginning with Suematsu (1949) and echoed in Western literatures (Reischauer and Fairbank 1958: 468-469; Sansom 1958, 16-17; Hall 1970: 37-43), have hypothesized that the socio-cultural and technological revolutions of the Middle Kofun were the result of Yamato conquest of southern Korea in the 4th century. Known as the "Mimana Nihonfu Hypothesis," based on questionable narratives in the *Nihon Shoki*, it holds that the Yamato government conquered southern Korea in 369 AD and ruled Kaya territory through a military/administrative base called "Mimana Nihonfu" until 562 when it was destroyed by Silla King Jinheung (540–576). The Yamato state, according to the advocates of this theory, used the base for 200 years to acquire advanced Korean culture and technology as well as to promote its interests in the Peninsula (Y Kobayashi 1961,41; Ishimoda 1962, 18-19).

During Japan's forced occupation of Korea, 1910–1945, the Japanese government in Korea, with the help of Japanese historians and archaeologists, made a massive effort, in finance and manpower, to map and investigate archaeological sites throughout the Peninsula.[1] One of the objectives was to find archaeological evidences for the "Mimana Nihonfu" in the lower Nakdong River basin where they believed it was centered. The purpose of such intensive effort on the part of Imperial Japan was to prove that southern Korea was historically under the Japanese rule and thereby to justify its control of Korea in the twentieth century.

Thirty-five years of effort, however, failed to find in the entire Kaya region a single keyhole-type tomb believed to be the physical symbol of the Yamato power's presence. Nor was there found a single piece of evidence supporting the existence of "Mimana Nihonfu" in southern Korea either in archaeology or in ancient historical records. In fact, Nihon (日本) as the state name of Japan did not even exist during 369–562. It appeared for the first time in history only in the late seventh century. Thus "Mimana Nihonfu" itself is a fictional term.

Furthermore, while ancient Chinese historians made detailed records about cultural, social, and political conditions of East Asia including the Korean Peninsula and the Japanese Archipelago of the said period, they made not a single mention of "Mimana Nihonfu" existing in the southern Peninsula.

Historically, the Archipelago was growing steadily in its socio-political complexity during the Kofun period, but during the Early Kofun period it still had no central government and its society was strongly agrarian. It was incapable of mobilizing massive military forces capable of launching wars across the sea in a foreign land, especially against the Korean Peninsula.

---

[1] Between 1917 and 1940, the Government General of Korea published a series of monographs on the archaeological and cultural sites of the Peninsula province by province under the general title: *Chosen Sotokufu Koseki Chosa Hokoku* (Reports on the Investigations of Ancient Cultural Sites by the Government General of Korea). During the same period, the Government General of Korea also published excavation reports of the tumuli of Korea's early states and the Lelang Chinese commandery in Pyongyang under the following general titles: *Chosen Sotokufu Koseki Chosa Tokubetsu Hokoku* (Special Reports on the Investigations of Ancient Cultural Sites by the Government General of Korea) and *Chosen Sotokufu Koseki Chosa Gaiho* (General Reports on the Investigations of Ancient Cultural Sites by the Government General of Korea).

Japan produced no iron until the sixth century, and after the demise of Lelang and Daifang in 313-314 it was dependent entirely on iron tools as well as raw iron imported from the Peninsula. Its military assault weapons were inferior. As TS Kim (2014b, 68) states:

> At that time, when the Wa could not produce iron, it was impossible for them to possess iron weapons better than those of Paekche, Kaya, and Silla... Kaya was being led by Geumgwan Kaya, the head of the Kaya Confederation, in Kimhae, which possessed heavy mounted military technology, consisting of iron body armor, iron helmet, horse paraphernalia, and iron weapons far superior to those of Wa.

Japan therefore was in no position – politically, militarily, or technologically – to conquer southern Korea, which was home to the powerful kingdoms of Paekche and Silla, as well as numerous Kaya polities fortified with lethal iron weaponry as well as mounted cavalry. (TS Kim 2014b, 169-179).

In addition, in 400 Koguryo dealt Wa elements on the southeast coast and Geumgwan Kaya in Kimhae a fatal blow and placed the territory of Silla and Kaya under its sphere of influence. Wa people could not dare encroach upon the region throughout the fifth century (H Suzuki 1987). They now sought to secure trading partners among the Kaya polities not affected by the Koguryo invasion of 400 such as Goseong So Kaya and Dae Kaya of Goryeong located in the outlying regions as well as among Mahan polities in the southwest and Paekche in the west-central Peninsula (GJEB 1994; KC Shin 2000, 190-191; SC Ha 2011, 95-140; Sakai 2013, 99; T.-S. Kim:2014a, 252, 258-264).

With its military and commercial position seriously jeopardized on the Peninsula's southern coast during the 5th century, Wa rulers repeatedly sought to enhance their political status and prestige in East Asia through diplomacy with the Liu Sung Dynasty (420–479) court in China. In this effort they sought to receive from the Chinese imperial court at least exalted political/military titles even over some Korean states. Chinese emperors, however, granted them titles a step below those granted to Koguryo and Paekche and refused to recognize the Wa kings' hegemony over any Korean state (H Inoue 1973: 3; TS Kim 2014b: 75-76).

In light of recent archaeological investigations in southern Korea and Japan and critical studies of the *Nihon Shoki*, leading Japanese scholars on the subject have either abandoned or radically revised the "Mimana Nihonfu" theory (Ukeda 1974; K Yoshida 1975; Kito 1976; Yamao 1978; H Inoue 1973; H Suzuki 1987; Naoki 1992; Y Suzuki 1985, Y Suzuki 1992, Y Suzuki 1995; T Tanaka 1992; Kimura 2005). The prevailing view advocated by Ukeda (1974), Yoshida (1975: 54-57), and Kito (1976) and generally affirmed by Korean historians (TS Kim 2014b: 327-334) is that the so-called "Mimana Nihonfu" consisted essentially of trading posts which various Wa polities in western Japan maintained on Korea's southern coast to acquire iron and other precious goods during the 4th–6th century.

To sum up, the notion that Yamato Japan ruled a portion of southern Korea through "Mimana Nihonfu" during the 4th–6th century cannot be sustained *historically* (Brown 1993: 123). In the early 8th century, when the *Nihon Shoki* was compiled by the Yamato court primarily to legitimize and glorify the Yamato regime often with fictional narratives (Tsuda 1924; Ikeuchi 1970; Kito 1976), the legendary trading posts of the bygone ages were metamorphosed into "Mimana Nihonfu" in the *Nihon Shoki*.

Underlying the horseriders' conquest theory and the Mimana Nihonfu hypothesis is the question of the primary actor during Japan's formative period. Who or which led the way in ancient Japan's revolutionary transformations? The Archipelago or the Peninsula? The Jomon/Wa/Yamato people or the Toraijin? This question has already been debated by Japanese scholars (Shimojo and Tanaka 2014: 279-324; Kanaseki and OYBH 1995: 236-247) as discussed in Chapter One: II, 6.

It is the old question of "chicken or egg." What caused what? Which came first? Archaeological and historical evidences inform that the chicken and the egg were there at the same time. One did not cause the other. They worked *simultaneously*. Jomon people's creativity and their superb adaptability for survival and cultural development on volcano-ridden islands were already there. *Without the creativity and adaptability, a prominent trait of the Japanese people, the Toraijin arrival, in every major period, would not have effected the revolutionary transformations of Japan's formative period.* That is how it has worked in all secondary civilizations. Native creativity and adaptability, combined with external stimulus through exchange and interactions, have resulted in socio-cultural and technological changes. That is how civilization emerged and advanced in the Peninsula as well in the broader context of what we call "The Yellow Sea Interaction Sphere" (Barnes 2015: 309-331).

CONCLUSIONS

In this book, we have sought to demonstrate, in light of archaeological and historical data, that the stimulus for Japan's formative period, came from the Korean peninsula. The archaeological data from the Peninsula and the Archipelago leave no doubt that it was the farmers of the Middle Mumun and the Songguk-ni culture that provided the catalysis for the birth of wet-rice farming in northern Kyushu and the onset of the Yayoi period.

The arrival of the Peninsular Middle Mumun people in northern Kyushu and their close interaction with the local Jomon people through intermarriages and in economic-technological affairs resulted in the first instance of major ethnic and cultural hybridization in the Archipelago. The very advent of the Yayoi people and the Yayoi society based on paddy-field rice production was the direct result of that hybridization.

The early Yayoi society became increasingly complex with a rapid increase of the Toraijin-type Yayoi population, resulting in inter-communal conflicts over land, water, and other vital resources. In this competing Yayoi society, the bronze-bearing Late Mumun people of the Peninsula arrived with their metal technology and other cultural features including new symbols of political authority/prestige (dagger, mirror, and comma-shaped jewel [*magatama*]). With the bronze weapons and bronze technology some of the local elites soon emerged as chieftains of the MiddleYayoi society, intensifying its social stratification (c. 300 BC–AD 50). During the subsequent Late Yayoi (c. 50–250 AD), the Archipelago witnessed the rise of "Wa kings" and "Wa queens" of various regional *kuni* (polities) throughout the Archipelago.

The archaeological information, along with ancient historical records, also make it abundantly clear that a large number of the Peninsular inhabitants came to the Archipelago during late Early~Middle Kofun period, bringing with them skills and technologies, especially in iron production which the Wa (Japanese) elites needed in the advancement of their civilization. It is also recognized that during the Late Kofun period (500–600 AD), Korean scholars, teachers, and skilled technicians in various fields came to teach and train the Wa (Japanese) ruling elites in the matters of a civilized society. According to Japanese paleo-demographic experts, in the course of a 1400 years between 800 BC and 600 AD, more than a million immigrants from southern Korea arrived in the Archipelago.

By the 8th century AD, according to the Hoki Year 3 section in the *Shoku Nihongi* (Chronicles of Japan Continued, compiled in 797), the Koreans and their descendants, including the powerful Yamato Aya clan, constituted the majority (80–90%) of the population in the Nara basin, the heartland of the Yamato power, even giving the basin a Korean name.

The name of Japan's famous city, Nara, is believed to have originated among the dominant Korean immigrant community in the Nara basin. In Korean, *nara* means "country." As expected, the Koreans living in the Nara basin would have called their new home "sae nara" meaning "new country." In the course of time, "sae nara" became simply "nara" as the "sae (new)" part was dropped.

Korean technicians, engineers, painters, and tile-makers constructed the first tile-roofed and foundation-supported buildings in Japan including the Asuka Temple, the first Buddhist temple in

Japan. Korean engineers built and operated iron industries, producing cutting-edge iron tools and iron weapons. They produced the highly coveted stoneware vessels, called *Sueki* in Japan. Korean craftsmen made and supplied precious jewels (gold earrings, gold pendants, decorated swords, jade ornaments) to local elites hungry for Korean-made prestige goods. Koreans skilled in equestrian culture operated horse-raising farms and revolutionized modes of transportation. Korean scholars taught the ruling elites reading, writing, and managerial wisdom and skills from the Confucian classics. Korean priests resided at Japan's first Buddhist temples, leading them in propagation and instruction.

Other Koreans including the Hata clan settled in the Kyoto basin in the 5th century. Controlling the Kadono River with their superior engineering skills they created the prosperous town of Heian-kyo, developing it into the royal city of Kyoto, Japan's imperial capital until 1867. They financed and built the impressive Fushimi Inari Shrine, Matsuo Shrine, and Koryuji Temple as well as imperial palaces. The powerful Korean elites in Kyoto also constructed for themselves at Sagano nearby great keyhole-shaped tombs to house their megalithic corridor burial chambers. One of them is the impressive Hebizuka Kofun, 75 m (225 feet) long. Others settled in Omi between Kyoto and Lake Biwa, in modern-day Otsu City of Shiga Prefecture.

Some of the Koreans and their descendants emerged not only as successful technocrats but also as powerful political functionaries during the late Kofun period, guiding and directing the state affairs. The most renowned among them was the Soga family. Through three Soga generations represented by Soga Iname, Soga Umako, and Soga Iruka, all of whom served as the prime minister of the Yamato government, the Soga family led Yamato for more than a century, during its most defining period, 536–645.

Around 600 AD, the Korean phase of Japan's formative period came to an end with Paekche's last cultural mission to the Yamato court in 603. In the meantime, through Paekche the Yamato court had learned about the events in China including the rise of Sui as the new empire in 589 and Paekche's close relationship with it. In 608, the Yamato court sent a sizable cultural mission intended to learn about the Chinese civilization with which to enrich its own civilization which it had been building with the people who had come from Mahan, Paekche and Kaya.

According to the *Nihon Shoki*: Suiko year 16, seven or all eight members of the cultural mission were scholars from the Yamato Aya Clan which comprised the descendants of Mahan, Paekche and Kaya people who resided in the Kinki Core Region. Upon their return they all functioned as officials in the Yamato government, grafting useful elements of the Chinese culture to the emerging Japanese civilization.

Following the demise of Paekche in 663, the best of the Paekche society, including scholar-officials, generals, skilled technicians, gold and silver smiths, and artists, among others, migrated to Yamato and other parts of the Archipelago, adding further civilizational talents to the newly emerging nation of Japan.

Underlying the Toraijin's crossing the Korea/Tsushima Strait at various times, beginning in the 9th century BC, to reach the Archipelago were *the dynamics of push and pull*. Undesirable conditions in the Peninsula such as climate changes, population pressure, and frequent inter-state wars pushed many of its inhabitants to leave, and favourable conditions in the Archipelago including fair climate, open lands for settlement, and the welcome mat spread out before them, pulled them in. In retrospect, it was akin to Europeans' crossing the Atlantic Ocean to reach the American continent. Like the Toraijin, they were fleeing their homeland to reach a new world to build a new life and a new home without the vexing problems of the motherland. And, in both cases, the immigrants had much to offer in the way of advancing the lifeways in their newly adopted country (Farris 1996: 16).

In light of Anthony's observations regarding migrations in history (1990: 903), we posit that the Korean migration to the Archipelago in the ancient times was not wave-like or sporadic but continually flowing "stream-like." "Earlier migrants create pathways by overcoming obstacles and providing routing information for later migrants. The route is therefore often just as finely targeted as the destination." Propelled by push-pull dynamics, a large number of Korean populations crossed the South Sea during a major crisis, but for one reason or another, some families and individuals migrated to the Archipelago even in peaceful times. As in modern days, there was an ongoing exchange of information between the migrants and their families and friends back home, prompting some of the latter to join the former.

Unlike the early European colonizers, the Peninsula immigrants intermingled culturally and ethnically with the native population of the Archipelago through intermarriages even at the highest level of the elites, giving birth to a new people called Nihonjin and a new nation called Nihon in the 7th century AD. The new civilization which emerged in the Archipelago during the 5th–7th century AD, was thus a creation of cooperative endeavour of two peoples of the Archipelago and the Peninsula. Essentially, it was a re-occurrence of the ethnic and cultural hybridization of the Archipelago which had taken place during the Initial and Early Yayoi period, only this time at a much grander scale.

This is a 1400-year long story of the Toraijin in Japanese history. Much more is yet to be known about them. This study, we hope, will encourage newly emerging scholars of Korean and Japanese history and archaeology to shed more light on the subject as well as on other relevant topics introduced. Ultimately, we hope, this study will contribute to the understanding, for the Koreans and the Japanese, that they have more in common than in opposing differences and thereby to the building of friendly relations, and perhaps even to the recovery of fraternity lost (Farris 1996: 1-2) during Japan's brutal invasions in 1592–97 and its forced, harsh, and exploitive occupation in the 20th century.

REFERENCES

Abbreviated References

In most cases, the institutional author also serves as publisher.

GBUB (Gungnip Buyeo Bangmulgwan [National Buyeo Museum]). 1992. *Buyeo Bangmulgwan Jinyeolpum Dogam* (Guide to the Exhibition Artifacts of Buyeo National Museum), edited and published by GBUB, Buyeo.

GCHB (Gungnip Cheongju Bangmulgwan [National Cheongju Museum]). 1997. *Cheolui Yeoksa* (History of Iron). Cheongju: GCHB.

GGOB (Gungnip Gongju Bangmulgwan [National Gongju Museum]). 1981. *Gongju Bangmulgwan Dorok* (Guidebook for National Gongju Museum). Gongju: GGOB.

___ 1999. *Ilbon Sojae Paekche Munhwajae Josa Bogoseo I: Kinki Jibang* (Report on Paekche Culture Remains in Japan I: Kinki Region). Gongju: GGOB.

___ 2002. *Geumgang: Choigeun Balgul 10-Nyeonsa* (Geum River: Most Recent Ten Years of Excavations). Gongju: GGOB.

___ 2004. *Gungnip Gongju Bangmulgwan* (GGOB). Gongju: GGOB.

___ 2006. *Hanseongeseo Ungjineuro* (From Hanseong to Ungjin). Gongju: GGOB.

GGWB (Gungnip Gwangju Bangmulgwan [National Gwangju Museum]). 1988a. *Hampyeong Chopo-ri Yujeok* (The Archaeological Site of Chopo-ri in Hampyeong). Gwangju: GGWB.

___ 1988b. *Naju Bannam Gobungun* (Bannam Tumuli in Naju). Gwangju: GGWB.

___ 2013. *Hwasun Daegok-ni Yujeok* (The Archaeological Site of Daegok-ni in Hwasun). Gwangju: GGWB.

GJEB (Gungnip Jeonju Bangmulgwan [National Jeonju Museum]) (ed.). 1994. *Buan Jukmak-dong Jesa Yujeok Yeongu* (Study of Archaeological Site of Buan Jukmak-dong Sacred Alter). Jeonju: GJEB.

___ (ed.) 2009. *Mahan, Sumshineun Girok* (Mahan, Breathing Records) Jeonju: Gungnip Jeonju Bangmulgwan.

GJIB (Gungnip Jinju Bangmulgwan [National Jinju Museum]). 2016. *Gukje Muyeokhang Neuk-do wa Haru-no-tsuji* (The International Trade Centers of Neuk-do and Haru-no-tsuji). Jinju: GJIB.

GJIB (Gungnip Jinju Bangmulgwan [National Jinju Museum]). 2002. *Cheongdonggi Shidaeui Daepyeong -Daepyeongin* (Daepyeong and Daepyeong People of the Bronze Age). GJIB.

GJIB/GSND (Gungnip Jinju Bangmulgwan [National Jinju Museum]/Gyeongsangnam-do (South Geyongsang Province). 2001. *Jinju Daepyeong-ni, Okbang 1 Jigu Yujeok II* (Site II of Okbang Areas I at Daepyeong-ni in Jinju). Jinju: GJIB/GSND.

GJUB (Gungnip Jung-ang Bangmulgwan [National Museum of Korea]). 1979. *Songguk-ni, 1: Bonmun* (Songguk-ni, 1: Text). Seoul: GJUB.

___ 1993. *Hangukui Seon – Weonsa Togi* (The Pottery of Prehistoric and Protohistoric Korea), Seoul: GJUB.

___ 1997. *Hanguk Godaeui Togi* (Korean Pottery of the Ancient Period), edited by GJUB.

___ 1998. *Hanguk Godaeui Gukka Hyeongseong* (State Formation Process in Ancient Korea), Seoul: GJUB.

___ 1999. *Teukbyeoljeon: Paekche* (Special Exhibition: Paekche), edited by GJUB.

___ 2008. *Galdae Batsogui Nara Dahori* (Daho-ri: A Nation in the Fields of Reeds), Seoul: GJUB.

GJUB and GGWB (Gungnip Jung-ang Bangmulgwan [National Museum of Korea] and Gungnip Gwangju Bangmulgwan [National Museum of Gwangju]). 1992. *Hanguk Cheongdonggi Munhwa* (Bronze Culture of Korea). Seoul: Beomwusa.

GKIB (Gungnip Kimhae Bangmulgwan [National Kimhae Museum]). 1998. *Gungnip Kimhae Bangmulgwan* (GKIB Guidebook). Kimhae: GKIB.

___ 1999. *Kayaui Geureut Batchim* (Pottery Stands of Kaya). Kimhae: GKIB.

GMUY (Gungnip Munhwajae Yeonguso [National Cultural Heritage Research Institute]). 1989a. *Mireuksa* (Mireuksa Temple). Seoul: GMUY.

___ 1989b. *Iksan Ipjeom-ni Gobun Balgul Josa Bogoseo* (Excavation Report of Iksan Ipjeom-ni Ancient Tomb). Seoul: GMUY.

___ 1991. Bukhan Munhwa Yujeok Balgulgaebo (Reports on Archaeological Sites of North Korea). GMUY.

___ 2008. *Hanguk Gogohak Sajeon* (Dictionary of Korean Archaeology). Seoul: GMUY.

GNB (Gungnip Naju Bangmulgwan {National Naju Museum}). 2013. *Gungnip Naju Bangmulgwan* (National Naju Museum). Naju: GNB.

GSBD (Gyeongsangbuk-do) (North Gyeongsang Province). 1998. *Kaya Munhwa Dorok* (The Catalogue of Kaya Culture). Edited by Hanguk Godaesa Yeonguhoe. Taegu: Yeseong Sajin Printing Company.

GSND–DDHB (Gyeonsangnam-do - Dong'a Dae Hakkyo Bangmulgwan [South Gyeongsang Province–Dong'a University Museum]).1999. *Namgang Yuyeok Munhwa Yujeok Balgul Dorok* (The Catalogue of the Excavations of the Nam River Culture Sites). Pusan: GSND–DDHB

JYYDPW (Choson Yujeok Yumul Dogam Pyeonchan Wiweonhoe (Editorial Committee for Archaeological Sites and Materials of Democratic Republic of Korea). 1989. *Choseon Yujeok Yumul Dogam 2* (Guide to Archaeological Sites and Materials of Democratic People's Republic of Korea 2). Pyongyang: JYYDPW.

MUJC and SNUM (Munhwajaecheong [Cultural Heritage Bureau], and Seoul National University Museum (editors). 1999. *Hanguk Jiseongmyo (Goindol) Jonghap Josa Yeongu* (Comprehensive Investigations of the Korean Dolmens). Seoul: MUJC and SNUM.

NKKFH (Nara Kenritsu Kashihara Kokogaku Kenkyusho Fuzoku Hakubutsukan [Nara Prefectural Kashihara Research Institute Associated Museum]). 1988. *Nara Kenritsu Kashihara Kokogaku Kenkyusho Fuzoku Hakubutsukan: Sogo Annai* (Nara Prefectural Kashihara Research Institute Associated Museum:(A Comprehensive Guide). Nara: Kashikoken.

___ 1999. *Yamato no Kokogaku 100 Nen* (100 years of Yamato Archaeology), edited by NKKFH: Nara: Kashikoken.

OFCAH (Osaka Furitsu Chikatsu Asuka Hakubutsukan [Osaka Furitsu Chikatsu Asuka Museum]). 2002. *Mitokutsu Kofun no Sekai* (The World of Unstolen Tombs). Osaka Furitsu Chikatsu Asuka Hakubutsukan.

___ 2003. *Kosen no Akusesari* (The Other World's Accessories). Osaka: Furitsu Chikatsu Asuka Hakubutsukan.

___ 2004. *Imaki no Tehito: Kofun – Asuka no Toraijin* (The Newly Arrived Skilled People of the Kofun and Asuka Periods). Osaka: Furitsu Chikatsu Asuka Hakubutsukan.

OYBH (Osaka Furitsu Yayoi Bunka Hakubutsukan [Osaka Prefecture Yayoi Culture Museum]). 1999. *Toraijin Tojo: Yayoi Bunkao hiraita Hitobito* (Arrival of the People Who Crossed the Sea: The People who Commenced the Yayoi Culture). Osaka: Yayoi Culture Museum.

___ 2004. *Yamato Okento Toraijin* (The Yamato Court and the Toraijin). Osaka: OYBH.

PJHGY and GDSGY (Pohang Jonghap Jecheol Jushik Hoesa Gisul Yeonguso [Pohang Combined Iron Industries Technological Research Institute] and Goryo Daehakkyo Saengsan Gisul Yeonguso [Korea University Production Technology Research Institute]). 1985. *Paekcheui Jecheol Gongjeonggwa Gisul Gaebal: Cheolgi Yumului Geumsokhakjeok Gochaleul Tonghaeseo* (Paekche's Steel Production Process and Technological Advancement: In Light of Metallurgical Analysis of Iron Artifacts). Seoul: PJHGY and GDSGY.

PUM (Pusan University Museum). 1996a. *Seonsa wa Godaeui Munhwa* (The Culture of Prehistoric and Ancient Periods). Pusan: Pusan University Museum.

___ 1996b. *Dongnae Bokcheon-dong Gobungun* III (Ancient Tumuli at Bokcheon-dong in Dongnae III). Pusan: Pusan University Museum.

SKHB (Sakai-shi Hakubutsukan) (Sakai City Museum). 2001. *Sakai Hakkutsu Monogatari: Kofun to Iseki kara mita Sakai no Rekishi* (The Story of Sakai Archaeological Excavations: The History of Sakai in Light of Ancient Tumuli and Archaeological Sites). Sakai: Sakai-shi Hakubutsukan.

SKAKH (Shiga Kenritsu Azuchijo Koko Hakubutsukan [Shiga Prefecture Azuchi Castle Archaeological Museum]). 2001. *Kankoku yori watarikite: Kodai Kokka no Heisei to Toraijin* (Crossing the Sea from Korea: Formation of [Japan's] Ancient State and the People Who Crossed the Sea). Omihachiman-shi: SKAKH.

Author listing

AHN, Jae-ho. 2000. Hanguk nonggyeong sahoeui seongnip (Formation of Korean agricultural society). *Hanguk Gogo Hakbo* 43: 41-46.

Aikens, C. Melvin, and Takayasu HIGUCHI. 1982. *Prehistory of Japan*. New York: Academic Press.

Allen, Chizuko T. 2008. Early migrations, conquests, and common ancestry: theorizing Japanese origins in relation with Korea. In *Sungkyun Journal of East Asian Studies*, 8(1): 105-130. Seoul: Sunggyunkwan University Academy of East Asian Studies.

AKAZAWA, Takeru. 1982. Culture change in prehistoric Japan: Receptivity to rice agriculture in the Japanese Archipelago. In *Advances in World Archaeology*, edited by F. Wendorf and A. Close, 151-211. New York: Academic Press.

AN, Zhi-min. 1985. Choko karyu iki senshi bunka no Nihon retto e no eikyo (Influence of the prehistoric culture of the lower reaches of the Yangtze River on the Japanese Archipelago). *Kokogaku Zasshi* 70.3: 297–311.

Anthony, David. 1990. Migration in archaeology: the baby and the bath water. *American Anthropologist* 92: 895-914.

Aston, W.G. 1972. *Nihongi: Chronicles of Japan from the Earliest Times to A.D. 697*, an English translation of the *Nihon Shoki*, compiled in 720 AD. Rutland and Tokyo: Charles E. Tuttle Company.

AZUMA, Ushio. 1999. *Kodai Higashi Ajiano Tetsuto Wa* (Ancient East Asia's Iron and Wa). Hiroshima: Keisuisha.

BABA, Hisao. 1997. Jomonjin (Jomon people). In *Jomon and Yayoi*, edited by the Organizational Committee for the 11th Open Symposium on Higher Education and Science, 26-37. Tokyo: Kuba Pro.

BAE, Jin-seong. 2006. Mumuntogisahoeui wisepumgwa gyecheunghwa (Stratification of Mumun society in light of funerary prestige goods. *In Gyecheungsahoewa Jibaejaui Chulhyeon* (Emergence of the Stratified Society and Elite Managers), edited by Hanguk Gogohakhoe (Korean Archaeology Society), 87-109. Yong'in-shi: Hanguk Gogohakhoe.

___ 2007. *Mumuntogi Munhwaui Seongripgwa Gyecheungsahoe* (Formation of the Mumun Pottery Culture and Stratified Society). Seoul: Seogyeong Munhwasa.

___ 2014. Kanhanto nanbu ni okeru shoki noko bunka no dotai: sekisei kogu o tsujite (State of the early agriculture in southern Korea: in light of stone tools). In *Retto Shoki Inasaku no Ninaite wa Dareka?* (Who Were the People in Charge of the Early Wet-Rice Cultivation in the [Japanese] Archipelago?), edited by N. SHIMOJO, pp. 49-77. Tokyo: Kodaigaku Kyokai.

Baker, P.T., and W.T. Sanders. 1972. Demographic studies in anthropology. *Annual Review of Anthropology* 1: 151-178.

BAN, Yasushi. 2018. *Sogauji no Kokogaku* (Archaeology of the Soga Clan). Shinsensha.

BAN, Yasushi, and Taisuke AOYAGI. 2017. *Katsuragi no Oto – Nango Isekigun* (The Royal Capital of Katsuragi – The Nango Archaeological Sites). Tokyo: Shinsensha.

___ 2018. *Soga Uji no Kodaigaku* (Ancient Period Studies of the Soga Clan). Tokyo: Shinsensha.

Barnes, Gina L. 1988. *Protohistoric Yamato*. Ann Arbor: University of Michigan.

___ 1989. Mahan, Paekche and state formation on the Korean Peninsula. *Mahan Munhwa Yeonguui Jemunje* (Various Issues in the Study of Mahan Culture). The tenth International Academic Conference Volume on Mahan – Paekche Culture, pp. 69-82. Iksan: Weongwang University Mahan – Paekche Research Institute.

___ 1991. Early Korean States: a review of historical interpretation, in *Hoabinhian, Jomon, Yayoi, Early Korean States*, edited by G.L. Barnes, 113-162. Oxbow Books.

___ 1992. The development of stoneware technology in southern Korea. In *Pacific Northeast Asia in Prehistory*, edited by C.M. Aikens and S.N. RHEE, 197-208. Pullman: Washington State University.

___ 1993. Miwa occupation in wider perspective, in *The Miwa Project: survey, coring and excavation at the Miwa site, Nara, Japan*, ed. by G.L. Barnes & M. OKITA, 181-192. BAR International Series 582. Oxford: Tempvs Reparatvm.

___ 2000. Archaeological armor in Korea and Japan: Styles, technology, and social setting. In *Clashes of Iron: Arms, Weaponry, and Warfare in Early East Asian States*, edited by G.L. Barnes, 60-95. Leiden: Brill.

___ 2007. *State Formation in Japan: Emergence of a Fourth Century Ruling Elite*. London: Routledge.

___ 2014. A hypothesis for early Kofun rulership. In *Japan Review*, No. 27: 3-29. Kyoto: International Research Centre for Japanese Studies, National Institute for the Humanities.

___ 2015. *Archaeology of East Asia: The Rise of Civilization in China, Korea, and Japan*. London: Oxbow.

Bausch, Ilona R. 2017. Prehistoric networks across the Korea Strait (5000–1000 BCE): 'early globalization' during the Jomon period in north-west Kyushu. In *The Routledge Handbook of Archaeology and Globalization*, edited by T. Hodos, 413-438. London: Routledge.

Best, Jonathan W. 1982. Diplomatic and cultural contacts between Paekche and China. *Harvard Journal of Asiatic Studies*, 42.2: 443-501. Cambridge: Harvard-Yenching Institute.

___ 2003. Buddhism and polity in early 6th century Paekche. *Korean Studies*, 26.2: 165-215. University of Hawaii Press.

___ 2006. *A History of the Early Korean Kingdom of Paekche*. Cambridge (MA) and London: Harvard University Asia Center.

___ 2016. Problems in the Samguk Sagi's representation of early Silla history. *Seoul Journal of Korean Studies* 29.1: 1-6.

Blanton, R.E., S.A. Kowalewski, O. Feinman, and J. Appel. 1981. *Ancient Mesoamerica*. Cambridge University Press.

Bokcheon Bangmulgwan (Bokcheon Museum). 1999. *Ancient Warriors: Ancient Weaponry*. Pusan: Bokcheon Museum.

Brown, Delmer. 1993. The Yamato Kingdom. In *The Cambridge History of Japan, Vol. 1, Ancient Japan*, edited by J.W. Hall *et al.* Cambridge University Press.

Burmeister, Stefan. 2000. Archaeology and migration: Approaches to an archaeological proof of migration. *Current Anthropology* 41: 539-567.

Byington, Mark E (ed.). 2009. *Early Korea: The Samhan Period in Korean History*. Cambridge, MA: Korea Institute, Harvard University.

___ (ed.) 2012. *Early Korea: The Rediscovery of Kaya in History and Archaeology*. Cambridge, MA: Korea Institute, Harvard University.

___ (ed.) 2016a. *The History and Archaeology of Koguryo Kingdom*. Cambridge, MA: Korea Institute, Harvard University.

___ 2016b. *The Ancient State of Puyo in Northeast Asia: Archaeology and Historical Memory*. Cambridge, MA: Korea Institute, Harvard University.

Carneiro, Robert L. 1970. A Theory of the Origin of the State. *Science* 169: 234-243.

Chamberlain, Basil H. 1902. *Things Japanese*. London: John Murray.

Chapman, Robert. 1990. *Emerging Complexity*. Cambridge University Press.

Cheongju National Museum. 2017. *Cheongju Bangmulgwan Dorok* (Cheongju National Museum Catalogue). Cheongju: Cheongju National Museum.

CHOI, Byeong-hyeon. 2015. Silla jogi Kyongju jiyeok mokgwakmyoui jeongaewa Saroguk naebuui tonghap gwajeong (Development of wooden chamber burials of the Kyongju region and the internal consolidation process of Saro-guk during the incipient Silla period). *Hanguk Gogo Hakbo* 95: 102-159.

CHOI, Mong-lyong. 1978. Jeonnam jibang sojae jiseogmyoui hyeongshikgwa bunryu (Typology of dolmens in South Jeolla Province). *Yeoksa Hakbo* 18: 1-50.

___ 1992. Trade system of the Wiman State. In *Pacific Northeast Asia in Prehistory*, edited by C.M. Aikens and S.N. RHEE. Pullman: Washington State University.

___ 1999. Hanguk Jiseongmyo eu giweon gwa jeonpa (Origin and diffusion of Korean dolmens). In *Hanguk Jiseongmyo (Goindol) Yujeok Jonghap Josa Yeongu* (The Comprehensive Study of Korean Dolmens), edited by Seoul National University Museum, pp. 9-17. Seoul: Munhwajaecheong and Seoul National University Museum.

___ 2009. Mahan yeonguui saeroun banghyanggwa gwaje (New approaches in issues in the study of Mahan). In *Mahan, Sumshineun Girok* (Mahan, Breathing Records), edited by National Jeonju Museum, 199-214. Jeonju: Gungnip Jeonju Bangmulgwan.

CHOI, Sung-rak. 1986. *Yeong'am Jangcheon-ni Jugeoji II* (Yeong'am Jangcheon-ri Dwelling Site II). Mokpo: Mokpo National University Museum.

___ 1993. *Hanguk Weonsamguk Sidae Yeongu* (A Study of the Culture of Korea's Proto-Three Kingdoms). Seoul: Hak'yeon Munhwasa.

___ 2017a. Yeongsangang yuyeok godae sahoewa Paekchee euhan tonghap gwajeong (The ancient society in the Yeongsan River basin and the political consolidation process under Paekche). *Jibangsawa Jibang Munhwa* 20.1: 279-299.

___ 2017b. Honam jiyeok cheolgimunhwaeu hyeongseonggwa byeoncheon (Formation and Changes of the iron age culture in the Honam region). *Doseo Munhwa* 49: 105-146.

CHOI, Wan-gyu. 2000. Honam jiyeokui Mahan bunmyo yuhyeonggwa jeon'gae (Types and development of graves in the Honam region). *Journal of Honam Archaeology* 11: 7-27.

___ 2001. *Mahan Bunmyo Yuhyeonggwa Jeon'gae* (Types of Mahan Burials and their Changes in Time). A special lecture delivered at the seventh History and Culture Lectureship, November 9, 2011. Iksan: Weongwang University.

___ 2009. Mahan myojeeu hyeongseonggwa Jeonbuk jiyeok eseoui jeon'gae (Formation of Mahan mortuary system and their development in the Jeonbuk region). In *Mahan, Sumshineun Girok* (Mahan, Breathing Records), edited by National Jeonju Museum, 247-259. Jeonju: Gungnip Jeonju Bangmulgwan.

___ 2013. Gimje Byeokkoljeui balgul seongkwawa keu euyi (Excavation results of the Byeokkol Dam and its significance). In *Byeokkoljeno Nazo'o Saguru* (In Search of the Mystery of the Byeokkol Dam). Sayama-ike symposium proceedings. Osaka: Sayama-shi Kyoiku I'inkai.

CHOI, Yeong-ju. 2007. Jojokmun togi eu byeoncheon yangsang (Changing Patterns of the jojokmun [bird footprint] pottery). *Hanguk Sanggosa Hakbo* 55: 79-114.

Crawford, Gary W. 2006. East Asian plant domestication. In *Archaeology of Asia*, edited by M.T. Stark, 77-95. Malden, MA: Blackwell.

___ 2008. The Jomon in early agriculture discourse: issues arising from Matsui, Kanehara and Pearson. *World Archaeology* 40.4: 445-465.

D'Andrea, A.C. 2007. Update: early agriculture in Japan – research since 1999. In *The Emergence of Agriculture: A Global View*, edited by T. Denham and J.P. White. London: Routledge.

Do, Yu-ho, and Gee-deok HWANG. 1957. *Gungsan Weonsi Yujeok Balgul Bogo* (Excavation Report on the Prehistoric Site of Gungsan). Pyongyang: Gwahakweon Chulpansa.

Earle, T.K. 1987. Chiefdom in archaeological and ethnohistorical perspective. *Annual Review of Anthropology* 16: 279-308.

Eckert, C., K.B. LEE, Y.I. LEW, M. Robinson, and E.W. Wagner. 1990. *Korea, Old and New: A History.* Cambridge, MA: Korea Institute, Harvard University.

Edwards, Walter. 1983. Event and Process in the Founding of Japan: The Horserider Theory in Archaeological Perspective. *The Journal of Japanese Studies* 1.2: 265-295.

EGAMI, Namio. 1967. *Kiba Minzoku Kokka* (Horse Riders' State). Tokyo: Chuo Koronsha.

___ 1992. *Egami Namio no Nihon Kodaishi: Kiba Minzoku Yonjugonen* (EGAMI Namio's Japan's Ancient History: Forty-five Years of Horse Riders). Tokyo: Taikosha.

EGAMI, Namio, and Makoto SAHARA. 2003. *Kiba Minzokuwa Kita?! Konai?!* (The Horse riders: Did they come or not?) Tokyo: Shogakkan.

Farris, William W. 1996. *Ancient Japan's Korean Connections. Korean Studies* 20: 1-22.

___ 1998. *Sacred Texts and Buried Treasures: Issues in the Historical Archaeology of Ancient Japan.* Honolulu: University of Hawai'i Press.

French, Howard W. 2002. Japan rediscovers its Korean past. *The New York Times,* March 11, 2002.

FUJIO, Shin'ichiro. 2007. Yayoi jidai no kaishi (The beginning of the Yayoi period). In *Jomon Jidaikara Yayoi Jidaie* (From the Jomon to the Yayoi Period), edited by T. NISHIMOTO, 7-19. Tokyo: Yuzankaku.

FUJIO, S., M. IMAMURA, and T. NISHIMOTO. 2010. Yayoi jidaino kaishi nendai – AMS tanso 14 nendai sokuteini yoru koseido nendai taikeino kochiku (The beginning date of the Yayoi period – constructing the precise chronology system in light of AMS C14 dating). *Sokendai Review of Cultural and Social Studies* 1: 69-96.

Fukuoka-shi Hakubutsukan (Fukuoka City Museum) (ed.). 2004. *Kudara Buneioto Wano Odachi: Himerareta Kokinno Seikiten* (King Munyeong of Paekche and Five Kings of Wa: Exhibition of the Hidden Era of Gold), 121-124. Fukuoka-shi: Fukuoka City Museum.

Fukuoka-shi Kyoiku I'inkai (Fukuoka City Education Committee). 1995. *Itazuke Iseki* (Itazuke Archaeological Site). Fukuoka-shi Maizo Bunkazai Chosa Hokokusho Dai 439-shu (Fukuoka City Buried Cultural Property Research Report No. 439). Fukuoka: Fukuoka Kyoiku I'inkai.

___ 1996. *Yoshitake Isekigun* (Yoshitake Archaeological Site Cluster). Fukuoka-shi maizo bunkazai chosa hokokusho Dai 461-shu. (Investigation report of Fukuoka City Buried Cultural Property #461). Fukuoka-shi: Fukuoka Kyoiku I'inkai.

FURUICHI, Akira. 2001. Kudara Konikishi-shi to Kudara-gun (The Konikishi [royal] clan of Paekche and Paekche-gun). In *Kodai Kawachito Kudara* (Ancient Kawachi and Paekche), edited by Hirakata Rekishi Forum Jikko I'inkai, 118–125. Hirakata: Daikoro Company.

FURUTA, Takehiko, and Masao SHIBURA. 1994. *Nihon Shokio hihan suru* (Criticising the *Nihon Shoki*). Tokyo: Shinzumi.

GANG, Dong-seok. 2019. Jiseongmyo sahoeui network gujowa seongkyeok (Structure and characteristics of network of the dolmen society). In *Hanguk Gogo Hakbo* 105: 6-43.

GANG, I.G., K.M. LEE, Y.H. HAN, and K.S. LEE. 1979. *Songguk-ni.* Seoul: Gungnip Jung-ang Bangmulgwan.

Gardiner, K.H.J. 1969. *The Early History of Korea.* Honolulu: University of Hawaii Press.

GU, Ja-bong. 1998. Samyeop hwandu daedoee daehayeo (On the long swords with palmetto-design pommel). *Gwagi Gogo Yeongu* 4: 69-96. Aju University Museum.

GWAK, Jang-geun. 2017a. *Paekche Munhwaui Kkot: Jeonbukeu Haeyang Munhwa* (The Blossoms of Paekche Culture: The Maritime Culture of Paekche). Jeonju: Jeolla Bukdo Hanguk Gojeon Munhwa Yeonguweon.

___ 2017b. Jangsu-gun jecheol yujeokui bumpo yangsanggwa geueumi (Distribution of iron production sites in Jangsu-gun and their significance). *Honam Gogo Hakbo* 57: 4-25.

Gyeongsang Namdo (South Gyeongsang Province). 1998. *Namgang Seonsa Yujeok* (Prehistoric Sites of the Nam River). Changweon: South Gyeongsang Provincial Government and Namgang Prehistoric Site Excavation Team.

Gyeongsang University Museum. 1990. *Hapcheon Okjeon Gobungun II: M3 Hobun* (Tomb M3: Okjeon Tumuli in Hapcheon II). Jinju: Gyeonsang University Museum.

___. 2000a. *Kimhae Daeseong-dong Gobungun I* (The Ancient Tombs of Kimhae Daeseong-dong I), edited by KC Shin and JW Kim. Kimhae: Gyeongseong University Museum.

___ 2000b. *Kimhae Daeseong-dong Gobungun II* (The Ancient Tombs of Kimhae Daeseong-dong II), edited by K.C. SHIN and J.W. Kim. Kimhae: Gyeongseong University Museum.

HA, In-su. 2006. Shinseokki shidae hanil munhwa gyoryu (Cultural exchange between Korea and Japan during the Neolithic period). *Journal of Korean Archaeology Society* 58: 4-39.

HA, Seung-cheol. 2011. Oeraegye munmuleul tonghaebon Goryeong So Kayaui daeoe gyoryu (Exchange and interactions of Goseong So Kaya in light of foreign type artifacts). In *Kayaui Poguwa Haesang Hwaltong* (Kaya Harbors and Seagoing Activities), edited by Kimhae-shi Haksul Wiweonhoe and Inje Daehakkyo Kaya Munhwa Yeonguso, 149-214. Kimhae: Inje Daehakkyo Kaya Munhwa Yeonguso.

HABU, Junko. 2004. *Ancient Jomon of Japan*. Cambridge University Press.

Hall, John W. 1970. *Japan from Prehistory to Modern Times*. New York: Delacorte Press.

HAM, Byeong-sam, and Keon-mu LEE. 1977. *Namseong-ni Seokgwanmyo* (A Cist Tomb at Namseong-ri). Seoul: National Museum of Korea.

HANADA, Katsuhiro. 2000. Okabe tatemono shurakuto Toraijin (Settlements of thick-walled buildings and Toraijin). *Kodaibunka* (*Cultura Antiqua*) 52.5: 287-300; 52.7: 407-417.

___ 2002. *Kodaino tetsu seisanto Toraijin: Wa seikenno keiseito seisansoshiki* (Ancient iron production and the Toraijin: formation of the Wa government and the production organization). Tokyo: Yuzankaku.

___ 2004. Kan tanya to Torai kojin shudan (Korean forging iron technology and the Toraijin technician groups). In *Kokuritsu Rekishi Minzoku Hakubutsukan Kenkyu Hokoku* (National History and Folklore Museum Research Report) 110: 55-71.

HARUNARI, Hideji. 1990. *Yayoi Jidaino Hajimari* (Beginning of the Yayoi Period). Tokyo: Tokyo University Press (in Japanese).

HARUNARI, Hideji, Shin'ichiro FUJIO, Mineo IMAMURA, and Minoru SAKAMOTO. 2003. Yayoi jidaino kaishi nendai (The beginning of the Yayoi period). In *Nihon Kokogaku Kyokai Dai 69 Kai Sokai Kenkyu Happyo Yoshi*, 65-68. Tokyo: Nihon Daigaku.

HANIHARA, Kazuro. 1984. *Nihonjin no Kigen* (The Origin of Japanese). Tokyo: Asahi Shinbunsha.

___ 1991. Dual structure model for the population history of the Japanese. *Japan Review* 2: 1-33.

___ 1993. Toraijin ni sekken sareta kodai Nihon (Ancient Japan overtaken by immigrants), in *Gen Nihonjin* (The Original Japanese), edited by Asahi Shinbunsha, 6-29. Tokyo: Asahi Shinbunsha.

___ 2000. The dual structure model: a decade since its first proposal. In *Newsletter Special Issue: Interdisciplinary Study on the Origin of Japanese Peoples and Cultures*, ed. by Keiichi OMOTO, p. 4. Kyoto: Nichibunken.

HASHIMOTO, Teruhito, and Yoshihiko KIBA. 2004. Akao Kuzuredani kofun-gun no chosa (Investigations of Kuzuredani ancient tombs). In *Imaki no Tehito: Kofun – Asuka no Toraijin* (The Newly Arrived Skilled People of the Kofun and Asuka Periods), edited by Osaka Furitsu Chikatsu Asuka Hakubutsukan, 86-87. Osaka: Furitsu Chikatsu Asuka Hakubutsukan.

HASHINO, Shimpei. 2003. Shiseki-bo denpa no prosesu – Kanhanto nandanbu–Kyushu hokubu o chushin to shite (Diffusion process of dolmens in light of the southern end region of the Peninsula and the northern part of Kyushu). *Nihon Kokogaku* (Journal of Japanese Archaeology) 16: 1-25.

___ 2014. Torai bunka no keisei to sono haikei (Formation of the Toraijin people's culture and their background). In *Retto Shoki Inasakuno Ninaitewa tareka?* (Who Were the People in Charge of the Early Wet-Rice Cultivation in the [Japanese] Archipelago?), edited by N. SHIMOJO, 79-124. Tokyo: Kodaigaku Kyokai.

HAURY, Emil W. 1958. Evidence at point of pines for a prehistoric migration from Northern Arizona. In *Migrations in New World Culture History*, edited by R.H. Thompson, 1-7. Tucson: University of Arizona Press.

HIGUCHI, Takayasu. 1986. Relationships between Japan and Asia in ancient times: Introductory comments, in *Windows on the Japanese Past: Studies in Archaeology and Prehistory*, edited by R. Pearson, K. Hutterer, and G.L. Barnes, 121–126. Ann Arbor: University of Michigan Center for Japanese Studies.

___ 1995. Konan kara no inasaku dempa (Diffusion of rice cultivation from the Yangtze River basin). In *Higashi Ajiano Inasaku Kigen to Kodai Inasaku Bunka* (Origins of Rice Cultivation in East Asia and Ancient Rice Agriculture) edited by K. WASANO, p. 282. Saga City: Saga University Department of Agriculture.

HIRAKORI, Tatsuya. 2013. *Mudeom Jaryorobon Cheongdonggi Shidae Sahoe* (Bronze Age Society in Light of Mortuary Materials). Seoul: Seogyeong Munhwasa.

HIRANO, Kunio. 2018. *Kikajin to Kodai Kokka* (Kikjin and the Ancient State). Tokyo: Yoshikawa Kobunkan.

HIROSE, Kazuo. 1997. *Jomon kara Yayoi e no Shinrekishizo* (New Historical Perspectives on Transition from Jomon to Yayoi). Tokyo: Kadokawa Shoten.

___ 2013. Yamashiro Hebizuka kofun o meguru 2, 3 no mondai (2, 3 problems surrounding the Yamashiro Hebizuka kofun). *Kokuritsu Rekishi Minzoku Hakubutsukan Kenkyu Hokoku*, 178: 143-176.

HIROSE, Yuichi. 2005. Daemahaeyeopeul saiedun hanil sinseokki sidaeui gyoryu (Korea/Japan exchange/trade during the Neolithic across the Tsushima Strait). *Hanguk Sinseokki Sidae Yeongu* 9: 41-54.

HOJO, Yoshitaka. 2000. Jeonbang Huweonbunui jeongaewa geu dayangseong (Development of zempo koen tumuli and their diverse characteristics). *Hangukui Jeonbang Huweonbun* (Keyhole Tumuli of Korea), edited by Paekche Research Institute, 29-44. Daejeon: Chungnam University Press.

HONG, Hyeong-wu. 1999. Ganghwa Jiseongmyo (Dolmens on Ganghwa Island.). In *Hanguk Jiseongmyo (Goindol) Yujeok Jonghap Josa Yeongu* (The Comprehensive Study of Korean Dolmens), edited by Seoul National University Museum, 213-224. Seoul: Munhwajaecheong and Seoul National University Museum.

HONG, Wontack. 2010. Ancient Korea-Japan Relations: Paekche and the Origin of the Yamato Dynasty. Seoul: Kudara International.

HORI, Masato. 2009. Toraijin no Haka (Tombs of the Toraijin). *Kiyo* 22: 13-22. Otsu City: Shiga-ken Bunkazai Hogo Kyokai.

HUDSON, M.J. 1999. *Ruins of Identity: Ethnogenesis in the Japanese Islands*. Honolulu: University of Hawai'i Press.

ICHIMURA, Kunio. 2004. Sono ato no Toraijin (Toraijin of the subsequent period). *Yamato Okento Toraijin* (The Yamato Court and the People Who Crossed the Sea), edited by Osaka Furitsu Yayoi Bunka Hakubutsukan, 48-49. Osaka: Yayoi Culture Museum.

IIDA, Teiji. 1912. *Shinyaku Nihon Shoki* (Newly Translated *Nihon Shoki*). Tokyo: Susebo.

IKEUCHI, Hiroshi. 1970. *Nihon Jodaishi no Ichi Kenkyu, Nissen no Kosho to* Nihon Shoki (A Study of Japan's Ancient History, Japan-Korea Interaction and *Nihon Shoki*). Tokyo: Chuokoron Bijutsu Shuppan.

IM, Hyo-taek, and Dong-cheol GWAK. 2000. *Yangdong-ni Gobun* (Yangdong-ni Tumuli). Pusan: Dongui University Museum.

IM, Yeong-jin. 2001. Paekcheui seongjanggwa Mahan seryeok geurigo Wae (Growth and Expansion of Paekche and Mahan Polities, and Wa). In *Kodai no Kawachi to Kudara* (Ancient Kawachi and Paekche), 48-73. Hirakata Rekishi Forum Jikko I'inkai. Hirakata: Daikoro Company.

IMAI, Kei'ichi. 1965. *Narato Kikajin* (Nara and the Immigrants). Edited by Sobundo, 30(5). Tokyo: Gyosei.

___ 1969. *Kikajin no Kenkyu* (Study of the Immigrants). Tokyo: Sogeisha.

IMAIZUMI, Tadayoshi. 1986. *Kundoku Shoku Nihongi* (Chronicles of Japan Continued with Japanese transcription). Kyoto: Rinsenshoten.

IMAMURA, Tomoyo, and Shin'ichiro FUJIO. 2009. Tanso 14 nen no kiroku kara mita shizen kankyo hendo – Yayoi bunka seiritsuki (The Yayoi culture formation period - changes in the natural environement in light of the C14 data). In *Yayoi Jidai no Kokogaku 2: Yayoi Bunka Tanjo* (The Archaeology of the Yayoi Period 2: Birth of the Yayoi Culture), edited by H. SHITARA, S. FUJIO, and T. MATSUGI, 47-58. Tokyo: Toseisha.

INOUE, Chikara. 2008. Dahori iseki ni mirareru Wa to kanren suru kokoshiryo ni tsuite (Regarding the archaeological materials related to Wa observed at Dahori site). In *Daho-ri Yujeok Balgul Seonggwawa Gwaje* (Daho-ri Excavations: Results and Prospects), edited by Gungnip Jung-ang Bangmulgwan, 235-255. Seoul: Gungnip Jung-ang Bangmulgwan.

INOUE, Hideo. 1973. *Mimana Nihonfu to Wa* (Mimana Nihonfu and Wa). Tokyo: Toshuppan Neirakusha.

INOUE, Mitsuo. 1991. Toraijin to Heiankyo (Toraijin and Heian Palace). In *Kodai Gozoku to Chosen* (Ancient Powerful Clans and Korea), edited by Kyoto Bunka Hakubutsukan (Kyoto Culture Museum), 81-130. Tokyo: Shinjinbutsu Oraisha.

___ 2000. Toraijin ga inakattara Nihon no rekishi wa 200-nen osoreteita. (If the Toraijin had not been, Japan's history would have been delayed by 200 years). In *Sapio*, edited by Sapio, 12 (10): 16-18. Tokyo: Shogakukan.

INOUE, Mitsusada. 1973. *Nihon no Rekishi I* (History of Japan I). Tokyo: Chuokoronsha.

INOUE, Mitsusada (with DM Brown). 1993. The century of reform. In *The Cambridge History of Japan, Vol. 1: Ancient Japan*, edited by D.M. Brown, 163-223. Cambridge University Press.

ISHIMODA, Tadashi. 1962. Kodaishi gaisetsu (An overview of the ancient history). In *Iwanami Koza: Nihon Rekishi* (Iwanami Lectures: Japanese History), 1-77. Iwanami Shoten.

ISHIWATARI, Shinichiro. 2001. *Kudara kara tora ishita Oujin Tenno* (Emperor Oujin who migrated from Paekche). Tokyo: San'ichi Shobo (in Japanese).

IWANAGA, Shoso. 1991. Nihon ni okeru seidobuki no torai to seisan no kaishi (Arrival of bronze weapons and the beginning of their local production). *Nikkan Koshono Kokogaku – Yayoiji daihen* (Archaeology of Japan-Korea Interaction – The Yayoi Period), edited by F. ODA and B.-S. HAN, 114-119. Tokyo: Rokko Shuppan.

___ 2005.Yayoi jidai kaishi nendai saiko, seidoki nendairon kara miru (Rethinking on the beginning of the Yayoi period, viewed from the chronology theory of the bronzes). *Bulletin of the Kyushu University Museum* 3:1-22.

JANG, Deok-weon. 2017. *Jincheon Seokjang-ni Yujeokui Jecheol Shiseol Seongkyeok Jaekeomto* (Re-examination of the Iron-Smelting Structures in Seokjang-ni, Jincheon). Cheongju: Jungweon Munhwajae Yeonguweon.

JEE, Geon-gil. 1979. Yesan Dongseo-ri seokgwanmyo chulto cheongdong ilgwalyumul (Bronze artifacts from a cist tomb at Dongseo-ri in Yesan. *Paekche Yeongu* (Journal of Paekche Research) 9. Paekche Research Institute of Chungnam University.

JEON, Yeong-nae. 1986. Nihon Inasaku bunka no denpa keiro (The diffusion route of Japan's rice cultivation). In *Ethnos in Asia* 30: 107-117, edited Naoichi KOKUBUN. Tokyo: Shin Nihon Kyoiku Tosho Kabushiki Kaisha.

___ 1987a. *Seokkiui Bigyo: Ilbongwaui Bigyo* (Lithic Implements Compared: With those of Japan). In Hanguksaron 17 (Essays on Korean History 17), 131-263. Guksa Pyeonchan Wiweonhoe.

___ 1987b. Geumgang yuyeok cheongdonggi munhwaui shinjaryo (New data on the bronze culture of the Geum River basin). *Mahan-Paekche Munhwa Yeongu* 10: 69-126.

JEONG, Jing-weon, and In-su HA.1998. Namhaean jibanggwa Kyushu shinseokki shidae munhwa gyoryu yeongu (Study of cultural exchanges during the Neolithic between Korea's southern coastal region and Kyushu). *Hanguk Minjok Munhwa 12* (Korean People and Culture 12), edited by Hanguk Minjok Munhwa Yeonguso (Research Institute of Korean People and Culture), 1-90. Pusan: Pusan University.

JEONG, Jing-weon, and Kyeong-cheol SHIN. 1984. Godae hanguk gapjue daehan sogo (A brief consideration on ancient Korean body armor and helmets). In *Yun Mu-byeong Baksa Hoegap Ginyeom Nonchong* (Festschrift in Honor of Dr. Mu-byeong Yun's 60th Birthday), edited by YUN Mu-byeong's 60th Birthday Celebration Publication Committee, 289-297. Seoul: Tongcheon Munhwasa.

JEONG, Su-ok. 2012. Hanbando chwisa munhwaga ilbon gobunshidaee michin yeonghyanggwa suyong gwajeong: bukbu Kyushuwa Kinki jiyeokeul jungshimeuro (Influence of Korean cooking culture on Kofun-period Japan and the process of adoption in light of archaeological remains from the Kyushu and Kinki region. *Hanguk Sangosa Hakbo* 76: 109-134.

JEONG, Ui-do. 2000. Namgang yujeokui hwanho yujeok (Moat-encircled cites at Namgang site). In *Jinju Namgamg Yujeokgwa Godae Ilbon* (Jinju Namgang Archaeological Sites and Ancient Japan), edited by Inje Daehakkyo Kaya Munhwa Yeonguso, 97-137. Kimhae: Kaya Culture Research Institute of Inje University.

JINAM, Timothy A., Hideki KANAZAWA-KIRIYAMA, and Naruya SAITOU. 2015. Human genetic diversity in the Japanese Archipelago: dual structure and beyond. *Genes & Genetic Systems* 9.3: 147-152.

JO, Beop-jong. 2010. Godae hanil gwan'gyeui seongrip (Formation of ancient Korea-Japan relations). In *Hanil Gwan'gyesa Yeongu Nonmunjip 11: Nonggyeong – Geumsog Munhwawa Hanil Gwan'gye* (Research Papers on Korea-Japan Relations 11: Korea-Japan Relations in Agriculture-Metallurgy Culture), edited by Hanil Gwan'gyesa Yeongu Nonmunjip Pyeonchan Wiweonhoe, 1-73. Seoul: Gyeong'in Munhwasa.

JO, Jin-seon. 2005. *Sehyeong Donggeom Munhwaui Yeongu* (A Study of the Korean Slender Bronze Dagger Culture). Seoul: Hak'yeon Munhwasa.

___ 2019. Jeon-geundaeui Hanil hangrowa Sehyeong donggeomui pageup gyeongro (Korea-Japan maritime route of the ancient and modern period and the diffusion of the slender-bronze dagger culture). *Hanguk Sangosa Hakbo* 105: 46-80.

JOYCE, Rosemary A. 2001. Burying the dead at Tlatilco: Social memory and social identities. In *Social Memory, Identity, and Death: Anthropological Perspectives on Mortuary Rituals*, edited by M.S. Chesson, 13-26. Archeological Papers of the American Anthropological Association, No. 10. Arlington: AAA.

JU, Bo-don. 2000. Baekje eu Yeongsan gang yuyeok jibae bangshik gwa jeonbang huweonbun pijangja eu seongkyeok (Paekche's governance method of the Yeongsan river region and the character of the buried person in the zempo koen tumuli). In *Hanguk eu Jeonbang Huweonbun* (Zempo Koen Tumuli of Korea), edited by Baekje Yeon'guso, 49-99. Daejeon: Chungnam Daehakkyo Chulpanbu.

KADOWAKI, Teiji. 1973. Sogashi no shutsuji ni tsuite (Regarding the Origin of the Soga clan). In *Nihon Bunkato Chosen* (Japanese Culture and Korea), edited by Chosen Bunkasha, 79-91. Tokyo: Shin Jinbutsu Oraisha.

___ 1991. Sogauji to Toraijin (The Soga clan and the immigrants) In *Kodai Gozokuto Chosen* (Ancient Powerful Clans and Korea), edited by Kyoto Bunka Hakubutsukan (Kyoto Culture Museum), 169-212. Tokyo: Shin Jinbutsu Oraisha.

KAMEDA, Shuichi. 1997. Kokogaku kara mita Kibi no Toraijin (Immigrants in the Kibi area in light of archaeology). In *Chosen Shakaino Shiteki Tenkaito Higashi Ajia* (Historical Development of the Korean society and East Asia). Tokyo: Yamakawa Shuppansha.

___ 2000. Tetsu to Toraijin (Iron and immigrants). *Fukuoka Daigaku Sogo Kenkyushoho* 240: 165–184.

___ 2003a. Toraijin no kokogaku (Archaeology of immigrants). In *Nanakuma Shigaku No. 4* (Nanakuma Historical Studies No. 4), edited by Nanakuma Shigakukai, 1-14. Fukuoka: Nanakuma Shigakukai.

___ 2003b. Michinoku no Toraijin – yosatsu (Immigrants in Michinoku – a preliminary observation). In *Kofun Jidai Togoku ni okeru Toraikei Bunka no Juyo to Tenkai* (Incorporation and Development of Immigrant Culture in Tokoku during the Kofun Period), edited by Senshu Daigaku Bungakubu, 55–65. Tokyo: Senshu University.

___ 2004a. Toraijin to kinzokugi seisan (Immigrants and the production of metallurgical implements). In *Kinzoku Bunka no Takaku-teki Tankyu (Multiple Approaches in the Study of Iron Culture)*, edited by Iron Culture Research Group, 75-94. Asaka: Tekki Bunka Kenkyukai.

___ 2004b. Nihon no shoki no kugi to kasugai ga kataru mono (Things revealed by Japan's early iron nails and braces). In *Kokogaku Kenkyukai 50 Shunen Kinen Ronbunshu [Bunka no Tayosei to Hikaku Kokogaku]* (The 50th Anniversary Volume of the Society of Archaeological Research [Cultural Diversities and Comparative Archaeology]), edited by Kokogaku Kenkyukai, 29-38. Okayama: Kokogaku Kenkyukai.

___ 2004c. Goseki no Kibi to Chosen hanto (Fifth-century Kibi and the Korean Peninsula). In *Kibi Chiho Bunka Kenkyu* 14: 1-19.

___ 2005. Chiiki ni okeru Toraijin no nintei hoho (Archaeological criteria for identifying immigrants in various regions). In *Dai Hachikai Kyushu Zempokoenfun Kenkyukai Shiryoshu: Kyushu ni okeru Toraijin no Juyu to Tenkai* (The Eighth Collection of Research Materials of Kyushu Keyhole Tombs Research Association: Adoption and Development of Immigrant Culture in Kyushu, edited by the Eighth Research Executive Committee on Kyushu Area Keyhole Tombs, 1-16. Fukuoka: Eighth Research Executive Committee on Kyushu Area Keyhole Tombs.

___ 2010. *Toraijin no Mura o sagasu* (In search of the immigrants' villages). A lecture delivered for a public forum, Asuka to Toraijin – Kodai Kokka o sasaeta Hitobito (Asuka and the Immigrants – the People who supported the Ancient State), 7/10/2010. Asuka: Asuka Mura Marugo to Hakubutsukan Foramu.

___ 2011. Kokogaku kara mita Nihon retto to Chosen hanto no koryu – Kofun jidai no Nishi Nihon Chi'iki o chushin ni (Exchange between the Japanese Archipelago and the Korean Peninsula – with a focus on western Japan during the Kofun period). *Higashi Ajia Sekaishi Kenkyu Senta Nenpo* 5: 111-130. Tokyo: Senshu Daigaku.

___ 2012. Toraijin no tokoku iju to Tago-gun kengun no haikei (Migration of the Immigrants to the Tokoku and the background of establishing the Tago-gun. In *Tagohi ga Kataru Kodai Nihonto Toraijin* (Ancient Japan and the Immigrants as revealed by the Tago memorial stone), edited by Y. HABUTA and Takasaki-shi, 77-146. Tokyo: Yoshikawa Kobunkan.

___ 2016. 4–5 seiki no Nihon retsudo no tekki seisan shuraku – Kanhanto no kakawari o chushin ni (Iron producing communities in the Japanese Archipelago during the fourth–fifth century – focusing on the relationship with the Korean Peninsula). In *Nikkan 4-5 Seikino Doki – Tekki Seisanto Shuraku* (Pottery-Iron Production and Settlements during the Fourth-Fifth Century Japan and Korea), edited by Nikkan Kosho no Kokogaku –Kofun Jidai Kenkyukai, pp. 283-321. Fukuoka: Nikkan Kosho no Kokogaku – Kofun Jidai Kenkyukai.

KAMIOBAYASHI, Shiro. 2004. Kofun – Asuka no Toraijin (Toraijin of the Kofun – Asuka Period). In *Imaki no Tehito* (Recently Arrived Skilled People), 61-68. Osaka: Osaka Furitsu Chikatsu Asuka Hakubutsukan.

KANASEKI, Hiroshi and OYBH. 1995. *Yayoi Bunka no Seiritsu – Daihenkaku no Shutai wa "Jomonjin" datta* (Formation of Yayoi Culture – the Main Actors of the Great Transformation were "Jomon People"), edited by H. KANASEKI and OYBH, 236-247.Tokyo: Kadokawa.

KANAZAWA-KIRIYAMA, Hideaki *et al.* 2017. A partial nuclear genome of the Jomons who lived 3000 years ago in Fukushima, Japan. *Journal of Human Genetics* 62: 213-221.

Kaner, Simon, and Ken'ichi YANO. 2015. Early agriculture in Japan. In *The Cambridge World History Vol II: A World with Agriculture, 12,000 BC–500 AD*, pp. 343-410, edited by G. Barker and C. Goucher. Cambridge University Press.

KANEYASU, Yasuaki. 1997. Omi no Torai Bunka (The Torai Culture of Omi). In *Toraijin*, edited by K. MORI and T. KADOWAKI, 61-84. Tokyo: Taikosha.

Karatsu-shi Bunka Shinko Zaidan (Karatsu City Culture Promotion Foundation). 1993. *Karatsu Matsurokan – Nabatake Iseki* (Karatsu Matsuro Hall – Nabatake Archaeological Site), edited by Karatsu-shi Bunka Shinko Zaidan. Karatsu: Karatsu City Culture Promotion Foundation.

Kashiwara-shi Kyoiku I'inkai. 1986. Takaida Yokoanagun I (Cliff tomb group of Takaida I). Kashiwara-shi Bunkazai Gaiho (Kashiwara City Cultural Property Report 1985-VI. Kashiwara: Kashiwara-shi Kyoiku I'inkai.

___ 1988. *Ogata Iseki* (The Ogata Site). *Kashiwara-shi Bunkazai Gaiho 1988-2* (Kashiwara City Cultural Heritage Report 1988-II), edited by Kashiwara City Board of Education, 1-55. Kashiwara City: Kashiwara-shi Kyoiku I'inkai.

___ 1994. *Hiraoyama Kofungun* (Hiraoyama Ancient Tumuli Group). Kashiwara Bunkazai Gaiho 1994-II (Kashiwara Cultural Heritage Report 1994-II). Kashiwara City: Kashiwara-shi Kyoiku I'inkai.

___ 1997. *Ogata no Tetsu* (The Iron of Ogata). Kashiwara City: Kashiwara-shi Kyoiku I'inkai.

KATAOKA, Koji. 1999. *Yayoi Jidai Toraijin to Doki – Seidoki* (The Toraijin Pottery and Bronzes in the Yayoi Period). Tokyo: Yuzankaku.

___ 2006. *Yayoi Jidai Toraijin kara Wajin Shakai e* (From the Yayoi Period Toraijin to Wa People's Society). Tokyo: Yusankaku.

KATO, Kenkichi. 1983. *Soga Uji to Yamato Oken* (Soga Clan and the Yamato Court). Tokyo: Yoshikawa Kobunkan.

KAWAE, Yoichi. 2014. Yayoitogi byeonhwawa hanbandogye togiui gwangyee daehan myeotgaji munje (Some issues regarding the relationship between changes in Yayoi pottery and the Korean Peninsula-style pottery found in northern Kyushu). *Hanguk Sangosa Hakbo* 86: 31-52.

KAZUHISA, Hirao (ed.) 2004. *Itokoku Rekishi Hakubutsukan* (Itokoku History Museum). Maebaru-shi: Itokoku Rekishi Hakubutsukan.

Kidder, J. Edward Jr. 1993. The earliest societies in Japan. In *The Cambridge History of Japan, Vol. 1, Ancient Japan*, edited by J.S. Hall *et al.*, 48-107. Cambridge University Press.

___ 1999. *The Lucky Seventh: Early Horyu-ji and Its Time*. Tokyo: International Christian University Hachiro Yuasa Memorial Museum.

KIM, Bum-cheol. 2010. Hoseo jiyeok Jiseongmyoui sahoegyeongjejeok gineung (Socioeconomic role of the dolmens in the Hoseo region). *Hanguk Sanggosa Hakbo* 68: 5-24.

KIM, Dae-hwan. 2017. Ilje Gangjeomgi Joseon Gojeok Josa Saeopgwa Hanguk Gogohaksa (Historical remains survey activities during Japan's forced occupation and the history of Korean archaeology). *Hanguk Sanggosa Hakbo* 97: 79-100.

KIM, Do-yeong. 2015. Dongbuk Ashia cheolgi munhwaui jeon'gaewa hanya'gongcheol jeongchaek (Development of iron culture and the policy of safeguarding iron production technology and distribution of ironware in northeast Asia). *Hanguk Gogo Hakbo* 94: 32-68.

KIM, Du-cheol. 2010. Gwansanggwa jeon'gi Kayaui myoje (Coffin platform and mortuary system of early Kaya). *Hanguk Gogo Hakbo* 75: 126-169. Pusan: Hanguk Gogohakhoe.

KIM, Gil-shik. 1994. Buyeo Songguk-ni yujeokui balgul josa gaeyowa seongkwa (A comprehensive analysis of Songguk-ni site excavations). In *Maeul eu Gogohak* (Archaeology of Village Settlements), edited by Hanguk Gogohakhoe (Korean Archaeological Society), 177-193. Seoul: Hanguk Gogohakhoe.

KIM, Gyeong-taek, Gi-seong LEE, Geon-il LEE, and Su-yeong IM. 2015. *Songguk-ni: Buyeo Songguk-ni Balgul Josa 40 Ju'nyeon Ginyeomjip* (Songguk-ni: 40 Years' Excavations of Songguk-ni). Buyeo: Korea National University of Cultural Heritage, Archaeological Research Institute.

KIM, Habeom. 2019. *An Emic Investigation on the Trajectory of the Songgukri [sic] Culture during the Middle Mumun Period (2900-2400 cl. BP) in Korea: A GIS and Landscape Approach.* Ph.D. dissertation, University of Orgon.

KIM, Hun-hee. 2011. Keolsuheyong yujarigiui byeoncheongwa eumi (Curlicued *yujarigi*: their evolution and significance). *Hanguk Gogo Hakbo* 81: 39-76.

KIM, Hyok-jung, 2020. Cheonan Dujeong-dong yujeok chulto ihyeong cheolgiui seongkyeok – Baekje chogi gapju yangsang keomto (The characteristics of iron objects excavated at the Dujeong-dong site (Cheonan) – An examination of Paekche's early body armor. *Hanguk Sangosa Hakbo* 108: 37-60.

KIM, Jae-hong. 2006. Gongju Suchon-ri, Geumsan Sudang-ri chulto Paekche salpo (Paekche *salpo* from Gongju Suchon-ri and Geumsan Sudang-ri). In *Hanseongeseo Ungjineuro* (*From Hanseong to Ungjin*), edited by Gungnip Gongju Bangmulgwan, 181-186. Gongju: National Gongju Museum.

KIM, Jang-suk. 2009. Hoseowa seobu honam jiyeok chogi cheolgi – weonsamguk sidae pyeonnyeone daehayeo (On the chronology of the Early Iron Age and the Proto Three Kingdoms Period in the Hoseo and Western Honam regions). *Honam Gogohakbo* 33: 46-69.

___ 2012. Namhan jiyeok jangranhyeong togiui deungjang (The appearance and spread of torpedo-shaped jars in southern Korea). *Gogohak* 11.3: 5-49.

___ 2018. Hanguk Shinseokki-Cheongdonggi shidae jeonhwangwa Jogi Cheongdonggi shidaee daehayeo (On the Neolithic-Bronze Age transition of Korea and the Incipient Bronze Age). *Hanguk Gogohakbo* 109: 8-39.

KIM Jang-suk and Jun-gyu KIM, 2016. Bangsaseong tanso yeondaerobon Weonsamguk sidae-Samguk sidae togi pyeonnyeon (Radio carbon dates and pottery chronology of the Proto-Three Kingdoms and Three Kingdoms periods). *Hanguk Gogohakbo* 100: 46-85.

KIM, Kyu-hyeok, and Jae-in KIM. 2001. Gwanchang-ni yujeok chulto suro mokchaekui sujong chosa (Analyses of logs used for irrigation ditches at Gwanchang-ni site). In *Gwanchang-ni Yujeok: B-G Jigu* (Gwanchang-ni B-G Section), edited by H.J. LEE *et al.*, 525-550. Seoul: Korea Daehakkyo Maejang Munhwa Yeonguso.

KIM, Kweon-ku. 1999. Gyeongsangbuk-do (North Gyeongsang Province). In *Hanguk Jiseongmyo (Goindol) Yujeok Jonghap Josa Yeongu* (The Comprehensive Study of Korean Dolmens), 673-854. Seoul: Munhwajaecheong and Seoul National University Museum.

___ 2003. *Cheongdonggi Shidae Yeongnam Jiyeokui Saengeopgwa Sahoe* (Bronze Age livelihood and society in the Yeongnam region). Ph.D. dissertation, Yeongnam University.

KIM, Minkoo. 2015. Rice in ancient Korea: status symbol or community food? *Antiquity* 89 345 (2015): 838-855.

KIM, Nak-jung. 2009. *Yeongsangang Yuyeok Gobun Yeongu* (A Study of the Ancient Tumuli in the Yeongsan River valley). Seoul: Hak'yeon Munhwasa.

KIM, Sang-min. 2019. Emergence and development of ironware manufacturing techniques in the southeast area of the Korean Peninsula. *Hanguk Sangosa Hakbo* 104: 36-70.

KIM, Seung-ok. 2006a. Bunmyo jaryoreul tonghaebon cheongdonggi shidae sahoe jojikgwa byeoncheon (Changes in the Bronze Age social organization as revealed in mortuary remains. In *Gyecheung Sahoewa Jibaejaui Chulhyeon* (Emergence of the Stratified Society and Elite Managers), edited by Hanguk Gogohakhoe, 39-82. Yong'in: Korean Archaeological Society.

___ 2006b. Songguk-ni munhwaui jiyeokkweon seoljeonggwa hwaksan gwajeong (Defining regional units of the Songguk-ni culture and its diffusional process). In *Geumgang: Songguk-ni Munhwaui Hyeongseonggwa Baljeon* (Formation of the Songguk-ni Culture and its Development). Gwangju/Jochiweon: Honam Gogohakhoe/Hoseo Gogohakhoe.

KIM, Tae-shik. 1993. *Kaya Yeonmaengsa* (History of Kaya Confederation). Seoul: Iljogak.

___ 2014a. Saguk Shidae eu Kayasa Yeongu (A Study of the History of Kaya during the Four States Period). Seoul: Seokyeong Munhwasa.

___ 2014b. *Saguk Shidaeui Hanil Gwan'gyesa Yeongu* (A Study of the Korea-Japan Relations during the Four States Period). Seoul: Seokyeong Munhwasa.

KIM, Tae-shik, and Kye-hyeon SONG. 2003. Gima Munhwaui ilbon jeonpa (Diffusion of Korean horse-riding culture to Japan). In *Hangukui Gima Minjok Ron* (Discussions on Korea as a Horse-Riders Nation), edited by T.S. Kim and K.H. SONG, 276-302. Seoul: Korean Equestrian Association Museum.

KIM, Yong-kan, and Kwang-jun SEOK. 1984. *Namgyeong Yujeok Yeongu* (A Study of the Namgyeong Site). Pyongyang: Kwahak Baekkwa Sajeon.

KIMURA, Makoto. 2005. Chosen Sankoku to Wa (Korea's Three Kingdoms and Wa). In *Nihon to Chosen* (Japan and Korea), edited by Y. TAKEDA. Tokyo: Yoshikawa Kobunkan.

KITANO, Kohei. 1989. Kofun jidai no doki to tetsuseisan kankei (Connections between Sue ware and iron production in Kofun period). In *Toshitsu Doki no Kokusai Koryu* (International Exchanges of Stoneware Pottery), edited by Otani Joshi Daigaku Shiryokan, 105-123. Tokyo: Tokyo Kashi Shobo.

KITO, Kioaki. 1976. Mimana Nihonfu no kento (Critical Examination of Mimana Nihonfu). In *Nihon Kodaikokuno Keiseito Higashi Ajia* (State Formation in Ancient Japan and East Asia). Tokyo: Azekura Shobo.

KOBAYASHI, Tatsuo. 2008. *Jomonno Shiko* (Thought Patterns of Jomon). Tokyo: Chikuma Shobo.

KOBAYASHI, Yukio. 1961. *Kofun Jidai no Kenkyu* (Research on the Kofun Period). Tokyo: Aoki Shoten.

Kokushi Daijiten Hensho I'Inkai. 1993. *Kokushi Daijiten 14* (Great Encyclopedia of National History). Tokyo: Yoshikawa Kobunkan.

KOMOTO, Masayuki. 1997. Kome, tetsu, haka (Rice, iron, and burials). In *Jomon to Yayoi* (Jomon and Yayoi), edited by Dai 11-kai [Daigaku to Kagaku] Kokai Shimpozium Soshiki I'inkai (The eleventh [Higher Education and Science] Open Symposium on Higher Education and Science), 104-110. Tokyo: Kuba Pro.

KOYAMADA, Koichi. 2001. Kodai Kawachi no kaihatsu to Toraijin (Development of ancient Kawachi and immigrants). In *Kodai Kawachi to Kudara* (Ancient Kawachi and Paekche, edited by Hirakata Rekishi Forum Jikko I'inkai, 94-97. Hirakata: Daikoro Company.

___ 2004a. Yamato Oken to Toraijin – Toraikei Joho (The Yamato court and the Toraijin – information from the Toraijin). In *Yamato Oken to Toraijin* (The Yamato Court and the Toraijin), edited by Osaka Furitsu Yayoi Bunka Hakubutsukan, pp. 28-35. Osaka: Yayoi Culture Museum.

___ 2004b. Torai shita sentan tanya gijutsu (The cutting-edge iron tool making technology). In *Yamato Oken to Toraijin* (The Yamato Court and the Toraijin), edited by Osaka Furitsu Yayoi Bunka Hakubutsukan, pp. 14-19. Osaka Yayoi Culture Museum.

Kunaisho (Imperial Household Agency). 2001. Tenno Heika no kisha kaiken (The emperor's press conference). In *Tenno Heika o Tanjobi ni Saishi* (On the Occasion of the Emperor's Birthday). Tokyo: Kunaisho.

Kurokawa, Mayo. 1880. Amenohiboko Kikajidai Ko (Thoughts on the Age of Amenohiboko's Naturalization). Tokyo. Bunkaisha.

KUSUMI, Takeo. 2004. Kofun Jidai shoto zengo no Hakata wangan iseki no rekishi-teki igi (Historical significance of the archaeological sites around the Hakata Bay on the eve and the aftermath of the advent of the Early Kofun period). In *Yamato Oken to Toraijin* (Yamato Kings' Power and the Immigrants), edited by Osaka Furitsu Yayoi Bunka Hakubutsukan, 54-61. Osaka: Yayoi Culture Museum.

KUWABARA, Hisao. 2015. Yayoi period. *Japanese Journal of Archaeology* 3: 54-56.

KWAK, Seung-ki, Gyeongtaek KIM, and Gyeoung-Ah LEE. 2017. Beyond rice farming: evidence from central Korea reveals wide resource utilization in the Songguk-ni culture during the late-Holocene. *The Holocene* 27.8: 1091-1092.

KWON, O-jung. 2013. The history of Lelang commandery. In *The Han Commanderies in Early Korean History*, edited by M.E. Byington, pp. 81-99. Cambridge, MA: Korea Institute of Harvard University.

KWON, Oh-young. 2005. *Godae Dong Asia Gyoryusaui Bit: Munyeong Wangneung* (Glorious Civilizational Exchanges in Ancient East Asia: King Munyeong's Tomb). Seoul: Doseo Publishing.

___ 2008. Paekcheui saengsan gisulgwa yutong chegye ihaereul wihayeo (Understanding of the production technology and distribution system of Paekche). In *Paekche Saengsan Gisului Baldalgwa Yutong Chegye Hwakdaeui Jeongchisahoejeok Hameu* (Socio-political Implications of the Development of the Production Technology and the Expansion of the Distribution System of Paekche), edited by Hanshin Daehakkyo Haksulweon, 11-38. Seoul: Hakyeon Munhwasa.

Kyoto Bunka Hakubutsukan (Kyoto Museum of Culture). 1989. *Umi o watatte kita Hito to Bunka* (The People Who Crossed the Sea and Their Culture), edited by Kyoto Bunka Hakubutsukan. Kyoto: Kyoto Museum of Culture.

Kyoto Kokuritsu Hakubutsukan (Kyoto National Museum). 1987. *Nihon no Kochu* (Body Armor and Helmet of Japan). Kyoto: Kyoto Kokuritsu Hakubutsukan.

Kyushu Rekishi Shiryokan (Kyushu Historical Resources Center). 1980. *Seido no Buki* (Bronze Weapons). In *Tenzuroku: Nihon Kinsoku Bunka no Reimei* (Tenzuroku: The Dawn of Japan's Metallurgical Culture). Fukuoka: Fukuoka Kenritsu Kyushu Rekishi Shiryokan (Fukuoka Prefecture Historical Resources Center).

Ledyard, Gari K. 1975. Galloping along with the horse riders: Looking for the founders of Japan. Journal of Japanese Studies 1.2: 217-254.

LEE, Byeong-ho. 2013. Asukasae pagyeondoen Paekche wabaksaui seonggyok (Characteristics of tile-making specialists commissioned to Asuka Temple). *Hanguk Sangosa Hakbo* 81: 35-56.

LEE, Chang-hee. 2011. Togirobon Kaya seongrip ijeonui hanil gyoryu (Korea-Japan relations prior to the emergence of Kaya states in light of the pottery). In *Kayaui Poguwa Haesang Hwaltong* (Kaya Harbors and Seagoing Activities), edited by Kimhae-shi Haksul Wiweonhoe and Inje Daehakkyo Kaya Munhwa Yeonguso. Kimhae: Inje Daehakkyo Kaya Munhwa Yeonguso.

LEE, Cheong-gyu. 2002. Yeongnam jiyeokui cheongdonggie daehan nonuiwa haeseok (Bronze mplements of the Yeongnam Region: Discussion and interpretation). In *Yeongnam Jibangui Chogi Cheolgi Munhwa* (The Late Bronze Age Culture of the Yeongnam Region), edited by Yeongnam Gogohakhoe, 23-37. Taegu: Yeongnam Archaeological Society.

LEE, Dong-ju. 2000. Namgangyuyeok shinseokkishidae munhwawa ilbonyeoldo (The Neolithic culture of the Namgang region and the Japanese Archipelago). In *Jinju Namgang Yujeokgwa Godae Ilbon* (Jinju Namgang Site and Ancient Japan), edited by Kaya Munhwa Yeonguso, 35-96. Kimhae: Kaya Munhwa Yeonguso, Inje University.

LEE, Eun-chang. 1968. Daejeon Goejeong-dong cheongdonggi munhwayeongu (Study of bronze culture at Goejeong-dong in Daejeon). *Asea Yeongu* 11.2: 7-99.

LEE, Gang-seung. 1987. Buyeo Gubong-ri chulto cheongdonggi ilgwal yumul (Bronze artifacts from Gubong-ri in Buyeo). In *Sambul Kim Won-yong Gyosu Jeongnyeon Toeim Ginyeom Nonchong* (Festschrift in Honor of Professor Won Yong Kim's Retirement), edited by the Festschrift Editorial Committee. Seoul: Ilchisa.

LEE, Gyoung-ah. 2003. *Changes in Subsistence Systems in Southern Korea form the Chulmun to Mumun Periods: Archaeological Investigation*. Ph.D. dissertation. University of Toronto.

___ 2005. Review of perspectives on Korean Neolithic cultivation from archaeological remains. *Hanguk Shinseokki Yeongu* 10: 27-49.

___ 2011. The transition from foraging to farming in Prehistoric Korea. *Current Anthropology*, 52, Supplement 4: S307-S329.

LEE, Han-sang. 1997. Jangsik daedoui hasae banyeongdoen 5-6 segi Silla eu jibang jibae (Silla's local governance as reflected in its gifting of decorated long swords during the 5th-6th century). *Gunsa* 35: 1-37. Gukbang Gunsa Yeonguso.

___ 2004. Samguk shidae hwandu daedoeu jejakgwa soyu bangshik (Manufacture of the long words with circular pommel and ownership methods during the Three Kingdoms period). *Hanguk Godaesa Yeongu* 36: 257-286.

___ 2006a. Hanseong Paekche jangshik daedoui jejak gibeop (Manufacturing methods of decorated long swords of the Paekche Hanseong period). In *Hanseongeseo Ungjineuro* (From Hanseong to Ungjin), edited by Gungnip Gongju Bangmulgwan, 166-170. Gongju: Gungnip Gongju Bangmulgwan.

___ 2006b. Jangsik Daedorobon Baekjewa Kayaui kyoryu (Exchange between Paekche and Kaya in light of the decorated long swords). In *Baekje Yeongu 43.* Chungnam University Baekje Yeonguso.

LEE, Hee-jun. 1998. Geumgwan Kayaui Yeoksawa Yujeok (History and Archaeology of Geumgwan Kaya). In *Kaya Munhwa Dorok* (The Catalogue of Kaya Culture), edited by Hanguk Godaesa Yeonguhoe, 154-156. Taegu: Yeseong Sajin Printing Company.

LEE, Hong-jong. 2007. Godae hanil gwangyereul tonghaeseobon Yayoi sahoeui hyeongseong (Emergence of Yayoi society in light of ancient Korea-Japan relations). In *Hanil Munhwa Gyoryu, Hanbandowa Ilbon Kyushu* (Korea-Japan Cultural Exchanges, the Korean Peninsula and Kyushu, Japan), edited by Gungnip Jung-ang Bangmulgwan, 24-35. Seoul: Gungnip Jung-ang Bangmulgwan.

LEE, Hyeon-hye. 1984. *Samhan Sahoeui Hyeongseong Gwajeong Yeongu* (Study of the Formation Process of Sam Han Society). Seoul: Iljogak.

LEE, Hyeong-gi. 2020. Munheoneurobon Kayaui gukkajeok seongkyeok (State characteristics of Kaya in light of written records). *Hanguk Sanggosa Hakbo* 107: 71-93.

LEE, Hyeong-gu. 2004. *Balhae Yeonaneseo Chajeun Hanguk Godae Munhwaui Bimil* (The Secrets of Korea's Ancient History Discovered in the Bohai Region). Seoul: Kimyeongsa.

LEE, Hyeong-gu, and Ro-hee PARK. 1996. *Gwanggaeto Daewang Reungbi Shinyeongu* (New Investigations of the Stele of King Gwanggaeto). Seoul: Donghwa.

LEE, Hyeong-weon. 2009. *Cheongdonggi Shidae Chwirak Gujowa Sahoe Jojik* (Settlement Structure and Social Organization during the Bronze Age). Seoul: Seogyeong Munhwasa.

LEE, In-sook. 1993. The Silk Road and Ancient Korean Glass. *Korean Culture* 14.4: 4-13.

LEE, Jong-cheol. 2000. *Namhan Jiyeokui Songguk-ni hyeong Jugeoje daehan Ilgochal* (A Study of Songguk-ni Settlement Type in Southern Korea). MA thesis, Jeonbuk National University.

___ 2015. *Songguk-nihyeong Munhwaui Chwirakchejewa Baljeon* (Settlement Organization and Development of the Songguk-ni Type Culture). Ph.D. dissertation, Jeonbuk National University.

LEE, Jong-wuk. 1982. *Silla Kukkaui Hyeongseong* (Formation of Silla State). Seoul: Iljogak.

___ 1994. *Go Choseonsa Yeongu* (A Study of Go Choson). Seoul: Iljogak.

LEE, Keon-mu. 1992a. Hanguk cheongdonggiui jejakgisul (Manufacturing technology of the Korean bronze implements). In *Hangukui Cheongdonggi Munhwa* (Korean Bronze Culture), edited by National Museum of Korea, 138-142. Seoul and Gwangju: Gungnip Jung-ang Bangmulgwan and Gungnip Gwangju Bangmulgwan.

___ 1992b. Hangukshik donggeom munhwa (Korean type bronze dagger culture). In *Hangukui Cheongdonggi Munhwa* (Korean Bronze Culture), edited by National Museum of Korea, 133-137. Seoul and Gwangju: Gungnip Jung-ang Bangmulgwan and Gungnip Gwangju Bangmulgwan.

___ 2002. Yeongnamjibangui chogi cheolgi munhwa (The early iron age culture in the Yeongnam Region). In *Yeongnamjibangui Chogi Cheolgi Munhwa* (The Late Bronze Age Culture of the Yeongnam Region), edited by Yeongnam Archaeological Society, 1-22. Taegu: Yeongnam Gogohakhoe.

___ 2007. Hanguk seon- weon-sa munhwawa Yoshinogari (Korean pre- and proto-historic culture and Yoshinogari). In *Hanil Munhwa Gyoryu, Hanbandowa Ilbon* (Korea-Japan Culture Exchange, the Korean Peninsula and Kyushu), edited by National Museum of Korea. Seoul: Gungnip Jung-ang Bangmulgwan.

___ 2008. Daho-ri yujeok balgului eui (Significance of Daho-ri site excavations). In *Daho-ri Yujeok Balgul Seonggwawa Gwaje* (Daho-ri Excavations: Results and Prospects), edited by National Museum of Korea, 7-15. Seoul: Gungnip Jung-ang Bangmulgwan.

LEE, Keon-mu, Gwang-jin YUN, Yeong-hun LEE, and Dae-gon SHIN. 1989. Euchang Daho-ri site Yujeokbalgul jinjeonbogo (Progress report of the excavations of Daho-ri site). *Kogohakji* 1: 5-174.

LEE, Ki-baek. 1988. *A New History of Korea*. Harvard University Press.

___ 2006. *Hanguksa Shinron* (New Perspectives of Korean History). Seoul: Iljogak.

LEE, Myeong-hun. 2016. Cheongdonggi shidae onggwanmyoui jeon'gae yangsang (Development of the Songguk-ni period jar burials). *Hanguk Sanggosa Hakbo* 93: 42-74.

LEE, Nam-gyu. 2008. Paekche cheolgui saengsangwa yutongee daehan siron (Preliminary considerations regarding iron production and its distribution system of Paekche). In *Paekche Saengsan Gisului Baldalgwa Yutong Chegye Hwakdaeui Jeongchisahoejeok Hameu* (Socio-political Implications of the Development of the Production Technology and the Expansion of the Distribution System of Paekche), edited by Hanshin Daehakkyo Haksulweon, 187-229. Seoul: Hakyeon Munhwasa.

LEE, Nam-seok. 2000. Paekche gobungwa geu yeonweon munje (Paekche tombs and issues regarding their origins). In *Paekchereul Chajaseo* (In Search of Paekche), edited by S.G. JEON et al., 149-157. Gongju: Gungnip Gongju Bangmulgwan.

LEE, Sang-gil. 1994. Changweon Deokcheon-ri yujeok balgul josabogo (Report on the archaeological investigations of Deokcheon-ri site in Changweon). In *Kyushu Gogohakhoe – Yeongnam Gogohakhoe Je 1-hoe Hapdong Gogohakhoe Balpyo Yoji*, July 23-24, 1994 (Kyushu Archaeological Society – Yeongnam Archaeological Society Combined Archaeological Societies Conference Volume, July 23-24, 1994), 83-100. Fukuoka: Kyushu Archaeological Society and Yeongnam Archaeological Society.

___ 2000. Cheongdonggi Maenapui seongkyeokgwa eumi (The characteristics and significance of burying bronze implements). *Hanguk Gogo Hakbo* 42: 23-55.

___ 2006. Jesawa gweollyeokui balsaeng (Emergence of ancestral veneration ritual and political power). In *Gyecheung Sahoewa Jibaejaeu Chulhyeon* (Emergence of Stratified Society and Elite Managers), edited by Korean Archaeological Society, 117-149. Yong'in: Hanguk Gogohakhoe.

LEE, Seong-ju. 1991. Weonsamgukshidae togiui ryuhyeong, gyebo, pyeonyeon, saengsan cheje (Types, genealogy, chronology, and production system of protohistoric pottery). *Hanguk Godae Nonchong* 2: 235-297.

___ 1999a. Jiseongmyo: Nonggyeongsahoeui ginyeommul (Dolmens: monumental objects of the agricultural society). In *Hanguk Jiseongmyo (Goindol) Yujeok Jonghap Josa Yeongu* (The Comprehensive Study of Korean Dolmens), edited by Seoul National University Museum, 423-441. Seoul: Munhwajaecheong and Seoul National University Museum.

___ 1999b. Gyeongsang Namdo (Gyeongsang Namdo). In *Hanguk Jiseongmyo (Goindol) Yujeok Jonghap Josa Yeongu* (The Comprehensive Study of Korean Dolmens), edited by Seoul National University Museum, 855-907. Seoul: Munhwajaecheong and Seoul National University Museum.

___ 2007. *Cheongdonggi – Cheolgi Shidae Sahoe Byeondongron* (Views on the Social Development and Changes during the Bronze – Iron Age). Seoul: Hakyeon Munhwasa.

LEE, Su-hong. 2014. Cheongdonggi shidae jugeo saenghwal byeonhwawa jiyeokseongui sahoejeok seongkyeok (Changes in residential patterns during the Bronze Age and their social significance in the regional context). *Hanguk Gogo Hakbo* 90: 4-35.

LEE, Taek-gu. 2008. Hanbando jungseobu jiyeokui Mahan bungumyo (Mahan Bungumyo in the west-central region of Korea. *Hanguk Gogo Hakbo* 66: 44-89.

LEE, Yang-su. 2007. Yoshinogariro ganeungil: hanbando nambueseo chulbaljeom (The path to Yoshinogari: the starting point from the southern region of the Korean Peninsula). In *Yoshinogari: Nihon no Naka no Kodai Kankoku* (Ancient Korean Culture in Japan), edited by Gungnip Jung-ang Bangmulgwan, pp. 266-293. Seoul: Gungnip Jung-ang Bangmulgwan.

LEE, Yeong-cheol. 2002. Honamjiyeokui 3-5 segi jugeojiui pyeonnyeon II (Periodization of the 3rd-5th century AD settlements in the Honam region II). *Yeongu Nonmun* (Research Essays) #2:48. Gwangju: Honam Munhwajae Yeonguweon (Honam Cultural Research Institute).

LEE, Yeong-hun. 1997. Jincheon Seokjang-ni cheol saengsan yujeok. (The iron production site at Seokjang-ni in Jincheon). In *Cheolui Yeoksa* (History of Iron), edited by National Cheongju Museum, 101-105. Cheongju: Gungnip Cheongju Bangmulgwan.

LEE, Yeong-mun. 1990. Yumulsang euro bon Honam jibang eu Jiseongmyo (Dolmens of southern Korea from in light of their associated artifacts). In *Hanguk Jiseongmyo Yeonguui Jemunje* (Issues in the study of Korean Dolmens), edited by Korean Archaeological Society, 31-60. Seoul: Hanguk Gogohakhoe.

___ 1998. Hanguk mandolin-hyeong donggeom munhwa e daehan gochal (Korean mandolin-shaped bronze dagger culture). *Hanguk Gogo Hakbo* 38: 63-104.

___ 1999. Jeolla Namdo (South Jeolla Province). In *Hanguk Jiseongmyo (goindol) Yujeok Jonghap Josa Yeongu* (The Comprehensive Study of Korean Dolmens), edited by Seoul National University Museum, 931-1010. Seoul: Munhwajaecheong and Seoul National University Museum.

LIN, Yun. 1990. *Zhong guo dongbeixi tongjian zailun* (Reexamination of the bronze daggers of Northeast China). A paper presented at Huan Bohai Kaogu Xueshutaohui (Circum Bohai Archaeological Conference) in Dalian, Liaoning Province. In *Kaoguxueshu Wenhualunji* (Essays on Archaeology Culture), edited by B. SU, 234-250. 1997. Beijing: Wenwu Chubanshe.

Lyons, Patrick D. 2003. *Ancestral Hopi Migrations*. Anthropological Papers of the University of Arizona, No. 68. Tucson: University of Arizona.

Maniwa-shi Kyoiku I'inkai. 2008. *Oyasada Kofungun* (Oyasada Ancient Tumuli). Okayama Maniwa-shi: Maniwa-shi Kyoiku I'inkai.

Manning, Patrick. 2013. *Migration in World History*. London and New York: Routledge.

MARUYAMA, Jiro. 1934. *Omi Kikajin no Anchi* (Settlement of the Immigrants in Omi). Tokyo: Iwanami Shoten.

MASUMOTO, Satoshi. 2004. Hiraishi kofungun no chosa seika (Investigation results of the Hiraishi Kofungun). In *Imaki no Tehito*. Osaka: Osaka Furitsu Chikatsu Asuka Hakubutsukan.

MATSUGI, Takehiko. 2002. Ilbon yeoldoe isseoseo daehyeong bunmyoui chulhyeon (Emergence of large tombs in the Japanese Archipelago). In *Dong Asia Daehyeong Gobunui Chulhyeongwa Sahoe Byeondong* (Emergence of Large Tombs and Social Changes in East Asia), edited by National Cultural Heritage Research Institute, 160-166. Seoul: Gungnip Munhwajae Yeonguso.

MATSUI, Akira, and Masa'aki KANEHARA. 2006. The question of prehistoric plant husbandry during the Jomon period in Japan. *World Archaeology* 38: 259-73.

MATSUMURA, H. 2001. Differentials of Yayoi immigration to Japan as derived from dental metrics. *Homo* 52.2: 135-156.

McBride II, Richard D. 2006. Is the *Samguk Yusa* reliable? Case studies from Chinese and Korean sources. *The Journal of Korean Studies* 11.2: 163-90.

MISHINA, Shoei. 1971. *Nihon Shoki Kenkyu* (A Study of the *Nihon Shoki*). Tokyo: Hanawa Shobo.

MIYAMOTO, Chiejiro. 1986. Jukyo to Soko (Residences and Storage Buildings). In *Yayoi Bunka no Kenkyu 7: Yayoi Shuraku* (Study of the Yayoi Culture 7: Yayoi Settlements), edited by H. KANASEKI and M. SAHARA, 9-23. Tokyo: Yusankaku Shuppan.

___ 1996. *Nihon Genshi Kodaino Jukyo Kenchiku* (Residential Construction of Prehistoric and Ancient Japan). Tokyo: Chuo Koron Bijutsu Shuppan.

MIYAMOTO, Kazuo. 2017. *Tohoku Ajia no Shokinoko to Yayo ino Kigen* (Early Agriculture of Northeast Asia and the Origin of Yayoi). Tokyo: Toseisha.

MIZOGUCHI, Koji. 2000. Burials of kings or of tribal leaders? Interpreting the evidence from monumental tombs in southern Japan. *Archaeology International* 4: 47-51.

___ 2002. *An Archaeological History of Japan, 30,000 BC to 700 AD.* Philadelphia: University of Pennsylvania Press.

___ 2009. Nodes and edges: A network approach to hierarchisation and state formation in Japan. *Journal of Anthropological Archaeology* 28: 14-26.

___ 2013. *The Archaeology of Japan: From the Earliest Rice Farming Villages to the Rise of the State.* Cambridge University Press.

___ 2014. The centre of their life-world: the archaeology of experience at the Middle Yayoi cemetery of Tateiwa-Hotta, Japan. *Antiquity* 88.341 (Sept. 2014): 836-950.

MIZUNO, Masayoshi. 1981. Gunshufun no kozo to seikaku (The structure and the characteristics of tumuli clusters). In *Kofunto Kokka no Naritachi* (Formation of the Kofun and the State), edited by T. Onoyama, pp. 143-158. Tokyo: Kodansha.

MIZUNO, Yu. 1967. *Nihon Kodai Kokka no Keisei: Seifuku Ocho to Tennoke* (Formation of Japan's Ancient State: Conquest Dynasty and the Imperial Household). Tokyo: Kodansha.

___ 1975. [Kiba minzoku settsu] hihan josettsu (Preliminary criticism [of Horserider Theory]. In *Ronshu Kiba Minzoku Seifuku Ocho* (Collection of Essays on Horseriders' Conquest Royal Dynasty Theory), edited by T. Suzuki, 319-321. Tokyo: Yamato Shobo.

MOON, An-shik. 2007. Goheung Gilduri gobun chulto geumdonggwangwa Paekcheui wanghuje (A gilt-bronze crown from the Gilduri tomb in Goheung and Paekche's tutelage system in local administration). *Hanguk Sanggosa Hakbo* 55: 33-51.

MORI, Koichi. 1982. Ilbonnaeui doraegye jipdangwa geu gobun (The Toraijin groups and their tombs in Japan). *Paekche Yeongu* 13: 161-164.

___ 2001. *Keitai Ocho to Kudara* (Keitai dynasty and Paekche). In *Kodai Kawachi to Kudara* (Ancient Kawachi and Paekche), edited by Hirakata Rekishi Forum Jikko I'inkai, 130-133. Hirakata: Daikoro.

MORI, Teijiro. 1985. *Ine to Seido to Tetsu* (Rice, Bronze, and Iron). Tokyo: Nihon Shoseki Kabushiki Kaisha.

MURAKAMI, Yasuyuki. 1999. *Wajin to Tetsu no Kokogaku* (The Wa People and the Archaeology of Iron). Tokyo: Aoki Shoten.

___ 2004. Nikkan no 3–4 seiki tekki gijutsu hikaku (Comparison of the third–fourth century iron technology of Japan and Korea). In *Yamato Oken to Toraijin* (Yamato Kings and the Immigrants), edited by Osaka Furitsu Yayoi Bunka Hakubutsukan. Sakai City: Yayoi Culture Museum.

___ 2007. *Kodai Kokka Seiritsu Katei to Tekki Seisan* (Ancient State Formation Process and Ironware Production). Tokyo: Aoki Shoten.

Murdoch, James. 1910. *A History of Japan.* London: Kegan Paul, Trubner and Co., Ltd.

NAKAHASHI, Takahiro, and Mazaru IZUKA. 1998. Hokubu Kyushu no Jomon-Yayoi ikoki ni kansuru jinruigaku-teki kosatsu (Anthropological examination regarding the Jomon-Yayoi transition in northern Kyushu). *Anthropological Science* (Japanese Series) 106.1: 31-53.

NAKAMURA, Daisuke. 2008. Cheongdongi sidaewa chogi cheolgi sidaeui pyeonnyeongwa yeondae (Periodization and chronology of the Bronze and Late Mumun). *Hanguk Gogo Hakbo* 68: 39-87.

NAKAMURA, Naokatsu. 1915. Omi to kikajin (Omi and the Immigrants). In *Rekishi to Chiri* (History and Geography), edited by Hashino Shoten, 7(6). Kyoto: Hashino Shoten.

NAKAMURA, Oki. 2002. Kaiso shakai (Ranked Society). *Kikan Kokogaku* 80: 38-41.

NAKAMURA, Shintaro. 1981. *Nihon to Chosen no Nisennen* (Two Thousand Years of Japan and Korea). Tokyo: Toho Shuppan.

NAKAYAMA, Kyotaku. 2003. Hokubu Kyushu no Shoki Shisekibo (Early dolmens in northern Kyushu). In *Dongbuk-a Jiseongmyoui Giweongwa Jeon'gae* (Origin and Development of Dolmens in Northeast

Asia), an academic conference volume, organized by Hanseo Godaehak Yeonguhoe, pp. 78-80. Jeonju: Hanseo Godaehak Yeonguso, Asia Sahakhoe.

NAM, Ik-hee. 2015. Ilbon Osakabu Doyama 1-ho bun chulto suekiui kyebowa jejak baegyeong (Genealogy and production background of the sueki from the Doyama Tomb #1 in Osakafu, Japan). *Hanguk Gogohakbo* 96: 140-159.

NAOKI, Kojiro. 1992. Kawachi Oken ni tsuite (Concerning the Kawachi king's political power). In *Kyodai Kofun to Kaya Bunka: 'Kuhaku' no 4-5 Seiki o Saguru* (Giant Tombs and Kaya Culture: In Search of the Fourth-Fifth Century 'Hiatus'), edited by T. NISHIJIMA, 135-157. Tokyo: Kadokawa Shoten.

Nara Kokuritsu Bunkazai Kenkyusho (Nara National Cultural Heritage Research Institute). n.d. *Asuka Shiryokan Annai* (Guide to the Asuka Historical Museum.) Nara: Nabunken.

Nara-ken Kyoiku I'inkai. 1977. *Niizawa Senzuka 126-gofun zumen – shashin* (Illustrations and Photos of Tomb #126 in Niizawa Senzuka), edited by Nara Kashihara Archaeological Institute. Kashihara: Kashikoken.

___ 1981a. *Niizawa Senzuka 139-go fun zumen-shashin* (Illustrations and photos of Tomb #139 in Niizawa Senzuka), edited by Nara Kashihara Archaeological Institute. Kashihara: Kashikoken.

___ 1981b. *Niizawa Senzuka 115-go fun zumen-shashin* (Illustrations and photos of Tomb #115 in Niizawa Senzuka), edited by Nara Kashihara Archaeological Institute. Kashihara: Kashikoken.

___ 1981c. *Niizawa Senzuka 109-go fun zumen-shashin* (Illustrations and Photos of Tomb #109 in Niizawa Senzuka), edited by Nara Kashihara Archaeological Institute. Kashihara: Kashikoken.

National Museum of Korea. 2003. *National Museum of Korea*, edited by K.M. YI et al. Seoul: National Museum of Korea.

___ 2007. *Yoshinogari: Ancient Korea in Japan*. Seoul: National Museum of Korea.

Nihon Shoki. See Aston, W.G.

NISHIMOTO, Toyohiro. 2006. *Yayoi Jidai no Hajimari* (Beginning of the Yayoi Period). Tokyo: Yuzankaku.

___ 2007. *Jomon Jidai kara Yayoi Jidai e* (From the Jomon to the Yayoi Period). Tokyo: Yuzankaku.

NISHITANI, Tadashi. 1997. *Higashi Ajia ni okeru Shisekibo no Sogo-teki Kenkyu* (Comprehensive Studies of Dolmens in East Asia). Fukuoka: Kyushu University Archaeological Research Institute.

NOH, Hee-suk. 1997. *Hanguk Seonsa Oge daehan Yeongu* (A Study on the Jade Stones of the Korean Prehistoric Period). MA thesis, Hanyang University, Seoul.

NOH, Jung-guk. 2003. Mahangwa Nagnang/Daebanggungwaui gunsa chungdolgwa Mokji-gukui soetoe (Military conflicts between Mahan and Lelang/Daifang and the decline of Mokji-guk). *Taegusahak* 71: 65-90.

___ 2009. Mahanui seongripgwa byeoncheon (Emergence and Changes of Mahan). In *Mahan, Sumshineun Girok* (Mahan, Breathing Records), edited by National Jeonju Museum, 215-223. Jeonju: Gungnip Jeonju Bangmulgwan.

ODA, Fujio. 1986. Hokubu Kyushu ni okeru Yayoi bunka no shutsugen josettsu (A preliminary view on the emergence of Yayoi Culture in Northern Kyushu). *Kyushu Bunkashi Kenkyusho Kiyo* 31: 143-145.

ODA, Fujio and Byeongsam HAN. 1986. *Nikkan Koshono Kokogaku: Yayoi Jidai-hen* (Archaeology of Japan-Korea Relations: The Yayoi Period). Osaka: Rokko Shuppan.

ODA, Fujio, Takao UNO, Mitsuzane OKAUCHI, Shozo IWANAMI et al. 1986. Yunyu Seidoki: 1. Chosen Hanto kara motarasareta seidoki (Imported Bronze implements: 1. Bronze implements obtained from the Korean Peninsula). In *Yayoi Bunka no Kenkyu 6: Doguto Gijutsu II* (Study of the Yayoi Culture 6: Tools and Technology), edited by H. KANASEKI and M. SAHARA, 35-44. Tokyo: Yuzankaku Shuppan.

OH, Yongje, M. Conte, S.H. KANG, J.S. KIM et al. 2017. Population fluctuation and the adoption of food production in prehistoric Korea: using radiocarbon dates as a proxy for population change. *Radiocarbon* 59.6: 1761-1770.

OH, Young-chan. 2006. Nagnang-gun Yeongu (A Study of Lelang-gun). Paju: Sagyejeol Chulpansa.

OH, Young-chan and Byington, Mark E. 2013. Scholarly studies on the Han commanderies in Korea. In *The Han Commanderies in Early Korean History*, edited by M.E. Byington, pp. 11-48. Cambridge, MA: Korea Institute, Harvard University.

OKAMURA, Hidenori. 1986. Chugoku no Kagami (Chinese[bronze] mirrors). In *Yayoi Bunka no Kenkyu 6: Dogu to Gijutsu II* (Study of the Yayoi Culture 6: Tools and Technology II), edited by H. KANASEKI and M. SAHARA, 69-77. Tokyo: Yuzankaku Shuppan.

Okauchi, Mitsuzane. 1996. *Kankoku no Zempo Koenfun* (Keyhole-shaped Tombs of Korea). Tokyo: Yusankaku.

Okazaki, Takashi. 1993. Japan and the Continent. In *The Cambridge History of Japan, Vol. 1, Ancient Japan*, edited by J.W. Hall et al., 268-316. Cambridge University Press.

OKUNO, Masao. 2012. *Kiba Minzoku no Kita Michi: Chose kara Kawachi ni Itaru Iseki Shutsudohin Zenchosa* (Tracing the Path of the Horseriders: Comprehensive Analysis of Archaeological Sites and Archaeological Finds from Korea to Kawachi). Fukuoka: Azusa Shoin.

Osakafu Kyoiku I'inkai. 1994. *Doyama Kofungun* (Ancient Tumuli of Doyama). Osaka-fu: Osaka-fu Kyoiku I'inkai.

OTSUKA, Hatsushige. 1992. Kofun bunka to Toraijin no yakuwari (Kofun culture and the role of immigrants). In *Kyodai Kofun to Kaya Bunka: 'Kuhaku' no 4-5 seiki o Saguru* (Great Tombs and Kaya Culture: In Search of the Fourth–Fifth Century 'Hiatus'), edited by T. NISHIJIMA, 50-68. Tokyo: Kadokawa Shoten.

OWA, Iwao. 1990. Hata-shi wa itsu doko kara, kitaka? (When and whence did the Hata clan come?). *Higashi Ajiano Kodai Bunka* 62: 196-226.

PARK, Bo-hyeon. 2006. Paekcheui gwanmowa sikri (Crowns and ceremonial gold and gilt-bronze shoes). In *Hanseongeseo Ungjineuro* (From Hanseong to Ungjin), edited by National Gongju Museum, 171-180. Gongju: Gungnip Gongju Bangmulgwan.

PARK, Byeong-wuk. 2015. Bangchucha bunseokeul tonghan cheongdonggishidae hoseojiyeok jesasul (Bronze age spinning technology of the west-central region of Korea in light of the analysis of spindle whorls). *Hanguk Gogo Hakbo* 94: 5-31.

PARK, Chan-heung. 2011. Paekche Seong wang, Wideok wangdaeui Waegye Paekche gwallyo (Paekche bureaucrats of Wa origin during the reign of King Seong and King Wideok). *Sarim* 39: 167-189.

PARK, Cheon-su. 1999. Gidaereul tonghayeobon Kaya seryeogui donghyang (Movement of the Kaya elites in light of the tall tubular pottery stands). In *Kayaui Geureut Batchim* (Pottery Stand of Kaya), edited by National Kimhae Museum, 93-106. Kimhae: Gungnip Kimhae Bangmulgwan.

___ 2002. Gochongeul tonghaebon Kayaeu jeongchijeok Byeondong (Political changes in Kaya in light of raised mound tombs). In *Dong Asia Daehyeong Gobunui Chulhyeongwa Sahoebyeondong* (Appearance of Large Tumuli and Social Changes in East Asia), edited by National Cultural Property Research Institute. Seoul: National Cultural Property Research Institute.

PARK, Jin-seok. 1996. *Koguryo Hotaewangbi Yeongu* (A Study of the Koguryo King Hotae Stele). Seoul: Bakijeong.

PARK, Shi-hyeong. 2007. *Gawanggaeto Wang Neungbi* (Mortuary Stele of King Gwanggaeto). Paju: Doseo.

PARK, Sun-bal. 2000. Paekcheui gukka hyeongseong (State formation of Paekche). In *Dong Aseaui Gukka Hyeongseong* (State Formation in East Asia), a conference volume for the tenth International Conference of Paekche Research, edited by the Paekche Institute, Chungnam University, 33-51. Daejeon: Chungnam Daehakkyo Paekche Yeonguso

___ 2001. Paekcheui namcheongwa Wae (Paekche's southward expansion and Wa). In *Kodai no Kawachi to Kudara* (Ancient Kawachi and Paekche), edited by Hirakata Rekishi Forum Jikko I'inkai, 25-46. Hirakata: Daikoro.

___ 2002. Daehyeong Gobunui chulhyeongwa Paekcheui gukka hyeongseong (Appearance of Large Tombs and the Formation of Paekche State). In *Dongasia Daehyonggobunui Chulhyeongwa*

Sahoebyeondong (Appearance of Large Tombs in East Asia and Social Changes). Seoul: Gukrip Munhwajae Yeonguso.

___ 2009. Mahan sahoeui byeoncheon (Transformation of the Mahan society). In *Mahan, Sumshineun Girok* (Mahan, Breathing Records), edited by National Jeonju Museum, 260-268. Jeonju: Gungnip Jeonju Bangmulgwan.

PARK, Sun-bal, Seong-jun Lee, Junko Habu, and Weon-jae Jeong. 2004. *Buyeo Gubong-Nohwari Yujeok* (Buyeo Gubong-Nohwari Site). Daejeon: Chungnam Daehakkyo Paekche Yeon'guso.

PARK, Yang-jin. 1999. [Dolmens of] Chungcheong Namdo. In *Hanguk Jiseongmyo (goindol) Yujeok Jonghap Josa Yeongu* (The Comprehensive Study of Korean Dolmens), edited by Seoul National University Museum, pp. 1067-1086. Seoul: Munhwajaecheong and Seoul National University Museum.

Pearson, Richard. 1976-78. Lolang and the rise of Korean states and chiefdoms. *Journal of the Hong Kong Archaeological Society*, VII: 77-90. Hong Kong Archaeological Society.

___ 2004. New Perspectives on Jomon Society. *Bulletin of the International Jomon Culture Conference* 1: 63-70.

___ 2007. Debating Jomon Social Complexity. *Asian Perspectives* 46.2: 361-399.

___ 2009. Fifth-century rulers of the Kawachi Plain, Osaka, and early state formation in Japan: some recent publications. *Antiquity*, 83.320: 523-527.

___ 2016. *Osaka Archaeology*. Oxford: Archaeopress.

Phillipi, D. L. 1968. *Kojiki*. A translation from classical Chinese with an Introduction and Notes. Tokyo: University of Tokyo Press.

Piggott, Joan R. 1997. *Emergence of Japanese Kingship*. Stanford University Press.

___ 2002. A review article of The Lucky Seventh: Early Horyu-ji and Its Time, by J. Edward Kidder, Jr. (1999). *Journal of Japanese Studies* 28(2): 460-464.

Reischauer, Edwin O., and John K. Fairbank. 1958 and 1960. *East Asia: The Great Tradition*. Boston: Houghton Mifflin Co.

RHEE, Song-nai. 1984. *Emerging Complex Society in Prehistoric Southwest Korea*. Ph.D. dissertation, University of Oregon, Eugene.

___ 1992a. Secondary state formation: The case of Koguryo. In *Pacific Northeast Asia in Prehistory*, edited by C.M. Aikens and Song-nai RHEE, 191-196. Pullman: Washington State University Press.

___ 1992b. Huanren-Jian region prior to the formation of Koguryo state from archaeological perspectives. In *Ancient Cultures of Northeast Asia: Their Origins and Development*, Mahan-Paekche Yeonguso, 123-140. Iri: Wonkwang University.

___ 1999a. [Dolmens of] *Jeolla Bukdo* (North Jeolla Province). In *Hanguk Jiseongmyo (Goindol) Yujeok Jonghap Josa Yeongu* (The Comprehensive Study of Korean Dolmens), edited by Seoul National University Museum, 909-930. Seoul: Munhwajaecheong and Seoul National University Museum.

___ 1999b. Society and culture of ancient Naju region in light of archaeology. In *Naju Jiyeok Godae Sahoe eu Seongkyeok* (Characteristics of the Ancient Society of the Naju Region), edited by Mokpo University Museum, 225-237. Mokpo: Mokpo University Museum.

___ 2002. Bokhap sahoeui baljeongwa Jiseongmyo munhwaui somyeol (Development of a complex society and the demise of the dolmen society). In *Jeonhwangiui Gogohak* I (The Archaeology of Transition Periods I), edited by Hanguk Sanggosa Hakhoe, 214-252. Seoul: Hak'yeon Munhwasa.

RHEE, Song-nai, C. Melvin Aikens, Sung-rak CHOI, and Hyukjin RO, 2007. Korean Contributions to agriculture, technology, and state formation in Japan: archaeology and history of an epochal thousand years, 400 BC–AD 600. *Asian Perspectives* 46.2: 404-459.

RHEE, Song-nai, and Mong-lyong CHOI. 1992. Emergence of complex society in prehistoric Korea. *Journal of World Prehistory* 6.1: 51-95.

Rouse, Irving. 1986. *Migration in History*. New Haven, CT: Yale University Press.

RYU, Chang-hwan. 2010. Samguk shidae gibyeonggwa gibyeong jeonsul (The cavalry and cavalry tactics of the Three Kingdoms Period). *Hanguk Gogo Hakbo* 76: 129-160.

SADAMORI, Hideo. 1991. Nihon to Chosen o musubu tamaki (The ring that connects Japan and Korea). In *Kodai Gozoku to Chosen* (Ancient Powerful Clans and Korea), edited by Kyoto Bunka Hakubutsukan, 213-230. Tokyo: Shin Jinbutsu Oraisha.

___ 1997. Chogi Suekiwa Hanbandoje Dojil Togi (Early Sue ware and stoneware of the Korean Peninsula). In *Hanguk Godaeui Togi* (Ancient Korean Pottery), edited by National Museum of Korea, 167-176. Seoul: Gungnip Jung-ang Bangmulgwan.

Saga-ken Kyoiku I'inkai (Saga-ken Education Committee) (ed.). 2008. *Yoshinogari iseki to Kodai Kanhan to: 2000 nen no Jiku o koete* (The Yoshinogari Site and the Ancient Korean Peninsula: Beyond 2000 years of Time and Space). Saga: Saga-ken Board of Education.

SAHARA, Makoto.1993. *Kiba minzoku wa konakatta* (The horse riders did not come). Tokyo: Nihon Hoso Shuppan Kyokai.

SAHARA, Makoto, and Hiroshi KANASEKI. 1981. *Inasaku no Hajimari* (The Beginning of Rice Cultivation). Tokyo: Kodansha.

SAKAI, Kyoji. 2004a. Sueki Seisan no Hajimari (The Beginning of the Sue Ware Production). *Kokuritsu Rekishi Minzoku Hakubutsukan Kenkyu Hokoku* 110: 339-365.

___ 2004b. Sueki seisanno juyoto hensen (Adoption and Variations of the Sueki). In *Imaki no Tehito* (Recently Arrived Skilled People), edited by Osaka Furitsu Chikatsu Asuka Hakubutsukan, 69-73. Osaka: Osaka Furitsu Chikatsu Asuka Hakubutsukan, 69-73. Osaka: Osaka Furitsu Chikatsu Asuka Hakubutsukan.

___ 2013. *Doki kara Mita Kofun Jidai no Nikkan Koryu* (Japan-Korea Exchange and Interaction during the Kofun Period in Light of the Pottery). Tokyo: Toseisha

Sakurai Shiritsu Maiso Bunkazai Senta. 2005. *Tairiku Bunka to Toraijin: Nara Bonchi Nambu ni okeru Toraikei Shudan no Doko* (Continental Culture and the Immigrants: Activities and Movement of the Immigrant Groups in the southern Nara Basin). Sakurai: Sakurai City Buried Cultural Heritage Center.

Samguk Sagi (see YI, Pyong-do)

Samguk Yusa (see YI, Pyong-do)

Sanders, W.T., and B.J. Price. 1968. *Mesoamerica: The Evolution of Civilization*. New York: Random.

Sansom, George B. 1958. *A History of Japan to 1334*. London: The Cresset Press.

SEKI, Akira. 1956. *Kikajin: Kodai no Seiji, Keizai, Bunka o Kataru* (The Immigrants: Revealing Politics, Economy, and Culture of the Ancient Period). Tokyo: Shibundo.

SEOK, Gwang-jun. 1979. Uri nara seobuk jibang goindolui byeoncheone daehayeo (Regarding the changes of dolmens in northwest Korea). Pyongyang: Yeoksa Gwahakweon.

SEONG, Jeong-yong. 1997. Daejeon Shindae-dong – Birae-dong cheongdonggi shidae yujeok (Bronze Age sites at Shindae-dong and Birae-dong in Daejeon). In *Honam Gogohakeu Jemunje* (Various Issues in Honam Archaeology), edited by Korean Archaeological Society, 205-236. Gwangju: Hanguk Gogohakhoe.

___ 2003. Hanseonggi Paekche maguui pyeonnyeongwa geu giweon (Chronology of the Hanseong period Paekche horse-trappings and their origin). In *Guksagwan Nonchong*, edited by Guksa Pyeonchan Wiweonhoe, #101: 1-28. Seoul: Guksa Pyeonchan Wiweonhoe.

___ 2006. 4–5-segi Paekcheui muljil munhwawa jibang jibae (Fourth–fifth century Paekche material culture and its local control). In *Hanseongeseo Ungjineuro* (From Hanseong to Ungjin), edited by National Gongju Museum, 209-227. Gongju: Gungnip Gongju Bangmulgwan.

___ 2009. Jungseobu jiyeok Mahanui muljil munhwa (Material culture of Mahan in the west-central region). In *Mahan, Sumshineun Girok* (Mahan, Breathing Records), edited by National Jeonju Museum, 233-246. Jeonju: Gungnip Jeonju Bangmulgwan.

Service, Elman R. 1971. *Primitive Social Organization: An Evolutionary Perspective*. New York: Random House.

___ 1975. *Origins of the State and Civilization*. New York: Norton.

SHICHIDA, Tada'aki. 2005. *Yoshinogari Iseki* (The Yoshinogari Archaeological Site). Tokyo: Toseisha.

___ 2007a. Yoshinogari iseki: Saga heiya ni kaika shita kanhanto no bunka (The Yoshinogari site: Korean Peninsula culture blossomed in the Saga Plain). In *Hanil Munhwa Gyoryu, Hanbandowa Ilbon Kyushu* (Korea-Japan Culture Exchange, the Korean Peninsula and Kyushu, Japan), edited by National Jung-ang Museum, 116-133. Seoul: Gungnip Jung-ang Bangmulgwan.

___ 2007b. Yoshinogari Iseki: Saga heiya ni okeru Yayoi bunka no seisei-hatten to Kanhanto (The birth and development of the Yayoi culture in the Saga plains and the Korean Peninsula). In *Yoshinogari: Nihon no Naka no Kodai Kankoku* (Ancient Korean Culture in Japan), edited by National Jung-ang Museum, 338-358. Seoul: Gungnip Jung-ang Bangmulgwan.

___ 2017. *Yamataikoku Jidai no Kuni no Miyako: Yoshinogari Iseki* (The Capital of the Yamatai Period Nation: The Yoshinogari Site). Tokyo: Shinzumi.

SHIM, Bong-keun. 1999. *Hangukeseobon Ilbon Yayoi Munhwaui Jeongae* (Emergence and Development of Yayoi Culture from the Korean Perspective. Seoul: Hak'yeon Munhwasa.

SHIMOJO, Nobuyuki. 2014a. Seisangu (masei sekki) kara mita shoki inasaku no ninaite (Those in charge of the early wet-rice cultivation in light of production [polished stone] tools). In *Retto Shoki Inasaku no Ninaite wa Dareka?* (Who Were the People in Charge of the Early Wet-Rice Cultivation in the [Japanese] Archipelago?), edited by N. SHIMOJO, 175-228. Tokyo: Kodaigaku Kyokai.

___ 2014b. Nishi Nihon ni okeru shoki inasaku to ninaite (Early wet-rice cultivation and those in charge of it in Western Japan). In *Retto Shoki Inasaku no Ninaite wa Dareka?* (Who Were the People in Charge of the Early Wet-Rice Cultivation in the [Japanese] Archipelago?), edited by N. SHIMOJO, 229-278. Tokyo: Kodaigaku Kyokai.

SHIMOJO, Nobuyuki, and Yoshiyuki TANAKA. 2014. *Toron: Retto shoki no inasaku no ninaite wa Dareka* (Discussions: Who were in charge of the early wet-rice cultivation in the Archipelago?). In *Retto Shoki Inasaku no Ninaite wa Dareka?* (Who Were the People in Charge of the Early Wet-Rice Cultivation in the [Japanese] Archipelago?), edited by N. SHIMOJO, 279-324. Tokyo: Kodaigaku Kyokai.

SHIMOMURA, Hiroshi.1993. *Nihonshi Daijiten* 2 (The Great Dictionary of Japanese History 2). Tokyo: Heibonsha.

SHIN, Gyeong-hwan, Gyeong-sook JANG, and Nam-gyu LEE. 2008. Paekche cheolgi jejo gongbeobui teukseong (Special characteristics of Iron tool manufacturing technology of Paekche). In *Paekche Saengsan Gisului Baldalgwa Yutong Chegye Hwakdaeui Jeongchisahoejeok Hameu* (Socio-political Implications of the Development of the Production Technology and the Expansion of the Distribution System of Paekche), edited by Hanshin Daehakkyo Haksulweon, 233-271. Seoul: Hakyeon Munhwasa.

SHIN, Hyeong-shik. 1981. *Samguk Sagi Yeongu* (A Study of the *Samguk Sagi*). Seoul: Iljogak.

SHIN, Kyeong-cheol. 1993. Choigeun Kaya jiyeokui gogohak seongkwa (Most recent archaeological results in the Kaya region). In *Kayasaron* (Essays on Kaya History), edited by Goryo Daehakkyo Hangukhak Yeonguso, pp. 99-119. Seoul: Korean Studies Institute, Goryo University.

___ 2000. Godae Naktonggang, Yeongsangang, geurigo Wae (The ancient Naktong river, the Yeongsan river, and Wa). In *Hangukui Jeonbang Huweonbun* (Keyhole Tumuli of Korea), edited by Paekche Research Institute, 163-198. Daejeon: Chungnam University.

SHIN, Kyeong-cheol, and Jae-wu KIM. 2000. *Kimhae Daeseong-dong Gobungun II* (Ancient Tombs at Kimhae Daeseong-dong II). Pusan: Gyeongseong University Museum.

SHIN, Na-hyeon. 2019. Godae janggunui byeoncheongwa sayong (Changes and use of barrel-shaped pottery vessel in the ancient times). In *Hanguk Gogohakbo* 105: 230-258.

SHIN, Sook-chung, Song-nai RHEE, and C.M. Aikens. 2012. Chulmun Neolithic intensification, complexity, and emerging agriculture in Korea. *Asian Perspectives* 51.1: 68-109.

SHIN, Yong-min. 2008. Daho-ri yujeok mokkwanmyosigiui yeongu (A study of the Burial system during the wood-coffin period at Daho-ri). In *Daho-ri Yujeok Balgul Seongkwawa Gwaje* (Daho-ri Excavations: Results and Prospects), edited by National Jung-ang Museum, 118-146. Seoul: Gungnip Jung-ang Bangmulgwan.

SHINKAWA, Tokio, and Mannen HAYAKAWA. 2011. *Shiryoto shiteno Nihon Shoki* (*Nihon Shoki* as a Historical Document). Tokyo: Tsutomu Shuppan.

SHINTAKU, Nobuhisa. 1994. Etsuji iseki no chosa (Investigations of the Etsuji Site). In *Kyushu Kokogakkai–Reinan Kokogakkai dai-ikkai godo Kokogakukai* (The First Joint Conference of the Kyushu and Yeongnam Archaeological Societies), 118-135. Fukuoka: Godo Kokogakukai Soshiki I'inkai.

SHIRAI, Katsuya. 2000. Nihon shutsudo no Chosensan doki/toki (The earthenware and stoneware of Korea unearthed in Japan). In *Nihon Shutsudo no Hakusai Toji* (Imported Pottery unearthed in Japan), edited by National Tokyo Museum, 90-120. Tokyo: Tokyo Kokuritsu Hakubutsukan.

___ 2001. Kudara doki – Mahan doki to Wa (Paekche pottery – Mahan pottery and Wa). In *Kodai no Kawachi to Kudara* (Ancient Kawachi and Paekche), edited by Hirakata Rekishi Forum Jikko I'inkai, 76-93. Hirakata: Daikoro.

___ 2004. Imaki no tehito: Toraijin shudan to Wakuni no bunmeika (Recently arrived skilled people: immigrants and their civilizing of Wa country), in *Imaki no Tehito* (Recently Arrived Skilled People), edited by Osaka Furitsu Chikatsu Asuka Hakubutsukan, 7-13. Osaka: Osaka Prefectural Chikatsuasuka Museum.

___ 2009. *Kokogaku kara mita Wakuni* (The Country of Wa in Light of Archaeology). Tokyo: Aoki Shoten.

SHITARA, Hiromi. 2006. Yayoi jidai kaitei nendaito koko hendo – Sakaguchi 1982 ronbun no saihyoka (The revised chronology of the Yayoi period and climate change – Re-evaluation of Sakaguchi 1982 thesis). *Komazawa Shigaku* 67: 129-154.

SHODA, Shin'ya. 2007. A comment on the Yayoi period dating controversy. *Bulletin of the Society for East Asian Archaeology* 1: 1-17.

___ 2009. *Cheongdonggi Shidae eu Saengsan Hwaldong gwa Sahoe* (Production Activities and Society of the Bronze Age). Seoul: Hak'yeon Munhwasa.

___ 2010. Radiocarbon and archaeology in Japan and Korea: What has changed because of the Yayoi dating controversy? *Radiocarbon* 52: 2-3.

___ 2015. Metal adoption and the emergence of stone daggers in northeast Asia. In *Flint Daggers in Prehistoric Europe*, edited by C.J. Frieman and B.V. Eriksen, 149-160. Oxford: Oxbow Books.

SHODA, Shinya, Oksana Yanshina, Jun-ho SON, and Naoto TERAMAE. 2009. New interpretation of the stone replicas in the Russian Maritime Province: re-evaluation from the perspective of Korean archaeology. *The Review of Korean Studies* 12.2: 187-210.

Shoku Nihongi. See IMAIZUMI Tadayoshi.

Shultz, Edward J. 2005. An introduction to the *Samguk Sagi. Korean Studies* 28: 1-13.

SO, Jae-yun. 2004. Paekche wakeonmuljiui byeoncheon gwajeonge daehan yeongu (A study of the changes of Paekche roof-tiled buildings. *Hanguk Sanggosa Hakbo* 45: 49–70.

SOHN, Myeong-jo. 2012. *Hanguk Godae Cheolgi Munhwa Yeongu* (A Study of Ancient Iron Culture of Korea). Gwacheon: Zininzin.

SONG, Eu-jeong. 2008. Daho-ri yujeok balgul josaui seongkwa (The results of Daho-ri excavations). In *Daho-ri Yujeok Balgul Seongkwawa Gwaje* (Daho-ri Excavations: Results and Prospects), edited by National Jung-ang Museum, 18-25. Seoul: Gungnip Jung-ang Bangmulgwan.

SONG, Eu-jeong, J.G. HONG, Y.H. YUN, S.M. KIM, and Y.B. LEE 2014. *Hwaseong Gian-dong Jecheol Yujeok* (Iron Production Site at Gian-dong, Hwaseong). Seoul: National Museum of Korea.

SONG, Jeong-shik. 2003. *Kaya-Sillaui Jongjang Pan'gap* (A Study on the Vertical Iron-Plate Body Armor). MA thesis, Pusan University.

SONG, Man-yeong. 2001. Namhan jibang nonggyeong munhwa hyeongseonggi chwirakui gujowa byeoncheon (Settlement patterns and their changes during the emergence of agriculture in southern Korea). In *Hanguk Nonggyeong Munhwaui Hyeongseong* (Formation of Agriculture in Ancient Korea), edited by Korean Archaeological Society, 75-110. Pusan: Hanguk Gogohakhoe.

___ 2006. Namhan jibang cheongdonggi shidae chwirak gujoui byeonhwawa kyecheunghwa (Changes in the settlement pattern and emerging social stratification during the Bronze Age of southern Korea). In *Gyecheung Sahoewa Jibaejaui Chulhyeon* (Emergence of a Stratified Society and Elite Manager), edited by Korean Archaeological Society, 9-37. Yongin: Hanguk Gogohakhoe.

Steponaitis, Vincas P. 1978. Locational theory and complex chiefdoms: A Mississippian example. In *Mississippi Settlement Patterns*, edited by B.C. Smith, 417-453. New York: Academic Press.

SUEMATSU, Yasukazu. 1949. *Mimana Koboshi* (History of the Rise and Fall of Mimana). Tokyo: Oyashima Shuppan. (Reprinted in 1956 and 1961 by Yoshikawa Kobunkan).

SUZUKI, Hideo. 1987. Kaya-Kudara to Wa – 'Mimana Nihonfu-ron' (Kaya-Paekche and Wa – 'Mimana Nihonfu Theory'). In *Chosenshi Kenkyukai Ronbunshu*, edited by Korean History Research Association 24: 63-95. Tokyo: Chosenshi Kenkyukai.

___ 1996. *Kodai no Wakoku to Chosen Shokoku* (Ancient Wa State and Various Korean States). Tokyo: Aoki Shoen.

SUZUKI, Kazunao. 2012. Cheongju Shinbong-dong Kofungunno tekkini miru hisoshashudan (The people buried in the ancient tumuli of Shinbong-dong of Cheongju in light of buried iron implements). In *Baekje Hakbo #8*, edited by Baekje Hakhoe, 105-132. Baekje Hakhoe.

SUZUKI, Takeki (ed.). 1975. *Ronshu Kiba Minzoku Seifuku Ocho* (Collection of Essays on Horseriders' Conquering the Royal Dynasty). Tokyo: Yamato Shobo.

SUZUKI, Yasutami. 1981. Mok Manchi to Soga Uji – Soga Uji Kudarajin settsu ni yosete (MOK Manchi and the Soga Clan – regarding the view that the Soga clan consisted of Paekche people). In *Nihon no Naka no Chosen Bunka* (Korean Culture in Japan), edited by Chosen Bunkasha, 50. Kyoto: Chosen Bunkasha.

___ 1985. *Kodai Taigai Kankeishi no Kenkyu* (A Study of Ancient Foreign Relations History). Tokyo: Yoshikawa Kobunkan.

___ 1992. Comments on the concept of Mimana and the question of "Did Mimana Nihonfu exist?" In *Kyodai Kofun to Kaya Bunka: 'Kuhaku' no 4-5 seiki o Saguru* (Great Tombs and Kaya Culture: in Search of the Fourth–Fifth Century 'Hiatus'), edited by T. Nishijima, 162-168. Tokyo: Kadokawa Shoten.

___ 1995. Kaya [Byeonhan] no Tetsu to Wa (The iron of Kaya [Byeonjin] and Wa). In *Kaya Jegukui Cheol* (Iron of Kaya States), edited by Kaya Culture Research Institute, Inje University, 35-62. Seoul: Doseo Chulpan.

TAKAHASHI, Mamoru. 1987. Ongagawa-shiki doki (Ongagawa-type pottery). In *Yayoi Bunka no Kenkyu 4: Yayoi Doki II* (Research on Yayoi Culture 4: Yayoi Pottery II), edited by H. KANASEKI and M. SAHARA, 7-16. Tokyo: Yuzankaku.

TAKAKU, Kenji. 1995. *Naknang Gobun Yeongu* (A Study of the Ancient Tombs in Naknang [Lelang]). Seoul: Hak'yeon Munhwasa.

TAKAKURA, Hiroaki. 1995. Chosen Hanto kara inasaku no dempa (Diffusion of rice cultivation from the Korean Peninsula). In *Higashi Ajia no Inasaku Kigen to Kodai Inasaku Bunka* (Origins of Rice Cultivation in East Asia and Ancient Rice Agriculture), edited by K. WASANO, 283-288. Saga: Saga University Department of Agriculture.

___ 2011. Kosa-nendai ketteiho ni yoru Yayoi jidai chuki–koki no jitsu nendai (The real dates of the Middle – Late Yayoi period according to the cross-dating methodology). In *AMS Nendai to Kokogaku*

(AMS Chronology and Archaeology), edited by H. TAKAKURA and Y. TANAKA, 203-232. Tokyo: Gakuseisha.

TAKATA, Kanta. 2014. *Kofun Jidai no Nitcho Kankei* (Japan-Korea Relations during the Kofun Period). Tokyo: Yoshikawa Kobunkan.

TAKESUE, Jun'ichi. 1997. Togiro bon Kayawa godae ilbon (Kaya and ancient Japan in light of the pottery). In *Kayawa Godae Ilbon* (Kaya and Ancient Japan), edited by Kimhae-shi Haksul Wiweonhoe, 93-126. Kimhae: Kimhae City Government.

___ 2001. Hokubu Kyushu no shuraku (Yayoi settlements in northern Kyushu). In *Yayoi Jidai no Shuraku* (Yayoi Period Settlements), edited by H. KANASEKI and Osaka Furitsu Yayoi Bunka Hakubutsukan, 102-117. Tokyo: Gakuseisha.

___ 2002. Buk Kyushu eu guk deungjang gwa jeon'gae (Emergence and development of 'countries' in northern Kyushu). *Yeongnam Gogohakbo* 30: 25–28.

___ 2005. Samhan to Wa no kokogaku (The archaeology of Samhan and Wa). In *Nihon to Chosen* (Japan and Korea), edited by Y. TAKEDA, 62-65. Tokyo: Yoshikawa Kobunkan.

___ 2008. Dahori iseki to Nihon (Dahori archaeological site and Japan). In *Daho-ri Yujeok Balgul Seonggwawa Gwaje* (Daho-ri Excavations: Results and Prospects), National Jung-ang Museum, 258-307. Seoul: Gungnip Jung-ang Bangmulgwan.

___ 2010. Kinkai Gusan-dong [金海龜山洞] Iseki A1 chiku no Yayoi-kei doki o meguru shomondai (Various issues regarding the Yayoi type pottery from A1 section of Kimhae Gusan-dong site). *Kobunka Danso* 65: 145-173.

___ 2012. Gensankoku jidai nendairon no shomondai (Various issues on the chronology of the proto three kingdoms). In *Weonsamguk – Samguk Shidae Yeokyeondaeron* (Issues on the Chronology of the Proto Three Kingdoms and the Three Kingdoms), edited by Sejong Munhwajae Yeonguweon, pp. 73-128. Seoul: Hak'yeon Munhwasa.

___ 2013. Shinhodo Kofungun ni mirareru Nihon bunka-kei yoso (Japanese culture type elements observed in the Shinbong-dong tumuli). In *Shinbong-dong Gobunguneul Saeropke boda* (New Perspectives on the Shinbong-dong Tumuli), edited by Chungbuk University Museum. Seoul: Hakyeon Munhwasa.

TAKESUE, Jun'ichi, Isaho IBA *et al.* 2011. Kinkai Heohyeon-ri [金海會峴里] kaizuka shusudo no Omi-kei doki (Omi type pottery excavated from Kimhae Hoehyeon-ri shell mound). *Kodaibunka* 63: 257-269.

TAKEUCHI, Rizo. 1948. *Kodai no Kikajin* (The Immigrants of the Ancient Period). In *Kokumin no Rekishi*, edited by Kokumin no Rekishi Kenkyukai, 2-6. Tokyo: Jitsugyo no Nihonsha.

TAMURA, Encho. 1978. *Kudara Bunka to Asuka Bunka* (The Paekche Culture and the Asuka Culture). Tokyo: Yoshikawa Kobunkan.

___ 1981. Asuka no Bukkyo (Buddhism of Asuka). In *Zusetsu: Nihon Bukkyo shi 1: Bukkyo to no Deai* (Pictorial Illustrations: The History of Japanese Buddhism 1: The Encounter with Buddhism). Kyoto: Hozokan.

TANAKA, Kyomi. 2004. Settsu – Kawachi no Toraijin (The immigrants in Settsu and Kawachi). In *Imaki no Tehito* (Recently Arrived Skilled People), edited by Osaka Furitsu Chikatsuasuka Hakubutsukan, 88-95. Osaka: Osaka Furitsu Chikatsuasuka Hakubutsukan.

TANAKA, Toshiaki. 1992. *Dai Kaya Renmei no Kobo t* (The Rise and Fall of Dae Kaya Confederation and [Mimana]). Tokyo: Yoshikawa Kobunkan.

___ 2001. Kudara to Wa no kankei (Relationship between Paekche and Wa). In *Kodai Kawachi to Kudara* (Ancient Kawachi and Paekche), edited by Hirakata Rekishi Forum Jikko I'inkai, 2-23. Hirakata: Daikoro.

TANAKA, Yoshiyuki. 2014. Iwayuru torai setsu no seiritsu kaei to torai no jisso (The formation process of the so-called Toraijin theory and the real picture of crossing the sea. In *Retto Shoki Inasaku no Ninaite wa Dareka?* (Who Were the People in Charge of the Early Wet-Rice Cultivation in the [Japanese] Archipelago?), edited by N. SHIMOJO. Tokyo: Kodaigaku Kyokai.

TATSUMI, Shunsuke. 2017. Hosokawa-dani kofungun no kiso-teki kenkyu (Preliminary study of the Hosokawa valley tumuli group). In *Asukamura Bunkazai Chosa Kenkyu Kiyo* (Bulletin of Research for Asukamura Cultural Heritage), edited by Asukamura Kyoiku I'inkai, . Asuka, Nara: Asukamura Kyoiku I'inkai.

Tenri University Sankokan Museum. 2014. *Sankokan Selection: Kanshiki-kei tsubo* (Sankokan Selection: Korean-type jar). Tenri City: Sankokan.

TERASAWA, Kaoru. 2001. Kango shuraku (Villages with encircling moat). In *Yayoi Jidai no Shuraku* (Yayoi Period Settlements), edited by H. KANASEKI and Osaka Furitsu Yayoi Bunka Hakubutsukan, 26-28. Tokyo: Gakuseisha.

Tokyo National Museum (ed.). 1992. *Kaya Bunkaten* (Exhibition of Kaya Culture). Tokyo: Asahi Shinbunsha.

TORAMA, Hideki. 1993. Kumeta kofungun no shoki Sueki (Early Sueki of the ancient tomb groups at Kumeta). In *Kanshiki-kei Doki Kenkyu* IV (Researches on Korean-Type Potteries IV), edited by Research Group on Korean Pottery Types. Osaka: Kanshikikei Doki Kenkyukai.

___ 1994. Kumeta kofungun no shoki Sueki (Early Sueki of the ancient tomb groups at Kumeta). In *Kanshiki-kei Doki Kenkyu* V (Researches on Korean Type Potteries V), edited by Research Group on Korean Pottery Types, xx . Osaka: Kanshiki-kei Doki Kenkyukai.

TOYAMA, Mitsuo. 2001. *Nihon Shoki wa nanio kakushite kita ka?* (What has the *Nihon Shoki* concealed?). Tokyo: Yosensha.

TSUDA, Soukichi. 1924. Kojiki *oyobi* Nihon Shoki *no Kenkyu* (A Study of the *Kojiki* and the *Nihon Shoki*). Tokyo: Iwanami Shoten.

___ 1948. *Nihon Koten no Kenkyu 1* (A Study of Japan's Ancient Classics 1). Tokyo: Iwanami Shoten.

___ 1950. *Nihon Koten no Kenkyu 2* (A Study of Japan's Ancient Classics 2). Tokyo: Iwanami Shoten.

TSUDE, Hiroshi. 2005. *Zempokoenfun to Shakai* (Keyhole-shaped Tombs and Society). Tokyo: Hanawa Shobo.

TSUJI, Zennosuke. 1969. *Nihon Bukkyo shi 1* (The History of Japanese Buddhism 1). Tokyo: Iwanami Shoten.

TSUJITA, Jun. 1924. *Kojiki Shinko* (New Lectures on the Kojiki). Tokyo: Meiji Shoin.

TSUNEMATSU, Mikio. 2011.Yayoi jidai chuki ni okeru Wajin no manazashi (A picture of the Wa people of the Middle Yayoi Period). In *AMS Nendai to Kokogaku* (AMS Chronology and Archaeology), edited by H. TAKAKURA and Y. TANAKA, 175-202. Tokyo: Gakuseisha.

UEDA, Masaaki. 1965. *Kikajin: Kodai Kokka no Seiritsu o megutte* (The Immigrants: Surrounding the Establishment of the Ancient State). Tokyo: Chuo Koronsha.

___ 1991. Kodaishi no naka no Toraijin (Toraijin in [Japan's] ancient history). In *Kodai Gozoku to Chosen* (Ancient Powerful Clans and Korea), edited by Kyoto Culture Museum, 45-80. Tokyo: Shinjinbutsu Oraisha.

UKEDA, Masayuki. 1974. *Roku Seiki Zenki no Nitcho Kankei - Mimana Nihonfu o Chushin to Shite* (Japan–Korea Relations Before the Early Sixth Century – Focussing on Mimana Nihonfu). Chosenshi Kenkyukai Ronbunshu (Korean History Research Association Collection of Essays), No. 11. Tokyo: Chosenshi Kenkyukai.

UMEZAWA, Iseso. 1962. *Kiki Hihan:* Kojiki *oyobi* Nihon Shoki *no seiritsu ni kansuru kenkyu* (A study on the establishment of the *Kojiki* and the *Nihon Shoki*). Tokyo: Sobunsha.

___ 1988. *Kojiki to Nihon Shoki no Kenso* (Investigations of *Kojiki* and *Nihon Shoki*). Tokyo: Yoshikawa Kobunkan. Im

WADA, Seigo. 1986. Political interpretations of stone coffin production in protohistoric Japan. In *Windows on the Japanese Past: Studies in Archaeology and Prehistory,* edited by R. Pearson, K. Hutterer and G.L. Barnes, 349-374. Ann Arbor: University of Michigan Center for Japanese Studies.

Walsh, Rory. 2017. *Ceramic Specialization and Exchange in Complex Societies: A Compositional Analysis of Pottery from Mahan and Baekje in Southwestern Korea.* Ph.D. dissertation. University of Oregon.

WASANO, Kikuo. 1995. Kodai Ajia no inatsubu to inasaku kigen (Rice grains of ancient Asia and the origin of rice cultivation). In *Higashi Ajia no Inasaku Kigen to Kodai Inasaku Bunka* (Origins of Rice Cultivation in East Asia and Ancient Rice Agriculture), edited by K. WASANO, 3-52. Saga City: Saga University Department of Agriculture.

WATANABE, Masahiro. 1999. Hokei shukobo no genryu (The origin of the square-shaped moat-surrounded tombs). In *Toraijin Tojo: Yayoi Bunka o Hiraita Hitobito (Arrival of the Immigrants: The People Who Commenced the Yayoi Culture)*, edited by Osaka Furitsu Yayoi Bunka Hakubutsukan, 82-85. Osaka: Osaka Furitsu Yayoi Bunka Hakubutsukan.

Weongwang University. 2000. *Iksan Yeongdeung-dong Yujeok (Iksan Yeongdeung-dong Site).* Iksan: Weongwang University.

WOO, Byeong-cheol. 2015. Samguk shidae jangshik daedoui jejak gisulgwa jiyeokseong (Manufacturing technology of the decorated long swords of the Three Kingdoms period and their local characteristics). *Hanguk Gogo Hakbo* 96: 104-139.

YAMADA, Hideo. 1972. *Nihon Shoki* no henshu katei to kinenho (Compilation process of the *Nihon Shoki* and the periodization method). In *Kojiki – Nihon Shoki I*, edited by Nihon Bungaku Kenkyu Shiryo Kankokai, 247-254. Tokyo: Yuseido.

___ 1991. *Nihon Shoki.* Tokyo: Kyoikusha.

YAMAGAMI, Hiroshi. 2004. Bashi no sato ga mittsukatta? (Has a horse-raising village come to light?). In *Imakino Tehito*, edited by OFCAH, 74-75. Osaka Furitsu Chikatsuasuka Hakubutsukan.

YAMAO, Yukihisa. 1977. *Nihon Kokka no Keisei* (Formation of the Japanese State). Tokyo: Iwanami Shoten.

___ 1978. Mimana ni kansuru shiron: shiryo no kento o chushin ni) (A working hypothesis regarding Mimana: in light of historical materials). In *Kodai Higashi Ajiashi Ronshu–Yasukazu SUEMATSU Hakase Koki Kinen Kaihen* (Collection of Essays on Ancient East Asian History–Festschrift in Honor of Dr. Yasukazu SUEMATSU's 70th Birthday), edited by Yasukazu SUEMATSU Hakase Koki Kinenkai, Vol. 2: 198-202. Tokyo: Yoshikawa Kobunkan.

___ 1984. *Nihon Kokka no Keisei* (Formation of the Japanese State). Tokyo: Iwanami Shoten.

YAN, Wenming. 1992. Dongbuk Asea nongeobui balsaenggwa jeonpa (Origin and diffusion of agriculture in Northeast Asia). In *Dongbuka Godae Munhwaui Weonryuwa Jeon'gae* (Ancient Cultures of Northeast Asia: Their Origins and Development), edited by Mahan-Paekche Research Institute, 95-100. Iksan: Weongwang University.

YANAGIDA, Yasuo. 1989a. Itokoku no Kokogaku (Archaeology of the Ito Region). In *Yoshinogari Isekiden* (Exhibition of the Yoshinogari Site). Omi: Shiga-ken Kyoiku I'inkai.

___ 1989b. Chosen Hanto ni okeru Nihon-kei ibutsu (Japanese-type artifacts found in the Korean Peninsula). In *Kyushu ni okeru Kofun Bunka to Chosen Hanto* (Kofun culture of Kyushu and the Korean Peninsula), edited by Fukuoka-ken Kyoiku I'inkai, 10-54. Tokyo: Gakuseisha.

___ 1992. [Munyeong jidai no Chosen Hanto nanbu ni mirareru Nihon Bunka (Japanese culture found in the southern part of Korea of the Proto-Three Kingdoms [Samhan] Period). In *Je 7-Hoe Hanguk Sangosa Hakhoe Haksul Balpyohoe* (The Seventh Academic Conference of the Korean Ancient Historical Society), edited by Hanguk Sanggosa Hakhoe, 31-40. Seoul: Hak'yeon Munhwasa.

Yemaek Munhwajae Yeonguweon (Yemaek Research Institute of Cultural Heritage). 2014. *Chuncheon Jungdo LEGOLAND KOREA PROJECT C-guyeoknae Yujeok Jeongmil Balgul Josa Bubun Wanryo (1 cha)*

221

Gyeolgwaseo (Interim Excavation Report on Section C of Chuncheon Jungdo LEGOLAND KOREA PROJECT). Chuncheon: Yemaek Munhwajae Yeonguweon.

YI, Hyunhae (aka Hyeon-hye LEE). 2009. The formation and development of the Samhan. In *The Samhan Period in Korean History* (Early Korea, vol. 2), edited by M.E. Byington, 17-59. Korea Institute, Harvard University.

YI, Pyong-do. 1972. *Samguk Yusa* (Anecdotes of the Three Kingdoms). Seoul: Daeyang Seojeok.

___ 1977 *Samguk Sagi* (Historical Records of the Three Kingdoms). Eulyu Munhwasa.

YOSHIDA, Akira. 1975. *Kodai Kokka no Keisei* (Ancient State Formation). Iwanami Koza: Nihon Rekishi, vol. 2 (Japanese History Lecture Series: History of Japan, vol. 2). Tokyo: Iwanami Shoten.

YOSHIDA, Kunio. 2005. Nendai sokutei no shin-tenkai (New development of ^{14}C dating). *Radioisotopes* 54.7: 233-255.

YOSHI'I, Hideo. 2001. Kudara bosei no donyu to tenkai (Adoption of Paekche tombs and its ramifications). In *Kodai Kawachi to Kudara* (Ancient Kawachi and Paekche), edited by Hirakata Rekishi Forum Jikko I'inkai, 104-117. Hirakata: Daikoro.

___ 2002. Ilbon chulto Paekche (Mahan) togiui jemunje (Various issues regarding the Paekche [Mahan] pottery found in Japan). *In Ilbon Sojae Paekche Munhwajae Josabogoseo III – Kinki jibang* (Investigative Report on Paekche Cultural Heritage in Japan III – Kinki Region). Seoul: National Gongju Museum.

___ 2007. Kodai higashi Ajia sekai kara mita Buneio [King Munyeong] no mokkan (King Munyeong's wooden coffin in light of the world of ancient East Asia). In *Nikkan Koryu no Kokogaku* (Archaeology of Japan–Korea Exchanges and Interaction), edited by M. Mogi. Tokyo: Toseisha.

YOSHIMURA, Kazuaki. 2000. Iron armor and weapons in protohistoric Japan. In *Clashes of Iron: Arms, Weaponry, and Warfare in Early East Asian States*, edited by G.L. Barnes, 104-111. Leiden: Brill.

INDEX

A

Abacus bead-shaped spindle whorls 124, 168
Agriculture i, iii, 2, 7, 12, 18, 27, 30, 32-33, 45-50,
    70, 74, 76, 82, 89, 95, 100, 118, 121, 132, 135,
    149, 163, 195, 197-198, 200, 202, 204, 211,
    215, 217-219, 221
Ajiki 99, 162, 170, 178
Akahage kofun 137
Akaokuzure-dani kofungun 143, 145
Akihito, Emperor xi, 184
Anra (or Aya)-guk 137-138
Arako 133, 134, 163
Ariake Sea 62
Ariyama kofun 154
Asabida of Kawachi Bu (Be) 136
Asakura Sueki kilns 149
Asuka period, glorious 141, 182, 186, 203
Asuka temple (also, Hokoji temple) 138, 175,
    184, 190
Asuka-mura 137, 139, 142, 145, 149

B

Baekchon River (battle of) 181, 183
Bannam (Naju) 113, 118, 193
Biwa Lake 127
bronze daggers (slender) i, 22, 27, 29-30, 51, 53,
    55, 57-58, 60-61, 64-71, 96, 210
bronze mirrors (Chinese trade 55, 80, 82, 84, 88,
    93-94, 152
bronze mirrors (multi-knobbed) 53-54, 55, 57-
    58, 60-61, 70-71
Buddhism in Paekche 99-100; in Yamato Japan
    xii, 6, 136, 140, 143, 147, 171-176, 180-181,
    184
Bungumyo 76, 117, 210
Buyeo (= Sabi) ix, 29, 55, 60-61, 79, 100, 118-119,
    134, 136, 140-141, 184, 186, 193, 204-205,
    207
Byeonhan ii, 73, 80-83, 86, 87, 89, 95-96, 102,
    104, 218

C

Chen Shou 10, 73
cheoljeong (tettei) 80
Chinese commanderies 83-85, 94
Chopo-ri (Hampyeong) 55, 57, 60-61, 69, 70, 193
Choson 61, 79, 83, 85, 194, 208
climate changes in prehistoric Peninsula 7, 24,
    32, 191
comma-shaped Amazonite stone 24-25, 26, 29,
    54, 57-58, 60-61, 166,
Confucianism in Paekche 99; in Yamato Japan
    xi, 6, 141, 162, 170-171, 180-181
corridor tombs in Paekche 116, 117; in Yamato
    Japan 127, 147, 150, 176-177

D

Dae Kaya 116, 122, 162, 186, 188, 219
Daegok-ni (Hwasun) 18, 55, 60, 193
Daepyeong-ni 12, 15, 18, 24, 26, 29, 30-32, 37, 39,
    46, 48, 193
Daho-ri 55, 61, 80, 83, 85, 95, 193, 201, 209, 219
Daifang ii, 6, 83-86, 92, 94, 96, 119, 122-123, 187, 212
decorated swords of Korea's early states 113,
    116, 137
Deokcheon-ri (Changweon) 209
Dolmens i, 15, 20, 24, 26-27, 30, 32, 35, 38-40, 60,
    64, 66, 81, 194, 197, 199, 205, 209, 212-215
Dongseo-ri 51, 60, 201
Dongseong 127, 179

E

Early Kofun and Middle Kofun period societies,
    compared 152-153
Echizen district 134
Egami, Namio (also, horse rider's conquest hy-
    pothesis) xii, 1, 152, 185-186, 198
Etafunayama kofun 164
Etsuji, an early Yayoi village 17, 37, 46, 48, 217

F

Fujinoki kofun 164, 167

223

T

U

W

Y